Do You Hear That Beat

Wisconsin Pop/Rock in the 50's & 60's

Gary E. Myers

Hummingbird Publishing

Do You Hear That Beat
by Gary E. Myers
©1994 by Gary E. Myers

Published by Hummingbird Publishing
P.O. Box 4777
Downey, CA 90241-1777
Printed in the United States of America

ISBN: 0-9643073-9-1
Library of Congress Catalog Card Number: 94-96410

Publisher's - Cataloging In Publication
        (Prepared by Quality Books, Inc.)

Myers, Gary E.
    Do you Hear that beat : Wisconsin pop/rock in the 50's & 60's / Gary E. Myers.
    p. cm.
    Includes biographical references.
    ISBN 0-9643073-9-1

    1. Rock music--Wisconsin--History and criticism. 2. Rock music--Wisconsin
--Collectors and collecting. I. Title.

ML3534.M94 1994   781.66'09775
                                   QB194-1788

Contents

Preface

Trivia question: What major hit (#2 on Billboard's Hot 100) from 1976 mentioned Wisconsin in the lyrics? (Hint: It's about an event that took place on the Great Lakes).

In the spring of 1993 a musician friend said that the only music he associated with Wisconsin was "On Wisconsin," a statement with which many may agree. Though I knew otherwise, I didn't realize the extent of it until the circumstances and research that led to this book. (By the way, the publishing rights to "On Wisconsin," rumored to be owned by Paul McCartney, are actually in the public domain).

I guess you could say the seeds for this book were planted during my own teenage years when I first heard "Thunder Wagon" by Milwaukee's Noblemen. Then came my own involvement in the scene, playing in bands in the area between January 1962 and September 1966. Add another 15 years or so of accumulating related information, a planned article on the Cuca label, the opportunity to contribute to Tom Tourville's Wisconsin discography book, nearly two years of additional research - and the tree has borne fruit.

Besides being a line from the song "Say Mama," my title also comes from the belief that we've probably all "heard the beat" of more Wisconsin music than we realize.

Trivia answer: "Wreck Of The Edmund Fitzgerald" by Gordon Lightfoot.

Acknowledgments

Each person who graciously answered my questions, or who trusted me with a photo, is listed as a source in the appropriate section. I wish to also acknowledge the following:

Clark Besch	Marlene Moore
Bill Conrad	Cathi Myers
Paul Curry	Dean Myers
Laurie Gorman	Jeff Naskrent
Doug Harper	George Paetzmann
Jeff Jarema	Jon Paris
Gary King (Nostalgia Records)	Mark Smith
Sherwin Linton	David Stanton
Jeff Lynn	Mike Stax
Michael McCall (Nashville Scene)	Ann Swan
Mean Mountain Music	David Vasquez
Darrell Meister	Carl Walden
Frank Merrill	Don Ward
John Miller	Wenzel's Music Town

The following people went a step further by sending additional material or helping with many referrals:

Jules Blattner
Jack Casper
Tom Davis
Mike Dellger
Deniel Edwards
Lucine Engstad
Bill Forseth
Denny Geyer
Rick Hoehn
Tom Lindemann

Jonathan Little
Dale Luther
Sam McCue
Bob Metzger
Dave Pilz
Ruth Primus
Eugene Recob
Doug Tank
Jim Van Puymbrouck

Special thanks to these individuals for their extra contributions:

Ken Adamany
Allen Bauman
John Cooke
Jim Kirchstein
Brian Lake

Phil Nee
Dean Nimmer
Robert Pruter
Rick Schurk
Tari Tovsen

And my main man:

Tom Tourville

About This Book

The following information will help you to understand who and what is covered in this book and, in some cases, why it's covered.

Time Period Covered

1. 1950- 1969. The artists or groups (with a Wisconsin connection) who recorded during that 20 year span.
2. If a particular artist began recording before 1969 and continued into the 70's or beyond, I've attempted to also include the later information (i.e., Al Jarreau's discography continues up to and beyond the writing of this book).
3. Historical artists whose recording careers began before 1950, but who were still active on disc after that, are covered by brief profiles and a list of biggest hits, rather than a complete discography.

Who Is Covered

1. Those who began recording in Wisconsin, regardless of any later relocation.
2. Those who began elsewhere but relocated to Wisconsin during the covered time period.
3. Artists who had some Wisconsin connection, but relocated before any recording activity, are covered in the same type of profile (and in the same section) as the historical artists in #3 above.
4. Beyond the obvious; i.e., groups who hit the national charts or who were well known locally, my original intention was to limit the next level of coverage with a set of admittedly arbitrary guidelines. I soon learned that those lines were difficult to draw. As the project grew, pieces of information about obscure and one-shot artists continued to pop up, so I decided that, although I couldn't seek out every recorded group, I would include whatever came to light. If it seems that some obscurities are included while others are not, this is the reason.
6. Music of, or closely related to, the pop/rock field is covered. This includes many better known, or more pop-related, country and jazz artists. However, I have not attempted an in-depth coverage of these fields.
7. For those who were there at the time, there were many non-recorded performing bands who will be more remembered than some of the obscure recorded groups. It is beyond the scope of this book to cover those bands, though some may be mentioned briefly in the context of other coverage.

Discographies

1. Only American releases are listed.
2. Reissues of hits are not included. However, reissues of obscure recordings (where known) are.
3. Where known, compilation albums that include reissues of obscure singles are mentioned. See listings at the end of the Cuca section and Around The State section.
4. Release dates may be estimated (especially when the month is shown). The estimate is based on other related information.
4. Footnotes are used to call attention to a point of interest about a particular song (where known), such as the name of the writer(s) or original artist.
5. (I) indicates instrumental (where known). Its placement before or after the slash shows which side it pertains to. Ex: (/I) means that the second side shown is an instrumental.
6. An underline on a particular song title shows that the song made a Billboard chart. The highest chart position is shown in parenthesis after the titles. A letter following the position indicates if it pertains to a chart other than the Hot 100. C=Country; ez=Easy Listening; r&b=Rhythm & Blues; all others=Hot 100 (a number over 100=Bubbling Under). Of course, if the title is an LP, it pertains to the LP chart.

Miscellaneous Information

1. All national chart information comes from Joel Whitburn's Record Research books.
2. To help the collector differentiate, unrelated groups with the same name as the covered group are listed by the label on which they appear.
3. Where known, date and place of birth are shown in parenthesis. If the city of birth is not followed by a state name, it can be assumed to be Wisconsin.
4. Nicknames are shown in quotation marks. Real names (as opposed to stage names) are shown in parenthesis.
5. Group line-ups shown in the left-hand column are generally either the known original members or those reported to be in the first recorded version of the group.
6. Later members are shown in the right-hand column. I have not attempted to show all the different line-ups or indicate which personnel were on any given record.
7. I have also not attempted to show where a musician is on vocal in addition to his instrument. Though many may consider the lead vocal to be the most important ingredient, I did not feel I could document that information with a sufficient degree of accuracy. There were simply too many bands who had more than one lead singer, duet vocals, etc., and too many conflicting memories. Probably the vast majority of group members did some background and/or lead vocals. "Voc" is shown only when that person was exclusively, or almost exclusively, a vocalist.
8. There are many artists for whom I found no information other than a listing of their recording(s). If these recordings are on a label covered in the book, they will be found in the label discographies. If they are on another label, they are listed in what is believed to be the appropriate geographical section. Also see the appendix.
9. Personnel in photos are identified from left to right, unless otherwise indicated.

Sources

1. This book would not exist were it not for *They Couldn't Tame Us - The Wisconsin 60's Rock Discography* by Tom W. Tourville. Though I contributed to that book, I was amazed at how much I learned from it. I had not realized there were so many Wisconsin acts that I had never heard of! Tom opened the door, I've gone in to dig and search. What a fun and interesting time it's been!

2. Joel Whitburn's Record Research books are THE source for Billboard chart information. The books I've used are: *Top Pop Singles, 1955-1990; Bubbling Under The Hot 100, 1959-1985; Top Pop Albums, 1955-1992; Top Adult Comtemporary, 1961-1993; Top R&B Singles, 1942-1988; Top Country Singles, 1944-1988.*

3. *The Directory Of American 45 RPM Records* from Ken Clee's Stak- O-Wax, Volumes 1-4, is an invaluable source of discography information.

4. Jerry Osborne's *Rockin' Records - Buyers-Sellers Reference Book and Price Guide* is a big help in finding what labels to search for particular artists, and for discovering various groups with the same name.

5. Some photos and records were purchased at Milwaukee's Mean Mountain Music.

6. Seemingly hundreds of telephone interviews and letters (I should be getting Christmas cards from AT&T and the U.S. Post Office this year), many of my personal recollections, a few in-person interviews - and the picture is completed.

Abbreviations

accord: accordion
B3: popular model of Hammond organ
bs: bass
CYO: Catholic Youth Organization
DJ: disc jockey
dr: drums
fl: flute
gtr: guitar
hca: harmonica
kb: keyboard

ld gtr: lead guitar
org: organ
perc: percussion
pno: piano
r&b: rhythm & blues
RAB: rockabilly
rh gtr: rhythm guitar
sx: sax
tb: trombone
tp: trumpet
voc: vocal

Wisconsin On The Charts

"This was a moment in rock history that was a great moment for dreams. Everybody had one and it almost happened for some people."
  - Jesse Roe (Messengers), 6/20/94

For a very few, it did happen. Though it may have been but a moment for some, 30 years later that moment remains. These are the Wisconsin artists who touched their dreams during the first two decades of the rock 'n' roll era.

These artists were all based in Wisconsin at the time of their initial released recording. Each executed that recording between 1950 - 1969 and each, at some point in his career, attained a position on Billboard's pop charts (Hot 100, Bubbling Under, or Hot LP's). In some cases the chart placing itself occurred after 1969. The artists are covered in descending order of highest chart position. This symbol (✳) calls attention to another noteworthy accomplishment of that artist. That accomplishment is considered relative our area of coverage, i.e., "Most Successful Country Artist" pertains to the artists covered in this book, not to all country artists.

1.	Fendermen		#5	11.	Steve Sperry	91
2.	Al Jarreau	LP	9	12.	Billy Thunderkloud	92
3.	Esquires		11		& the Chieftones	
4.	Underground Sunshine		26	13.	A.B. Skhy	100
5.	Dave Dudley		32	14.	Robbs	103
6.	Thee Prophets		49	15.	Love Society	108
7.	Messengers		62	16.	Unchained Mynds	115
8.	Chico Holiday		74	17.	Junior & the Classics	134
9.	Harvey Scales & Seven Sounds		79	18.	Tracy Nelson	LP 145
10.	Tim Davis		91	19.	Corporation	LP 197

Chronologically
(Date of first pop chart placing)

1. Chico Holiday	5/59	11. Thee Prophets	3/69
2. Fendermen	5/60	12. Unchained Mynds	4/69
3. Dave Dudley	6/63	13. Underground Sunshine	7/69
4. Junior & the Classics	9/64	14. A.B. Skhy	12/69
5. Robbs	6/66	15. Tim Davis	9/72
6. Messengers	4/67	16. Tracy Nelson	10/74
7. Esquires	8/67	17. Billy Thunderkloud	6/75
8. Harvey Scales & the Seven Sounds	10/67	& the Chieftones	
9. Love Society	8/68	18. Al Jarreau	8/76
10. Corporation	3/69	19. Steve Sperry	6/77

In addition to the musicians covered in this section, there are many individuals who went on to achieve chart status as members of other non-Wisconsin based acts. These accomplishments are included in the sections of the book that deal with their Wisconsin careers. For instance, a member of Tony's Tygers has gone on work with 90's superstar Michael Bolton. That information is found in the Milwaukee section under "Tony's Tygers."

Fendermen: Phil Humprhey, Jim Sundquist (courtesy Alan Clark)

Fendermen
(Madison)
Mule Skinner Blues - #5 - 1960

Phil Humphrey - gtr (11/26/37; Niagara)
Jim Sundquist - gtr (11/26/37; Stoughton)
Denny Dale (Gudim) - bs (2/26/41; Northfield, MN)
Johnny Hauer - dr

"Good mornin', Captain!" shouted Phil Humphrey from radios and jukeboxes in the summer of 1960, and two young men leaped from a small bar near Madison to national prominence. A 30-year old country song, recorded in a basement with no bass or drums, and released initially on a tiny label, "Mule Skinner Blues" was an unlikely hit if there ever was one.

A few pertinent facts:
1) The song was originally "Blue Yodel No. 8" by country great Jimmie Rodgers in 1931.
2) A mule skinner doesn't really skin mules - he drives them.
3) Yes, the Fendermen named themselves after the brand of guitar they played.

Born on the same day, perhaps it was destined that Humphrey and his partner, Jim Sundquist, would meet 20 years later. It was at a beer party in Milwaukee that the pair first made music together. Each went his own way and another year passed. Then one day Humphrey, while working as an Omar Bread delivery man, recognized Sundquist's name on an apartment and left a message. "I didn't even know who Phil Humphrey was," says Sundquist. "Then it dawned on me and I remembered what a good singer he was and we got together."

Their first gig was at the *Oats Bin*, "an old farmer place in Stoughton," recalls Sundquist. Having no idea what to charge, the boys offered to do an hour for free beer and, if the owner liked them, $5 apiece to finish the night. Continuing there regularly, they soon added "Mule Skinner Blues" to their repertoire. Humphrey had picked it up from a bluegrass record by Joe D. Gibson (Released on Tetra 4450).

While the two musicians were gigging at the *Ideal Bar* in Madison, Bill Gregor, a fan and part owner of a music store, suggested recording it. They cut it on a VM recorder in Gregor's basement and Gregor took it to Jim Kirchstein, owner of the new Cuca label. "Cuca didn't even have a studio," says Sundquist. "All it was, was a label. He bought (equipment for) a beautiful studio with the money he got from Mule Skinner Blues."

Sundquist and Humphrey had 500 copies pressed and spent a few months trying to sell them. "We had a trunk full of Cuca records and nobody would buy them," says Sundquist. "We had given up on it totally. It wasn't even jukebox level. When you put it on a jukebox, nothing would come out. You had to go behind the bar and turn up the volume all the way."

The Fendermen found work playing between movies at theaters and they were spotted by La Crosse DJ Lindy Shannon. "He got us on a Cavalcade of Stars type of show and when we did Mule Skinner Blues it brought the house down. He said, 'Gosh, you guys ought to cut that thing. That'd be a hit!' I said, 'We already have - here, have a box." Shannon started playing it and things began to change. Reaching the top spot on WKBH in La Crosse on March 28, 1960, it caught the attention of a representative from Soma records of Minneapolis.

Label owner Amos Heilicher (Soma is Amos spelled backwards) had the duo come to Kay Bank Studios to re-record the song and cut a different flip side (Heilicher apparently preferred putting instrumentals on the flip side of vocals). The record hit Billboard's Hot 100 on May 23, beginning an 18-week chart run. "Lindy's the one that popped that thing for us," says Sundquist. "If it hadn't been for his radio play, Mule Skinner Blues would have never gone anywhere."

The song hit both pop and country and their first big show was with Johnny Cash at the Minneapolis Auditorium. "When we walked out on that stage, it was just the two of us, and all that applause came all at once - 10 or 20,000 people, it was just overwhelming," recalls Sundquist. At first I was just petrified. Then all of a sudden I started laughing and I looked at Phil and we almost died laughing. We looked at the people and we couldn't get started." When they finally did their hit, they got several curtain calls. "It was just the biggest thrill of my life,"[1] says Sundquist.

In addition to live shows with many name acts, the Fendermen did Dick Clark's TV show on June 11, 1960, in a setting complete with two buckboards and two mules. The other guests were Paul Evans, Bobby Darin, and the Skyliners.

With the addition of Johnny Hauer of La Crosse on drums and Denny Dale (Dennis Gudim) of Minneapolis on bass, the Fendermen saw their follow-up, "Don't You Just Know It," stall at number 110 on the charts. The boys were not receiving their royalties and they joined with Cuca's Jim Kirchstein in a lawsuit against Heilicher. Because of the litigation, the release of the LP was held up for a year, a development that certainly didn't help sales.

By the end of the year the original partners amicably decided to split. "The last time I saw Phil Humphrey we were flipping a coin to see who was going to buy the turkey dinner as we said goodbye," recalls Sundquist. "We were in Minneapolis at the 620 Club. I wished him luck and he wished me luck. We sat down and we had a turkey dinner together and a couple of drinks. Then he went his way and I went mine."

Humphrey hired a seven piece band out of Canada and continued on the road as Phil Humphrey & the Fendermen, while Sundquist returned to the Cuca studio, recording as both the Muleskinners and Jimmy Sun & the Radiants. One of his musicians, bassist Tom Gress, went

---

[1]Bream, Jon. "Rewind." <u>Minneapolis Star Tribune</u> 5/7/89: 8F. - courtesy Jim
      Sundquist

on to produce and form his own record label in Milwaukee. Gress even had Sundquist come in years later and record, of all things, a jazz version of "Mule Skinner Blues."

An odd sidelight is the fact that Soma released records by several other groups with names very similar to the Fendermen. It was apparently mostly coincidence, but it does appear as if they were trying to come up with a name that sounded familiar to the DJ's and the record buyers. These names include Thundermen, Echo Men, Voo Doo Men, Embermen and Fenderbenders.

Fendermen bassist Denny Dale (eventually changed to Dale Denny to eliminate confusion with his son who now performs as Denny Dale) has continued as a recording artist as well as producer and co-host of a cable TV show.

Though Sundquist has remained in music, he left it as full time occupation around 1968 when he decided, "I was tired of being broke all the time and got a job at Twin City Arsenal." A frequent highlight over the years has been the testimony of many younger guitarists on the influence of his "Mule Skinner Blues" solo. In the 90's Sundquist and his wife, Sharree, write and perform gospel music. "I do a musical ministry for the Lord," he says. "That's where my heart is. I don't drink anymore or smoke anymore or pop pills anymore. It's quite a sight to all these people that knew me before, when I could hardly stand up on the stage." Fortunately for the old fans, he still plays "Mule Skinner Blues."

Cuca	1003	Mule Skinner Blues/Janice			1/60
Soma	1137	<u>Mule Skinner Blues</u>/Torture	(/I)	(#5, 16C)	4/60
	1142	<u>Don't You Just Know It</u>[1]/Beach Party	(/I)	(110)	9/60
	1155	Heartbreakin' Special/Can't You Wait[2]			11/60
LP:					
Soma	1240	Mule Skinner Blues			/61

Muleskinners/Jimmy Sun & the Radiants

Don Phillips - rh gtr

Tom Gress - bs (7/19/41)

John Christanovich - dr

Dave Vasser - hca

Shorty DeLongchamp - bs

Johnny Zolinski - dr

Ray Peters - dr (Brainerd, MN)

Cliff Johnson (Brizendine) - gtr

Bob Edmondson - bs

Ray Peters recorded with several Minnesota bands from 1959-65. Bob Edmondson later wrote songs in Nashville under the name Kandy Kane.

---

[1]Huey Smith & the Clowns, 1958
[2]w: Dorsey Burnette

Jimmy Sun & the Radiants
Cuca	1046	Cocaine Blues[1]/Molly And Ten Brooks[2]	10/61
		(Side 2 reissued on *The Cuca Story, Vol. 2*)	
	6636	The Engineer's Last Ride/Rockpile[3]	3/66

Muleskinners
Cuca	1139	Galloping Paul Revere/Rocky Road Blues[4]	8/63
		(Side 2 reissued on *The Cuca Story, Vol. 3*)	
Sara	63101	Brody's 97/Good Woman's Love[5]	10/63
Soma	1414	Wolfman/Everglades[6]	10/64
Twin Town	708	Muleskinner Blues '65/Our Last Night	/65
Water Street	8596	Muleskinner Blues/Whiskey	/70

Phil Humphrey & the Fendermen
| Sassy | 0284 | Popeye/Don't You Just Know It | /62 |
| Dab | 102 | Raindrop/Fas-Nacht Kuechel | |

Denny Dale
LeJac	3002	Mr. Moon[7]/Why Did You Leave Me	9/65
	3003	One More For The Road/Love You Everyday	9/65
		(Denny & Jack)	
Soma	1447	Mr. Moon/Why Did You Leave Me	10/65
Homely	1935	Why Am I So Ugly/Crawl In Back	6/80
Brandy	1200	Why Me/Love You Everyday	1/85
	1201	Meaning Of A Man/Sweethearts In Heaven	4/85
	1202	Home In Minnesota/Beginning Of The End	11/88
Door Knob	1032	The Beginning	10/93

Also see: The Cuca Story
    Pro-Gress Records - Wisconsin Labels, Underground Sunshine (Tom Gress)
    Dick Hiorns - Stevens Point/Wausau
    Dave Vasser - Cuca
    Johnson Brothers - Madison (Cliff Johnson)
    Crossfires - Cuca (related material)
    Night Beats - Milwaukee (related material)
Sources: Sharree Sundquist letter, 5/28/91
    Jim Sundquist telephone interviews, 1993-94
    Dennis Gudim letter, 12/13/93

---

[1]Roy Hogsed, 1948
[2]Bill Monroe
[3]aka "Gotta Do My Time" - Johnny Cash
[4]Gene Vincent, 1958
[5]Bill Monroe
[6]Kingston Trio, 1960
[7]Coachmen, 1966

Minneapolis Star Tribune, 5/7/89 - courtesy Jim & Sharree Sundquist
Phil Nee Show; WRCO, 5/22/93 - courtesy Phil Nee
Whitburn, Joel. <u>Record Research</u>. Menomonee Falls: Record Research, 1992.
Clee, Ken. <u>Directory of American 45 R.P.M. Records</u>. Philadelphia: Stak-O-Wax, 1992.
Hill, Randal C. <u>Collectible Rock Records</u>; Orlando: House of Collectibles, 1979.

Muleskinners: Jim Sundquist, Tom Gress, John Christanovich (courtesy Tom Gress)

Al Jarreau - Milwaukee weekly entertainment guide, 11/6/64 (courtesy Les Czimber)

Al Jarreau
(3/12/40; Milwaukee)
(LP) Breakin' Away - #9 - 1981, (45) We're In This Love Together - #15 - 1981

✳ **Biggest Star**

It may be news to many people to learn that Al Jarreau is from Milwaukee, and most will be surprised to discover that he recorded there as long ago as 1965. Jarreau had begun harmonizing with his brothers at the age of four but his professional career developed at a very gradual pace. He began sneaking into a few clubs not long after graduating from Lincoln High. Though he remembers Harvey Scales and some of the other groups around town, he has no recollection of being in the *Continental Caravan* (a show that several acts put on in various clubs) as some have claimed. "I don't recall that the stuff I did was part of any sort of broader program," he reflects. "During those days I was doing more jazz than things that would have been part of the same kind of show those guys were doing." A 1961 concert at Lincoln Memorial Center featured Jarreau and a quartet augmented by the Jazz All Stars big band.

"I forgot about 'Room Boom'," he chuckled when reminded of one of his early recordings. Those first sessions came about through Dave Kennedy, owner of the Raynard label. "I knew Dave Kennedy from those early days," says Jarreau. "Dave had a band and I think I might have done some dates with him, and he just discovered this young singer that he wanted to do some work with." After those first two singles Jarreau did not record professionally for ten years.

From 1958-62 he attended Ripon College and was in Milwaukee only during summer vacations and holidays, doing his early gigs with pianist Les Czimber. "It began with Les and I at the Driftwood Lounge on Capitol Drive," he says. "It was shortly after that when we began to do a lot of dates around town." Those dates included the Holiday House, the Pfister Hotel, and Sardino's, as Czimber recalls. "We came in with Jarreau and put in one ad to see what happens. We went in there and you couldn't move. Sardino's was like sardines." The Indigos, a four-part vocal group that Jarreau formed in Ripon, also did occasional gigs in Milwaukee.

Not yet convinced that music was a viable way to make a living, Jarreau earned a Master's Degree in vocational rehabilitation from the University of Iowa. Some live recordings at a club during that period surfaced many years later. "I was singing at a club called the Tender Trap in Cedar Rapids and we recorded some things for our own purposes at the time. It might have been just after the 'Breaking Away' LP that the people who had those tapes released some stuff on a label that I think was called Bainbridge."

Jarreau and Czimber headed for the West Coast shortly after the singer graduated from Iowa. "I moved to San Francisco and started working as a rehabilitation counselor and singing nights," he explains. "We worked for Abe Todah, who owned a club in Santa Clara called the Mecca. He had been the owner of the Driftwood Lounge in Milwaukee."

It wasn't long before the night time job took precedence. Jarreau did some club work with pianist George Duke in San Francisco, then relocated to Los Angeles and appeared at Dino's, the Troubador and the Bitter End West. He gained national television exposure via Johnny Carson, Merv Griffin and Mike Douglas.

Finally, while opening for singer/pianist Les McCann at the Troubador in 1974, Jarreau was signed by Warner/Reprise. The biggest part of the initial recording success came in Europe. The LP *We Got By* won a Grammy Award in Germany. Acclaim in the jazz field began to grow and singles began to trickle on to the r&b and Bubbling Under charts. A live album recorded in Europe cracked the top 50 in 1977 but it was still another four years before the major pop breakthrough.

Appropriately titled *Breakin' Away*, the album broke the top ten, won two Grammys and gave

Jarreau his biggest hit single. Jay Graydon, producer and co-writer of much of the material, had also worked with Manhattan Transfer, George Benson and Earth, Wind & Fire. (Graydon's father, Joe, had been a big band singer and scored a top hit with "Again" in 1949 with Gordon Jenkins).

In the years since, Jarreau has won additional Grammy nominations, critics' polls, and NAACP Image Awards. "Moonlighting," which he co-wrote for the mid-80's TV series, is another of his best known pop hits.

Before heading west with Jarreau, Les Czimber performed a record 79 hour piano marathon in the window of a clothing store. The stunt was done to promote the movie *Song Without End*, the story of Franz Liszt. He later worked in Las Vegas with singer Odia Coates who was featured on a 1975 Paul Anka hit. Czimber still plays in Orange County, California.

Raynard	10022	I'm Not Afraid/Ska-Bobbi		/65
	10024	Shake Up/Room Boom		/65
Reprise	1374	Rainbow In Your Eyes/Hold On Me	(#92 r&b)	9/76
Warner	8443	Take Five[1]/Loving You	(91 r&b)	8/77
	8481	We Got By/So Long Girl		10/77
	8677	Thinkin' About It Too/Fly	(55 r&b)	10/78
	8751	All/She's Leaving Home		2/79
	49234	Never Givin' Up/Distracted	(102, 26 r&b)	5/80
	49538	Gimme What You Got/Spain	(63 r&b)	8/80
	49588	Distracted/Alonzo	(61 r&b)	10/80
	49746	We're In This Love Together/Alonzo	(15, 6 r&b)	7/81
	49842	Breakin' Away/(Round, Round, Round)Blue Rondo A La Turk[2]		
			(43, 25 r&b)	11/81
	50032	Teach Me Tonight[3]/Easy	(70, 51 r&b)	3/82
	29893	Your Precious Love/Monmouth College Fight Song		
			(102, 16 r&b)	10/82
	29720	Mornin'/Not Like This	(21, 6 r&b)	2/83
	29624	Boogie Down/Our Love	(77, 9 r&b)	5/83
	29501	Trouble In Paradise/Step By Step	(63, 66 r&b)	8/83
	29446	A Christmas/One Love		12/83
	29262	After All/I Keep Callin'	(69, 26 r&b)	9/84
	29091	Raging Waters/Fallin'	(42 r&b)	1/85
	28295	Pretend/Black And Blues		7/85
	28626	L Is For Lover/	(42 r&b)	7/86

---

[1]Dave Brubeck, 1961; w: Paul Desmond
[2]Dave Brubeck Quartet - *Time Out* LP, 1960
[3]DeCastro Sisters, 1954

	28538	Tell Me What I Gotta Do/	(37 r&b)	10/86
MCA	53124	Moonlighting[1]/	(23, 32 r&b)	5/87

LP's:

Reprise		We Got By		/75
	2248	Glow	(132)	7/76
Warner Bro.	3052	Look To The Rainbow/Live In Europe	(49)	5/77
	3229	All Fly Home	(78)	9/78
	3434	This Time	(27)	5/80
	3576	Breakin' Away	(9)	7/81
Bainbridge		(see text)		
Warner Bro.	2380	Jarreau	(13)	3/83
	25106	High Crime	(49)	10/84
	25331	Al Jarreau In London	(125)	8/85
	25477	L Is For Lover	(81)	9/86
Reprise	25778	Heart's Horizon	(75)	11/88
	26849	Heaven And Earth	(105)	6/92

Sources: Al Jarreau telephone interview, 3/21/94
　　　　Les Czimber telephone interview, 5/22/93
　　　　Al Jarreau bio - courtesy Pat Rains & Assoc., 4/28/93
　　　　Whitburn. Record Research
　　　　Clee. American 45 R.P.M. Records

Esquires

(Milwaukee)

"Get On Up" - #11 - 1967

✳ **Highest R&B Position (#3)**

Gilbert Moorer (8/20/41; Birmingham)	**Sam Davidson**
Alvis Moorer (1/18/40; Birmingham)	**David Bursey**
Sam Pace (9/22/44; Kansas City, MO)	**Danny Reed**
Sean Taylor	**Ortez Guzman**
Millard Evans	**Clint Mosley**

The Esquires' story begins about 10 years before they hit the charts with their first release. Siblings Gilbert, Alvis and Betty Moorer formed a vocal group around 1957, inspired, taught and supported by their father, Gilbert Moorer, Sr., who had spent many years singing in gospel groups. While attending North Division High School, the three continued their efforts as many other members, including Harvey Scales, passed in and out of the group. (Gilbert also attended

---

[1]From the television series starring Bruce Willis and Cybill Shepherd

Lincoln Middle School along with Oprah Winfrey). Isn't it interesting that the Esquires' "Get On Up" and Scales' "Get Down" charted within two months of each other?

Sam Pace joined around 1961 and Betty dropped out to go solo. The Esquires contributed background vocals to Betty's 1963 Cuca release and to an album by Milwaukee's Bonnevilles that same year. An additional Cuca session, "You Don't Care," surfaced on a compilation LP several years later.

Sean Taylor joined in 1965 and in 1966 the foursome went to the Dave Kennedy Studio and cut a demo of Gilbert's original, "Get On Up." When they took it to the Impressions in Chicago, Sam Gooden and Fred Cash were interested. Unfortunately, leader Curtis Mayfield was tied up with the Five Stairsteps and the Esquires were unable to make any headway.

Back in Milwaukee later that year, WAWA DJ O.C. White gave them a contact with Gene Page, a Chicago-based producer for ABC who, in turn referred them to Bill "Bunky "Sheppard. Sheppard liked the demo but thought something was missing from the song and called in his friend Mill Edwards for an opinion. Edwards had been in two Chicago vocal groups of the early 60's, the Bel Aires and the Sheppards.

"I told him there's a hole there," says Edwards. "They're singing 'Get On Up' and then there's a big hole there. 'Well,' he said, 'You know it's not there so do something, give me something.' I worked on it and came up with the bass parts for the song."[1] Besides Edwards bass parts, the record blended a number of tasty ingredients; bright, upbeat singing, a punchy horn arrangement by Tom Washington, and a vocal insertion of the well-known horn intro from "Knock On Wood."

In exchange for putting the bass parts on "Get On Up," the Esquires provided the backup for Edwards record, "Things Won't Be The Same," released as Mill Evans. Of course, "Get On Up" became the hit and Edwards became a member of the Esquires.

Shortly after their first big gig at New York's Apollo theater, Sean Taylor was dismissed from the group by manager Bunky Sheppard. Taylor, a fatherless youth when he joined the Esquires, was "just one of those guys who screws off a lot,"[2] says Gilbert Moorer. Taylor did a pair of solo singles for the Magic Touch label at this time.

It was common practice at the time for record companies to try to duplicate the sound of an artist's initial hit with a follow-up while, at the same time, avoiding just a re-hash job. The Esquires accomplished this with "And Get Away" which charted 22 pop and 9 r&b.

---

[1]Pruter, Robert. <u>Chicago Soul</u>. Chicago: University of Illinois Press, 1991.
[2]see footnote 1

Things began to fade with next release, however, and it wasn't until moving to the Wand label in the fall of 1968 that the Esquires returned to the top 30 of the R&B charts with "You've Got The Power."

In 1971 Sean Taylor returned to the fold and sang lead on "Girls In The City" which, though it only bubbled under pop, made #18 on the Soul chart. This was to be their last real "hurrah," however, as far as the charts were concerned, though the Esquires have continued to record and perform.

Mill Edwards left in 1971 to go into the jewelry business, coming back long enough to reprise his bass vocal on the group's update of "Get On Up '76," which brought a final chart appearance. The group disbanded for a short time, then came back with some personnel changes. In the 90's the Moorer brothers and Sam Pace continue as the Esquires.

Bunky	7750	Get On Up/Listen To Me	(#11, 3 r&b)	7/67
	7752	And Get Away/Everybody's Laughing	(22, 9 r&b)	10/67
	7753	You Say/State Fair	(126, 41 r&b)	1/68
	7755	Why Can't I Stop/The Feeling's Gone	(48 r&b)	4/68
	7756	I Know I Can/How Could It Be		7/68
Wand	1193	You've Got The Power/No Doubt About It	(91, 29 r&b)	11/68
	1195	I Don't Know/Part Angel	(37 r&b)	3/69
	11201	Whip It On Me/It Was Yesterday		6/69
B&G	7751	Ain't No Reason/Baba Daba Dop		/69
Capitol	2650	Reach Out/Listen To Me		10/69
Lamar	1001	Girls In The City/Ain't Gonna Give It Up	(120, 18 r&b)	1/71
Rocky Ridge	403	Danced A Hole In The World/That Ain't No Reason		7/71
Hot Line	103	Henry Ralph/My Sweet Baby		/72
New World	101	Stay/Let Me Build You A New World		/74
JuPar	104	Get On Up '76/Feeling's Gone	(62 r&b)	9/76
Lasco	1101	The Fish/My Lady		/79

LP's:

Bunky	300	Get On Up And Get Away	/67
Cuca	4500	Badger A Go Go	/69

(This compilation LP includes "You Don't Care" by the Esquires and "Long Hot Summer" by Betty Moore with backing vocals by the Esquires)

Mill Edwards

Constellation	170	Things Won't Be The Same/I've Got To Have Your Love (Mill Evans)	/66
Bunky	7761	Don't Forget About Me/Use What You Got	/69
Cutlass	8143	I Found Myself/	/72

Sean Taylor

Magic Touch	2003	Never Do I Worry (About You)/Funky Soul Dance	/67
	2008	Put Me Down Easy/Too Late To Turn Back Now	/67

Also see: Harvey Scales
        Betty Moore - Milwaukee
Unrelated Esquires: Album, Alley, Audio Fidelity, CFP, Columbia, Dot, Durco, Feature,
        Glenvalley, Hi-Po, Phalanx, Raven, Salem, Scratch, Smog City, Tower
Sources: Sam Pace telephone interview, 12/4/93
        Tori Moorer Jackson/Gilbert Moorer telephone interview, 7/28/94
        Pruter, Robert. "Get On Up … And Get Away." It Will Stand 5/82: 6-9.
        Whitburn. Record Research
        Clee. American 45 R.P.M. Records
        Osborne, Jerry & Pat Brown. Rockin' Records: Buyers-Sellers Reference Book & Price
            Guide. Port Townsend, WA: Jellyroll Publications, 1993.

Esquires: Sean Taylor, Alvis Moorer, Sam Pace,
Gilbert Moorer (courtesy Tori Jackson)

Underground Sunshine: Chris Connors,
Jane Little, Berty Kohl, Frank Kohl

Underground Sunshine
(Montello)
"Birthday" - #26 - 1969

Rex Rhode - gtr
Jane Little (Whirry) - kb (1/22/51; Portage)
Bert "Bertie" Kohl (Koelbl) (8/18/49; Waldkierchen, Germany) - bs
Frank Kohl (Koelbl) (9/30/47; Waldkierchen, Germany) - dr
        Chris Connors (John Dahlberg) (10/2/46; Milwaukee)
        Dave Wayne (Waehner) - org
        Mike Hoolihan - bs

One change the Beatles brought to pop music was the inclusion of album cuts on "Top 40" radio playlists. This resulted in an unprecedented popularity of many tunes that were simply not available on singles. Since many bands were trying to "out-Beatle" each other anyway, it wasn't much of a stretch for the bands or their management/record labels to conclude that a sound-alike 45 might have a ready made market. Underground Sunshine certainly was not the first to try, nor were they the most successful (That honor probably goes to the #18 hit version of "Michelle." Can you name the artist?), but they were close.

Initially a hard rock trio guided by Madison radio personality Jonathan Little, the band decided, after recording some demos, that they needed a keyboard. Little (who was music director of WISM at the time) says it was to add more of a "Doors"-type flavor to their sound, but bassist Bert Koelbl says they "needed a keyboard to do the Beatles solo." Enter Little's sister - or little sister - Jane.

"I was a senior in high school and I was going with the drummer," says Jane. "I could play the piano and sing, so I would go to the practices with them, and it came to a point where they asked if I wanted to just get a keyboard and play along."

The four musicians and their manager trekked to Milwaukee for their meeting with fate. "The Dave Kennedy studios were in kind of a tough part of town," recalls Jonathan Little, "and there was a bar down below. We were up on the second floor, the elevator didn't work, and we had to haul all of the equipment upstairs. Harvey Scales & the Seven Sounds were down below performing that night. We actually had to run down two different times and say, 'Can you guys just hold up for about 15 minutes. We're trying to get the tracks down right now." Tom Gress reportedly did the production for a flat fee.

Through his many friends in radio, Little secured some airplay even before releasing the record on his own Earth label. Then came further response, a switch to the Intrepid label (a division of Mercury), and things began to change in many ways.

The musicians had signed an agreement to pay a 20% commission to a local backer in return for his supplying equipment. An attorney advised them to break the agreement, considering the amount excessive. Guitarist Rex Rhode didn't concur. "He quit because he was such good friends with this other person," says Jane Little. "And we were supposed to be going to do Dick Clark in just a few weeks. The silly guy quit at that time!"

The band advertised in *The Milwaukee Journal* and auditioned for a replacement, settling on Chris Connors. Connors had chosen his stage name on a train ride to college in 1964. "A girl on the train told me I reminded her of this guy named Chris Connors. I liked it and have used it ever since," he explains. (Connors apparently was unfamiliar with female jazz vocalist Chris Connor from the 50's, or with r&b singer Chris Kenner from the early 60's).

Underground Sunshine went on to do *American Bandstand, Upbeat*, and extensive touring. The album charted and the follow-up single bubbled under. Jane Little and Frank Koelbl got married, but all was not well.

Jonathan Little attributes the demise of the band to "substance abuse problems." Jane Little says, "We were all pretty innocent Montello High School kids and he (Connors) came in with Milwaukee ideas and big time thoughts. I couldn't handle the groupies coming to the motel room afterward. The whole thing was really tacky to me."

Bert Koelbl: "I left because the biggest paycheck I ever got was $325.00 and I was doing an awful lot of work. And quite frankly, management was not fulfilling my needs."

Chris Connors: "Bert Koelbl fell in love and stopped appearing for jobs. Jane was removed from the band by her parents because the rest of the band was using pot. Frank and Jane married and then Jane pulled Frank out of the group. This is simplistic but pretty much covers the facts."

Frank Koelbl: "The Little's think (drugs are) what broke the band up, but it wasn't. There was some conflict there because he was making a little more money than we were. It wasn't because of drugs. We were never into drugs a whole lot. We did some pot but none of us are pot-heads or dope-heads. It got blown out of proportion. How many bands back in the 60's did, in fact, smoke pot? (Underground Sunshine) gave us a lot of opportunities and I had a lot of great experiences - got to see a lot of the country, got to see a lot of different things."

(Trivia answer: The hit single of "Michelle" was by David & Jonathan, a pseudonym for Roger Greenaway & Roger Cook. I've disqualified the Silkie's "You've Got To Hide Your Love Away" because it included Beatles involvement.)

Epilogue:

Chris Connors, Bert Koelbl and David Wayne later formed a short-lived band called Eden Stone. Connors continues to play clubs in a duo with his wife, Debbie.

Bert and Frank Koelbl reunited with original guitarist Rex Rhode as Underground Sunshine (or U.S., as the members not-always-affectionately refer to it) around 1989-1991. Bert also had a booking agency from 1973-1991 and has since gone into writing and producing his own Christian music. "It's been a very, very good learning experience," he says of the Underground Sunshine days. "Even the way it was done, I would not trade anything for it."

After a divorce from Frank, Jane remarried and is now teaching piano "and loving it."

Earth	100	Birthday[1]/All I Want Is You		/69
Intrepid	75002	Birthday/All I Want Is You	(#26)	7/69
	75012	Don't Shut Me Out[2]/Take Me Break Me	(102)	10/69
	75019	Nine To Five/Rotten Woman Blues		/69
	75029	Jesus Is Just Alright[3]/Six O'clock		/70

LP:

Intrepid	74003	Let There Be Light	(161)	11/69

Also see: Challengers - Milwaukee (Chris Connors, David Wayne, Mike Hoolihan)
　　　　Picture - Milwaukee (Mike Hoolihan)
　　　　Pro-Gress Records - Wisconsin Labels, Fendermen (Tom Gress)
Sources: Jonathan Little telephone interview, 1/93
　　　　Jane Trahms telephone interview, 11/14/93
　　　　Frank Koelbl telephone interview, 11/14/93
　　　　Bert Koelbl telephone interview, 11/14/93
　　　　Chris Connors letter and telephone interview, 11/93
　　　　Phil Nee Show; WRCO, 3/12/94 - courtesy Phil Nee
　　　　Whitburn. Record Research
　　　　Clee. American 45 R.P.M. Records

Dave Dudley
(David Pudraska; 5/3/28; Spencer)
Six Days On The Road - #32 - 1963

✳ **Most Successful Country Artist**

At age 35, with ten previous releases, recording a cast-off song for an unknown label, Dave Dudley was not a likely candidate to score a top country hit, cross over to pop, and establish a song as a standard in the field. But with a biting hard-edged guitar sound, a unique background vocal, and his big baritone voice, Dudley created a trucker's anthem that launched the rest of his career.

Baseball had claimed Dudley's interest initially and things looked promising. After a 15-3 record in 1949, his first year pitching for Stevens Point, he began to step up in the minors. When an arm injury halted that progress, he returned to Wisconsin to work for the railroad. A visit to a friend at a local radio station one evening put him on a different track.

---

[1]Beatles - *The White Album*, 1968
[2]Bread - *Bread* LP, 1969
[3]Byrds, 1970

"I was just sitting there waiting for him to get through with his shift so we could go grab a couple beers," recalls Dudley, "and I picked up a guy's guitar in the corner and I started fooling around with it. The program director, Vern Shepherd, heard me and asked me if I wanted to sing a few songs in the mornings. Heck, I thought he was kidding." After Dudley failed to show up the next morning, he quickly discovered that Shepherd was serious when the program director angrily phoned Dudley's mother. When he learned there would be money involved, Dudley began the AM serenading regularly, earning $5-10 a show singing his favorite Hank Thompson and Eddie Arnold tunes.

After a while he formed a band and began to work clubs and write songs. In 1955 Dudley traveled to Cincinnati with the hope of placing some tunes with King Records whose roster included Cowboy Copas and Hawkshaw Hawkins. King not only liked the songs, they liked Dudley's voice and style, and put out three singles.

These were followed by releases on NRC, Starday and Circle Dot, a company co-owned by Dudley. "Maybe I Do," on a label owned by pop star Bobby Vee, became Dudley's first country chart entry in late 1961. Next came a song that Dudley had written with the hope of getting it to Leroy Van Dyke who was just coming off his major hit, "Walk On By." Released first on the New Star label, "Under Cover Of The Night" was picked up by Jubilee and attained a respectable #18 on Billboard's Hot C&W Sides. But Dudley wasn't sure which way to go at this point.

"I had to make a decision," he says. "I was thinking that things weren't happening very fast. We weren't getting that hot and I figured if I had to be local all the time, that's no way to live for the rest of your life." Dudley went into partnership with Jim Madison in Minneapolis to get into the production end of the business. The agreement was for him to produce a line of country artists for Madison's label and continue to record as a solo artist for the company.

"I had this song Jimmy C. Newman gave me," he explains. "It was at the Grand Ole Opry. Some guy had given him this song, 'Six Days On the Road', and he said to me, 'That song is not for me, I can't sing a song like that,' so he threw the tape in my guitar case. So, we were one song short at Kay Bank Studios in Minneapolis and I was paying for the time. We had finished three songs, we had 45 minutes left and I wanted to get my money's worth so I reached in my guitar case and I said, 'Let's see what we got here.' The girl was typing it up while the tape was playing and I just learned it right there on the spot. We did it in 45 minutes and that's when we invented that guitar sound. Then we used our local singers that we had taken just at random and used them as back-up singers. We put them on the record and they did great."

The song seemed to capture a bit of a 50's rockabilly flavor with an almost simultaneous feeling of country shuffle rhythm and rock n' roll eighth notes. (The same way some early rock n' roll records did when it seemed as if they weren't yet sure which way to play it). The background vocal created a kind of windy effect, and you could almost feel an 18-wheeler barreling past you down a Tennessee hill. The record attracted attention in a hurry.

Mercury Records felt that the label name, Golden Wing, was an infringement on their Wing budget label. Reportedly planning to have George Jones cover the tune, they called to register their complaint. Dudley's reply was, "I'm gonna tell you right now. This song is gonna be on this label as long as it's hot. If you want to sue me, go ahead and sue me. You or nobody else is gonna stop me from making this record a hit!" The two companies came to an agreement allowing Dudley to use Golden Wing on that record with a change to Golden Ring thereafter. Jones never showed up to record the cover version and, ironically, Dudley soon signed with Mercury.

With that kind of success it was inevitable that Dudley's previous labels would attempt to cash in on his name. "They put out some real trash," he says. "I think Starday was the guiltiest of all. They turned out some demos I'd done and they were just terrible."

"Six Days On The Road" even showed up on Soma a little later. "I don't know too much about that," says Dudley. "Soma was the distributor for Golden Ring so they might have made a deal to get all the mileage they could out of it."

Sadly, two of the people responsible for the record ended their lives early. According to Dudley, guitarist Jimmy Colvard committed suicide after having done studio work in Nashville. Songwriter Bob Montgomery suffered a similar fate. "Montgomery, he killed himself," says Dudley. "He was hoping that he always could write songs as big as 'Six Days' and I guess it just kind of overwhelmed him and he never could live up to that expectation again. It just got to him. The other guy, (co-writer) Earl Green, he's still around."

Dudley recorded for Mercury for ten years, moving to Rice (a company he co-owned) in 1973. Next came United Artists, back to Rice, then Sun. The most unusual item during the later years is probably a 1978 release on Columbia (10851) that puts Dudley on the flip side of a Bob Dylan cut. "That's one I don't even know about," he says. From 1961 to 1980 he placed a staggering 41 singles on Billboard's country charts. "Cowboy Boots," his follow-up to "Six Days," graced the pop chart for just one week and he bubbled under three more times over the next three years.

Dudley lived in Nashville from 1965 to 1980, then returned to northern Wisconsin. "I just got kinda tired of the old rat race thing over there," he laughs. "You know it's business as usual from sun-up till - sun-up!"

Pre-Mercury Discography:

King	1508	This Is The Last Time/Cry Baby Cry		/55
	4866	Ink Dries Quicker Than Tears/I'll Be Waiting For You		/56
	4933	I Guess You Know You're Right/Rock And Roll Nursery Rhyme		6/56
Starday	364	Cry Baby/Careless Fool		/58
NRC	024	Where There's A Will There's A Way/I Won't Be		
			Just Your Friend	4/59
Starday	499	It's Gotta Be That Way/Where Do I Go From Here		6/60

Circle Dot	101	Picture Of My Heart/Your Old Standby		/60
Vee	7003	<u>Maybe I Do</u>/I Wouldn't Wait Around	(#28 C)	9/61
New Star	6420	Under Cover Of the Night/Please Let Me Prove (My Love For You)		/62
Jubilee	5436	<u>Under Cover Of The Night</u>/Please Let Me Prove (#18C) (My Love For You)		8/62
Golden Wing	3020	<u>Six Days On The Road</u>/I Feel A Cry Coming On	(32, 2 C)	5/63
Pelham	4504	You're The Only One/I Wouldn't Wait Around		8/63
King	5792	Ink Dries Quicker Than Tears/I'll Be Waiting For You		/63
Golden Ring	3030	<u>Cowboy Boots</u>/I Think I'll Cheat	(95, 3 C)	10/63

Sources: Dave Dudley telephone interview, 11/13/93
    Shestack, Melvin. <u>Country Music Encyclopedia</u>. NY: Crowell, 1974.
    Fred Masotti, 1993
    Clee. <u>American 45 R.P.M. Records</u>
    Whitburn. <u>Record Research</u>

Dave Dudley (courtesy Dianna Key,
Southern Arts Music)

Thee Prophets: (top) David Leslie, Brian Lake,
(bottom) Chris Michaels, Jim Anderson (courtesy Brian Lake)

Thee Prophets
(West Allis)
"Playgirl" - #49 - 1969

Brian Lake - org (6/20/49; West Allis)
Jim Anderson - gtr (2/23/48; West Allis)   **Mark Sandusky** - gtr
Dave Leslie (Stimac) - bs (7/27/49; West Allis)   **Tony Gazzana** - voc
Chris Michaels (Michael Mashock) - dr (4/21/49; West Allis)
                                                      Joe Kopecky - sx
                                                      Jerry George - sx
                                                      Jose Salazar - tp
                                                      Dave Maciolek - bs
                                                      Lee Johnson - gtr

This exuberant teen pop record began edging its way across national airwaves in early 1969, achieving top ten positions in some markets. The record was produced by the same team that had scored with the Buckinghams' "Kind Of A Drag" two years earlier. The ingredients for the hit began to mesh when leader Brian Lake met producer Carl Bonafede while trying to secure more prestigious bookings for his group.

Lake credits Elvis' "Hound Dog" (on a 78 brought home by his father) as one of his first musical influences. When the Legends became his local heroes a few years later, he started guitar lessons at West Allis Music, with Doug Tank of the Royal Lancers as his teacher. In 1962 he recruited neighborhood friends Jim Anderson and Dave Stimac to form a band, and the three of them convinced Mike Mashock to buy a set of drums and take lessons.

In an effort to set the music apart from other guitar-oriented bands, Lake picked up a Wurlitzer electric piano. That soon gave way to a Farfisa organ, which was a little closer to what he really wanted. "Through listening to a Jimmy Smith record, I discovered the Hammond B3," he says. "I immediately fell in love with that instrument and really still am to this day."

The B3 was purchased in 1966 and the band was developing more of an r&b sound. Two saxes, a trumpet and a lead singer were added, expanding the group to eight pieces. Within a year, however, the horns were dropped and Jim Anderson left temporarily to be replaced by Mark Sandusky. The band leaned more toward top 40 material and in 1967, with a bit of Association-type sound, they cut their first single for the Appleton based Tee Pee label.

The next step was Lake's trip to Chicago in an attempt to obtain bookings through Chartwell, a major agency that handled many name acts. Representative Carl Bonafede was impressed with the tape but told Lake he couldn't book them without a hit record. A second tape and a second trip brought the same result but, fortunately, Bonafede continued to hear about the group and finally went to see them at a club in Racine. The live appearance did the trick and Thee Prophets were signed to a management-production deal.

"Playgirl" and "Shame, Shame" were selected from a batch of demos and recorded at Sterosonic in Chicago in August 1968. They decided to hold "Shame" as a likely second single, believing it too strong for a "B" side. Bonafede shopped the tapes in New York and selected Kapp, thinking they would devote more effort to promotion than larger labels with more name artists.

Meanwhile, plans for "Shame, Shame" fell by the wayside as the Magic Lanterns released their version of it and Thee Prophets watched it climb into the national top 30.

"Playgirl" came out about November and was first played by Tex Meyer at WRIT. It didn't really start to move for a few months, however, finally entering Billboard's Hot 100 on March 8, 1969. While peaking at 41 in Record World and 39 in Cash Box, it made the top ten in Boston, Tulsa and Los Angeles and ascended all the way to number one at WLLR in Lowell, Massachusetts. It has always been somewhat of a sore spot with Lake that they only reached number 15 in Milwaukee, where they thought they would do the best.

Jay & the Americans had gained a recent success with a remake of the Drifters' "This Magic Moment," prompting Lake to suggest another Drifters oldie, "Some Kind Of Wonderful," for a follow-up. The label was pushing for an album, but the wind was beginning to shift.

The LP, cut at Chess' famous 2120 South Michigan Avenue studio, was rushed and the band members were not happy with the material. Leaning in an "underground rock" direction, they had been playing Hendrix and Cream tunes in their shows and had hoped to record their version of Hendrix' "Fire" on the album. They were excited about recording with a 50-piece orchestra but disappointed in the mix-down. Says Lake, "The entire album was pretty much a textbook example of the group itself having no say whatsoever."

The LP charted briefly and "Some Kind Of Wonderful" bubbled under. Thee Prophets did their hit on TV shows like *Upbeat* and *Mike Douglas* while continuing to fill their concerts with covers of Hendrix, Cream, Electric Flag, Chicago, and Blood, Sweat & Tears.

Bonafede and Kapp pressed them to record more teen bubblegum material. "It was all stuff that we, as musicians, were not into at all," recalls Lake, "so musically we were at totally opposite ends." With their contract tying them up for five years, it was either record what they were asked or not record at all. They chose the latter. "It really didn't bother us that much that we weren't recording," claims Lake. "We had gained such a big name from 'Playgirl' and the other records and most of our money was from touring. We never really saw any record royalties." Anderson and Leslie left after a while and, when Lake grew disenchanted with the travel, Thee Prophets disbanded in October 1972.

Jim Anderson was last known to be in Texas and Dave Stimac in Minneapolis. Mike Mashock is a pharmacist in Seattle and Tony Gazzana went into radio. Lake did behind-the-scenes work for WISN-TV, then joined Sight & Sound Publishing. He has been involved with distribution for Casio keyboards since 1981 and he still owns the same Hammond B3.

| Tee Pee | 4529/4530 | To Be With You/If You Would Leave Me | | 9/67 |
| Kapp | 962 | Playgirl/Patricia Ann | (#49) | 12/68 |

	997	<u>Some Kind Of Wonderful</u>[1]/They Call Her Sorrow	(111)	5/69
	2038	Rag Doll Boy/It Isn't So Easy		8/69
	2087	A Little Bit Of Love/Come To Me Girl		4/70
	2097	Some Kind Of Wonderful/They Call Her Sorrow		9/70

LP:

Kapp	3596	<u>Playgirl</u>	(163)	6/69

Also see: Dynastys - Milwaukee (Dave Maciolek)
      Triumphs - Milwaukee (Tony Gazzana, Jerry George)
      Messengers (related story)
Unrelated Prophets: Atco, Chess, Delphi, Epic, Jairick, Smash, Stephayne
Sources: Brian Lake telephone interview and tapes, 3/93-5/93
      Whitburn. <u>Record Research</u>
      Clee. <u>American 45 R.P.M. Records</u>

Messengers
(Milwaukee)
"That's The Way A Woman Is" #62 - 1971

✳ **Most Bizarre Story**

Suppose you decided to write a novel, or maybe a sitcom, about a 60's band, and this is your plot:

Your teenage hero, Greg, starts a band in Minnesota and they put out an obscure record. Then, he goes off to school in Milwaukee and starts another band with the same name. They get pretty good - so good that a large, hip label is interested in them. Alas, the organ player's parents won't let him sign a contract.

While deciding what to do about this, they cut a record in their home studio. Well, maybe not really a record, maybe just a favor for DJ friend Paul. But Paul takes it to Chicago and it becomes a record after all. In fact, it starts selling. But Greg and his band don't want to be involved with it because they're still courting the large, hip label.

Well, Paul and the Chicago record company want a band to promote the record and cut a follow-up, so they:
      a) create one from various Chicago musicians,
      b) find one in a Chicago bar,
      c) get one from Boston (!),
      d) all of the above,

---

[1]Drifters, 1961

and they put a fictitious guy named Michael at the head of it. By this time the record is a regional hit. The other band (the guys from a, b, c, or d; above) do the follow-up and THAT'S a regional hit!

Meanwhile, Greg's band has replaced the under-age organ player and signed with the large, hip label. Their first record comes out and THAT'S a regional hit! There are hits all over the place! In spite of all this, the large, hip label, for some strange reason, doesn't release a follow-up. After a while, Greg's band gets tired of waiting around for the company to do something, and they put out a record on their own label. Even THAT'S a local hit!

Oh yes, they also hire a guy named Michael. A real guy, not the fictitious one from that phony band. (He even has the same name as another real guy from another real band in town. This has nothing to do with our story but it fits perfectly with the confusion!).

Finally, about two and a half years after the first record, the large, (and maybe not so) hip (after all) label releases an album - but no single! For that, they wait another year and a half! Well, it finally comes out and it's the biggest hit yet! Even in Japan! All right! Now we're cooking! But wait!

The band breaks up and they are never heard from again.

Yes, it's ridiculous, it'll never work. It's far too complicated and weird. But, as we all know, truth is stranger than fiction, and this is the true story of the Messengers.

Minnesota Messengers (just for the record)**:**
Greg Jeresek - bs
Greg Bambenek - gtr
Roy Burger - gtr
Chip Andrus - kb
Mike Murphy - dr

Soma   1427 My Baby/I've Seen You Around   3/65

Milwaukee Messengers:
Greg Jennings (Jeresek) - bs (7/3/47; Winona, MN)
Jesse Roe - org (9/16/47; Bayshore, Long Is., NY)
Peter Barans - gtr/bs (6/23/46; Chicago, IL)   **Rob Leslie** - org
Jeff Taylor - voc (3/10/47; Detroit, MI)   **Michael Morgan** - org
Augie Jurishica - dr (5/2/47; Milwaukee)   **Mike Demling** - dr

                                  John Hoier - gtr/bs (3/25/49; El Segundo, CA)
                                  Bob Cavallo - dr (11/16/48; Milwaukee)

Formed by Greg Jeresek and Peter Barans at Marquette University in 1966, the Messengers included Mark Kapov and one or two other members before settling on the line-up that appeared on the first record (Milwaukee Messengers shown above). During the year preceding that record, the band benefitted from a big break for the Robbs.

Con Merten was the manager of both groups and, when the Robbs got the call to do the television show, *Where The Action Is,* in Los Angeles, Merten called on the Messengers to fill many of the Robbs dates. "That really was a springboard for us," says drummer Augie Jurishica. "It got us traveling around with a bunch of groups that summer - Herman's Hermits, Wayne Fontana & the Mindbenders, the Animals and so on." Mercury Records had some interest in the group (probably through Merten, since the Robbs had signed with Mercury) but no deal was consummated.

An engagement as the opening act for the Dave Clark Five at Chicago's McCormick Place provided an important contact, as well as some pre-show panic. "We got down there to do the gig," recalls organist Jesse Roe, "and the special cord from the Hammond organ to the speaker was missing. We're going nuts - 'What are we gonna do?' - and Greg called and had a pilot break into our house up in Menomonee Falls, get the cord, get to the airport and fly it in! We had about ten minutes till show time and the pilot brings the cord in! I'll never forget that."

After the show Jeffrey Bowen of Motown approached the group. "He was saying words I had not even heard about," laughs Greg Jeresek. "He kept telling us we were the baddest white group he had ever seen, and we were kind of scratching our heads about why did this man come back to complain?"

Motown flew the band to Detroit for auditions and meetings (A charter flight in the midst of an airline strike). "We walked into Motown studios when Levi Stubbs (of the Four Tops) was singing 'Reach Out'" says Roe. "Holland-Dozier-Holland wanted to produce us. They dangled 'You Keep Me Hanging On' to us." However, Roe's parents wouldn't clear the way for their underage son to sign and the band returned to Milwaukee.

Jeresek had an engineering background and had built a recording studio in the house where they were all living. One evening the members gathered there, along with WOKY DJ Paul Christy and Brian Lake, leader and organist of Thee Prophets. Jesse Roe recalls the proceedings of that fateful night:

"It's a classic story that shouldn't be told," he laughs. "Christy wanted to have some teenage band to record 'Midnight Hour' and asked as a favor would we 'just do it the way you do it,' because we were doing the Rascals version. He said, 'Do it fast,' and we did this kind of twinky version of it - extremely fast. It wasn't thought out. It was a joke. We did 'Hard Hard Year' seriously and then he wanted something else and we did a jam, a song of mine."

Brian Lake added some background vocals (which got buried in the mix) but learned that the real reason he had been invited was to be offered the gig as Jesse Roe's replacement. The members had mutually agreed to take that step in order to sign with Motown. Lake opted to stay with his own group and Rob Leslie stepped in when Roe left to return to his family in New York.

Augie Jurishica and Greg Jeresek offer slightly differing memories of the record's release:

Jurishica: "We made an agreement with Bob Golden at USA Records. The only reason we went with him was the Buckinghams had just had 'Kind Of A Drag' (a hit for the company) and he was a local and we could get a distribution-only contract with him, where we didn't owe him anything else."

Jeresek: Paul (Christy) negotiated the deal with USA and it got kind of sticky from that point on, because it was one of those gentlemen's agreements between Paul and myself. What Paul and USA agreed, I was never privy to. I learned my first lessons of how things were done in the music industry, because a lot of contracts were signed with my name on it that I had not signed."

While "Midnight Hour" began to gather airplay, the Messengers signed with Motown. USA, needing a band to promote the record, issued subsequent pressings showing the group as "Michael & the Messengers," then came up with a band (or bands?) to fill that bill. They also omitted the original flip side, replacing it with Jesse Roe's jam instrumental from the original session and titling it "Up Till News." "Midnight Hour" reportedly made number 3 in Chicago while bubbling under nationally at number 116. (More on the consequences of this later).

Possibly the first white group signed to Motown, the Messengers released a single on the Soul subsidiary. It also bubbled under, while the flip side, "California Soul," would become a hit for the 5th Dimension a year later. Jurishica claims the song was written for the Messengers.

"We then ran into Motown politics," says Jeresek. Things were beginning to unravel between Holland-Dozier-Holland and Berry Gordy, and also between Diana Ross & the Supremes. Seeds were being sown for the company's move to Hollywood. "The whole core of what Motown was at the time of our signing was disintegrating all around us, so we were kind of lost in a limbo and assigned to different producers. Really the whole album thing turned into a whole ordeal of nothingness."

Personnel changes took place in the group, also. Organist and lead singer Michael Morgan came aboard. Though there was no connection, this helped to fuel the confusion about Michael & the Messengers. Despite the presence of Morgan, the Milwaukee group was never known as "Michael & the Messengers." (Unrelated to the Messengers, but perhaps adding a bit more confusion, there is a Michael Morgan in Milwaukee who played guitar for Little Artie & the Pharaohs). Disappointed with the situation at Motown, the Messengers released a self-produced, live single on their own Home Made label and it achieved some local success.

The album finally came out in early 1970 with no single released. Over a year passed before the release of "That's The Way A Woman Is," which reached its respectable #62 position during a nine-week chart run in the fall of 1971. It achieved greater success in Japan and the Messengers undertook a tour that Jeresek hoped would rejuvenate the band. "We were treated like royalty," he says. "It stuck as the number one hit for months over there. Unfortunately, what happened was just the reverse of what I expected. When we returned to the states it was such a big let-down, it was the unofficial end."

Epilogue:

Greg Jeresek had already removed himself from live performing to concentrate on the engineering and management of the group. He continued to build sound equipment and he provided the sound for Milwaukee's *Summerfest* for several years before moving to California. He eventually returned to Minnesota where he has a video production company.

Peter Barnes (changed from the original spelling of Barans) was the only member who played every Messengers gig from start to finish. He and Michael Morgan then formed a duo and toured from Florida to California and up to Seattle. "That was probably the most fabulous experience that I've had," says Barnes. The pair then returned to Milwaukee and co-hosted the *Sunday Night Special* on Channel Six (WITI-TV). Morgan & Barnes then convinced a San Francisco entertainer named Uncle Vinty to add a group to his solo act, in which all the members would be featured in various combinations. This modern vaudeville-type show was introduced on the TV show and performed at colleges for the next year. When Vinty decided to go back to being a single, Morgan & Barnes, along with drummer Ted Medbury, went to New York as the Movies. The name proved appropriate when the trio, while recording for Arista, placed a song in the Jane Fonda-George Segal film, *Fun With Dick And Jane*. Barnes has since gone on to do writing, production and music for television in Milwaukee, Ft. Worth, and Los Angeles. Morgan reportedly became a minister in Texas.

Jeff Taylor, through a call from Reed Kailing of the Destinations, became one of the Hardy Boys, a group created to capitalize on and promote an animated cartoon TV series. They charted one LP briefly in late 1969. Taylor followed that with a series of recordings with Gary Loizzo of the American Breed ("Bend Me, Shape Me," 1968). "We put out a lot of 45's under different group names," says Taylor, "hoping one would catch on and then we would have put a group together. Unfortunately, it never got quite to the point where we wanted it to." Taylor, now a goldsmith in Oconomowoc, has continued to perform with The Plumb Loco Band since about 1986. During the interview he interjected "When is Greg going to get the Messengers back together?"

Jesse Roe returned to Milwaukee and worked briefly in a band with Augie Jurishica and future actress Amy Madigan. Roe and Madigan then joined with Fred Bliffert and went to Los Angeles where they recorded for Asylum as Jelly.

Bob Cavallo returned to his pre-Messengers family business, photography.

John Hoier moved to Los Angeles and operated a recording studio for many years, also doing studio work with the Turtles. He gave up the studio in 1987 and went on to work in sound mixing and editing for Warner Brothers.

"The experience that the Messengers went through affected each one of us greatly," says Greg Jeresek. "We really kept at it and gave it our all and were looking for some support outside of ourselves. When you get none from your management company and none from the record company, it really wears on you. I think the ramifications of that are probably pretty significant throughout all of our lives."

USA	866	In The Midnight Hour[1]/Hard Hard Year[2]		4/67
	866	<u>In The Midnight Hour</u>/Up Til News	(#116/I)	5/67
		(2nd pressing shown as Michael & the Messengers, however this is still the Messengers. The above three songs were all recorded at the same session.)		
Soul	35037	<u>Window Shopping</u>/California Soul[3]	(132)	10/67
Home Made	1	I Gotta Dance/Right On		/69
Rare Earth	5032	<u>The Way A Woman Is</u>/In The Jungle	(62)	9/71

LP:

Rare Earth	509	The Messengers		2/70

Movies

Arista	0202	Dancin' On Ice/		8/76
	0235	Ahead Of The Game/Satellite Touchdown		2/77
	0261	Hello Hello Young Lovers/Cricket She Jump	(/I)	8/77

LP:

Arista	4085	The Movies		/76

Michael & the Messengers

So, who were the real Michael and the Messengers? Or was there even such a band? Where did they come from? Was Jesse Roe involved?

Greg Jeresek: "That group was kind of just a Scotch Tape® and bailing wire creation - just one that Christy kind of threw together with people from Milwaukee that he knew and people from Chicago that USA knew." Believing that Jesse Roe was involved, Jeresek says, "That was kind of bizarre. His folks were kind of pressuring him to get out of the Messengers so he did kind of reluctantly. The next thing I know he had teamed up with Christy and was out on the road with them for a while."

---

[1]Wilson Pickett, 1965
[2]Hollies LP
[3]5th Dimension, 1969

Augie Jurishica: "After we went with Motown, Christy got a little group together with Jesse in it. He put 'Up Til News' on our recording and listed himself as the writer and producer of it. They were together a very short time. They were all Chicago people. I don't know who they were."

Peter Barnes: "They made more money than we did. That was our first good screwing."

Jeff Taylor: "When Jesse left and went to Chicago, I believe, and started that, then I don't know what happened. We haven't seen a residual since the day we cut the record."

John Hoier: "From what I've been able to gather, there were many (Michael & the Messengers) groups. Promoters would throw something together."

Bob Cavallo: "They got Jesse Roe and they threw the group together. We never saw a penny of that (money from USA Records)."

(Hoier and Cavallo were both later members and were not involved in that record).

Paul Christy (Christides): "We came up with the name so we could have a follow-up to the record. The new group was a bar band that USA picked up out of Chicago. Bob Monaco from USA found them and he dealt with them."

Christy used the name Wesley Willard to take production credit on the label. He could not remember any of the members' names and has no recollection of any involvement by Jesse Roe. (Christy also produced the Milwaukee band the Next Five. Eric Olson of that group claims that Christy asked them to become Michael & the Messengers). After leaving WOKY, Christy had been with Chicago's WCFL and many other stations. He eventually went to work for the syndication division of Bonneville Broadcasting near his native Detroit.

Bob Monaco has been quoted as saying the band was from Woburn, Massachusetts (suburb of Boston). This seemed like the most unlikely scenario of all until I heard Jesse Roe's story.

Jesse Roe: "I was living in New York and I was driving to Boston with a friend and I heard 'Up Til News' on the radio. That annoyed me no end. I went around trying to find out what I could do about this. ASCAP said you need a lot of money to sue. Then I found out that Christy and Bob Monaco were booking bands all over the Midwest under the name Michael & the Messengers. I didn't get anything out of it so I went to Premier Talent in New York and they took a group from Boston called the Del Mars and shipped them to Chicago. I was never in that band although my picture was taken with them once. (The agency) promised me zillions of dollars but I never got anything out of this other than to throw a monkey wrench into what Christy and Monaco were doing. There was no Michael & the Messengers. It was up for grabs. I rode with them once in a limo to get the picture taken and that was it."

(Roe laughingly recalled another encounter with Monaco a few years later while in California with Jelly. "We were somewhat auditioning him to be our producer and he says, 'If I had a heart attack, Jesse would crawl over my body to get to the board,' - so he didn't forget!") Despite all the hassles connected with the Messengers, Roe says, "I love all those guys and it's the greatest memories of my life. I want to put that on record - the most beautiful people."

Whoever Michael and the Messengers were, they weren't afraid to go right into the Messengers home territory. *Action*, a Milwaukee teen publication from June 6, 1967 includes a story describing the local teens' disappointment to find the "wrong band" playing at the Thiensville Teen Center. The real Messengers had played there several times.

And Now - (drum roll) - The Unveiling:

Wayne Beckner - voc
Jack DeCarolis - org (11/29/43; Fitchburg, MA)
Ron Gagnon - bs   **Ken Menehan** - gtr (Fox Lake, IL)
Tom Fini - gtr   **Jerry Goodman** - gtr
Paul "Michael" Cosenza - dr

The Del Mars began in Leominster, MA, and had been working clubs in Boston, Rhode Island, New York City, and other locations. The group was heavily influenced by the Rascals and the Vagrants, whose visual, physical presentation they emulated. In the spring of 1967 they were working at the Peppermint Lounge and Wagon Wheel in New York City and were signed with Premier Talent through an agent named Alan Slater. "We were a very good club band," says Jack DeCarolis, "pretty seasoned because we been playing for quite a few years around the Boston area.

"Slater evidently knew the people at USA Records in Chicago, Jim Golden and Bob Monaco. We were playing in New York City and just getting by, and one day we got a call from Slater saying that there was an opportunity and a kind of a weird situation happening in the Midwest. What I heard was that USA had some kind of a deal for this tape and subsequently the Messengers went on to Motown. The story, as I was told, was that there was one member of the Messengers left. The other guys had all signed and went on and there was a guy who appeared in our original pictures." (DeCarolis did not at first recall Roe's name but recognized it immediately). "The deal was that Jesse was going to join our group and we would become Michael & the Messengers. They had this record in Chicago and the thing was moving up the charts fast, and they were looking for a group that could cover the record and mimic the tune. We had the same instrumentation, basically, so we said, 'Sure, what the heck'.

"We were supposed to start out in Chicago and join up with him because they had bookings lined up. So we were driving out, we had no money, and we were hearing this record playing on the radio all the way out there. We were thinking, 'This is pretty nice'. So we got to Chicago and met with Jim Golden and Bob Monaco. I can't tell you what happened with Jesse. I don't know whether they intentionally meant to keep him out of the picture, or he was going back to school, or his parents didn't want him to do it. I never got that story straight, but it eventually boiled down to the fact that we were going to assume the name of the group and we signed a contract with USA and started playing. The only time I met Jesse was when we had the pictures taken in New York.

"Some of the first jobs we played were up in the Milwaukee area and, let me tell you, we were met with some pretty weird situations. We didn't really know what was going on. We were a bunch of naive kids. People would come up and say, 'Where's da-da-da,' and we didn't know what they were talking about." Regarding the previously mentioned May 12 Thiensville gig, DeCarolis said he couldn't imagine why the management booked them there and, to make things worse, he thinks they arrived late! Twenty-seven years after the fact, having now seen the 1967 *Action* review for the first time, he says, "When I read that article everything sort of fell into place. I never really understood why the response was like it was."

That type of problem was remedied by concentrating the bookings in Illinois, Indiana and the Dakotas. The next record, "Romeo And Juliet" was really Michael & the Messengers but, since it was an attempt to capture the sound of "Midnight Hour," still not representative of the group's live presentation.

That sound turned out to be something that was never captured on record. The remaining two Michael & the Messengers singles were done primarily by studio musicians with the vocal overdubbed by either DeCarolis or Wayne Beckner. Producer Bob Monaco sang a duet with DeCarolis on "Run And Hide," and the track for "Gotta Take It Easy" saw double duty by backing the Cherry Slush version of the tune a few releases later (#904).

Guitarist Ken Menehan from Fox Lake, Illinois, replaced Tom Fini and toured back to the East Coast with the group. At some point later, Menehan apparently formed his own band back in Chicago using the Michael & the Messengers name. (An illegitimate version of an already illegitimate band?) Musicians included organist Mel Carlson and bassist John Brizzolara. Carlson says they later worked as "Faith - formerly Michael & the Messengers."

Menehan's replacement with the real(?) Michael & the Messengers was Jerry Goodman, who subsequently joined the Flock as a violinist. (An odd sidelight here is the fact that, a few years later, ex-Flock member John Billings worked in pick-up band in Milwaukee with ex-Messengers Augie Jurishica and - Jesse Roe!). Those who are aware of Jerry Goodman's later success with John McLaughlin's Mahavishnu Orchestra would probably be amazed at this footnote to his career.

DeCarolis believes that the idea for the "Michael" part of the name came from Dionne Warwick's 1966 hit "Message To Michael." "I never really knew, but in my mind that sort of made sense," he says.

As the group was fading, DeCarolis says he got a call from Jim Golden (at USA) about auditioning for a new band called CTA (Chicago Transit Authority, the original name of superstar group Chicago). Feeling burned out on the business, he declined. He has worked as a biologist for DuPont since 1978 and has his own jazz group. Wayne Beckner is believed to be a traveling evangelist. Tom Fini was last known to have a talent agency in Nashua, New Hampshire. Paul Cosenza is out of the music business and living quietly back in Leominster. Well, how about that? They don't seem like such bad guys after all.

Between Ken Menehan's spinoff group and the possibility of other bands purporting the name, the number of musicians claiming membership in Michael & the Messengers may one day approach the number of spectators at Woodstock.

USA	874	Romeo And Juliet[1]/Lies (Don't Mean Nothin')	(#129)	7/67
	889	Run And Hide/She Was The Girl		10/67
	897	Gotta Take It Easy/I Need Her There		/68

Unrelated Messengers: Beam, Era, MGM
Unrelated Movies: A&M, CBS Associated, RCA
Sources: Augie Jurishica telephone interview, 6/6/93
    Greg Jeresek telephone interview, 7/25/93
    Paul Christy telephone interview, 9/30/93
    Bob Cavallo telephone interview, 12/93
    Brian Lake telephone interview, 12/93
    John Brizzolara telephone interview, 12/93
    Mel Carlson telephone interview, 12/93
    Jeff Taylor telephone interview, 1/25/94
    Peter Barnes telephone interview, 1/26/94
    John Hoier telephone interview, 1/28/94
    Jesse Roe telephone interview, 1/8/94
    Jack DeCarolis telephone interview, 5/29/94
    Clee. American 45 R.P.M. Records.
    Whitburn. Record Research.
    Osborne - Brown. Rockin' Records
    Posniak, Alan. "Badger Beat." Milwaukee Journal (date unknown) - courtesy Brian Lake
    Kreiser, Dawn. "Will the Real Messengers Please Stand Up." Action 6/6/67: 3 - courtesy
        Clark Besch, 1994
    Jarema, Jeff. "We're Not Nice - Punk on USA Records." Here 'Tis #6, 1994

---

[1]Reflections, 1964. The Michael & Messengers version also appears on the Electra LP, *Nuggets,* 1972.

Messengers: Peter Barnes, Michael Morgan, Mike Demling, Greg Jeresek (courtesy Peter Barnes)

Michael & the Messengers: (top) Jack DeCarolis, Paul Cosenza, Jesse Roe (never worked with group), (bottom) Wayne Beckner, Ron Gagnon (courtesy Jack DeCarolis)

Chico Holiday (courtesy Chico Holiday)

Chico Holiday
(Ralph Vergolino, 8/24/34; Waukesha)
"Young Ideas" - #74 - 1959

✳ Earliest to chart nationally

This summertime hit seems to sparkle with the excitement the young singer was feeling on his first trip to New York City. A bright, bouncy tune written by country star Sonny James (whom Holiday has yet to meet), the song was recorded in RCA's new 24th St. studios in the early spring of 1959.

Holiday's father, a dog trainer, owned Chico's Kennels on Bluemound Road across from the Bluemound Drive-In, thereby acquiring the nickname "Chico." It wasn't long before young Ralph was given the same nickname by the regular customers. RCA added the "Holiday" part several years later.

While attending Waukesha High, Holiday had begun to play guitar and sing country-western songs. A few years later, in 1954, the National League's Boston Braves moved to Milwaukee and the town was excited. Mary and Nancy Bigg, two sisters from Waukesha, wrote a song about it titled "Braveland Boogie." With the sisters on background vocals, Holiday recorded it under the name Chico Verlin. "It was when the Braves first came in," recalls Holiday. "It talked about Joe Adcock and everybody. We performed it one night there at the stadium and I remember the groundskeeper yelling at me for walking on the grass."

The Bigg sisters went on to do local radio commercials. Holiday did some country gigs, but he became more attracted to the pop sounds and rhythms of records like Perry Como's "Catch A Falling Star" and Dean Martin's "Sway." He recorded an EP on Milwaukee's Raynard label and started sending out demos.

When his father did some work for Oakton Manor Resort in Pewaukee, Holiday heard about their showroom and secured a booking there where he met Chicago DJ Marty Fay. "He had a radio program called *Marty's Morgue* where he would just destroy people," explains Holiday. "He'd be playing their record and all of a sudden you'd hear 'Zip! Crash!' and he'd say 'That's a piece of garbage.' I found out he was in the audience and I didn't even want to go on." Fay liked what he heard, however, and helped Holiday get some material to producers Hugo (Peretti) and Luigi (Creatore) who were about to leave Mercury for RCA.

"I'll never forget the day I got the call," says Holiday. "It was a guy named Larry Auerbach from William Morris and he said, 'I've been contacted by RCA and they'd like to have you come to New York.' After my heart stopped beating - I mean this was like something you read about - I said, 'You mean they want me to come and audition?' He said, 'No, they want to sign you."

It was a heady time for the singer. "They're talking to Dick Clark on the phone and booking me on that show and all these other things. I remember walking down Broadway looking at the buildings that I was going to buy - 'I'll take the Pan Am Building' - you know."

Holiday did Clark's show several times along with the Buddy Deane Show in Baltimore, Alan Freed in New York, Robin Seymour on CKLW in Windsor and many others. "Young Ideas" spent six weeks on Billboard's Hot 100.

It was another two years, however, before Holiday saw another hit record and this time his thunder was stolen by a cover version. Back in Hartland, Wisconsin, John Dolan had started the New Phoenix label. He brought Holiday an unfinished song titled "God, Country And My Baby," inspired by the Kennedy-Kruschev Berlin Wall crisis. Holiday worked on it and went to New York to record it with arranger Billy Muir who had done his RCA sessions. The record began to get action and was picked up by Coral but Dolan had also sent it to Liberty who covered it with Johnny Burnette. Holiday's original did well in the East but failed to chart nationally while Burnette's climbed to number 18 in late 1961 (his final chart appearance). With a lyric about a young man going off to war, the song aroused some controversy. "There was an article in Time Magazine," recalls Holiday, "about the record being banned by the BBC because it reflected the hysterical attitude of the Berlin Crisis in the United States."

Holiday continued to record, including some 1964 sessions in Detroit using some of the same musicians who would become mainstays of the Motown Sound. Though he feels these were some of his best efforts, they were never released. Perhaps his involvement with a song with "God" in the title was prophetic, as he turned to Christian music in the 70's, and eventually to the ministry. Two of his inspirational albums on the Melodyland label were very successful.

Married to Sally since 1960, Holiday has lived in New York, Pittsburgh, Detroit, Seattle and Oregon. 35 years after "Young Ideas" he has settled in Anaheim Hills, California, where he is a minister for the Calvary Chapel Church.

Star	1007	Braveland Boogie/Why Am I Blue Without You (Chico Verlin)		/55
Raynard	EP 10065	What Did I Do/Just Because You're You/Calypso Song/Riddle Song (Chico)		/58
RCA	7499	Young Ideas/Cuckoo Girl	(#74)	4/59
	7549	Lulu Had A Baby/Your Kid Sister		7/59
	7574	Please Don't Touch/Lonesome Stranger		9/59
	7621	I Believe, I Believe/Rockin' Horse To Rockin' Chair		11/59
New Phoenix	6190	God, Country And My Baby/Fools		9/61
Coral	66291	God, Country And My Baby/Fools		10/61
Coral	62304	Johnny Was Late For The Wedding/Twelve O'clock Midnight		3/62
	62319	Blue Tattoo/It Won't Be Me		6/62
	62363	Lonely Cinderella/Love Is Born		6/63

Karate	512	Big Boat Up The River/500 Miles	/65
	518	Show Us The Way/She Gave Me Love	/65
Shamley	44108	Now I Taste The Tears/Boy Meets Girl	/69

LP's (All songs Christian/inspirational)

Singspiration		I've Never Known A Love Like This	/73
Melodyland	1975	Chico Holiday Sings	/75
	1975-2	Holiday At Melodyland	/75
	31-24	Just As I Am	/77
	30-26	My Life's A Better Picture	/78
Eagle Wing		Wings Of An Eagle	/89
Aseph		Wings Of An Eagle	/89

Sources: Chico Holiday interview, 3/9/93
    Nancy Bigg telephone interview, 3/93
    Whitburn. <u>Record Research</u>
    Clee. <u>American 45 R.P.M. Records.</u>
    Tourville, Tom W. <u>They Couldn't Tame Us - The Wisconsin 60's Rock Discography</u>.
      Fairmont, MN: Midwest, 1992.

Harvey Scales (courtesy Ken Adamany)

Harvey Scales & the Seven Sounds
(Milwaukee)
"Get Down" - #79 - 1967

Harvey Scales - voc (9/27/43[1]; Osceola, AR)
Rudy Jacobs - gtr
Rollo Armstead - ten sx
Ben Petrey - bari sx   **Roy Scott** - tp
Monnie Smith - tp/pno   **Billy Stonewell** - dr
Al Vance - bs (6/20/43; Rockford, IL)   **Melvin Taylor** - ten sx
Vic Pitts - dr

From twist to disco and beyond, Harvey Scales continues to perform, record, write and produce into his fourth decade in the business. While he was a child his family moved from Arkansas to South Bend, Indiana, and on to Milwaukee, where Scales attended Roosevelt Jr. High. He did some of his early singing with the Esquires and Al Jarreau.

Scales took on the name "Twistin' Harvey" when Chubby Checker was appearing in Milwaukee. "I had a twist contest with Chubby Checker and I beat him out," he says. "That's how I got the name." His first recording, "The Clock" on Cuca, employed the backing of the Del Reys. That band never recorded on their own, but drummer Craig Krampf went on to much success with the Robbs and his own studio career.

After this initial release, Scales began to write with Al Vance, bassist of the Seven Sounds. The two acts decided to join forces and they did a few more sessions for Cuca before switching to Lenny LaCour's Magic Touch label. With distribution by Stax, they scored with their first release. "Otis (Redding) came up here and saw us and took us back directly to Stax," says Scales. Al Vance says Stax had big plans for the group but things fell apart. "We had Isaac Hayes and David Porter writing songs for us, Booker T. and the M.G.'s doing our arrangements - then a whole lot of silly stuff went down, stuff you couldn't believe."

With "Get Down" on the charts, Scales & the Seven Sounds toured with name acts. "Wilson Pickett didn't want us on the show because we were kicking his butt for 30 days," claims Vance. "Broadway Freeze," a similar funky dance tune was the follow-up but it did not enjoy similar success. Some of the Magic Touch sides were distributed by Chess and it appears that LaCour's label continued to release material after the group left for Mercury. Scales also did some work with producer Don Davis, a connection that would prove to be very important.

In 1970 things seemed to be on the up-swing when the band signed with Chess. "We recorded 'The Yolk'," recalls Vance. "Leonard (Chess) was so pleased. He said, 'We've always wanted you guys and everything's going to be lovely.' Three weeks later the man had a heart attack.

---

[1]Date given by Scales. 9/27/41 has been previously published.

Marshall Chess said, 'No, no, I'm selling everything to GRT Records."

But if "Get Down" was Scales' first big league bass hit, it was a grand slam homer that he clobbered in 1976 when Johnny Taylor recorded his "Disco Lady." "Don Davis called me in Oakland," explains Scales, "and said, 'Hey, I love the song. Why don't we do it on Johnny Taylor.' Johnny Taylor hated the song. He put it on as an extra song after talking to him about it for a few months - finally got him to do it on the album. At that time it became the fastest selling single in the history of r&b." The Columbia 45 hit Billboard's Hot 100 in February, rode to the top on 19-week run, and became the first certified platinum single in history.

"After 'Disco Lady' deals came from everywhere," says Scales. "Deals as an artist, deals as a writer, deals as a producer, publisher. I started doing a lot of stuff with the O'Jays, Dramatics, Tavares, Patty Brooks, Millie Jackson, Cissy Houston, everybody."

Even before the "Disco Lady" explosion, Scales had enjoyed a bit of a preview when the J. Geils band covered his "Love-Itis" (from the flip side of "Get Down") on their *Hotline* LP in late 1975. It is probably one of his most covered tunes to date.

After spending much of the 80's in Concord, California, and Atlanta, Georgia, Scales returned to Milwaukee in 1990, where he continues his career.

Cuca	1132	The Clock/Every Step Of The Way		6/63
		(Twistin' Harvey)		
	1155	(On The Streets Of) New York City/Glamour Girl		2/64
		(Harvey & the Seven Sounds)		
	1271	I Want To Apologize/Independence		4/66
	1311	Monkey Time '67/Bootleg		1/67
		(Harvey & the Seven Sounds)		
Magic Touch	2007	Get Down/Love-Itis	(#79; 32 r&b)	10/67
		(Harvey Scales & the Seven Sounds)		
	16001	Broadway Freeze/I Can't Cry No More		1/68
		(Harvey Scales & the Seven Sounds)		
	2069	Too Good To Be True/Love Is A Gas		4/69
	2072	Don't You Ever Let It End/The Sound Of Soul		/69
	2077	Welcome Home/Trackdown		/69
	3002	Trying To Survive/Bump Your Thing		/69
Mercury	72937	Shake Your Power/The Sun Won't Come Out		7/69
Chess	2089	The Yolk/Funky Yolk		/70
	2093	Get Down 1970/Funky Football		/70
Cadet Concept	7029	Electric Robot/Leave It For The Trashmen		/71
	7030	I'll Run To Your Side/The Trashmen		/71
Stax	0126	I Wanna Do It/What's Good For You		6/72
Magic Touch	7006	Groove On Sexy Lady/Rock The World		/75

	8002	Groove On Sexy Lady/Rock The World	5/76
	9003	Follow The Disco Crowd/Love Thief	/76
Casablanca	954	Shake-A-Matic/Universal Love	1/79
	990	Rock Your Body/Baby Let's Rock	6/79
	2223	I Get Off On You/Disco Fire	11/79
Earthtone	001	Spend The Night Forever/Single Girls	/86
Kashgold	004	Are You Still In Love/Versions	/90
Earthtone	002	All In A Night's Work/We Can't Go On Meeting Like This	/91

LP's:

Casablanca	7109	Confidential Affair	7/78
	7164	Hot Foot	/79

(The Seven Sounds also have two pre-Harvey Scales sessions on the Cuca compilation LP *Badger A Go Go* - see Cuca section)

Also see: Cheaters (Several of the Seven Sounds played in this group)
Sources: Harvey Scales telephone interview, 9/6/93
    Al Vance telephone interview, 4/3/94
    Clee. <u>American 45 R.P.M. Records.</u>
    Whitburn. <u>Record Research.</u>
    Gordon, Davie & Scott Taylor. "Harvey Scales." <u>Voices From The Shadows #17</u>, 1991.

Tim Davis & the Chordairs: Davis, Denny Geyer, Curley Cooke (courtesy Dennis Geyer)

Tim Davis
(11/29/43; Milwaukee - 9/20/88; Las Vegas, NV)
"Buzzy Brown" #91 - 1972

"Tim was such a great guy that people focused on that," says Paul Chitwood, guitarist and high school friend of Davis', "but he was also a great drummer. He was the best shuffle drummer around."[1]

Davis' drumming, singing and songwriting took him from his first record, on Janesville's tiny Leaf label, to working with the Steve Miller band on five albums, and finally to his own LP's. (Those solo LP's included contributions from many of his old Wisconsin friends. His sole chart appearance came with a song written by Wisconsin guitarist Curley Cooke). Unfortunately, the Metromedia label was headed downhill at the time and most of Davis' solo efforts were lost in the sunset.

An adopted child, Davis was raised in Janesville, the only black family in town at the time. He became a swimming and track star in high school and did not start playing music until his graduation. The early Wisconsin gigs often included Miller, Boz Scaggs, Ben Sidran, and Ken Adamany. The "Workout" side of his first record was recorded live at Mother's in Madison with Mother herself playing maracas.

Sometime after Miller had defected to San Francisco, he called Davis who then headed west along with Jim Peterman and Dick Personett of the Chordairs. Besides drumming, Davis also contributed some lead vocals to four of the early Miller LP's.

Davis left Miller in 1970 and, after a European tour with singer Terry Reid, began work on his solo career. He continued writing after the Metromedia efforts and contributed two songs to Steve Miller's 1984 *Italian X-Rays* album. By 1987 diabetes had taken both of his legs. Reflecting on Davis' funeral which took place the following year, keyboardist Jim Peterman said, "It was a very sad occasion. It was so much more than a loss musically. Tim was a friend to nearly everyone he met."[2]

Tim Davis & the Chordairs:

Tim Davis - dr

Jim Marcotte - gtr (5/15/44; Milwaukee)

David Chaffee - bs

Curley Cooke - gtr (11/12/44, Wausau)

Jim Peterman - kb (8/26/44; Milwaukee)

Dick Personett - bs (2/8/47; Janesville)

Denny Geyer - gtr (9/18/43; Milwaukee)

---

[1]Milam, Stan. "Tim Davis was more than a great drummer." <u>Janesville Gazette</u> 10/17/91: 2C

[2]Milam. "Tim Davis"

Leaf	6467	Wine, Wine, Wine/Workout		/64
		(Tim Davis & the Chordairs)		
Metromedia	253	Buzzy Brown/On The Rocks	(#91)	8/72
	263	Boogie Woogie F.C.B./Don't Mention The Lady's Name		1/73
	0102	Only Yesterday/Take Me As I Am		
		(Without Silver, Without Gold)		4/73
	0104	Winter Song/Baby Won't You Come Out Tonight		10/73

LP's:

Metromedia	1054	Pipe Dream	4/72
	1075	Take Me As I Am (Without Silver, Without Gold)	4/73

Also see: Playboys - Madison/Janesville (Jim Peterman)
     Ray Kannon & the Corals - Around The State (Curley Cooke, Jim Marcotte)
     A.B. Skhy (Denny Geyer, Jim Marcotte)
     Legends - Milwaukee (Paul Chitwood)
     Nigh Tranes - Madison (Ken Adamany, Ben Sidran, Denny Geyer
Sources: Tommy Davis letter, 10/25/93
     Tourville. Wisconsin . . . Discography.
     Whitburn. Record Research.
     Clee. American 45 R.P.M. Records.
     Milam, Stan. Janesville Gazette, 10/17/91

Steve Sperry

(10/3/41; Ft. Atkinson)
Flame - #91 - 1977

✳ **Longest time between first release and first chart appearance (17 years).**

"You and my mom are the only two people that know about it," says Steve Sperry of his 1960 release on Cuca. That record, produced by Vilas Craig, was done around the same time that Sperry played lead guitar for the Crossfires. Sperry left that band to form his own trio and then joined the Jim Langdon Trio, another group that recorded for Cuca.

While with the Langdon Trio, Sperry got introduced to the world of jingles, recording for producer Jerry Swayzee in Madison. In 1968 Swayzee relocated to Chicago to work in the jingle business for Dick Marx (father of 80's singing star Richard Marx), and Sperry followed in 1969. He has been successful in that field ever since.

For a few years before the Chicago move, Sperry and Sam McCue (of Milwaukee's Legends) had been producing many of Ken Adamany's bands for release on the Rampro label. There were groups from both Wisconsin and Illinois, including Rockford's Paegens with Brad Carlson (later known as Bun E. Carlos of Cheap Trick) on drums. Sperry also did some work with New Blues, a Milwaukee band that became A.B. Skhy.

When Sperry finally came out with his second solo release, it wasn't exactly a calculated move. "I hadn't even planned on releasing it," he explains. "I'd written it when I lived in Nashville in 1976 and I played it for a couple of friends and they said, 'When we're doing a jingle some day, why don't we record that.' So we did and I played it for my attorney, Dick Shelton. He said, 'Why don't you take that over to my friend Robin McBride at Mercury and see if there's any interest. Sure enough, they put it out and they claimed at one point we had about 300 radio stations on it across the country."

The song was covered by Bobby Vinton and recorded, but not released, by Dolly Parton. Despite all that, there was no follow-up. "I wasn't a working musician, per se," says Sperry, "so there was nothing they could tap into as far as my gigging or anything."

As a writer, Sperry also had seven songs used on the television show *Fame* and its five cast LP's. In the 90's he has taken some time away from the jingles to create a project for children called *The Music Critters,* and to write a stage musical about the Harley Davidson titled *The Milwaukee Vibrator.*

Cuca	1008	That Ain't So/Our Summer Love		8/60
		(Side 1 reissued on *The Cuca Story, Vol. 2*)		
Mercury	73905	<u>Flame</u>/Comin' Through To You	(#91)	6/77

Also see: Crossfires - Cuca
      Jim Langdon Trio - Cuca
      Playboys - Madison/Janesville
      Feature/Rampro Records - Wisconsin Labels
      A.B. Skhy
      Vilas Craig - Around The State
Sources: Steve Sperry telephone interview, 3/8/94
      Whitburn. <u>Record Research</u>
      Clee. <u>American 45 R.P.M. Records.</u>

Billy Thunderkloud & the Chieftones
(British Columbia/Boaz)
What Time Of Day - #92 - 1975

Billy Thunderkloud (Vincent Clifford) - gtr (5/7; Kispiox, BC)
Jack Wolf - ld gtr (10/29; Ayanish, BC)
Barry Littlestar - bs (4/8; Kispiox, BC)
Richard Grayowl - dr (5/25; Kitwancool, BC)

These four musicians are all members the Tsimshian Indian Nation. After growing up in Northwest British Columbia, they met at an Indian residential school in Edmonton, Alberta. There it was discovered that Thunderkloud and Littlestar were brothers who had been separated at a very young age. They formed the Chieftones and moved to Wisconsin in the 60's. They were reportedly working on a ranch in Boaz at the time of their first recording for Cuca.

The Chieftones soon moved to Nashville and, though they appeared all over the U.S. and Canada, they seemed to find their greatest success in the East and booked out of Boston for many years. Thunderkloud was honored as "Indian Of The Year" in 1975. He continues performing occasionally while the other members have retired from music. Though they made just one appearance on the Hot 100, they managed five entries on the country charts in 1975-76. Thunderkloud never responded to numerous attempts for an interview.

Billy Thunderkloud & the Chieftones: Thunderkloud, Jack Wolfe, Barry Littlestar, Richard Grayowl (Mountain lion is Sim-Au-Git, a gift from Walt Disney). (courtesy Ruth Primus)

Cuca	1287	Do Lord[1]/Shouldn't Have Done What I Did	8/66
Claremont	5590	Rang-Dang-Do/Indian Moon	
	5596	Steal Away/A Closer Walk	
Youngstown	3472	I Wonder/Don't Dare	/68
Scepter	12234	I Wonder/Don't Dare	11/68
Superior	104	All Through The Night/	/74
20th Century	2116	Come To Me/You Touched My Life	7/74

---

[1]Spiritual based on 19th century British melody. (Same tune used for pop/country hit "Gotta Travel On" - Billy Grammer, 1958). Reissued on *Badger A Go Go* LP.

	2164	Kick The Can/I'm Havin' A Party		1/75
	2181	What Time Of Day/When Love Is Right	(#92, 16 C)	4/75
	2239	Pledging My Love[1]/I Will Love You Until I Die	(37 C)	9/75
Stable	66601	His Kind Of Woman/		5/75
Polydor	14321	Indian Nation[2]/I'm Going Right To Where I Do Wrong	(54 C)	5/76
	14338	Try A Little Tenderness[3]/Natural Feelin'	(47 C)	7/76
	14362	It's Alright/The Wanderer[4]	(77 C)	11/76
	14383	Let Me Be Your Man/100 Years From Now		4/77
	14412	Oklahoma Wind/Trouble With Angel		9/77
	14449	Let Me Love You/My Lady		2/78

LP's:

Superior	103	All Through The Night	/74
20th Century	452	Off The Reservation	9/74
	471	What Time Of Day	/75

Sources: Ruth Primus, 8/94
     Fred Masotti, 1993
     Tourville. Wisconsin . . . Discography
     Whitburn. Record Research
     Dick Neumann, 8/94

A.B. Skhy
(Milwaukee/San Francisco)
Camel Back - #100 - 1969

Dennis Geyer - gtr (9/18/43; Milwaukee)
Howard Wales - kb
Jim Liban - hca (11/20/47; Milwaukee)   **Gary Karp** - kb
Jim Marcotte - bs (5/14/44; Milwaukee)   **Curley Cooke** - gtr (11/12/44)
Terry Anderson - dr   **Rick Jaeger** - dr

What better way to exit the Hot 100 than at the final position. With a one week visit there, this transplanted group made the briefest possible appearance on the coveted Billboard list, though they did bubble under for four weeks. They also did it just in time to make this book - a few weeks before the onset of the 70's.

---

[1]Johnny Ace, 1955
[2]Don Fardon, 1968; Raiders, 1971 (Indian Reservation)
[3]Ted Lewis, 1933; Otis Redding, 1967; Three Dog Night, 1969; many others
[4]Dion, 1961

It could also be argued that, according to my own category definitions, A.B. Skhy should be placed in the "relocated" section, since they did not record as a group until after leaving Wisconsin. In fact, they apparently didn't even take their name until leaving. It is a borderline case but, since most of the members had previously recorded in Wisconsin, it seemed that they deserved to be included here.

Even the time of the name change varies in different memories. They were known initially as New Blues and one former member thought the name was changed shortly before they left Milwaukee. Dennis Geyer says the new moniker was chosen on the drive to San Francisco in spring of 1968. Explaining the reason for the trip, he says "We couldn't get any (record company) interest (in Milwaukee), and Steve Miller and a lot of our friends had come out to California and were getting a lot of interest. We were encouraged by Miller and a number of other friends that were in his band to come out."

Before the move New Blues had at various times included Sam McCue (who left to rejoin the Everly Brothers), Jim Peterman (who preceded the others to California to join Miller), and Steve Sperry. Many of the musicians had also worked with several bands while attending the University of Wisconsin in Madison. "There was just this clan of musicians that all revolved around Ken Adamany's booking agency," says Geyer. "It was a wonderful thing."

Geyer also recorded with the Stoval Sisters on Reprise in 1971, as a member of Gideon & Power on Bell in 1972, and with zydeco artist Queen Ida (with whom he worked extensively for seven years) in the 80's. Several of his songs have been covered by other artists, including Canned Heat and Coke Escovido.

A.B. Skhy: Dennis Geyer, Curley Cooke, Jim Marcotte, Rick Jaeger(courtesy Dennis Geyer)

Other members who continued with notable success include Howard Wales (Jerry Garcia and others), Rick Jaeger (Dave Mason, studio work), Curley Cooke (Steve Miller, Boz Scaggs and others), and Jim Liban (Milwaukee band Short Stuff, studio work).

MGM	14086	Camel Back/Just What I Need	(#100)	12/69

LP's:

MGM	4628	A.B. Skhy	/69
	4676	Ramblin' On	/70

Also see: Tim Davis (Dennis Geyer, Jim Marcotte, Curley Cooke, Jim Peterman)
      Bonnevilles, Greenmen - Milwaukee (Howard Wales)
      Legends - Milwaukee (Rick Jaeger, Terry Anderson)
      Steve Sperry
      Playboys - Madison/Janesville (Jim Peterman)
Sources: Dennis Geyer letter and telephone interview, 3/12/93, 9/25/93
      Whitburn. Record Research

Robbs

(Milwaukee)
"Race With The Wind" - #103 - 1966

✳ **Most "Bubbling Under" Records Of Any Act That Never Made The Hot 100.**

Dee Robb (David Donaldson) - gtr (6/21; Ann Arbor, MI)
Bruce Robb (Robert Donaldson) - org (10/22; Ann Arbor)
Joe Robb (George Donaldson) - sx (9/16; Ann Arbor)
Dick Gonia - ld gtr   **Teddy (Salvatore) Peplinski** - dr (10/7/42; Milwaukee)
Dennis Sachse - dr (dec)   **Craig Robb (Krampf)** - dr (8/25/45; Milwaukee)

"We were the kings of the *Bubbling Under* chart," says Craig Krampf of the Robbs' dubious distinction. Counting their release under the name Cherokee, the group placed six titles on the Almost-Making-It roster, including two at the number 103 position.

The Donaldson family, with three musical brothers, had moved from Michigan to Florida, then to Wisconsin while Dee was in junior high. While in high school he formed Dee & the Starliners, taking the stage name "Robb" from his grandmother's maiden name.

Neighbor and good friend Con Merten joined as manager in the early days in Oconomowoc. Applying their budding entrepreneurial skills, the boys put together a venture for the town's *Maxwell Street Days*. Merten drove the flatbed truck, the band set up on the back, and they stopped to play in front of each business to whom they had sold advertising time.

Around 1961 the group landed a gig backing Del Shannon and spent much of the following year on the road. Despite being considered a Milwaukee area band, the Robbs never spent much time in the city's club scene. "We always felt like we were kind of outside because we lived in so many different places," says Dee. "There was a really cliquish thing."

Their first record, "The Prom" came out on Argo, a division of Chess/Checker, and received some national airplay. The next two, for two different companies, followed in quick succession. "Those records were done at approximately the same time," explains Dee, "and we were signed to Argo, so we had to do the others surreptitiously under different names, which was very common in those days." Robb and Merten had initially taken "The Prom" to Mercury Records but had suffered a very negative experience there. It was a memory that would resurface a few years later in an ironic twist.

During the first few years, the Robbs had gone through a few drummers, including former Bonneville Teddy Peplinski. When Peplinski left, Craig Krampf came in. "They needed a drummer for some major show happening at the Milwaukee Auditorium," Krampf recalls, "so we got together, everything clicked, and I went on with Dee Robb & the Robins. I think that first big show was opening for the Beach Boys." Generally assumed to be a cousin or even a brother, Krampf became known as Craig Robb.

In 1965 the band was signed to RCA and, though they never had a release for the label, they were sent out on tour backing Little Peggy March ("I Will Follow Him," 1963). Having previously met Dick Clark, they made it a point to renew their acquaintance when the tour reached Los Angeles in May. "We went to Dick Clark's office and just sat in the lobby literally," says Dee, "and Dick Clark came out and remembered us and was glad to see us. In this conversation he started to tell us about this giant promotion he was doing next year called *Dick Clark's Young World's Fair* and the test fair was going to be in Chicago. It was a pretty amazing undertaking. He had every manufacturer from automobiles to cosmetics, clothing, anything that related to kids. There must have been 10 or 12 major acts playing every show. It was probably the biggest pop promotion that had ever been done at that time. He introduced us to this guy who was promoting it."

The Robbs returned to the Midwest, guitarist Dick Gonia was drafted, and the "classic" four piece line-up was in place. That fall, Clark's promoter arrived in Chicago to begin preparations for the big event.

"As I've found over the years," continues Dee, "with everything that ever has worked in the entertainment and music business that we've been involved in; be it Rod Stewart or Ringo Records, no matter who it is; besides having to have the talent and all the basic things in place - it's timing. It just seems that a certain energy surrounds certain things at certain times. We had that energy at that time.

"We'd gone from a very slick, almost r&b show band kind of image to being kind of folky, hippy kind of guys. We changed the style of music and we had a fair following in the Midwest.

This thing just started to snowball. We'd be out-drawing major acts that were appearing in town.

"So (the promoter) came to some of these gigs and from the first gig that we played in Chicago, a spark lit. From then on, every time we played Chicago it was sold out. There were people standing around the block, there were mobbings, it was like a little microcosm of superstardom. He saw this happening and he realized there was something here."

The Robbs were slated to take part in a battle of the bands along with many top Chicago groups; the Buckinghams, Cryan Shames and Shadows Of Knight. The winner would get one show in the *Young World's Fair*. "He was already figuring he was going to get a piece of our action," says Dee. "He later told us that his plan was to fix the playoff but the amazing thing was he didn't have to."

Dick Clark was about to become reacquainted with the band. "I can remember Dick Clark coming to town and going, 'Who the hell are the Robbs," relates Craig Krampf, "and why are they playing on this big stage show with all the top artists in the country?' By the third day we couldn't leave the dressing room to go back to our hotel. It was like Beatlemania. It was just girls chasing after us, tearing at our clothes. It was like a movie, just unbelievable. It's an incredible memory."

And this was only the beginning. As Dee explains: "Clark had brought the whole *Where The Action Is* to tape in Chicago. Well, the Mama and Papas got busted in New York for acid the night before and couldn't be on the show so he had this open slot. So the day before it's supposed to tape, they call us up and say, 'Okay, you've got a shot on *Where The Action Is,*' and we almost died! This was the biggest thing that's ever happened to us in our lives! And they said, 'You've gotta have a tape of something brand new.' We didn't have any tape. So we dashed down and recorded 'Race With The Wind' and the B side.

"It happened that in the studio that night was a staff Mercury producer named Lou Reisner. Frankly, I had had a bad experience with Mercury. Before we signed with Argo I went to Charlie Fach of Mercury and we played our demo for him. In the middle of the song he just ripped the needle right across our demo - soft acetate in those days - and destroyed it and just brutalized us! I was on the verge of tears. I couldn't believe it. So, I had this bad taste from Mercury. So we do the shoot for *Where The Action Is* and here's all these guys from Mercury Records and they take us to dinner!"

The Robbs booking on the *Young World's Fair* was extended. They continued playing opposite such acts as the Rascals and Sam The Sham & the Pharaohs while Mercury continued to pursue them. "We'd get off stage and here would be six executives in suits all dressed up from Mercury Records and Irv Steinberg, the president of the label, brings his kids to get autographs!" relates Dee. "For ten days they kept this up. They took us to dinner, they took us to clubs and finally, out of exhaustion, we signed a deal with them."

The Robbs moved to California in May 1966 to replace Paul Revere & the Raiders as the house band on *Where The Action Is* for 26 weeks. And they continued to bubble under. "One of the reasons was, having the show turned to be not such a blessing," says Bruce. "What it meant was, every label we signed with figured, 'My God, we've got all the promotion we need.' 'Race With The Wind' sold like a gold record but it did this over a period of two years."

The band moved to Atlantic in 1968 with no luck, then to Dunhill in 1969 and a return to the *Bubbling Under* chart. The final label change to ABC brought them back to their previous chart high of number 103, but the group was leaning toward country-rock and it was time for a change.

As the new sound took shape, they felt a new name was needed. Touring and looking for a word that "looks great and sounds great," they picked Cherokee off the name of a truck stop in Oklahoma. ABC, however, didn't know what to make of the new sounds and, despite appearances by Chris Hillman, Sneaky Pete and Gib Gilbeau, the musicians were not completely satisfied with the resulting LP. Years later producer Steve Barri remarked to Bruce Robb that, "You guys were the Eagles and we didn't know it!"

It was this dissatisfaction that led the band to the building of their own studio. It was initially used for their own demos and those of some friends but the pace stepped up within a few years. The Robbs did their final performance as a band in 1973. They made the plunge into new studio equipment when they were offered the opportunity to record Steely Dan's *Pretzel Logic* LP. Then, when they had to turn down Poco due to lack of space, they decided to expand. The brothers purchased a property vacated by MGM and moved in to 751 North Fairfax in Los Angeles on January 2, 1975. Cherokee Studios continues to be a very successful operation.

Craig Krampf had dropped out shortly after the performing ended and was doing demo sessions. "A year later the boys were doing extremely well and driving Cadillacs and Corvettes," says Krampf, "and my wife and I were on food stamps and I'm going, 'Did I make the right decision?'" Eventually, it turned out that he did. As a studio musician Krampf became one of the top five L.A. studio drummers. He has played on over 200 albums and won gold and platinum record awards. As a songwriter he co-wrote Steve Perry's 1984 mega-hit, "Oh Sherrie" and won a Grammy for a song in the *Flashdance* soundtrack. Krampf moved to Nashville in 1987 where he continues as a very successful producer/musician/songwriter. "To this day I love making records more than anything," he says.

Argo	5439	The Prom/Bye Bye Baby	/63
		(Dee Robb)	
Todd	1089	Surfer's Life/She Cried[1]	/63
		(Robby & the Robins)	

---

[1]Jay & the Americans, 1962

Score	1006	Say That Thing/He's Got The Whole World In His Hands[2]		/64
		(Dee Robb & the Robins)		
Mercury	72579	Race With The Wind/In A Funny Sort Of Way	(#103)	6/66
	72616	I Don't Feel Alone/Next Time You Call Me		9/66
	72641	Bittersweet/End Of The Week		12/66
	72678	Rapid Transit/Cynthia Loves	(123)	5/67
	72730	Girls, Girls/Violets Of Dawn		10/67
WRIT (EP)	--	You've Got Your Troubles/Louie Louie/		/68
		(Other cuts by Skunks, Tony's Tygers)		
Atlantic	2511	Castles In The Air/I Don't Want To Discuss It		4/68
	2578	A Good Time Song/Changin' Winds		11/68
Dunhill	4208	Movin'/Write To You	(131)	9/69
	4233	Last Of The Wine/Written In The Dust	(114)	3/70
ABC	11270	I'll Never Get Enough/It All Comes Back	(103)	7/70
	11295	All The Way Home/Rosiana		4/71
	11304	Girl, I've Got News For You/All The Way Home	(116)	7/71
		(Cherokee)		

Robbs: (top) Joe Robb, (bottom) Craig Krampf, Bruce Robb, Dee Robb (courtesy Alan Clark)

---

[1]Laurie London, 1958

LP's:

Mercury	61130	<u>The Robbs</u>	(200)	/67
ABC	719	Cherokee		/71

Also see: Bonnevilles - Milwaukee (Teddy Peplinski)
      Legends, Renegades - Milwaukee (Dennis Sachse)
Unrelated Cherokee(s): Challenge, Grand, Guyden, MGM, Peacock, Ranwood, UA
Sources: Interview with Dee, Bruce and Joe Robb, 5/20/93
      Craig Krampf telephone interview, 9/26/93
      Tourville. <u>Wisconsin . . . Discography.</u>
      Whitburn. <u>Record Research.</u>
      Clee. <u>American 45 R.P.M. Records.</u>
      Osborne-Brown. <u>Rockin' Records.</u>

Love Society
(Plymouth)
"Do You Wanna Dance" - #108 - 1968

Dave Steffen - ld gtr (3/4/51; Plymouth)
Mike Holdridge - org   **Duane Abler** - rh gtr
Keith Abler - rh gtr (10/14/51; Plymouth)
Steve Gilles - bs
Mike Dellger - dr (5/4/50; Plymouth)

Love Society: (top) Steve Gilles, Mike Holdridge, Keith Abler, (bottom) Dave Steffen, MikeDellger
(courtesy Dave Steffen)

From Bobby Freeman's 1958 original to the Ramones 20 years later, "Do You Wanna Dance" has made six appearances on the Billboard Hot 100. At number 108, the Love Society almost got there. The group's initial Tee Pee release came almost exactly ten years after Freeman's hit and was picked up nationally by Scepter. The dreamy arrangement was probably lifted off the Mamas & Papas first album in 1966. The latter group then released it as a single in late 1968, three months after the Love Society.

"We were just bunch of farm boys from Plymouth," says drummer Mike Dellger. "Suddenly you're signed to a major label before you graduated from high school. In a way that was a little bit disconcerting because it goes to your head right away. You think, 'Well, I'm not going to need anything. I'm gonna be rich!"

The recording came about when Target label owner Al Posniak went to hear the group after they won a battle of the bands in Sheboygan. The song went to number one on Green Bay's WDUZ and the boys' first big show was with the Brooklyn Bridge at Milwaukee's *Summerfest*. Scepter's follow-up, another re-make with "Tobacco Road," got some action but not enough to keep the company interested, so Target released another single that been recorded earlier.

When Keith Abler left and joined Phase III, Love Society added Abler's younger brother, Duane. A contract with RCA led to still another remake, the Beach Boys "Don't Worry Baby." After a second RCA single and an unreleased album, Keith Abler rejoined and the band went to Mercury for their final release.

The demise of Love Society led to the formation of Sunblind Lion, a group that included members from both Love Society and Phase III. 1993 finds Abler in a group called Flashback, still getting requests for the old version of "Tobacco Road" and "playing songs from that era of time where I think music is going to last," he says.

Tee Pee	3878	Do You Wanna Dance[1]/Without You		4/68
Scepter	12223	<u>Do You Wanna Dance</u>/Without You	(#108)	7/68
	12236	Tobacco Road[2]/Drops Of Rain		12/68
Target	1006	Let's Pretend (We're Making Love)/You Know How I Feel		/69
		(Side 2 reissued on Pebbles *Highs In The Mid 60's, Vol. 10*)		
RCA	0257	Don't Worry Baby[3]/You Know How I Feel		11/69
	9821	Bang On Your Own Drum/Candle Waxing		5/70
Mercury	73130	America[4]/Wanda		11/70

---

[1]Bobby Freeman, 1958; Del Shannon, 1964; Beach Boys, 1965; Mamas & Papas, 1968; Bette Midler, 1973; Ramones, 1978
[2]Nashville Teens, 1964; w: John D. Loudermilk
[3]Beach Boys, 1964; Tokens, 1970; B.J. Thomas, 1977
[4]Simon & Garfunkel - *Bridge Over Troubled Water* LP, 1970; Yes, 1972

Also see: Phase III - Appleton/Fox Cities (Keith & Duane Abler)
        Faros - Appleton/Fox Cities (related material)
Sources: Keith Abler telephone interview, 8/21/93
        Mike Dellger telephone interview, 1994
        Tourville. Wisconsin . . . Discography.
        Whitburn. Record Research.

Unchained Mynds
(La Crosse)
We Can't Go On This Way - #115 - 1969

✳ **Youngest band to chart**

Randy Purdy - kb (10/31/51; La Crosse)
Wayne Bentzen - gtr   **Doug Krupinski** - gtr
Clare Troyanek - bs
Dan Hansen - dr

The members of the Unchained Mynds ranged in age from just 14 (bassist Troyanek) to 19 (guitarist Bentzen) when they went into the Coulee Studio for their first recording session. "It was like the American dream," says lead singer Randy Purdy. "We just wanted to be part of the music scene. We ordered 500 copies, then we had to order them again, and then one more time, so it was almost 1500 copies here in town. We just couldn't believe it, but yet we were kind of going with the flow." These were impressive figures for a town the size of La Crosse. Manager Lindy Shannon was sending the record out to stations around the country even as a follow-up was released.

In Milwaukee Jon Hall picked up the record for his Teen Town label and took over the management of the group. When the song became a hit there, Hall placed it with Buddah for national distribution.

Guitarist Bentzen was drafted to Viet Nam and replaced by Doug Krupinski. The boys toured to New York and Pennsylvania and made two appearances at the Nashville Pop Festival alongside Bobby Goldsboro, Roy Orbison, Grand Funk and B.J. Thomas. "I think a lot of the DJ's knew that we were real inexperienced," recalls Purdy. "They would say something after the song was finished like, 'I think he went flat on that last note" (laughs).

Unfortunately, the song's title proved to be prophetic and by 1972 the group was history. Troyanek moved to Arizona, joining a band called *Tennessee*, and Purdy performs in a duo for dinner cruises and restaurant gigs.

Transaction	705	We Can't Go On This Way[1]/Goin' Back To Miami		/69
	707	Hole In My Shoe/Warm Smoke		/69
Teen Town	109	We Can't Go On This Way/Goin' Back To Miami		/69
Buddah	111	<u>We Can't Go On This Way</u>/Goin' Back To Miami	(#115)	4/69
	119	Everyday/		6/69
	140	Everyday/You, Me And My Yoyo		10/69

Also see: Today's Tomorrow - La Crosse (Troyanek)
Sources: Randy Purdy telephone interview, 4/93
     Whitburn. <u>Record Research.</u>
     Clee. <u>American 45 R.P.M. Records.</u>

Junior & the Classics
(Milwaukee)
"The Dog" - #134 - 1964

Junior Brantley - org (Milwaukee)
Dennis Madigan - vibes (7/9/41; Milwaukee)   **Keith Dreher** - gtr (dec; circa 1972)
Kent Ivy - sx   **Vic Pitts** - dr
Brand Shank - bs (8/19/40; Milwaukee)
Jerry Sworske - dr (4/8/42; Milwaukee)

"The guy from RCA originally came down to listen to Little Artie & the Pharaohs," says Jerry Sworske, "but he came down on the wrong night and we were there. We never told Little Artie that." RCA's Groove subsidiary released Junior & the Classics' version of "The Dog" just about the time that Billboard had expanded their Bubbling Under chart enough to accommodate it. Other than club work as usual around Milwaukee, the only additional benefit of the record action was a few gigs around Chicago. Sworske also reports that the Classics did some studio work backing other artists at Dave Kennedy Studios. The group had no more releases for three years until Lenny LaCour's Magic Touch label made a few attempts.

Junior Brantley joined Short Stuff in the early 70's and recorded two LP's and several singles with the band. He worked with the Fabulous Thunderbirds in 1986, the year the Texas band scored big with "Tuff Enuff." The following year Brantley joined Roomful Of Blues and stayed with them until 1992 when he joined the American Super Stars Show. He does the Little Richard impersonation for the Las Vegas review. In spite of all these accomplishments Brantley was reluctant to discuss his history. Expressing the concern that this type of story might be detrimental to his career, he perhaps prefers to hide his early 60's beginnings rather than take pride in his longevity.

---

[1]Teddy & the Pandas, 1966

Unchained Mynds: (top) Randy Purdy, Dan Hanson, Clare Troyanek, (bottom) Wayne Bentzen, Denny Lawrence (left before recording) (courtesy Dan Hanson & Randy Purdy)

Junior & the Classics: Brand Schank, Jerry Sworske, Dennis Madigan, Kent Ivy, (front) Junior Brantley

Groove	0043	The Dog[1]/Birmingham	(#134)	9/64
Magic Touch	2001	Wise Up/Stock Blues In D		/67
	2003	Wise Up/Mix Up A Go Go		/67
	2008	Marching Around Your Heart/Mix Up		/67
	2009	Kill The Pain/Please Make Love To Me		/68
Birdie	2909	You're So Lucky/Jr. MacKinley		/82

Also see: Mid-Knighters - Milwaukee(Keith Dreher)
     Cheaters (Vic Pitts) - Milwaukee
     Noblemen - Milwaukee (Brand Shank, Jerry Sworske)
     Bonnevilles, Continentals - Milwaukee (Dennis Madigan)
     Darnells - Milwaukee (Jerry Sworske)
Sources: Junior Brantley telephone interview, 10/24/93
     Dennis Madigan telephone interview, 5/14/94
     Jerry Sworske telephone interview, 8/8/94
     Jim Liban telephone interview, 1993
     Clee. American 45 R.P.M. Records.
     Whitburn. Record Research.
     Tourville. Wisconsin . . . Discography.

Tracy Nelson
(12/27/44; French Camp, CA)
Tracy Nelson - #145 LP - 1974

Tracy Nelson is an artist who has attained a respected name and reputation in the business without the benefit of significant chart success. None of her singles have appeared on Billboard's Hot 100 and her highest placing on the LP chart came as a member of the group Mother Earth in 1969.

Conceived in Madison but born in California while her father served in the Navy, Nelson was raised back in Madison and began her performing there. While attending the University of Wisconsin and singing folk and blues, she met producer Sam Charters at a party. Charters took her to Chicago to record her first LP for Prestige, an album that was later reissued and remained in print for many years.

Nelson interacted with many other musicians who were attending college in Madison, including Steve Miller and Boz Scaggs. Like them, she also left for greener pastures. "(For) all of us who played music in Madison, there was no real club scene," she says. "We did fraternity gigs and you could only go so far and have so much fun with that."

---

[1]Rufus Thomas, 1963

She relocated to the San Francisco area where Mother Earth was formed. That group recorded a movie soundtrack album for United Artists in 1968. A second LP charted on Mercury and the group moved to Nashville. In the early 70's, Nelson made the transition back to a solo artist. In 1974 she received a Grammy nomination for the single "After The Fire Is Gone" with Willie Nelson (no relation). She continues to record for independent labels while residing in the Nashville area.

Mother Earth

United Artists	50503	Revolution/Stranger In My Own Home		5/68
Mercury	72878	Down So Long/Goodnight Nelda Greeby		12/68
	72909	Mother Earth/I Did My Part		4/69
	72943	I Wanta Be Your Mama Again/Wait, Wait, Wait		8/69
Reprise	1019	Soul Of Sadness/Temptation Took Control Of Me And I Fell		6/71
	1041	I'll Be Long Gone/Bring Me Home		10/71

Tracy Nelson

Mercury	72995	Sad Situation/Stay As Sweet As You Are		11/69
Atlantic	4028	After The Fire Is Gone/Whisky River (Tracy & Willie Nelson)		/74
	3235	It Takes A Lot To Laugh, It Takes A Train To Cry[1]/ Lean On Me[2]		2/75
MCA	40479	Nothing I Can't Handle/Sweet Soul Music		12/75

LP's:

Tracy Nelson

Prestige	7303	Deep Are The Roots		/65
	7726	Deep Are The Roots (reissue)		/69
Columbia	31759	Poor Man's Paradise		/72
Atlantic	7310	<u>Tracy Nelson</u>	(#145)	9/74
MCA	494	Sweet Soul Music		/75
	2203	Time Is On My Side		/76
Flying Fish	052	Home Made Songs		/81
	209	Come See About Me		/82
Audio Directions				
	101	Doin' It My Way		/82
Adelphi		Doin' It My Way		/83
Rounder	3123	In The Here And Now		/93
		I Feel So Good		1/95

Mother Earth

United Artists	5185	Revolution (soundtrack)		/68
Mercury	61194	<u>Living With The Animals</u>	(144)	1/69
	61226	<u>Make A Joyful Noise</u>	(95)	7/69

---

[1]Bob Dylan - *Highway 61 Revisited* LP, 1965
[2]Bill Withers, 1972

Mercury	61230 Mother Earth Presents Tracy Nelson Country		/70
	61270 Satisfied		/70
Reprise	6431 <u>Bring Me Home</u>	(199)	4/71
	2054 Tracy Nelson's Mother Earth		/73

Unrelated Tracy Nelson: Nelson has often been confused with actress Tracy Nelson, the daughter of the late Rick Nelson.
Sources: Tracy Nelson telephone interviews, 8/21/93, 3/6/94
      Whitburn. <u>Record Research.</u>
      Clee. <u>American 45 R.P.M. Records.</u>

Corporation
(Milwaukee)
The Corporation - #197 LP - 1969

Danny Peil - voc
John Kondos - gtr/pno/flute/harp
Gerry Smith - ld gtr
Pat McCarthy - org (11/11/47; Milwaukee)
Ken Berdoll - bs (12/14/43; Milwaukee)
Nick Kondos - dr

The Corporation was born at Cudahy's Galaxy Club circa early 1968 when the Kondos brothers joined the remnants of a group called Eastern Mean Time. Several months later the band bought into the Bastille, a club near Lincoln & Howell. They then connected with Detroit producer John Rhys who brought some Capitol Records people in to hear them. The group was signed and an album was recorded at Tera Shirma Studios in Detroit.

Coupling one side of originals with a full side of John Coltrane's "India," it became a regional hit. "It made number three in Milwaukee in March of '69," says bassist Ken Berdoll. " There were a couple other parts of the country where it really hit well, like Little Rock, Arkansas."

Negotiations for a second shot with Capitol broke down and the group recorded several songs at Dave Kennedy Studios. When the band broke up later that year, this material was released on two albums and a single on Age Of Aquarius, a custom label of Cuca.

After Berdoll ran into harmonica ace Jim Liban in a laundromat (Liban having just returned from working with A.B. Skhy in San Francisco), the two of them formed Short Stuff. That band was later joined by Junior Brantley (of Junior & the Classics) and existed off and on in various formations for the next 16 years.

(courtesy Tracy Nelson)

Corporation: Danny Peil, Patrick McCarthy, Gerard Smith, Ken Berdoll, Nick Kondos, John Kondos
(courtesy Rick Schurk)

Capitol   2467 I Want To Get Out Of My Grave/Highway   4/69
Age Of Aquarius   1496 Sitting By The Sea/You Make Me Feel So Good   /70
LP's:
Capitol   175 The Corporation   (#197)   2/69
Age Of Aquarius   4150 The Corporation   /70
                   4250 Hassles In My Mind   /70

Also see: Danny Peil & the Apollos - Milwaukee (Peil)
 Rock-A-Fellers - Milwaukee (Ken Berdoll)
 John Kondos & the Galaxies- Milwaukee (John & Nick Kondos)
 Eastman Blues Band - Milwaukee (John & Nick Kondos, Gerry Smith)
 James Hanns & the Soul Entertainers (Patrick McCarthy)
 Karen Wells - Black Knights - Appleton/Fox Cities (Danny Peil)
Unrelated Corporation: ABC, Musicor
Sources: Ken Berdoll telephone interview, 1/93
 Rick Schurk
 Clee. American 45 R.P.M. Records.
 Whitburn. Record Research.
 Bruckner, Bill. "Milwaukee's Music & Musicians." Bugle American 11/75: 151-152.

Historical and Relocated Chart Acts

The following artists were active on record between 1950 and 1969, but began their recording careers prior to that time or after leaving Wisconsin (or both). They are presented in alphabetical order.

1. Jackie Cain
2. Chordettes
3. Jerry Cole
4. Bobby Hatfield
5. Woody Herman
6. Hildegarde
7. Tommy James
8. Pee Wee King
9. Liberace
10. Steve Miller
11. Vaughn Monroe
12. Les Paul
13. Boz Scaggs
14. Glen Yarbrough

Jackie Cain
(Jacqueline Ruth Cain - 5/22/28; Milwaukee)
(Jackie Cain & Roy Kral)

Singer Jackie Cain left Milwaukee at the age of 18 to work jazz gigs in Chicago. It proved to be the right move when she met singer-pianist Roy Kral. They were married June 27, 1949 and have remained in a lifelong partnership of matrimony and music.

Cain and Kral worked with saxophonist Charlie Ventura before going out on their own. With extensive performing in Las Vegas in the 50's, they became well known in the jazz world and recorded for Storyville, Columbia, Atlantic, Roulette, Capitol, CTI and Studio Seven. In the early 60's they moved to New York and have recorded many radio and television commercials.

Chart Single:

Time And Love	#36 ez	/72

Sources: Feather, Leonard. Encyclopedia Of Jazz In The 60's. NY: Horizon, 1966.
      Feather, Leonard. Album liner notes. Concerts By The Sea, Studio Seven 402, 1976.
      Whitburn. Record Research.

Chordettes
(Sheboygan)

Jinny Osborn Lockard	**Lynn Evans**
Janet Buschman Ertel	**Margie Needham**
Dorothy Hummitzsch Schwartz	**Nancy Overton**
Carol Buschman	**Joyce Weston**

Formed in 1946, the Chordettes own the unique distinction of being the only female barbershop quartet ever to cross over to the pop charts. With Jinny Osborn's father presiding over the *Society for the Preservation and Encouragement of Barbershop Singing in America*, the girls sang at shows all over the country. They were talked into auditioning for *Arthur Godfrey's Talent Scouts* and won with a performance of "Ballin' The Jack" (a song from 1914). The Chordettes became regulars on Godfrey's television show from 1949 to 1953, along with singer Julius La Rosa and musical director Archie Bleyer.

The group's first recordings were for Columbia. Barbershop material had never been a big seller on record before, so the company was "quite flabbergasted that they did so well," says Carol Buschman.

Bigger things were in store upon leaving Godfrey, however. "We were one of the first to be fired," reports Buschman. "Arthur didn't want anybody to become too independent of him and his show." When Bleyer left, he started Cadence Records with the Chordettes as one of his first artists. Buschman credits Bleyer with a great deal of their success, from picking songs to laying out the arrangements. "It was his idea to put the intro to 'Mr. Sandman'," she says, "and I think that's what sold it."

Bleyer and Janet Ertel married in 1954 and the quartet charted 14 singles from 1954 to 1961, finally disbanding around 1964. In 1991 Lynn Evans and Nancy Overton added two new members and reactivated the name under the management of another 50's veteran, Herbie Cox of the Cleftones. Both "Mr. Sandman" and "Lollipop" have been used in several movies and Carol Buschman says, "I'm very happy with my memories."

Biggest Chart Hits:

Mr. Sandman	#1	/54
Born To Be With You	5	/56
Just Between You And Me	8	/57
Lollipop	2	/58
LP:		
Harmony Time	3	/50

Sources: Whitburn. Record Research
      Garvey, Dennis. "The Chordettes." Goldmine 7/10/92: 13-18
      All quotes from Carol Buschman interview - Phil Nee Show; WRCO, 7/91 - courtesy
          Phil Nee

Jerry Cole
(9/23/39; Green Bay)

Cole was a highly respected guitar player in his early days around Green Bay with his band, the Flaming Coals, but he didn't record until he joined the Champs ("Tequila," 1958) in California. Though he has often claimed to be on their famous hit, Cole actually joined the group in the fall of 1961.

He recorded as a solo artist for Capitol, Crown, Custom (aka Jerry Kole), Happy Tiger, Midget and Warner Brothers between 1963 and 1975; and as a member of The Id on RCA in 1967. An excellent guitarist, he has done a great amount of studio work and backed many name artists over the years. He continues to gig around Los Angeles in the 90's.

Chart Single:
Warner 8101 Susanna's Song (In The California Morning)   #20 ez   /75
          (Jerry Cole & Trinity)

Also see: Jerry Williams & the Rockets - Appleton
Sources: Myers, Gary. "The Champs - Tequila!" Goldmine 8/82: 8-12
      Whitburn. Record Research.

Bobby Hatfield
(8/10/40; Beaver Dam)

Hatfield left Wisconsin early in his life when the family moved to Southern California. It was in Santa Ana in 1962 that he teamed up with Bill Medley. As the Righteous Brothers they became the most popular "blue-eyed soul" act of the 60's. The duo placed 18 singles on the Hot 100 between 1963 and 1967, hitting the top spot twice. When they split up Hatfield recorded solo for Verve.

Reuniting in 1974, the Righteous Brothers scored three more top 40 hits. They continue to appear together off and on, and it's Hatfield singing the classic "Unchained Melody" that came back to the charts via the movie *Ghost* in 1990.

Biggest Chart Hits (with the Righteous Brothers):

You've Lost That Lovin' Feelin'	#1	/65
Unchained Melody[1]	4	/65
Ebb Tide[2]	5	/66
(You're My) Soul And Inspiration	1	/66
Rock And Roll Heaven	3	/74
LP's:		
You've Lost That Lovin' Feelin'	4	/65
Just Once In My Live	9	/65
Chart Single (solo):		
Only You (And You Alone)[3]	95	/69

Sources: Whitburn. <u>Record Research</u>

Woody Herman
(Woodrow Charles Herrmann - 5/16/13; Milwaukee -
10/28/87; Los Angeles)

Woody Herman was born for a lifetime of music. Beginning with local vaudeville at the age of six and leaving high school to join a big band, he virtually spent his life on the road.

From the early start as a child song and dance man, Herman added clarinet and saxophone and soon had his own radio show on WTMJ. He went on the road with the bands of Harry Sosnik, Gus Arnheim and Isham Jones before starting his own in 1936. From 1937 to 1964 Herman amassed 53 chart singles and five chart LP's while recording for Decca, Columbia, Mars, Capitol, MGM, Phillips and Verve.

---

[1]Les Baxter, Al Hibbler, 1955, many others
[2]Frank Chacksfield, Vic Damone, 1953, many others
[3]Platters, 1955, many others

Herman also continued to sing with the band, which remained one of the most active and contemporary big bands throughout the years. Never afraid to experiment, he recorded material ranging from classical to rock (including an album with guitarist Mike Bloomfield in the 70's). Herman won the Lifetime Achievement Grammy in 1987.

Biggest Chart Hits:

At The Woodchopper's Ball	#9	/39
Blue Flame (The band's theme song)	5	/41
Blues In The Night	1	/42
Laura	4	/45
Caldonia	2	/45
Sabre Dance	3	/48

Sources: Whitburn. __Record Research__
　　　　　Feather. __Encyclopedia Of Jazz__

Hildegarde!
(Hildegarde Loretta Sell - 2/1/06; Adell)

Certainly among the earliest of the First-Name-Only entertainers (and with an exclamation point, no less), Hildegarde's initial success came in England. Upon returning to the states she became one of the most popular radio personalities of the 40's. She charted seven singles on Columbia and Decca between 1936 and 1947, three of them with the Guy Lombardo Orchestra.

Billed as "The Incomparable Hildegarde!," she lives up to the title by continuing to perform and win awards. In 1992 she was inducted into the Wisconsin Performing Arts Hall Of Fame, and she has received a lifetime achievement award from the Manhattan Association of Cabarets and Clubs. In 1993, at the age of 87, she opened her *First Annual Farewell Tour* at New York's Algonquin Hotel, showcasing her as a living link to many of the great songwriters of past years, including Cole Porter, George and Ira Gershwin and Irving Berlin.

Biggest Chart Hits:

June Is Bustin' Out All Over[1]	#11	/45
The Gypsy	7	/46

Sources: Don Dellair telephone interview, 7/9/93 (Tommy Wonder & Don Dellair Mgmt.)
　　　　　Whitburn. __Pop Memories.__

---

[1]from the Broadway musical *Carousel*

Tommy James
(Thomas Jackson - 4/29/47; Dayton, OH)

60's star Tommy James lived briefly in Monroe, Wisconsin, when his father managed a hotel there. James told DJ Phil Nee that it was in Wisconsin at the age of nine that he first heard Elvis. The family moved out of the area about two years later. (David Gates of Bread reportedly spent some summer vacations with an uncle in Monroe).

James recorded his first hit at the age of 16 for a small label in Michigan. However, it didn't become a hit until two years later when a DJ in Pittsburgh broke it. The master was then purchased by Roulette and, with his newly recruited band, the singer racked up a string of hits for the next six years. James recorded for Snap, Red Fox, Roulette, ABC, RCA, Fantasy, Millennium and Twenty-One from 1963 to 1983, charting 32 singles and 10 LP's.

Biggest Chart Hits:

Hanky Panky	#1	/66
I Think We're Alone Now	4	/67
Mony Mony	3	/68
Crimson And Clover	1	/69
Sweet Cherry Wine	7	/69
Crystal Blue Persuasion	2	/69
Draggin' The Line	4	/71
LP:		
Crimson And Clover	8	/69

Sources: Phil Nee, 1993
        Whitburn. Record Research.

Pee Wee King
(Julius Frank Kuczynski - 2/18/14; Abrams)

With two major standards and many other well known tunes to his credit, Pee Wee King is probably Wisconsin's most covered songwriter.

An accordionist, King did his early performing on radio station WRJN in Racine. He soon shifted his base of operations to Louisville, Kentucky. King and his band, *The Golden West Cowboys*, worked often on the *Grand Ole Opry* between 1936 and 1947. He was the first Opry performer to bring in drums, first with a trumpet and first with an electric instrument (steel guitar).

King gained exposure working with Gene Autry and went on to record extensively for Bluebird and RCA through 1958. Later label affiliations were Todd, Jaro, Landa, Briar, Starday and Cuca. His credits include two films, *Country Western Hoedown* and *Durango Kid*.

With singer/co-writer Redd Stewart, King's two most successful compositions are "You Belong To Me" (four covers in the top 12; 1952-62) and "Tennessee Waltz" (11 charted singles; 1948-64). Other oft-covered songs include "Slow Poke" and "Bonaparte's Retreat."

King was voted into the *Country-Western Hall Of Fame* in 1974.

Biggest Chart Hits:

Slow Poke	#1	/52
Silver And Gold	18	/52

Sources: Whitburn. <u>Record Research</u>
    Shestack, Melvin. <u>Country Music Encyclopedia</u>. NY: Crowell, 1974.

Liberace
(Wladziu Valentino Liberace - 5/16/19; West Allis -
2/4/87; Palm Springs, CA)

Believe it or not, Walter Busterkeys was the first stage name for this flamboyant pianist when he made his early club appearances in New York in 1940. Known more as a television and Las Vegas performer than a pop recording artist, he did chart six singles and five LP's on Columbia between 1952 and 1954.

Biggest Chart Hits (LP's):

Liberace At The Piano	#1	/52
Liberace by Candlelight	6	/53
Concertos For You	7	/54

Sources: Whitburn. <u>Record Research</u>
    Slonimsky, Nicholas. <u>Baker's Biographical Dictionary of Musicians, 7th Edition</u>. NY:
        Schirmer, 1984.
    <u>Who's Who In Entertainment.</u> Chicago: Marquis, 1992-93

Steve Miller
(10/5/43; Milwaukee)

Miller's family moved to Texas when he was about five years old and he grew up in Dallas. His father was a doctor and a friend of Les Paul (probably from the Milwaukee days), and Miller credits meeting Paul as high point in his young life.

The Marksmen, Miller's first band in Dallas, included Boz Scaggs who had moved there from Ohio. The two musicians continued to work together after moving to Madison to attend the University of Wisconsin. Both of them occasionally played with Ken Adamany's Nigh Tranes as well as Miller's Ardells.

Miller's first recording was done in Chicago in late 1965 with the Goldberg-Miller Blues Band on Epic. Soon after that he moved to San Francisco and served as somewhat of a pipeline for Madison area talent to migrate there. Several musicians from the Ken Adamany clan either worked in Miller's band or went to the West Coast on his referral. He developed a reputation in those days of being difficult to work with. One source referred me to another of Miller's old friends, saying that "He's only one who's known Steve for that long and is still speaking to him."

Miller has recorded for Capitol since 1968, charting 19 singles and 19 LP's.

Biggest Chart Hits:

The Joker	#1	/74
Rock'n Me	1	/76
Fly Like An Eagle	2	/77
Jet Airliner	8	/77
Abracadabra	1	/82

LP's:

The Joker	2	/73
Fly Like An Eagle	3	/76
Book Of Dreams	2	/77
Abracadabra	3	/82

Also see: Boz Scaggs
        Nigh Tranes - Madison
Sources: "Steve Miller Band." Capitol Records Media & Artist Relations - courtesy Tom Davis
        Gary Gerlach telephone interview; 7/9/94
        Whitburn. <u>Record Research.</u>

Vaughn Monroe
(11/7/11; Akron, OH - 5/22/73)

Monroe's Wisconsin connection was brief but his family lived in the Milwaukee suburb of Cudahy for a short time during his teen years. While attending Cudahy High School, Monroe won the state trumpet championship at age 14.

The family moved to Pennsylvania before Monroe graduated and he went on to tremendous success as a band leader with a rich baritone voice. Recording for Bluebird, Victor and RCA Victor from 1940 to 1960, Monroe enjoyed five chart LP's and an amazing 71 chart singles, nine of which went all the way to the top spot.

Biggest Chart Hits (all were number one):

There I Go	/40
My Devotion	/42
When The Lights Go On Again	/43

Let's Get Lost	/43
There! I've Said It Again	/45
Let It Snow! Let It Snow! Let It Snow!	/46
Ballerina	/47
Riders In The Sky	/49
Someday	/49

Sources: Whitburn. <u>Record Research</u>
  Corenthal, Michael. <u>Illustrated History Of Wisconsin Music</u>. Milwaukee: MGC, 1991

Les Paul
(Lester William Polfuss - 6/9/15; Waukesha)

Having enjoyed great success as a pop/jazz guitarist, Les Paul may be equally remembered by some for his advances in electronics, both in guitars and recording techniques. Beginning with country music, Paul first called himself Red Hot Red, then Rhubarb Red. A gig at WRJN in Racine brought wider exposure and Paul eventually traveled to Hollywood and New York, recording with Bing Crosby and the Andrews Sisters.

Paul's first recording was as Rhubarb Red on the Montgomery Ward label in 1936. He went on to record for Vocalion, Okeh, Decca, Capitol, Columbia and RCA. It was with Capitol in 1948 that he began his string of 45 chart singles and five LP's, mostly with his wife Mary Ford (Colleen Summer - 7/7/28 - 9/30/77). The pair became a sensation at the dawn of the 50's with the sound of their multi-tracked vocals and guitars. Nearly all of their big hits were re-makes or covers.

Paul and Ford were married December 29, 1949, and divorced in 1963. Paul continues to play regularly in New York in 1994.

Biggest Chart Hits (solo):

Nola[1]	#9	/50
Whispering[2]	7	/51
Meet Mr. Callahan	5	/52
Lady Of Spain[3]	8	/52
With Mary Ford:		
Tennessee Waltz[4]	6	/51

---

[1]Vincent Lopez, 1922, many others
[2]Paul Whiteman, 1920, many others
[3]Ray Noble, 1931, many others
[4]Pee Wee King, 1948, many others

Mockin' Bird Hill[5]	2	/51
How High The Moon[2]	1	/51
The World Is Waiting For The Sunrise[3]	2	/51
Just One More Chance[4]	5	/51
Tiger Rag[5]	2	/52
Bye Bye Blues[6]	5	/53
Vaya Con Dios	1	/53
I'm A Fool To Care	6	/54
Hummingbird	7	/55
LP's:		
New Sound - Vol. 1	7	/51
New Sound - Vol. 2	3	/51
Bye Bye Blues	2	/53

Sources: Whitburn. Record Research
      Shaughnessy, Mary Alice. Les Paul: An American Original; NY: Morrow, 1993

Boz Scaggs
(William Royce Scaggs; 6/8/44, OH)

Boz Scaggs attended high school in Dallas where he met Steve Miller and played in the Marksmen, Miller's first teen-age band. Both musicians moved to the Madison area around 1962 to attend the University of Wisconsin. Though he did not record while in Wisconsin, Scaggs did fill in as a sideman with Ken Adamany's Nigh Tranes, Steve Miller's Ardells, and various other bands. How did "Boz" come out of William Royce? "(It was) a nickname from high school," he says. "Short for 'Bosley'. I don't really know where it came from."

Scaggs traveled to Sweden and recorded an album of folk-style material for the Karusel label in 1965. After returning to the states he reunited with Miller for two LP's. His initial solo deal in the States was with Atlantic in late 1969 and he first charted on Columbia in 1971.

Biggest Chart Hits:

Lowdown	#3	/76
Lido Shuffle	11	/77
Breakdown Dead Ahead	15	/80
Jojo	17	/80

---

[1]Patti Page, 1951, others
[2]Benny Goodman, 1940, many others
[3]Isham Jones, 1922, many others
[4]Bing Crosby, 1931, many others
[5]Original Dixieland Jazz Band, 1918, many others
[6]Bert Lown, 1930, others

Look What You've Done To Me	14	/80
Miss Sun	14	/81
LP's:		
Silk Degrees (LP)	2	/76
Down Two Then Left (LP)	11	/78
Middle Man (LP)	8	/80

Also see: Steve Miller
      Crossfires - Cuca
      Nigh Tranes - Madison
Sources: Boz Scaggs letter, 3/26/94
      Whitburn. <u>Record Research.</u>
      Clee. <u>American 45 R.P.M. Records.</u>

Glen Yarbrough
(1/12/30; Milwaukee)

Glen Yarbrough formed the Limeliters in Hollywood, California, in 1959. The folk trio went on to chart ten albums between 1961 and 1964 (nine on RCA, one on Elektra). After leaving to go solo, he scored another nine chart LP's with RCA and one on Warner Brothers. His final Billboard appearance came in 1969.

Biggest Chart Hit:

Baby The Rain Must Fall	#12	/65

Sources: Whitburn. <u>Record Research</u>

(courtesy Jeff Naskrent)

Jim Kirchstein

Dave Peterson (Jaguars) in Cuca studio

(courtesy Tom Sumner)

The Cuca Story
(James Kirchstein - 3/28/31; Sauk City)

"Kirchstein was the only person who really gave people like us a chance. He was a real Godsend."
> - Mike Morgan (Little Artie & the Pharaohs), 6/8/94

"He had an amazing operation there."
> - Bill Sherek (Tikis, Talismen), 8/94

"Sooner or later we all recorded at Cuca."
> - Roger Loos (Temptations, Bob Mattice & the Phaetons, others), 3/94

Wisconsinites and geography fans know that Madison is the state capital but few would guess that nearby Sauk City had once been the state's recording capital. In this tiny town on the Wisconsin River (not to be confused with Saukville, which is near Lake Michigan), Jim Kirchstein built a recording studio that provided an outlet for hundreds of groups and artists from the entire region. The discography is sprinkled liberally with polkas - always a favorite in Wisconsin - but the incredible quantity of material released (over 700 singles and 200 albums and still counting) runs the gamut of musical categories.

Kirchstein attended the University of Wisconsin and served in the Korean Conflict. Upon his return home in 1954 he opened a record store in the basement of his brother's toy shop in Sauk City, which is about 20 miles northwest of Madison . By late 1959 he had set up a recording studio, choosing the unlikely name of Swastika for his label.

"That was a very dumb thing I did," says Kirchstein. "This was in the 50's and the horrors of World War II were just 15 years before that. I had the idea of creating a series of German related type music and the swastika was basically a symbol of good luck, a symbol of the sun. RCA actually pressed (the first records) - RCA was largely Jewish. I got a call from Bill Leonard and he said, 'I don't know - we can't do this, we're raising a lot of eyebrows,' and I said, 'Bill, it's a dumb thing. Throw them all away'. The first two were on that label. We changed to Cuca halfway through the second one."

Of course, this makes the Swastika label a real rarity but it was the new name (Cuca was a nickname for a Mexican cousin of Kirchstein's wife) that proved to be the good luck charm. The company hit paydirt just two releases later with two local musicians who named themselves for the brand of guitar they played. The Fendermen's "Mule Skinner Blues" was a rockabillyish novelty version of a song written in 1931 by country-western great Jimmie Rodgers. The musicians had brought in a tape recorded in a friend's basement and it was released on Cuca 1003. Kirchstein recalls the action starting when a college station in Lincoln, Nebraska, played it constantly for an entire day. It soon hit the top spot at WKBH in La Crosse where DJ Lindy Shannon reigned. The young company was not prepared for a national release so the record was sold to Soma in Minneapolis. A re-recorded version went to number five on Billboard's Hot 100 during the summer of 1960.

"The Fendermen were two guys, Jim Sundquist from Kingsbury, Michigan, and Phil Humphrey from Stoughton, which is just a little ways from here," explains Kirchstein. "They were performing at a tavern and I heard about them. After they got their hit their lives became very wild. They made a lot of money, they were driving Cadillacs and they ended up in a Mexican prison." (When asked about the prison, Jim Sundquist replied, "I have no idea. That must have been Phil Humphrey and the rest of the guys.")

The record firmly established the company and financed a larger studio. "Those days were fun," says Kirchstein. "Everything was pioneering. The record industry was owned by RCA and Capitol and a couple others, and for a little town in South Central Wisconsin to have a little studio, so what, you know. A little later we started doing our own mastering. By 1961 we had built our major studio and we had groups every day throughout the week, coming from as far away as Fargo, North Dakota."

By 1963 the studio had begun to attract many outside artists. "Bobby Vee, Bobby Bare, Cheap Trick was just starting a little bit later," recalls Kirchstein. "Bobby Bare, just after he came in, had a big hit called 'Detroit City'. Bobby mainly did producing of some groups he brought up from Iowa. Lawrence Welk was quite interested in the label and we kept in touch for many years."

Cuca was also gaining a reputation around Chicago and artists and producers from the Windy City were making the trip out to the peaceful countryside. "Chicago liked us because we were a little hick town and nobody was tapping our studios. In Chicago they tap the studios, literally," claims Kirchstein. "Out in Sauk City that didn't happen so we had a lot of strange groups come out. Very often the promoters would come into the booth and when they'd sit back in their chair we'd see a gun pop out of their shoulder holster."

Jan Bradley was one of the Chicago artists who visited. Her number 14 pop hit, "Mama Didn't Lie," was produced there. According to Kirchstein, at one point Cuca products made up four of the top ten on Nashville's r&b giant, WLAC.

By this time the company was doing a lot of custom work. There were several different label names and a few different numbering systems, making it nearly impossible to complete the discography. Beginning in 1963 and running concurrent with the original system, the procedure for custom work was to have the first two digits designate the year, the next digit(s) for the month, and finally the sequence of release. Thus, 6494 would indicate 1964, ninth month, fourth release of that month. Then, if no more product were issued that month, the next release would be 64101 (for 1964, 10th month, first release). So, although the dating information is a blessing, the other aspects are a nightmare: a mix of four and five digit numbers, and no way of knowing what the final release was in any given month. It might also seem that a number such as 64111 could mean the 11th release in January as well as the first one in November, but Kirchstein says the number of custom releases in a month never got that high. (However, copies of ledger cards show a 67410 and 67412 - oh well, maybe that never happened in January!) It also seems that there may have occasions when the same number was used under two different label names.

(It also appears as if several other small labels in the state used this system. Some have turned out to be custom labels of Cuca clients. Others have not, leading to speculation as to why this came about.)

Besides all that, Kirchstein had already gone to using a 3000 series and a 5000 series intended for different musical categories. He also states that many outside projects were completed in a matter of a few days, with only 300-500 copies pressed, and were never even logged. A band could come in, do their session, and get 300 records for $37.50.

Sara (for Kirchstein's first wife) was the most commonly used alternate label name. Others include Age Of Aquarius, American, Banana, Butternut, Dee Jay and Night Owl. Often the client would use their own label name with the Cuca number.

Album-wise, the company did well with its ethnic line and old time folk music. Various items are occasionally sought for reissue in other parts of the world. "I get probably four or five orders a week for records that I haven't had for 10 or 15 years," says Kirchstein. "We quite often find a tape made of some of our selections that we know nothing about. I do know that 'Mule Skinner Blues' has been released many times. We try to follow up."

"The record business is probably one of the worst in the world as far as being misused. A lot of the labels were Mafia controlled. A lot of real good artists who never made it. A lot of very honest people within a largely dishonest world."

In 1964 Kirchstein built radio station WVLR (for Very Live Radio. It later became WMIL) and in 1966 he opened his own pressing plant which ran until 1972. In 1968 he joined the University of Wisconsin as a consultant and has been an engineer for the state for over 20 years. He still does an average of one LP per year along with audiovisual projects for non-profit organizations. In a remark sure to break the heart of many collectors he says, "Not long ago we donated over a million records to the federal penal institutions. We just ran out of storage space. They came down with a huge semi."

With many happy memories of the artists he recorded, Kirchstein says, "Every once in a while I hear someone shout at me when I'm in the city and it's one of the musicians. We end up talking for an hour even though they may have only had one session."

(Many Cuca artists are covered in other sections of the book. Please see index).
Sources: Jim Kirchstein interview, 8/29/88; many subsequent telephone conversations

Sharon Arnold

Cuca	1074	Cold Cold Heart[1]/Little Bitty Tear[2]	3/62
	1110	I Walk/Tennessee Waltz[3]	11/62

Believed to be from the Green Bay area, Arnold is backed by Dave Kennedy's Ambassadors on her second release.

Source: Tari Tovsen telephone interview, 1/93

Birdlegs & Pauline
(Rockford, IL)

Sidney "Birdlegs" Banks (10/13/29; Chicago, IL)
Pauline Shivers Banks (4/28/33; Memphis, TN)

Cuca	1125	Spring/So Many Ways		2/63
Vee Jay	510	Spring/So Many Ways	(#94, 18 r&b)	5/63
LP:				
Cuca	4000	Birdlegs		9/64
Pauline Shivers				
Expo	102	No Messin' Around/Please Bless Our Home (Pauline & Bobby)		8/68
Opex	109	Stopped/Tough Stuff		/69
	110	You Better Tell Him No/Boom Boom		/69
	111	You're A Devil/Won't You Come Back Home		/70

"Big hit," says Kirchstein of 'Spring' by this artist. "Birdlegs and his group came out of Rockford. His wife, Pauline, was one of the finest vocalists I've ever heard. I put out the record really for the flip side, 'So Many Ways', which Pauline sang. About that time Milwaukee had a DJ named O.C. White who was really getting hot. I sent him the record and he played the flip side and I got a call from Abner of Vee Jay and we leased it to them. They sold over 100,000 but the problem was they went bankrupt about the time after we got our first check. We never

---

[1]Hank Williams, Tony Bennett, 1951; many others
[2]Burl Ives, 1962
[3]Pee Wee King, 1948; Patti Page, 1950; many others

heard anymore, but we had the publishing so it was a good thing for us. Could have been a lot of money if they had stayed in business. We did an album on them shortly after that. 'Spring' wasn't on the album because the single was still licensed out."

Sidney Banks picked up his nickname as a skinny youngster playing basketball in Chicago. He had been performing for nearly 10 years before the opportunity came for the first recording. "When I first come to Rockford I hadn't ever recorded yet," he recalls, "But Tyrone Davis was my valet." Davis, of course, went on to much success on the soul charts in the late 60's and early 70's.

Banks' group, the Versatility Birds, included Mack and Floyd Murphy who later worked with the Blues Brothers. The group toured the South and made many appearances with Ike & Tina Turner, B.B. King, Magic Sam and Little Milton. There were a few more recording attempts but, with the financial problems at Vee Jay, no more singles were released.

When the couple got divorced near the end of the 60's, Pauline returned to Chicago and recorded under her maiden name. She left the business about 10 years later and has confined her singing to the church since then. "I never really got anything from the record financially," she says, "and that discouraged me in a lot of ways. When I came into the church it was comfortable for me and so I stayed in the church."

Banks left the music business around 1969 and has also been involved in church work since 1976. He remains the rare artist who had a hit with the only single he ever released.

Sources: Jim Kirchstein interview, 8/29/88
        Sidney Banks telephone interview, 5/91
        Pauline Shivers Gogins telephone interview, 4/9/94
        Whitburn. Record Research.

Dick Buscher & the Cliches
(Dubuque, IA)

Dick Buscher - rh gtr
Nick White- ld gtr   **Benny Bryson** - ld gtr
Tom Weig - bs   **Denny Tranel** - bs
Harry Bluett - dr   **Terry Williams** - dr

| Cuca | 1040 | Outlaw/Wayward Wind[1] | 6/61 |
| | 1054 | Two Hearts In Love/Carioca[2] | 11 /61 |

---

[1]Gogi Grant, 1956
[2]Enric Madriguera, 1934; Les Paul, 1952; many others

1077	I Wonder Why[1]/Love, Love, Love		4/62
1105	Run Boy Run/16 Tons[2]		8/62
1168	Baby (Come On Home)/Blue Heart		4/64
1235	Don't Say You're Sorry/Stagger Lee[3]		6/65

One source has this singer nicknamed "The Blonde Swede," though a friend says he never heard him called that. Buscher's recordings include several remakes; some in an early rockabilly style, others with a more poppish Rick Nelson flavor. "Run Boy Run" was probably his most successful record. Buscher's hobby was flying and he was killed in the crash of his own small plane around 1967.

Sources: Joe Hudspeth telephone interviews, 4/93, 8/17/94
            Tourville. <u>Wisconsin . . . Discography.</u>

Coreys
(Reedsburg)

Bob Corey - sx (4/10/47; Milwaukee)
Tom Corey - org
Ross Corey - bs

| Cuca | 6981 | The Summer's Gone/Movin Out | (/I) | 8/69 |
| **LP:** | | The Ross Corey Sound | | /78 |

This family group did MOR pop material.

Sources: Cuca ledger card - courtesy Jim Kirchstein
            Bob Corey telephone interview, 8/21/94

Crossfires/Ace & the Crossfires
(Whitewater)

Allen "Ace" Bauman - gtr (7/9/40; Lake Mills)
Steve Sperry - gtr (10/3/41; Ft. Atkinson)
Todd Langmack - sx   **Denny Geyer** - gtr (9/18/43; Milwaukee)
Leo Weidenfeld - bs (2/18/40; Milford)   **Phil Alagna** - bs/sx (5/10/43; Milwaukee)
Harry Jay (Johnson) - dr

---

[1] w: Tomsco-Tharp (Fireballs)
[2] "Tennessee" Ernie Ford, 1955; others
[3] Archibald, 1950; Lloyd Price, 1959; others

Crossfires: Phil Alagna, Ace Bauman, Harry Jay, Denny Geyer (courtesy Allen Bauman)

Cuca	1027	When My Blue Moon Turns To Gold Again[1]/Young Love[2] (I/I)	1/61
Leaf	6238	All American Twister[3]/This Should Go On Forever[4]	/62
		(Ace & the Crossfires)	

Related:

Arcolia	46560	A.D.C. Baby/You Cheated	
		(Harry Jay & Group Therapy)	

In spite of having only two singles released, this band is significant because of the additional recording activities of many of its members. Steve Sperry recorded solo and eventually hit the national charts in 1977; Dennis Geyer touched the charts with A.B. Skhy in 1969; and Phil Alagna did some work with the Legends' Sam McCue before moving to California with the Mojo Men. Also, leader Ace Bauman and bassist Leo Weidenfeld had previously appeared on two early Wisconsin rock 'n' roll releases with the Teddy Boys and Scotty Stewart.

The Crossfires were booked by Ken Adamany. Fill-in musicians on some gigs included Steve Miller and Boz Scaggs. "Ken's booking agency was really based upon the Crossfires and the

---

[1]Cindy Walker, 1944; Cliffie Stone, 1948; Elvis Presley, 1956
[2]Sonny James, Tab Hunter, Crew Cuts, 1957
[3]Bill Parsons (Bobby Bare), 1959
[4]Rod Bernard, 1959

Nigh Tranes (Adamany's own group) because he always knew that we were going to be there to do the jobs," asserts Bauman. "I remember Adamany telling us he's got a bass player for us to use such and such a night. He said, 'His name's Scaggs,' and that's the only reason I happen to remember it, is the name left an impression. I remember he wasn't very good." (laughs)

Of the early gigs, Bauman says, "A lot of the places had never had rock 'n' roll bands, so it was either turn down and play softer music or everybody just went crazy. It didn't seem to be any halfway-in-between."

Both of the Crossfires' singles made some area charts but the band was nearly involved in something much bigger. "This guy came in with his guitar and he said he needed a band to back him up," says Bauman, recalling a demo session at WTTN in Watertown. "We backed him up and actually even put it on tape. The song was kind of a weird, different, bizarre song, so we told him we didn't have time to fool with that because we had to get these demo tapes ready. Well, the guy was Phil Humphrey and the song was 'Mule Skinner Blues'."

Since Humphrey's partner, Jim Sundquist, reports having no knowledge of the incident, Humphrey must have been scouting around on his own with the idea of augmenting their duo for the recording.

Adamany produced and played on the bands' Leaf release, "All American Twister." The song was Bauman's rewrite of the 1959 hit "All American Boy." "Ken sent that record to ABC-Paramount and they offered me a contract on that one," says Bauman. "The problem was that was the beginning of the Viet Nam Conflict and I was classified 2S and as soon as I graduated I would have been gone. I went into teaching and if I wouldn't have taught, I probably would have been drafted right away, so there wouldn't have been anything I'd have been able to do."

Bauman has been a teacher and wrestling coach in Mineral Point for many years while Leo Weidenfeld has been a pilot for United Airlines since 1964.

Unrelated Crossfires: Capco, Lucky Token, Rhino, Strand, Tower
Also see: Scotty Stewart, Teddy Boys (Allen Bauman)
        A.B. Skhy (Denny Geyer)
        Mojo Men (Phil Alagna)
        Steve Sperry
        Nigh Tranes
Sources: Allen Bauman letters, 1/20/93, 3/93
        Dennis Geyer telephone interview, 1/93
        Phil Alagna telephone interview, 4/93
        Leo Weidenfeld telephone interview, 6/4/94
        Allen Bauman interview on Phil Nee Show, WRCO - courtesy Phil Nee, 4/93

Doc De Haven
(6/20/31; Madison)

Cuca 1098, 1175, 1200, 1223, 1302, 1435
LP's: 3000, 3100, 3200, 3300, 3400

This jazz trumpet player has led his own combo since 1955 when he first played at the Campus Inn on State Street. Before that he had played while in the Air Force and as a student at the University of Wisconsin. Most of his releases consisted of pop and jazz standards.

Continuing throughout the 80's and 90's, DeHaven received a proclamation as "Madison's Jazz Personality of the Year" in 1990 and has been a regular winner as the best local jazz and dance band. DeHaven recorded on Neophonic in 1991.

Source: Doc DeHaven resume - courtesy Lea DeHaven, 1993

Andy Doll
(Oelwein, IA)

Mastertone	1014	Muskrat Ramble/		
Starday	345	That's Life/You Can't Stop Me From Dreaming		/57
AD	109	The Butterfly/Hawaiian War Chant	(I/I)	
	0989	Stockade Rock/Letters Have No Arms	(I/)	
	3409	Wild Side Of Life/Sandy Haired Stranger		
	4627	Boogie Walk/Yankee Rouser		
	4784	Wild Desire/Wait		
Starday	587	Honey Dew/Goodbye Mary Ann		
Jay Jay	300	Hot Chicken/Milwaukee Waltz		/64
Cuca	1259	Mixer Polka/Little Jessie		2/66
Audio	LP1001	On Stage		

Sources: Tourville. Wisconsin . . . Discography
      Clee. American 45 R.P.M. Records.
      Osborne-Brown. Rockin' Records.

Don & the Dominos
(Wisconsin Rapids)

Don Zabel
Harry

Cuca	1062	Wabash Cannon Ball/Give A Little, Take A Little	11/61
		(Don & Harry)	

1088	Just Let Me Be/Too Blue To Cry	6/62
	(Side 1 reissued on *The Cuca Story - Vol 1*)	
1109	Weary Blues/Whole Lotta Love	10/62
	(Side 1 reissued on *The Cuca Story - Vol 1*)	
1143	Cherokee Boogie/Domino Theme	8/63

With an obvious country slant, the familiar sounding titles above are probably re-makes of the well-known tunes by Hank Williams and others. However, leader Don Zabel would not be interviewed or provide any information, so I was unable to confirm this.

Sources: Cuca ledger cards - courtesy Jim Kirchstein
Clee. American 45 R.P.M. Records.

First Garrison
(Des Moines, IA)

Larry Dowd

Damion	6532	Tell Me No Lies/Mama Say Blue	3/65

Dowd previously recorded with Larry Dowd & the Rock-A-Tones on the Spinning label.

Source: Tourville. Wisconsin . . . Discography

Five Chords

Probable members:
J. Woodward
H. Kellett

Jamie	1110	Love Is Like Music/Don't Just Stand There	9/58
Soma	1151	I Need Your Loving/Belinda Brown	11/60
Cuca	1031	Jeannie/Red Wine	2/61
Macon	104	Sally/Chicago	
Boom	LP 4949	Wild Are The Five Chords	

A traveling show band, possibly from Michigan or Indiana.

Sources: John Cooke telephone interview, 1/94
Cuca ledger cards - courtesy Jim Kirchstein, 8/13/94
Tourville. Wisconsin . . . Discography.

Fortunes
(Darlington)

Roger Hessling

Cuca   1173   You Got The Right/Candy Man   9/64

Also see: Vilas Craig & the Viscounts (Roger Hessling)
Unrelated Fortunes: This band is probably not related to any other Fortunes on record.
Source: Cuca ledger cards - courtesy Jim Kirchstein

Joey Gee & the Bluetones: Bill Morrison, Craig Sorensen, Ricky Bates, Joey Gee
(courtesy Joe Giannunizio)

Joey Gee & the Bluetones/Come-Ons
(Iron Mountain, MI/Milwaukee)

Joe Giannunzio - voc/hca (9/17/42; Iron Mountain, MI)

Bluetones:	**Come-Ons:**	
Craig Sorensen - gtr (Iron Mt., MI)	**Mike** - ld gtr	
Billy Morrison - bs (Kingsford, MI)	**Don** - rh gtr	
Rickey Bates - dr (Iron Mt., MI)	**Tom** - bs	**Vaughn Ryan** - bs
	Paul - dr	

Sara	6451	Don't You Just Know It[1]/Little Searcher	5/64
		(Joey Gee & the Bluetones)	
	6599	She's Mean/You Know - Till the End Of Time	9/65
		(Joey Gee & the Come-Ons)	
		(Side 1 reissued on Pebbles *Highs In The Mid 60's, Vol. 10* - Side 2 on Vol. 15)	

Joey Gee & the Come-Ons: (top) Don, Joey Gee, Tom, (bottom) Paul, Mike (courtesy Joe Giannunzio)

Joe Giannunzio left his first band, the Bluetones, in Iron Mountain to attend broadcasting school at Career Academy in Milwaukee. While there he ran an ad for musicians and the Come-Ons were formed. The band's most notable gig was probably opening for the Turtles at the Scene. Giannunzio returned to the Upper Peninsula and, along with radio work, continued singing until 1968. Since 1972 he has worked in Seattle for KING, KOMO and KJR under the name Joe Cooper.

Unrelated Joey Gee: ABC
Sources: Joe Giannunzio telephone interview and letter, 8/14/94, 8/19/94
      Clee. <u>American 45 R.P.M. Records.</u>
      Tourville. <u>Wisconsin . . . Discography.</u>

---

[1]Huey Smith & the Clowns, 1958

Bobby Hankins
(Olewein, IA)

Cuca	6533	White Lightnin'[1]/Lonesome Hours	3/65
	6563	Hawaiian War Chant/Rollin' On	6/65
	1256	Root Beer Song/How's Things	2/66
White Lightnin'	500	White Lightnin'/Root Beer	
Cuca	6681	Just Between The Two Of Us/Boy Oh Boy (A Heartache)	8/66

Sources: Tourville. <u>Wisconsin . . . Discography</u>
    Jim Kirchstein, 1994

Ron Harvey
(Ronald Bothe)

KFIZ	2924	Santa & The Elf/ (same)

Ron Harvey did several big band recordings on Cuca. This novelty record was done at a Fond du Lac radio station where he worked as a DJ.

Sources: Dale Luther telephone interview, 6/12/94
    Tourville. <u>Wisconsin . . . Discography.</u>

Henchmen VI
(Ontonagon, MI)

Scott Keinski - ld gtr (White Pine, MI)
Joe DeHut - rh gtr (6/23/48; Ontonagon, MI)
Art Moinlenen - org
Bob Durant - bs
Jay Jackson - dr

Cuca	6731	All Of The Day/Is Love Real	3/67

This band is not related to the Scarlet Henchmen on Night Owl.

Unrelated Henchmen: Guillotine, Leaf, Monument, Punch, Swan, United Artists
Sources: Joe DeHut telephone interview, 8/14/94
    Tourville. <u>Wisconsin . . . Discography.</u>
    Osborne-Brown. <u>Rockin' Records.</u>

---

[1]George Jones; 1959 (w: J.P. Richardson=Big Bopper)

Bobby Hodge
(Madison - 7/16/32; Gastonia, NC)

Nashville	5014	Carolina Bound/You're Always Welcome	
		To Cry On My Shoulder	/61
Cuca	1066	Sitting On Top Of The World/So Easy To Love	2/62
		(Side 1 reissued on *The Cuca Story - Vol 3* LP)	
	1140	It's Almost Tomorrow/Impossible To Get You Off My Mind	7/63
Golden Wing	3040	Alligator Man/Taxicab Driver	/63
Stop	161	Great Lakes Dan/So Easy To Love	3/68
Cuca	68101	Blue Christmas/Sing A Song Of Christmas	10/68
Stop	266	Scarlet Water (Known As Wine)/Your Love Passed Away	4/69
	1550	Bus Driving Son Of A Gun/I Can't Fight The World	/69
Volunteer	4000	Close Up The Honky Tonks/	
		You Took Her Off My Hands[1]/I Wish I Could Fall In Love Today	

Bobby Hodge appeared on the Grand Ole Opry in 1961 and some of his Nashville sessions included top country studio musicians. Between touring he frequently fell back on his old job as bus driver for the city of Madison. He also worked as a DJ for WKOW. His best selling record was "Scarlet Water (Known As Wine)." After an unsuccessful campaign for sheriff around 1970, Hodge moved to Tampa, Florida, where he has done well as a race horse owner and night club proprietor.

Sources: Bobby Hodge telephone interview, 8/10/94
    Tourville. <u>Wisconsin . . . Discography.</u>
    Clee. <u>American 45 R.P.M. Records.</u>

Earl Hooker
(Earl Zebedee Hooker - 1/15/30; Clarksdale, MI - 4/21/70; Chicago)

Rockin'	513	Sweet Angel/On The Hook	5/53
King	4600	Race Track/Blue Guitar Blues	/53
Argo	5265	Frog Hop/Guitar Rumba (sic)	3/57
Bea & Baby	106	Trying To Make A Living/Dynamite	3/60
Checker	947	Trying To Make A Living/Dynamite	5/60
		(Above two by Earl Hooker & Bobby Saxton)	
Chief	7016	Galloping Horses, A Lazy Mule/Blues In D Natural	8/60
		(Earl Hooker & Junior Wells)	
	7020	Calling All Blues/Knocking At Your Door	9/60
		(2nd side shown is by James, both sides were credited to him)	

---

[1]Ray Price, 1963

	7021	Messing With The Kid/Rockin' Wild	10/60
		(Earl Hooker & Junior Wells)	
	7031	Rockin' With The Kid/Rockin' Wild	12/60
CJ	605	Senorita Juanita/Sweet Soozie	/60
		(Earl Hooker with Earl Tidwell)	
	613	Do the Chickin (sic)/Yea Yea	/61
		(Earl Hooker & his Roadmasters)	
	619	Your Lovin' Arms/Happy I Long To Be	/61
		(Earl Hooker with Al Perkins & Bette Everett)	
Chief	7039	Messing With The Kid/Rockin' Wild	/61
Age	29101	This Little Voice/Apache War Dance	/61
		(Earl Hooker & A.C. Reed)	
	29106	Blue Guitar/Sweat To Tell The Truth	/62
	29111	These Cotton Picking Blues/How Long Can This Go On	/62
Checker	1025	Tanya/Put Your Shoes On Willie	11/62
Age	29114	That Man/Win The Dance	/63
		(Earl Hooker with the Earlettes)	
Mel-Lon	1000	Want You To Rock Me/Down In My Heart	/64
	1001	The Leading Brand/Blues In D Natural	/64
Mel	1005	Messing With The Kid/Come On In This House	/64
Cuca	1194	Bertha/Walkin' The Floor	11/64
		(Earl Hooker & the Soul Twisters)	
CJ	643	Chicken/Wild Moments	11/65
		(Earl Hooker & his Roadmasters)	
Jim Ko	-	You Can't Hide/Won't Be Down Long	/65
Sue	392	Calling All Blues/ (see Chief 7020)	9/65
Cuca	6793	Dynamite/End Of The Blues	9/67
		(Earl Hooker & the Soul Thrillers)	
	1445	Dust My Broom/You Took All My Love	/69
Blue Thumb	103	Boogie, Don't Blot/Funky Blues	8/69
Arhoolie	521	Wah Wah Blues/You Don't Want Me	/70

LP's:

Cuca	4100	The Genius Of Earl Hooker	/68

Reissued material on Arhoolie, Blue Thumb, Bluesway, Blues On Blues

Blues guitarist Earl Hooker was another of Cuca's Chicago visitors. Hooker was the cousin of blues great John Lee Hooker and, from another side of the family, r&b singer Joe Hinton.

"Earl called and set up a 7:00 appointment," relates Kirchstein. "At about midnight I gave up and then they came in. They were very tired after a long day of travel and finding us, but we got a few bottles of wine - my folks had a grocery store next door - and we got baloney and bread. About 2AM we got recording and it was one of the finest sessions. We recorded all night. Earl had recorded with other labels but those tapes got lost in a fire and they said we had the only master tape of Earl Hooker."

Kirchstein is apparently referring to the album, since Hooker had recorded singles for numerous labels since 1953. His Cuca LP is entirely instrumental, as Hooker seldom sang. It includes a version of "Sleepwalk" retitled "Bertha" for his wife, and Sam & Dave's "Hold On, I'm Coming," on which Hooker took the liberty of crediting himself as writer.

The guitarist did six or seven sessions at Cuca over a period of a few years and, though the initial LP was done around 1964, the vinyl did not see daylight until nearly four years later. "Earl died very young from tuberculosis," says Kirchstein. "Terrible loss. A great talent and a pioneer in Chicago blues type guitar."

Sources: Jim Kirchstein interview, 8/29/88
      Danchin, Sebastian. Earl Hooker - The Life & Death of a Ghetto Hero. Unpub. -
         courtesy Sebastian Danchin, 3/13/93.
      Clee. American 45 R.P.M. Records.
      "Earl Hooker." Living Blues Vol 1, No. 2. Summer 1970 - courtesy Robert Pruter.

Jerry & the Continentals
(Portage)

Jerry Karow - ld gtr
Larry Barden - rh gtr   **Tom Nennig** - ld gtr (2/3/50; Portage)
Jerry Nennig - bs (7/20/43; Portage)   **Dean Packard** - rh gtr
Tom Roland - dr   **Rich Hartley** - org
                     Mike Jordan - dr

Night Owl   6791   I've Had It[1]/A Heart Of Stone   9/67
                  (Side 1 reissued on *Badger A Go Go* LP)

"It's your run-of-the-mill happy days things," is Jerry Nennig's brief description of his Continentals days, which lasted from 1959-72. The band was one of many that drew early inspiration from the Ventures. So much so that, according to Nennig, they were the first in the state to use Mosrite guitars, the line introduced by the Ventures.

Sources: Cuca ledger cards - courtesy Jim Kirchstein
      Jerry Nenning telephone interview, 9/6/94

---

[1]Bell Notes, 1959

Dave Kennedy
(Milwaukee)

Dinamo	1002	Pizza Pie/	/59
Cuca	1004	Accidentally/Joanie	3/60
Soma	1138	Accidentally/Joanie	4/60
Bolo	721	Where Did My Darling Go/Please Don't Leave Me Alone	/61
Job	502	Night Train/Dave's Blues	
Raynard/Page		(see Raynard Records - Wisconsin Labels)	

Oddly enough, there were two different Dave Kennedy's on Cuca. This one was a more mainstream pop artist who had his own label, Raynard, in Milwaukee. A multi-instrumentalist, he overdubbed all the parts on some of his records.

Also see: Raynard/Page Records
Sources: Clee. <u>American 45 R.P.M. Records</u>

Dave Kennedy & the Ambassadors
(La Crosse)

Dave Kennedy - rh gtr (9/22/42; Auburndale)
Tari Tovsen - ld gtr (10/25/42; La Crosse)
Ronnie Rink - bs   **Tom Eisenman** - dr
Tom Neary - dr   **Al Banasik** - gtr
                                                  Chuck Sargeant - kb
                                                  Jerry Oliver - bs
                                                  George Eberdt - dr

Lindy	101	Blue/Me Neither	(/I)	/60
		(Dave Kennedy with the Super-phonics)		
Cuca	1036	Wooden Heart[1]/You Didn't Listen		5/61
		(Side 2 reissued on *The Cuca Story, Vol. 1*)		
	1050	Lili Marlene[2]/You Can't Be True Dear[3]		9/61
	1058	Do Not Forsake Me[4]/You Don't Want Me Anymore		11/61
	1079	Don't You Ever Go/I'm Afraid You'll Put Me Down		5/62
		(Chuck Sargeant & the Ambassadors)		
	1093	Little Red Rented Rowboat[5]/That's Where Lonesome Lives		7/62

---

[1]Elvis Presley - *G.I. Blues* LP, 1960
[2]Perry Como, 1944
[3]Ken Griffin, others, 1948
[4]aka "High Noon" - Frankie Laine, 1952
[5]Joe Dowell, 1962

	1107	Peepin' And Hidin'[1]/Kiss Me Quick[2]	11/62
		(Side 1 reissued on *The Cuca Story, Vol. 1*)	
	1133	Zombie Jamboree/Lonely Is A Word	6/63
		(Side 1 reissued on *Badger A Go Go* LP)	

LP:
Coulee   1001   Breaking Up Is Hard To Do   /64
Related:
Sabina   521   Nothing In Return/Summertime Time   /64
                       (Belmonts - backing by the Argoes/Good Times)

Good Times
Kama Sutra   215   She Makes It Hard On Me/That's When Your Heartaches Begin[3]   9/66
             215   Hard Life/That's When Your Heartaches Begin   10/66
             247   You Got The Fever/Mr. & Mrs. Arthur Thompson Request   /68
Changing Times (Tari Tovsen)
Transaction   714   Diana/We Got To Live Together[4]   /70

Dave Kennedy & the Ambassadors: Tom Eisenmann, Tari Tovsen, Dave Kennedy, Al Banasik, Chuck Sargeant

[1] aka "Baby What You Want Me To Do" - Jimmy Reed, 1960
[2] Elvis Presley - *Pot Luck* LP, 1962
[3] Elvis Presley, 1957
[4] Buddy Miles, 1970

David Kennedy & the U.S.A. Band

Audem		9130	She Wore Red Dresses[1]/I Hear You Knocking[2]	/89
Eli	LP	881	For Openers	

Cuca's second Dave Kennedy was an 18-year old singer-guitarist with his group from La Crosse. They were brought in by their manager, DJ Lindy Shannon, for whom Kennedy had recorded one previous single.

Kennedy started out singing at an A&W in Marshall for burgers and root beers, but a skirmish with the law caused him to be sent to St. Michael's Home in La Crosse. While there he learned a few more chords and wrote his first song, impressing one of the nuns. Sister Mary John (with whom Kennedy has remained in close touch) got the song to Shannon who recorded it for his Lindy label. The backing band was the Super-Phonics and two of the members eventually joined Kennedy's Ambassadors.

The first trip to Cuca came the following year. "Dave came in when Presley had just released his movie, *G.I. Blues,*" explains Jim Kirchstein, "and in that he sang 'Wooden Heart'. Lindy Shannon got the idea of releasing a single so we did it. In fact, when Andy Doll came up from Iowa to record, we were working with the Kennedy master. He thought it was a great idea and he went back and told a friend of his about it. His friend is the guy who had the hit, Joe Dowell."

"Warner Brothers wanted to buy us," says Kennedy. "They would have bought the group and the master for a little over $1,000. Jim Kirchstein wouldn't let the record go. He had given up 'Mule Skinner Blues' to Amos Heilecher at Soma and he said this was his second shot at a hit record and he wasn't going to give this one up. But he didn't have the distribution power that Mercury/Smash had. Joe Dowell had my record in the studio along with Elvis' record. Lindy was told that by the man from Mercury. If he would have let us go to Warner Brothers we would have had the (hit) record."

Cuca responded to Dowell's hit by recording two answers; "You Don't Have A Wooden Heart" by Linda Hall and "I, Too, Have No Wooden Heart" by Rhea Renee. They then had Kennedy cover Dowell's later hit, "Little Red Rented Rowboat." "Our way of getting even," laughs Kirchstein.

(It was late in 1962 when I first encountered Kennedy. Each of us dated the same Green Bay girl often over the next several months, much to the dismay of her old high school boyfriend - whom she eventually married after all!)

---

[1] w: Dwight Yoakam
[2] Smiley Lewis, Gale Storm, 1955

When draft notices began arriving in early 1964, the Ambassadors recorded a parting LP on the Coulee label. About that same time, a New York band called the Argoes lost their lead singer while playing in Ishpeming, Michigan. On the club owner's referral they called Kennedy who accepted and relocated to the East Coast.

The Argoes backed the Belmonts (several years after their split with Dion) on one record and worked with Del Shannon, the Ronnettes and other name acts. With a name change to the Good Times, the band signed with Kama Sutra. The initial release, "She Makes It Hard On Me," received some negative feedback about the title, causing subsequent pressings to be issued as "The Hard Life." After another single, label owner Artie Ripp offered Kennedy the chance to go solo. "Like an ---hole I said, 'No, I have to stay with the band," recalls Kennedy. "That was a major career mistake on my part."

The Good Times continued to play clubs for another six years before their demise. Kennedy continues going strong as David Kennedy & the U.S.A. Band. Ambassadors guitarist Tari Tovsen joined the Shy Guys and recorded in the 70's with Changing Times. He continues playing in the 90's. Tovsen has also been the primary force in organizing the Lindy Shannon tribute-reunion concerts of 1992 and 1994.

Also see: Shy Guys (Tari Tovsen)
          Jesters III (Tom Eisenman)
          Super-Phonics (Al Banasik, George Eberdt)
          Greenmen - Milwaukee (George Eberdt)
Sources: Jim Kirchstein interview, 8/29/88
          David Kennedy letter and telephone interview, 2/6/93, 3/10/93
          Tari Tovsen letter, 1/20/93
          Clee. American 45 R.P.M. Records.

Jim Langdon Trio
(Madison)

Bill Lengacher - banjo, conga
Don Tollefson - gtr
Steve MacEnroth - gtr   **Steve Sperry** - gtr (10/3/41; Ft. Atkinson)
John Segerstrom - bs   **Dean Kaul** - bs

Cuca		1129	Billy Sol/Rickety Rockety	3/63
	EP	1149	Maryann/Billy Sol/Overland/Egypt	10/63
	LP	1100	The Jim Langdon Trio	/63

Strangely enough, the Jim Langdon trio was neither a trio, nor did it have a Jim Langdon. It seems that the original four members cared for a paraplegic professor at the University named Jim Grasscamp. The musicians were residing at One Langdon St. (Langdon also being the name of Fraternity Row in Madison). A combination of the professor's first name and the street name produced the folk group's mythical leader. The "trio" part referred to the three vocalists, Bill Lennaker being the non-singing member. Steve Sperry became successful in the advertising business and hit Billboard's Hot 100 with his own single in 1977.

Also see: Steve Sperry - On The Charts
Sources: Steve Sperry telephone interviews, 3/8/94, 5/14/94
         Clee. <u>American 45 R.P.M. Records.</u>

Jim Langdon Trio: Dean Kaul, Don Tollefson, Steve Sperry, Bill Lengacher (banjo)

Bobby Lee

Cuca	1065	It Takes Breaks/Connie	12/61
	1076	King Size Love/Twist It	4/62
Mustang	1115	It Takes Breaks/	

This must be one of the most common names in the music business. There are Over 25 Bobby Lee records on the following labels: A-B-S, Ara, Confederate, D, Falew, Gold Coast International, Little Richie, Mandy, Musicor, Port, Ramco, Sage & Sand, Squaw Man, Stoneway, Sue, Tonka, Trac, Vistone. I have been unable to determine if any of these are related to the Cuca Bobby Lee. This artist was apparently connected with a Colorado songwriter/truck driver named James Ed Keele. All four of Lee's Cuca sides were written by Keele with various co-writers from the greater Denver area. Lee's initial Cuca release was one of the company's first national promotions and it received some airplay around the country.

Unrelated Bobby Lee: Decca, Coulee (Showmen with Bobby Lee)
Sources: Osborne-Brown. Rockin' Records
      Fred Masotti
      Clee. American 45 R.P.M. Records.

Denny Lee

(Denny Lee Frey - 10/27/45; Marshfield)

Owl	1036	Judy's Clown/Cooly Mooly	(/I)	/63
	253	Diane/My Daddy		/64
Cuca	1278	Fortune Teller/You're The One		6/66
Age of Aquarius				
	1556	Searchin'/Evil Girl		/70

(Denny Lee Incorporated Plus)

Denny Lee Frey performed from 1959-85, the last 12 years in a duo with his brother. Lee plays piano and organ. The Owl label was owned by Wausau country singer Hoot Roberts.

Unrelated Denny Lee: This artist has no connection with guitarist Denny Lee (Sesso) of the Greenmen and other bands.
Sources: Denny Frey telephone interview, 8/13/94
      Tourville. Wisconsin . . . Discography.

Fred Lowrey

Cuca	1288	Yellow Bird[1]-Walk Right In[2]/Happy Whistler[3]-Mocking Bird	9/66
LP	7100	Whistling In Heaven	

This blind whistler was featured on Leroy Holmes 1954 hit, "The High And The Mighty" and had appeared with Horace Heidt and Vincent Lopez. Kirchstein contacted him and flew him in to record.

Sources: Jim Kirchstein interview, 8/29/88
      Whitburn. Record Research.
      Clee. American 45 R.P.M. Records.

---

[1]Mills Brothers, 1959; Arthur Lyman Group, 1961; others
[2]Rooftop Singers, 1962; others
[3]Don Robertson, 1956

Bob Mattice (courtesy Bob Mattice)

Bob Mattice & the Phaetons

Bob Mattice - voc (10/24/38; Red Granite)
Tom Loos - ld gtr
Roger Loos - sx (11/28/40; Oshkosh)
Tom Reischl - rh gtr (4/13/43; Oshkosh)
Ralph Barfell - bs/org
Jim Kelly - dr   **Jerry Kowall** - dr (11/10/40; Menominee, MI)

Cuca	1016	What's All This/Kaw-Liga[1]		9/60
		(Both sides reissued on *The Cuca Story, Vol. 2*)		
	1034	Safari/Camel Walk	(I/I)	4/61
		(Side 1 reissued on *The Cuca Story, Vol 2*)		

"Mattice was one of Wisconsin's first rock 'n' rollers," says Alan Posniak. "He could imitate Elvis, Buddy Holly, Johnny Cash, Roy Orbison and others to a tee." After his discharge from the armed forces, Mattice appeared frequently as a featured guest with Posniak's Catalinas. Phaetons drummer Jim Kelly had already joined the latter band.

The Phaetons' two Cuca releases were done before Mattice's military service. "What's All

---

[1]Hank Williams, 1953

This," described by Jerry Kowall as an answer to "Mule Skinner Blues, reportedly reached number 20 on Milwaukee's WTMJ. In the 90's Mattice continues to play rockabilly, laughing as he reports, "I still have a band and I still play the same songs!"

Unrelated Phaetons: Hi-Q, Sahara, Vin, W.B.
Also see: Catalinas
          Temptations (Roger Loos)
          Karen Wells (Jerry Kowall)
Sources: Bob Mattice telephone interview, 7/10/93
          Jerry Kowall telephone interview, 5/23/94
          Posniak, Alan. "Organizer of Rock 'n' Roll Band Says Enthusiasm Is Key to Success."
          <u>Milwaukee Journal,</u> date unknown - courtesy Alan Posniak, 8/93

Dick Miller

Gold Star	105	It/I Took My Baby To The Movies	
		(Dick Miller & the Saddle-Ites)	
Pageant	117	A Tear, A Heartbreak, A Love/Cigarettes And Coffee Blues	
		(Dick Miller & the Rhythmasters)	
Cuca	1049	Cherokee Songs/A Lonely Game	9/61
		(Dick Miller & the Wranglers, side 1 reissued on *The Cuca Story-Vol 3*)	

Miller is believed to be from Juneau and may have also recorded on Happy Hearts and M&M. There may also be a connection with Sylvia & the Saddle-Ites on Cuca 6554.

Source: Tourville. <u>Wisconsin . . . Discography</u>

Millionaires
(Michigan)

Ron Van Horn - pno/bs/gtr
Bill Saxon - gtr/bs

                              Bob Bierd - dr (1/12/43; Madison)

Cuca	6463	I Got A Woman[1]/Without Love	6/64
Sounds of Wisconsin			
	6814	The Packer Backer/Patriotic Medley	1/68

The Millionaires relocated to Green Bay and worked there as a duo in the late 60's.

Also see: Zakons - Madison/Janesville (Bob Bierd)

---

[1]Ray Charles, 1955

Unrelated Millionaires: Davis, Shar
Probably unrelated: Big Bunny, Bunny, Cadillac, Phillips, Specialty
Sources: Bob Bierd telephone interview, 7/30/94
  Osborne-Brown. Rockin' Records.

Steve Mutimer & the Rhythm Kings
(Rockford, IL)

Cuca	1009	El Disco/Maj	8/60
Int. Artists	2121	Stuck On Me/Don't Sweat The Small Stuff	/60

Both records produced by Vilas Craig, owner of International Artists label.

Sources: Vilas Craig letter, 1993
  Tourville. Wisconsin . . . Discography.

Night Beats
(Wausau)

Vern Kasten - voc
Dick Lodholz - gtr (12/4/43; Wausau)
Jim Drwek - bs   **Dick Sternberg** - dr (11/29/43; Wausau)
Paul Pritzl - dr   **Ken Heldt** - bs/gtr

Cuca	1001	Night Rider/Johnny B. Goode[1]	(I/)	11/59

It seems that there were two number 1001's on Cuca, the first being the switch-over from the Swastika label with Willie Tremain's Thunderbirds. Thus, the Night Beats earn the distinction of having the first release using only the Cuca name. The record also featured a picture sleeve.

According to Dick Lodholz, the band's drummer Paul Pritzl holds another distinction, that of playing drums on the Mar-Keys 1961 hit, "Last Night." This seems surprising since the Mar-Keys were Memphis musicians. However, Lodholz says the session was done in Chicago where Pritzl was living at the time, and the regular drummer was unavailable.

Lodholz was a highly respected guitarist and the Night Beats also backed singer Robin Lee on one record. The band broke up around 1968 and Lodholz went into the retail end of the music business.

---

[1]Chuck Berry; 1958

Also see: Robin Lee
       Starfires - Stevens Point/Wausau (Dick Sternberg)
Unrelated Night Beats (Nightbeats, Nitebeats): Peach, Sound, Tide, Zoom,
Sources: Dick Lodholz telephone interview, 9/19/93
       Dick Sternberg telephone interview, 7/12/94
       Tourville. <u>Wisconsin . . . Discography.</u>
       Osborne-Brown. <u>Rockin' Records.</u>

Nocturnes
(Stoughton/Oregon)

Ron Thompson

| Cuca | 6373 | Cyclone/Jambalaya Rock[1] | | 7/63 |
| | 64103 | Little One/Hello Josephine[2] | | 10/64 |

Possibly related:

| Soma | 1108 | Hot Night/Switchblade | | /59 |
| | | (Ron Thompson) | | |

Sources: Clee <u>American 45 R.P.M. Records</u>
       Cuca ledger cards (courtesy Jim Kirchstein)

Orbits
(Portage)

Jerry Raimer - ld gtr (9/13/37; Portage)
Bill Alexander - bs
Bob Hoffer - dr

| Cuca | 1006 | Orbit Rock/Slow Burn | (I/) | 4/60 |
| | | (Side 1 reissued on *The Cuca Story-Vol 2*) | | |

This group is not connected with the Orbits from Stevens Point who also had a Cuca release.
Guitarist Jerry Raimer later joined the Zakons and Shane Todd's Shane Gang.

Source: Jerry Raimer telephone interview, 8/3/94

---

[1]Hank Williams ("Jambalaya"), 1952; Fats Domino, 1961; many others
[2]aka "My Girl Josephine" - Fats Domino, 1960

Ravens: Mike McCabe, Butch Wield, Don Wendt, Denny Thompson, Mark Strause
(courtesy Butch Wield)

Ravens
(Shawano)

Mark Strauss - voc
Mike McCabe - ld gtr/steel gtr
Merlin "Butch" Wield - sx/bs (11/27/44; Antigo)
Dennis Thompson - bs
Don Wendt - dr

Sara   6383   Moon Over My Window/The Shuck[1]   (/I)   8/63

Lead singer Mark Strauss wrote "Moon Over My Window" after breaking up with his girlfriend.
The Ravens continued for several years and Butch Wield played until the late 80's in a family
band.

Unrelated Ravens: No other Ravens records are connected with this group.
Sources: Butch Wield telephone interview, 6/22/94
        Tourville. Wisconsin . . . Discography.

---

[1]Ventures - *The Ventures* LP, 1961

Lorraine Rice

Cuca 1293, 1300; Butternut 1299

Lorraine is the sister of country artist Bobby G. Rice, who appears on at least one of her singles.

Sources: Phil Nee, 1993
        Clee <u>American 45 R.P.M. Records</u>

Jimmy Russell

Cuca	1167	Gotta Find Me A Job/Somewhere There's An Angel	2/64
	1233	Moo-Moo Part 1/Moo-Moo Part 2	6/65
Tylja	1111	Nursery Rhyme Rock & Roll/Please Don't Go	
Odessa	2001	Come Here My Love/Soft Feeling	

Source: Tourville. <u>Wisconsin . . . Discography</u>

Silver Notes
(Markesan)

Larry Pfaff - ld gtr
Lowell Lindberg - stl gtr
Bee Pfaff - bs
Phil Steinberg - dr

Sara	6881	Zip Code 54923/The Girl I Love The Most	8/68

Bassist Bee is the wife of Larry in this country band and the couple still performs in the 90's.

Sources: Cuca ledger cards - courtesy Jim Kirchstein
        Bee Pfaff telephone interview, 8/21/94

Gene Ski

Sara	6632	Six Foot Down/Feelin' Bad	3/66
Tee Pee	1004	To Hell With Love/The Urge For Going	1/69

Kicks Magazine says, "When it comes to burial-related discs, Gene leads the league." Backing group is the Troubadours who probably also backed Marv Duncan on Night Owl 1535. Ski is also involved in Cuca 67122 by Mack & Sandy Ford.

Sources: <u>Kicks</u> #7: 54
        Prellberg, Mark. "Target/Tee Pee Records." <u>Lost and Found</u> #2, 1993: 70
        Cuca ledger cards - courtesy Jim Kirchstein

Stage-Men
(Fond du Lac)

Wally Messner - ld gtr (5/26/48; Fond du Lac)
Bob King - rh gtr
Ed Lenop - bs
Eric Henry - dr

Cuca   6472   Fallout/Can't You See   (I/)   7/64

The Stage-Men went through various stages between 1953-68. In the early 70's Wally Messner did studio work, both in Wisconsin and Nashville. His Nashville work included some releases with Chuck Glaser of the Glaser Brothers. Messner also recorded back in Wisconsin with Radio Flyer on End Of The Trail Records. He continues to play in the 90's.

Source: Wally Messner telephone interview, 6/22/94
        Dale Luther telephone interview, 6/12/94

Stage Men: Bob King, Eric Henry, Wally Messner, Ed Lennop (courtesy Dale Luther)

Strangers
(Fargo, ND)

Bill Velline - ld gtr (9/3/38; Fargo, ND)
Ken Harvey - rh gtr
Dick Dunkirk - bs
Bob Korum - dr (3/18/40; Fargo, ND)

Liberty	55481	Toy Soldier/Loco	(I/I)	9/62
	15550	Card Shark/Mind Reader	(I/I)	5/63
Cuca	1172	Runaway[1]/John Henry		4/64
Dick Dunkirk & the Strangers				
Bangar	652	Don't You Believe Them/You Can't Lie To A Liar		/64
Soma	1424	Don't You Believe Them/You Can't Lie To A Liar		1/65
Bobby Vee & the Shadows				
Soma	1110	Suzie Baby/Flyin' High	(/I)	6/59
Liberty	55208	Suzie Baby/Flyin' High	(/I)	8/59
Related:				
Vee	1001	Leave Me Alone/What'll I Do		2/60
		(Bill Velline & the Shadows)		
Soma	1154	Maybe Baby[2]/Fools Like Me		/60
		(Dave Johnson & the Shadows)		

This was Bobby Vee's band, originally known as the Shadows. They changed their name to the Strangers due to the growing reputation of England's Shadows (who originally backed Cliff Richard). Vee produced an album's worth of material, all instrumental, at Cuca, but Liberty never released the LP. "They had the Ventures," says Vee, "and figured one instrumental band was all the world needed at that time."

Guitarist Bill Velline is Vee's brother. Dick Dunkirk and Bob Korum also did some session work for country artists Wade Ray and Freddie Hart. Korum has been working in sales for a Montana TV station since the late 70's, while continuing to play occasionally.

Dave Johnson (Soma 1154 above) was not a member of the Shadows, but a singer from Gettysburg, South Dakota, who hired the band to back him on record.

Unrelated Strangers: Chattahoochie, Checker, Choice, Christy, Jubilee, KCM, King, KL, Maske, Linda, Salsoul, Titan, Warner Bro.

---

[1]Del Shannon, 1961
[2]Buddy Holly, 1958

Sources: Bobby Vee telephone interview, 7/11/94
      Bob Korum telephone interview, 7/3/94
      Tourville. <u>Wisconsin . . . Discography.</u>
      Clee. <u>American 45 R.P.M. Records.</u>
      Osborne-Brown. <u>Rockin' Records.</u>

Supremes Four
(Milwaukee)

Lovelace Redmond
Homer Walton
Carl Campbell
Phillip Green

Sara   1032   I Lost My Job/I Love You Patricia   3/61

A belated answer to the Silhouettes 1958 hit, "Get A Job," this may be the first release to use the "Sara" name. The Supremes Four was a black vocal group. Guitarist on the session is Denny Lee, later known as Deniel Edwards, who worked with the Greenmen and many other groups.

Also see: Greenmen, Ramrods (Denny Lee)
Sources: Deniel Edwards
      Clee. <u>American 45 R.P.M. Records.</u>
      Osborne-Brown. <u>Rockin' Records.</u>

Tempests
(Watertown)

Dan Fendt - voc (9/15/46; Watertown)
Mike Fendt - ld gtr (3/20/--; Watertown)
Jim Rosenow - rh gtr
Ron Fendt - bs
Danny Kopp - dr

Sara   6453   Bop-A-Shimmy/(I Wanna) Love My Life Away[1]   5/64
             6561   I Need Your Love, I Do/Hello Amy[2]   6/65

---

[1]Gene Pitney, 1961
[2]Everly Bros., 1964 (B side)

Reflection   --   Pretty Woman[3]/Let's Hang On-Sherry-Bye Bye Baby[4] (medley)   /77
                        (Reflection)

With two brothers and a cousin, and mom helping out with the career, the Tempests began as a family affair. Mike Fendt's original, "I Need Your Love, I Do," is an interesting Beatlesque (via Knickerbockers?) number. Sometime after the Sara singles, three of the members fulfilled their military obligation. Reuniting after their discharge in 1968, they renamed the band Reflection. The group evolved into a traveling show band and continued into the late 70's. Mike Fendt eventually moved to the Twin Cities and kept it going until 1986. "It was one of the more satisfying parts of my whole life," says Fendt, who still does some playing and booking along with his work as a psychologist.

Unrelated Tempests: Century, Fujimo, Panorama, Polydor, Smash, Southern Wing
Sources: Catherine Fendt telephone interview, 8/27/94
        Cuca ledger cards - courtesy Jim Kirchstein
        Osborne-Brown. Rockin' Records.

Tempests: Ron Fendt, Mike Fendt, Jim Rosenow, Dan Fendt, Danny Kopp (courtesy Catherine Fendt)

---

[1]Roy Orbison, 1964
[2]Four Seasons, 1965-62-65

Tornadoes with Richie Wynn
(Fargo, ND/Moorhead, MN)

Richie Wynn (Richard Sapa) - rh gtr (2/20/43; Fargo, ND)
Chet Priewe - ld gtr   **Bill Velline** - ld gtr
Terry Erdman - bs   **Freddie Swenson** - bs
Al Johnson - dr   **Mark Rowe** - dr

Soma	1182	You're Too Late/Spookin'	/61
Cuca	1099	Loneliest Guy In The World/It Always Makes Me Cry	8/62

Given the output of the Cuca studio and the frequent usage of some 60's band names, perhaps some duplication was inevitable - but three different Tornados within four months?

This band was traveling around the Midwest when they did their Wisconsin session. Guitarist Bill Velline is the brother of singer Bobby Vee. Dick Sapa (aka Richie Wynn) says Vee wrote "You're Too Late" for them. Sapa has owned the Blue Moon Saloon in Kalispell, Montana, since the early 70's.

Also see: Strangers (Bill Velline)
Unrelated Tornados/Tornadoes: see below
Sources: Dick Sapa telephone interview, 8/28/94
        Bob Korum, 1994
        Cuca ledger cards - courtesy Jim Kirchstein, 8/13/94

Tornados
(Woodruff)

Gordy Hastreiter - gtr (6/27/46; Woodruff)
Bob Olson - sx/gtr (Chicago)
Teddy Vernick - gtr   **Dick Saykally** -gtr
Denny Hastreiter - bs (8/25/44; Woodruff)   **Cookie Bushar** - voc
Dan Peterson - dr

Cuca	1092	Scalping Party/7-0-7	(I/I)	6/62
	6361	Last Date/		6/63

This Tornados group started as teenagers playing sock hops in 1959 and lasted until 1966. "We also played for a lot of the private groups like Mars Candy Co. and Johnson's Wax. They all had these big estates up here," says Denny Hastreiter. "As a result of that we had a lot of good bookings down in suburban Chicago and places like that."

Dan Peterson later became a band instructor in New London and Bob Olson went on to conduct the Omaha Philharmonic Orchestra. (Do you suppose he tells the musicians about his obscure rock 'n' roll records?) Fill-in member Dick Saykally is now a scientist at U.C. Berkeley, CA.

Unrelated Tornados/Tornadoes: ABC-Paramount, Aertaun, Bumble Bee, Cuca (1099, 1104),
        Date, Josie, London, Phalanx, Soma, Tower
Sources: Denny Hastreiter telephone interview, 8/16/94
        Clee. American 45 R.P.M. Records.
        Osborne-Brown. Rockin' Records.

Tornados

This group remains a mystery. They are not Dennis Sundlie's Tornados from Minneapolis (who remain active in 1994).

Cuca   1104   Standing Watch/Hey There   10/62

Unrelated Tornados/Tornadoes: (see above)
Source: Clee American 45 R.P.M. Records.

Willie Tremain's Thunderbirds
(Mauston)

Swastika	1001	Midnight Express/Frankie's Rock	(I/I)	7/59
Cuca	1001	Midnight Express/Frankie's Rock	(I/I)	8/59

(Both sides reissued on *The Cuca Story, Vol. 1*)

This is the only record that appears on both labels, with the name switched during the pressing.

Sources: Label photo on *Best of Cuca, Vol 1* LP - courtesy Rick Schurk

Trodden Path
(Mequon)

Tim Urban - ld gtr
Mike Frommer - rh gtr (5/9/48; Whitefish Bay)
Steve Turner - bs (2/18/48; Ames, IA)
Tom Szymarek - dr

Night Owl   6711   Don't Follow Me/Can't You See   1/67
                        (side 1 reissued on Pebbles *Highs In The Mid 60's, Vol. 10*)

This teen age band worked under the name B.E.A.T. Ltd. until they recorded. They had considered calling themselves the Yellow Pipe but Mike Frommer says Cuca vetoed that name.

"It was named after the pipes that ran around my parents' basement where we practiced," he reports, "but the label was not going to release the record with that name because it connoted marijuana smoking. This was 1966, remember, and Donovan had just had 'Mellow Yellow'." DJ Ken Wright produced the disk. Paul Zukowski, who functioned as a manager and co-writer, recalls wearing wigs, "because you really couldn't grow your hair long and stay in high school." ·

Bassist Steve Turner, recalling "an episode of my life that was near and dear to me," says, "The record did amazingly well - considering it was warped." Turner now has the interesting occupation of doing scrimshaw (a type of engraving) on walrus tusks and artifacts for sale in Alaska.

Sources: Paul Zukowski telephone interview, 8/20/94
   Mike Frommer telephone interview, 8/25/94
   Steve Turner telephone interview, 8/29/94
   Crofty Thorp, 1993
   Tourville. <u>Wisconsin . . . Discography.</u>

Dave Vasser

Sara	63102	New Orleans/Blue Mountain	10/63

Vasser played harmonica and yodeled with the Muleskinners, Jim Sundquist's post-Fendermen group. Since the next Sara number is also a Muleskinners release, it seems likely that they are backing him on this record, though Sundquist says he doesn't remember it.

Also see: Fendermen
Sources: Jim Sundquist telephone interview, 7/3/94
   Tourville. <u>Wisconsin . . . Discography.</u>

Vigilantes
(Hancock/ Houghton, MI)

James Brogan - voc
Don Hermanson - gtr
Greg Coby - sx   **Lee Sterbenz** - gtr
Don Kaekala - bs   **John Mitchell** - gtr/bs
Jay Mihelich - dr (3/7/43; L'Anse, MI) **Lloyd Hugo** - bs

Cuca	1042	Ramblin' On/Someday (Someone Will Come To Me)	8/61
		(Side 1 re-titled "Travelin' On" on 2nd pressing, reissued on *The Cuca Story, Vol. 3)*	
	1064	Highland Fling/No Never (reportedly not released)	12/61
Hermi	001	Warm Wind/Caterpillar Crawl	/62

Related:

Heartbeat	60	Harlem Nocturne[1]/Blue Moon[2]	(Playboys)	/63
Sunny	1	Temptation[3]/Blue Tango[4]	(Lovers)	/63
Limelight	3007	King Of Fools/Mary	(Pastels)	/63
	3014	Drag Strip USA/Mary	(Flagmen)	/64
Cuca	6481	Dream Girl/Everything I Do	(Jim Brogan)	8/64

All Nighters

GMA	1	You Talk Too Much[5]/Summertime Blues[6]	/64
Erie	001	Hey Baby[7]/Talk To Me[8]	/65
	002	Girl Don't Go/Hello	/65
LP	1	Live At The Barn	/65

Besides the above releases with various versions of this band, the same basic group backed Jay Johnson on USA 749, Richard Parker on Phillips 40133, and Johnny Tucker on Sonic 30864. Beginning as high school friends in the Michigan Upper Peninsula, the band traveled extensively around the area. They were based in Chicago when much of the recording took place in 1963. Jay Mihelich now has a record store in Muskegon, MI.

Unrelated Vigilantes: JCP
Sources: Jay Mihelich letter and telephone interviews, 8/92, 9/92, 5/15/94
     Osborne-Brown. Rockin' Records.
     Clee. American 45 R.P.M. Records.

Willie & the Zerkons

Cuca	1163	Out Of Here/End Of Something	3/64
Bagdad	1007	Going Places/Surfing In The Sunset	

Source: Tourville. Wisconsin . . . Discography

---

[1]Herbie Fields, 1953; Viscounts, 1960
[2]Glen Gray, Benny Goodman, 1935
[3]Bing Crosby, 1934
[4]Leroy Anderson, 1952
[5]Joe Jones, 1960
[6]Eddie Cochran, 1958
[7]Bruce Channel, 1962
[8]Little Willie John, 1958; Sunny & the Sunglows, 1963

Discography

Swastika

| 1000 | Don Chambers | I Overlooked An Orchid/Riding Down The Canyon | 7/59 |
| 1001 | Willie Tremain's Thunderbirds | Midnight Express/Frankie's Rock | 7/59 |

Cuca

1001	Willie Tremain's Thunderbirds	Midnight Express/Frankie's Rock	8/59
1001	Night Beats	Night Rider/Johnny B. Goode	/59
1002	Montereys	Rockin' Fool/Rocker	/59
1003	Fendermen	Mule Skinner Blues/Torture	1/60
1004	Dave Kennedy w/Rose Marie	Accidentally/Joanie	3/60
1005	Judy Vyne	Hell's Bells/San Diego	5/60
1006	Orbits	Orbit Rock/Slow Burn	6/60
1007	Herman Feller, Jr.	Swiss Teen Song/New Glarus Waltz	
1008	Steve Sperry	Our Summer Love/That Ain't So	8/60
1009	Steve Mutimer & Rhythm Kings	El Disco/Maj	8/60
1010	Furys	This Way Out/St. Louis Blues	
1011	Six Shooters	Don't You Just Know It/Spin	
1012	Nigh Tranes	Hangover (Swamp Fever)/Rockin' Abe	9/60
1013	Roger Bright & Polka Jacks	I Love To Yodel/Ski Waltz	
1014	Clarence Zahira	Pocatello Polka/Westphalia Waltz	9/60
1015	Dave Kennedy	Two New Stars/Garden Of Love	9/60
1016	Bob Mattice	What's All This/Kaw-Liga	9/60
1017	Caravans	Rock & Roll Christmas/Caravan	11/60
1018		My Son's Lullaby/	
1019	Dick Sherwood	Goldie's Waltz/Pee Wee's Polka	
1020	Ronnie Premier & Royal Lancers	So Loved Am I/Angel In My Eyes **Sara**	12/60
1021	Teen's Men	Spin Out/Like New	
1022	Ambassadors	Christmas Polka/Little Drummer Boy	12/60
1023	Minnesota Marv & Vanguards	Sweet Little Wife/Nobody's Darlin'	1/61
1024	Johnson Brothers	Like Rachel/Julie Dear	1/61
1025	Minnesota Marv & Ed Cree & Vanguards	White Lightning/Little Boy Blue	1/61
1026	Billy Raye	Melody Of Love/Begin The Beguine	
1027	Crossfires	Young Love/When My Blue Moon Turns To Gold Again	1/61
1028	Joey Tantillo	Gunnar Polka/Tic-Toc Polka	
1029	Joey Tantillo	Your Cheatin' Heart/I Walk Alone	
1030	Norman Feller, Jr.	La Adelita Polka/Gigi Polka	
1031	Five Chords	Jeannie/Red Wine	3/61
1032	Supremes Four	I Lost My Job/I Love You, Patricia **Sara**	3/61
1033	Zakons	Trackin'/Wasted	4/61
1034	Bob Mattice & Phaetons	Safari/Camel Walk	4/61
1035	Karen Wells	Believe Him/Never Gonna Let Him Go	5/61
1036	Dave Kennedy & Ambassadors	Wooden Heart/You Wouldn't Listen	5/61

1037	Rustad & Wierman (Rockford, IL)	Meanwhile Back At The Pad/(Part 2)		6/61
1038	Bards	Unicorn Song/Yellow Bird		6/61
1039	Rock-A-Fellers	Say Mama/Reaction		6/61
1040	Dick Buscher & Cliches	Outlaw/Wayward Wind		6/61
1041	Robert Berndt	False Dreams/After Hours		7/61
1042	Vigilantes	Ramblin' On/Someday (Someone Will Come To Me)		8/61
1043	Jelly Swiss Boys	Goldust Polka/Where Are The Days Of Youth		
1044	Linda Hall	You Don't Have A Wooden Heart/Treat Me Nice		
1045	Rhea Renee	I Too, Have No Wooden Heart/Switzerland	**Sara**	8/61
1046	Jimmy Sun & Radiants	Cocaine Blues/Molly And Ten Brooks		
1047	Dick Hiorns	The Gods Were Angry/I'm Movin' On		
1048	Twilighters	Can't You Stay A Little Longer/Restless Love	**Sara**	
1049	Wranglers	A Lonely Game/Cherokee Song		
1050	Dave Kennedy & Ambassadors	Lili Marlene/You Can't Be True Dear		
1051	Boyds Solo Band	Hillbilly Auctioneer/Hillbilly Polka		
1052	Kenny Kotwitz Quintet	Wooden Heart/Adelita		10/61
1053	Tony Grecco	Say Mama/Some Tears Must Fall	**Big Beat**	10/61
1054	Dick Buscher & Cliches	Two Hearts In Love/Carioca		
1055	Darnells	Little Sheila/Besame Mucho	**Sara**	
1056	Mack Johnson Combo	In The Dog House/Hip Shakin' Mama	(not released)	
1057	Paul Weingardt	Sweet Marguerite/Sweet Potato Polka		
1058	Dave Kennedy & Ambassadors	High Noon/You Don't Want Me Anymore		
1059		Little Darlin'/Toothache		
1060	Dan Ronald	Little Drummer Boy/Silent Night		11/61
1061	Shane Todd	Today/Lonely For You	**Dutch**	11/61
1062	Don & Harry	Wabash Cannonball/Give A Little, Take A Little		11/61
1063	Continentals	Tic Toc/Sue		
1064	Vigilantes	Highland Fling/No Never	(not released?)	
1065	Bobby Lee	It Takes Breaks/Connie		12/61
1066	Bobby Hodge	Sitting On Top Of The World/So Easy To Love		2/62
1067	(not released)			
1068	Myrna Robbins	Silver Wings/Lili Marlene		
1069	(not released)			
1070	Linda Hall	Almost Always True/G.I. Guy		2/62
1071	Bobby Smith & Neat Beats (Dubuque, IA)	Be My Baby/St. Louis Twist		2/62
1072	Vilas Craig/Badgers	Skinny Minnie Twist/Badger Twist		3/62
1073	Vibratones	Money/Side-Winder		3/62
1074	Sharon Arnold	Cold Cold Heart/Little Bitty Tear		
1075	Night Owls	Waitin' By The School/Please Don't		4/62
1076	Bobby Lee	King Size Love/Twist It		
1077	Dick Buscher & Cliches	I Wonder Why/Love, Love, Love		
1078	Ray Kannon & Corals	Muleskinner Twist/Please Don't Leave Me		5/62
1079	Chuck Sargeant & Ambassadors	I'm Afraid You'll Put Me Down/Don't You Ever Go		
1080	Jimmy Hartwig	Jeannine Polka/Ragtime Cowboy Joe		

1081	Bobby Price & Dynamics	Come Go With Me/Money Honey	4/62
1082	Leroy Gilbertson	Russian Rumble/Anniversary Song	
1083	Vic Martinson & the 3 Bears	Boo On You/So Lonely Tonight	4/62
1084	Sammy Eggum	Trombone Waltz/Stoughton Special	5/62
1085	Three Naturals	Ooo-La-La Polka/Village Tavern Polka	5/62
1086	Robby & the Teens (Bemidji, MN)	The Angel You Sent Me/ She'll Never Be Back **Sunderland**	5/62
1087	Rhea Marquita	Meet Me Tonight/Without Your Love	5/62
1088	Don & the Dominoes	Just Let Me Be/Too Blue To Cry	7/62
1089	Robbie's Alpiners	Swiss On Rye/Rudy's Polka	7/62
1090		As I Ride/Lonesome Lonesome Blues	
1091	Edelweiss Stars	Teach Me How To Yodel/Es Strussi	
1092	Tornados	Scalping Party/7-0-7	
1093	Dave Kennedy & Ambassadors	Little Red Rented Rowboat/ That's Where Lonesome Lives	7/62
1094	Temptations	Call Of The Wind/Bluer Blues	
1095	Bobby Price & the New Dynamics	Oh, I Like It Like That/Is It True	
1096	Vikings	Rawhide/Rave On	
1097	Furys	Run To Him/Jenny	**Dee Jay**
1098	Doc De Haven Combo	I Can't Get Started/I Love Paris	
1099	Tornados	Loneliest Guy In The World/It Always Makes Me Cry	
1100	Jimmy Hartwig	Tap Room Polka/Sittin' And Waitin'	
1101	Kenny King & the Be Bops	I'm Gonna Love You/You're Alright	
1102	Tune Toppers	Cocktail Waltz/Laughing Song	
1103	Nor-Trons	Pretty Music Polka/Be Love Be Faithful	
1104	Tornados	Hey There/Standing Watch	7/62
1105	Dick Buscher & Cliches	16 Tons/Run Boy Run	
1106	Ray Kannon & the Corals	Little Baby/Dance	
1107	Dave Kennedy/Ambassadors	Kiss Me Quick/Peepin' And Hidin'	
1108	Jimmy Carson	Please Don't Want Me Back Again/I've Got A Right To Know	
1109	Don & the Dominos	Weary Blues/Whole Lotta Love	
1110	Sharon Arnold	I Walk/Tennessee Waltz	
1111	Lonnie Walker	I Slipped, I Stumbled, I Fell/Let's Talk About Us	11/62
1112	Jo Davis	Christmas Vacation/Jamaican Holiday	11/62
1113	- 1121 (various polka artists)		
1122	Ray Kannon & the Corals	Rendezvous/Barbara	
1123	- 1124 (polka)		
1125	Birdlegs & Pauline & Versatility Birds	Spring/So Many Ways	2/63
1126	Bobby Smith & the Shades	I Can't Keep From Crying/Come Back Laurie	
1127	- 1128 (polka)		
1129	Jim Langdon Trio	Billy Sol/Rickity Rockety	
1130	Lavenders	Aw Shucks/Down By The Sea	
1131	Vern Meisner	Strollin'/Time Out	

1132	Twistin' Harvey	The Clock/Every Step Of The Way	
1133	Dave Kennedy/Ambassadors	Lonely Is A Word/Zombie Jamboree	6/63
1134	Betty Moore	Long Hot Summer/Voo Doo Walk	
1135	- 1137 (polka)		
1138	Frank Gay & Gayblades (Rockford, IL)	Hades/Downbound Train	8/63
1139	Mule Skinners	Galloping Paul Revere/Rocky Road Blues **Sara**	8/63
1140	Bobby Hodge	Impossible To Get You Off My Mind/It's Almost Tomorrow	
1141	Raylene & the Dairylanders	Sentenced/This Is The Last Time	8/63
1142	Little Artie & the Pharaohs	The Fox And The Hound/My Symphony	8/63
1143	Don & The Dominos	Cherokee Boogie/Domino Theme	8/63
1144	Louie Byk	Honey/Soon We'll Be Married	
1145	Johnny & the Shy Guys	Born To Be With You/Moon Dawg	
1146	Vernon Yancey Combo	I Can't Stand It/Crazy Rock	9/63
1147	Freddie Patton (Rockford, IL)	Tell Me Why/Have Mercy	
1148	Norman Trio	Cathy, Where Are You/Little Senorita	9/63
1149	Jim Langdon Trio	Maryann/Billy Sol/Overland/Egypt (EP)	10/63
1150	Alvin Styczynsky	Back Home Polka/Haymaker's Polka	10/63
1151	Spike Michael	Billy Boy/Mary Lou	10/63
1152	Lavenders	They Call The Wind Maria/White Lightnin' Effin'	
1153	Russ Wilson Orchestra	Dutchman Waltz/California Polka	
1154	Ron Harvey	I'll String Along With You/Girlfriend	11/63
1155	Harvey & the Seven Sounds	(On The Streets Of) New York City/Glamour Girl	
1156	Ron & the Continentals	Rebound Baby/Rollin' Stone	11/63
1157	Little Artie & the Pharaohs	Impossible/It Puzzles Me	11/63
1158	Ron Harvey Orchestra	Just Another Polka/Wisconsin Polka	
1159		Somewhere There's An Angel/Gotta Find Me A Job	
1160	Teen Tones	Sands Of Arabia/Be Careful	
1161	Vern Meisner	Julyda Polka/Judy Waltz	
1162	Little Artie & the Pharaohs	Foxy Devil/I'll Take Care Of You	3/64
1163	Willie & the Zerkons	Out Of Here/End Of Something	
1164	Ray Kannon & Corals	Let's Surf/Diane	
1165	Paul Kruegal Orchestra	Trollie's Waltz/Mark Polka	
1166	Jimmy Carson	Big Midnight Special/Tears Are Only Mine	3/64
1167	Jimmy Russell	Gotta Find Me A Job/Somewhere There's An Angel	
1168	Dick Buscher & Cliches	Baby (Come On Home)/Blue Heart	4/64
1169	Billie Duncans	September Song/Slow Walk	4/64
1170	Jerry Gilbertson Orch.	Dream Time/Little Tiger	4/64
1171	Syl Liebl	Old Lady Polka/Chicken Polka	4/64
1172	Strangers	Runaway/John Henry	4/64
1173	Fortunes	You Got The Right/Candy Man	9/64
1174	Freefall Three	616/Walk On The Wild Side	9/64
1175	Doc De Haven Combo	Hello Dolly/Billy Boy	9/64
1176	- 1181 (polka)		
1182	Pee Wee King	Petticoat Junction/Tennessee Waltz	9/64

1183	Dick Rodgers	Foundling Waltz/Just Because	9/64
1184	Goose Island Ramblers	Mrs. Johnson Turn Me Loose/Cannonball	9/64
1185	T-Bones	Mary Ann Waltz/City Hall Polka	10/64
1186	Dixie Drifter	Little Hero/Rings On My Fingers	10/64
1187	Collins	Hey Good Lookin'/Oh Lonesome Me	
1188	Yeomen (Columbus, OH)	I Never Will Marry/This Little Light Of Mine	
1189	Vern Meisner	The High Life/Taffy	10/64
1190	Badger Brass Band	Hail To The Chief/Peace Corp Song	
1191	(not released)		
1192	Franklin Ray	A Broken Heart/Closer	10/64
1193	Uncle Ozzie Orchestra	Anna Marie/Sauerkraut Polka	
1194	Earl Hooker	Bertha/Walkin' The Floor	11/64
1195	- 1196 (polka)		
1197	Bill Davis	Longer Than Forever/They'll Never Guess I'm Lonely	11/64
1198	Ole Gerald Orchestra	Red Raven Polka/Chicago Waltz	11/64
1199	Bill Davis	I'll Be There When You Call/Lonely Mr. Blue	12/64
1200	Doc De Haven	Preacher/What's New	12/64
1201	- 1205 (polka)		
1206	Rod and Terry	That's All Right/I Still Love You	1/65
1207	Pee Wee King	Guitar Polka/Wings Of A Dove	1/65
1208	- 1209 (polka)		
1210	Swingalongs	Don't Call Me, I'll Call You/Please Don't Want Me Back Again	
1211	- 1215 (polka)		
1216	Collarmen	Ebony/Their Hearts Were Full Of Spring	3/65
1217	- 1221 (polka)		
1222	Swingalongs	Goodnight Irene/Ode To The Little Brown Shack Out Back	5/65
1223	Doc De Haven Combo	Dream On, Little Dreamer/Chim Chim Cheree	5/65
1224	- 1231 (polka)		
1232	Jack Leonard	Missing You/(There's Been) Too Much Said Already	6/65
1233	Jimmy Russell Trio	Moo-Coo Part 1/Moo-Coo Pat 2	6/65
1234	Verne Meisner	Apple Blossom Time/Orange Peelings	6/65
1235	Dick Buscher & Cliches	Don't Say You're Sorry/Stagger Lee	6/65
1236	Joan Malone	Admit It/Don't Talk Baby	6/65
1237	- 1246 (polka)		
1247	Pee Wee King	Danny Boy/I Am Praying For The Day	12/65
1248	Jack Leonard	Fate Of A Fool/You'll See The Day	12/65
1249	- 1255 (polka)		
1256	Bobby Hankins	Walk By Myself/Root Beer	2/66
1257	Goose Island Ramblers	Hurley Hop/Nikolina	2/66
1258	Syl Liebl & Jolly Swiss Boys	St. Paul Waltz/Long John Polka	
1259	Andy Doll	Mixer Polka/Little Jessie	
1260	Bobby Lanz & Celtics	How Long Will It Last/Much Too Much	2/66
1261- 1263 (polka)			

1264	Bill Davis & Knight Riders	Talking In Your Sleep/Yesterday About This Time	
1265	Jerry Hartman	When You're Away/Highways Are Happy Ways	3/66
1266	- 1269 (polka, etc.)		
1270	Joan Whitney	Fate Of A Fool/Sil Vous Plait	4/66
1271	Harvey Scales	I Want To Apologize/Independence	4/66
1272	- 1274 (polka, etc.)		
1275	Pee Wee King	History Repeats Itself/Hope, Faith And Love	4/66
1276	Jolly Cholly's Trio	Dummy Doll/Squaws Along The Yukon	5/66
1277	Connie Caddell	That's When/The Little Puppet	5/66
1278	Denny Lee	Fortune Teller/You're The One	6/66
1279	- 1280 (polka)		
1281	Don King & Rhythm Kings	Crazy Arms/Moon Over Naples	8/66
1282	Rhythm-Aires	It's Polka Time/Give Back My Heart	8/66
1283	Lorraine Rice	Tippi Toeing/Shoes	
1284	Bek Brothers & Collarmen	My Rhonda/Today	
1285	- 1286 (polka)		
1287	Chief Tones	Do Lord/Shouldn't Have Done What I Did	
1288	Fred Lowrey	Yellow Bird/Walk Right In/Happy Whistler/Mocking Bird (EP)	
1289	- 1291 (polka, etc.)		
1292	Vern Meisner	Somewhere My Love/Blue Eyes Crying In The Rain	9/66
1293	Lorraine Rice	Tippi Toeing/Shoes	9/66
1294	Bek Brothers	Today/My Rhonda	
1295	- 1298 (polka, etc.)		
1299	Lorraine Rice	We'll Pray Part 1/We'll Pray Part 2 **Butternut**	10/66
1300	Lorraine Rice	Happy Holidays/If Jesus Came To Your House	10/66
1301	Dick Noel	Little Lost Angel/Brush Those Tears From Your Eyes	
1302	Doc De Haven Combo	Green Dolphin Street/Swanee River	10/66
1303	John Doremus	What Is A Boy/Dear World	10/66
1304	- 1308 (polka or no information)		
1309	Up-Stairs	Operator Please/Be My Baby	1/67
1310	Cal Calloway	Oh How I Miss You Tonight/A Garland Of Old Fashioned Roses	
1311	Harvey Scales & 7 Sounds	Bootleg/Monkeytime '67	1/67
1312	Cannons	Day To Day/Love Little Girl **Night Owl**	1/67
1313	- 1314 (polka or no information)		
1315	Redd Stewart & Pee Wee King	Too Many Years/I Want To Light A Candle	
1316	Hal Wayne & Pee Wee King	Night Friends/Alone In San Antone	
1317	Tony Rademacher Orch.	Southside Polka/Waltz Medley	
1318	John Krepansky	San Antonio Rose/Your Cheatin' Heart	2/67
1400	Dick Kaye & Kaydettes	Swiss Boy Waltz/Dick's Polka	
1401	Dick Kaye & Kaydettes	Hear My Plea/Pistol Packin' Mama	
1402	- 1416 (polka, etc.)		
1417	Collarmen	Georgy Girl/Hee Nay Mah Toi	
1418	- 1419 (polka)		

1420	Pee Wee King	I'm In Love With The Bridesmaid/(No One) Unless It's You	
1421	- 1434 (polka, etc.)		
1435	Doc De Haven Combo	Santa Claus/Christmas Medley	11/68
1436	- 1444 (polka)		
1445	Earl Hooker	Dust My Broom/You Took All My Love	/69
1446	- 1456 (polka, etc.)		
1457	Challengers of Who	It's Love/Leave Me Be	**Night Owl**
1458	- 1459 (polka)		
1460	Mel Henke	Woman In Space/Built For Comfort	
1461	- 1466 (polka)		
1467	Betty Moore & Seven Sounds	The Long Hot Summer/Voo Doo Walk	
1468	- 1492 (polka, etc.)		
1493	Flying Machine	I'll Find You Anyway/Flying On The Ground	
1494	- 1495 (polka, etc.)		
1496	Corporation	You Make Me Feel Good/Sitting By The Sea	**Age of Aquarius**
1497	- 1499 (polka, etc.)		
1500	Challengers	Hear My Message/I Wanna Hold You	**Age Of Aquarius**
1501	Gary Chamberlain & Country Cats	Muleskinner Blues/Don't Be Angry	**Top Gun**
1502	- 1503 (polka)		
1504	Tom Shehan	God Help The World/Garbage Can Song	5/70
1505	Francis Becker	Musicians Play All Night/It's Your Fault Polka	5/70
1506	Sound Control	I'll Be Back Again/When Will It End	**Night Owl** 5/70
1507	Country Cousins	White Lightnin'/Alabamy Bound	
1508	Dick Kapusta & Troubled Mind	Forgotten People/Is This Free	5/70
1509	George Marshall	Wisconsin/Friends Of Mine	**Sara**
1510	- 1511 (polka)		
1512	Cords	Cords, Inc./Trink	/70
1513	Cords	Ghost Power/Waiting Here For You	
1514	- 1515 (polka, etc.)		/70
1516	Major & Lieutenants	Love, Peace And Soul/Communicating	
1517	Bill Savatski	Village Inn Polka/Moonlight Waltz	
1518	Minnesota Ranch Hands	Wabash Cannonball/Chime Bells	
1519	Minnesota Ranch Hands	Hu La La/Big House On The Corner	
1520	Bob Heil & the Mavericks	Part Of Mine/I Can't Stay	**Top Gun**
1521	Tommy Kaye Show	I Need Someone Now/Man Without a Name	**Embers**
1522	Seltaeb	I Want You/Looking For You	**Banana**
1523	- 1525 (gospel, etc.)		
1526	Leonard Pickett	Ballad Of Sittin' Bull/Legend Of The White Buffalo	
1527	Rear Exit	Thinking Of You/Summertime	**Night Owl**
1528	- 1532 (polka, etc.)		
1533	Jimmy Rogers	I'm Fallin' Out With Myself/I'm Reapin' Wild Seeds	
1534	Holy Providers	When Did You Reach Paradise/Surely He Did	
1535	Fabulous Troubadours w/Marv Duncan	Tribute To Jimi Hendrix/Cheater	**Night Owl**

1536	- 1537 (polka)		
1538	Friends	Jane/Can't Make It Without You	**Sara**
1539	Paul Kay	Swiss Maiden Waltz/Firehouse Polka	
1540	Minnesota Ranch Hands	Honky Tonk Angel/Under The Double Eagle	
1541	Gary Reinke	This War's Over And Done/Being Carried Away	**Sara**
1542	Gene Heier Orchestra	Gypsy Polka/After We're Married Waltz	
1543	UW Waukesha Rock Band	Spinning Wheel/25 Or 6 To 4	
1544	- 1545 (polka)		
1546	Jumpin' Jerry	She Told Me She Loves Me/In The Mood	
1547	Short Stuff	Talk Is Cheap/Bread And Butter Woman	**Age Of Aquarius**
1548	Tayles	Bizzaro Ben/She Made Me That Way	**Age Of Aquarius**
1549	Tayles	Funny Paper Sam/It's High Time	**Age of Aquarius**
1550	Seltaeb	You're The Only Girl For Me/What I Am	**Banana**
1551	- 1553 (polka, etc.)		
1554	Peaceful Coalition	Let's Try To Be One/False Alarm Love	**Age Of Aquarius**
1555	Syl Groeschl	Mein Hut Der Hat Drei Eichen/Dorf Muzik	
1556	Denny Lee Inc. Plus	Searchin'/Dream Girl	**Age Of Aquarius**
1557	Ericksons	Talk Of Love/Yesterdays	**Age Of Aquarius**
1558	Pynk Peach Mob	No Tears/Love Captured Me	**Night Owl**
1559	- 1564 (polka, etc.)		
1565	Jumpin' Jerry	Please Release Me/Somebody Else	
1566	Drifters	River Waters/Danny Boy	**Age Of Aquarius**
1567	Johnny & the Poor Boys	The Fightin' Side Of Me/Alabama Jubilee	
1568	Francis Becker	Morning Star Polka/Lonely Laendler	
1569	Continentals	Girls/Stay Near Me	
1570	Intrepid	Where Have They Gone, What Have Done/Stone Woods	**American**
1571	Harrison Trio	Run, Little Girl/La Fraja	**Evil**
1572	Sue Wallenhorst	How Can Anything So Right/Over And Over Again	
1573	Jumpin' Jerry	Jump's Polka/Elmer's Tune	
1574	Dick Dombreck	Oh Lonesome Me/Summertime Vienna	
1575	What's New	Buccaneer/Whenever She's Alone	**American**
1576	Brother Hayes & Farmer Singers	You Must Be Born Again/I Got A Home	
1577	James Cardman	Soldier's Lament/Find A Little Peace Of Mind	
1578	Western Gentlemen	Muleskinner Blues/Occasional Wife	
1579	- 1590 (gospel, polka)		
1591	Sundog	Eat At Home/Rockin' Rollin' Feely	
1592	-1603 (gospel, polka)		
1604	Baby Grand	Nature's Way/12 Bars Of Blues	**Hemisphere**
1605	Lloyd Amasker		
1606	Concepts Prod.	We Are/	
1607	- 1636 (gospel, polka)		
3001	Kenny Kotwitz	C'est Magnifique/Skyliner	11/61
3301	Citations	Moon Race/Slippin' And Slidin'	**Sara** 4/63

101   Brad Meyers & Citations   Just For You/I Don't Love Her Anymore **Sara** /64

The releases in the following 5000 series seem to skip around over a period of 10 years or more.

5016 Denny King   Fate Of A Fool/Don't Talk Baby   **Sara** /61
5005 Blue Notes   Never Gonna Leave You/
5011 Ziggy & the Zoo   Little Star/Come Go With Me
5024 Thomas Cats (Kingsford, MI)   Dream On Little Dreamer/The Seashell   **Sara**
5026   Never Ending Song Of Love/Mexicali Rose
5027   El Rancho Grande/I'm Gonna Sing About You
5035   Hey Daddy/You Win Again
5036 Paco & the Citations   Cheryl, Moana, Marie/Chime Bells   **Sara**
5045 Laverne Montgomery   He's Your Prize/I'd Like To Help You Out
5046   Stand By Me/Wind Storm
5051 Cathy Reeve   Missouri River/Wanderin' In My Mind
5052 Sir Richard & the Knights   Never Happened That Way/   **American**
5054 Sundog   Going Back To California/Gimme Some Lovin'   **American**
5055 Marg Andrews   Longing For A Swiss Boy/You're Someone Special To
                                                      Someone I Know
5059 Kids From Wisconsin   Guess I'll Never Know/Sun Down Lover   **American**
5060 Step By Step   She's Gone/Time After Time
5061 Georgette Beltran   This Lovely Day's Mine/Suddenly I Feel Lonely

Dates on the following releases are shown by the record numbers (see text).

6311 Dick Marshall & Nighthawks   Jitterbug Joe/The Hawk   **Sara**
6333 Tex Smith   We're In The Same Boat/Have You Seen Her Before Old Moon
6334 Vilas Craig   Gotta Find My Baby/Love You; If I May **International Artists**
6335 Vilas Craig   It's All Over/Chumba   **International Artists**
6336 Vilas Craig   Heartbreak Hotel/Black Out   **International Artists**
6337 Vilas Craig   Poor Loser/Summer's Over   **International Artists**
6342 Teen Kings   I Might Have Known/It's Too Late   **Sara**
6343 George Smith   Frog Liver Quiver/East Avenue Drive
6344 Centurys   Her Love/Wayward Wind   **Micro**
6352 Jerry Dee & Intruders   Bo Diddley/Sugar Corsage   **Sara**
6354 Grand Prix's   Linda/San Jose   **Sara**
6361 Tornados   Last Date/
6363 Tommy Lee & Starfires   Lost Love/Nervous Breakdown   **Sara**
6371 Playboys   Look At Me/Shout
6372 Thundermen   Blues Stay Away From Me/Night Train
6373 Nocturnes   Cyclone/Jambalaya Rock
6375 Nobels   Tossing & Turning/Hideaway
6381 Chevrons   Good Good Lovin'/For Your Love   **Sara**

6382	Judy Lee & Playboys	Low Voltage/I Wonder Could It Be You	**Darly**
6383	Ravens	Moon Over My Window/The Shuck	**Sara**
6392	Catalinas	By My Window/Wo Wo	**Sara**
6393	Jack Calvert	Everyday I Have The Blues/After Hours	**Sara**
63102	Dave Vasser	New Orleans/Blue Mountain	**Sara**
63103	Muleskinners	Good Woman's Love/Brody's 97	**Sara**
63104	Ray Allen & Trendells	Who's Gonna Cry/Go On (Play Your Game)	
63114	Dick Allen & Fairlanes	Dreamin'/Night Twist	
6431	Bel-Airs	I'll Be Forever Loving You/Hey Little Girl	**Sara**
6451	Joey Gee & Bluetones	Don't You Just Know It/Little Searcher	**Sara**
6453	Tempests	Hello Amy/Bop-a-Shimmy	**Sara**
6462	Chevrons	Please Don't Make Me Cry/Still In Love With You	**Sara**
6463	Millionaires	I Got a Woman/Without Love	
6465		Let Go Of My Love/P.S. Dear, I Love You	
6471	Clyde Kelly	I'll Cry Tomorrow/Please Don't Leave Me Anymore	
6472	Stage Men	Fall Out/Can't You See	
6473		Basin Street Blues/Maryland	
6474	Frankie Ray & Bel Airs	Country Boy (With Big Guitar)/Puff Away	
6481	Jim Brogan	Dream Girl/Everything I Do	
6492		In The Mood/Woodchopper's Ball	
6494	Gary Lane & Mad Lads	Henrietta/What Do You Do When	**Sara**
64103	Nocturnes	Hello Josephine/Little One	
64111	Flames	The Bird/Worthless Dreams	
64112	Jackie & Jill	I Want The Beatles For Christmas/Jingle Bells	
64121	Casuals	Come One (Pretty One)/Angel On My Shoulder	
64122	Jerry Nash	Tears/Wasting My Time	
64124	Nate Landrum	You Got Me Beat/Love Is A Golden Ring	
6521	Will Eske Trio	Charlie Was A Boxer/All I Do Is Dream Of You	
6522	Golden Tones	Beyond The Reef/Cocktail Waltz	
6523	Virginians	Lonesome As Me/Wapadego	
6531	Twilights	You Make Me Feel So Good/007	
6532	First Garrison	Tell Me No Lies/Mama Say Blue	**Damion**
6533	Bobby Hankins	White Lightnin'/Lonesome Hours	
6541	Larry Phillipson	Bitter Feelings/Talkin' To Myself	
6542	Jaguars	Boney Maronie/I've Had It	
6544	Ray Allen & Trendells	Look At Me/I Love You (And I Really Mean It)	
6551	Les Barney Gugel	My Hog's Gone Wild/Stompin' At The Surf	
6552	Les Barney Gugel	Darling, I Love You/Devil Woman	
6553	Country Hilbillys	Blue Eyes Crying In The Rain/Cold Cold Heart	
6554	Sylvia & the Saddle-Lites	Poor Nate's Mountain Dew/Mr. Thunder	
6561	Tempests	Hello Amy/I Need Your Love, I Do	**Sara**
6562	Ray Allen & Trendells	Shake A Tail Feather/I'm So Glad	
6563	Bobby Hankins	Hawaiian War Chant/Rollin' On	
6564	Notables	Another Night/Living In The Past	

6565	Larry Lee Phillipson	Milwaukee Road/Little Miss Teardrop	
6566	Dick Hiorns	Alimony/Every Time The Phone Rings	**Sara**
6567	Paramounts	Shake A Tail Feather/Try Me	**Sara**
6583	Jaguars	Things We Said Today/What's The Use Of Love	**Sara**
6584	(same as 6564)		
6593	Duane & the Drifters (Epworth, IA)	Tell Me/Misty	**Sara**
6599	Joey Gee & the Come-Ons	She's Mean/You Know -'Til The End Of Time	**Sara**
65101	Bobby Pierce & Country Kings (Zion, IL)	We Could/Mr. Lonesome, Mr. Blue	
65111	Attila & the Huns	The Lonely Huns/Cheryl	**Sara**
65112	Ken Reitz	Willing Consent/Bullgine Run	**Sara**
65123	Connie Gorton	You Wouldn't Believe Me/Lovin' From You	**Sara**
65125	Originals	Little Bit Of Everything/Watermelon Man	**Sara**
65126	Originals	Jive Samba/Taste Of Honey	**Sara**
65128	Marksmen	Black Pepper/Sharon	**Sara**
6611	Little Lee Babcock	You're The Only One I Know/Have You Ever Been Lonely	
6614	Robin & the Batmen	Batskinner/Louie Louie '66	**Sara**
6624	Quarrymen (E. Dubuque, IL)	Don't Try Your Love/Why	**Sara**
6632	Gene Ski	Six Foot Down/Feelin' Bad	**Sara**
6633	Raylene & Blue Angels	Canadian Sunset/Shakin' All Over	
6635	Barbara Lee Mac	Big Fat Mama/One More Memory	
6636	Jimmy Sun & the Radiants	Rockpile/The Engineer's Last Ride	
6641	Tikis	We're On The Move/Rick-O-Shay	**Sara**
6642	Skip 'n' Gail	I Still Miss Someone/Funny How Time Slips Away	
6644	IV Dimensions (Rock Falls, IL)	My Babe/End That Stompin'	**Sara**
6645	Kenny Bee & Rog Winters	The Writing's On The Wall/The Plainsman	
6646	Kenny Bee & Rog Winters	Come Back Home/Orange Blossom Special	
6647	Julie Durocher	Please Mr. D.J./Bad News	
6648		Ain't It Sad/Things Are Going My Way	
6649	Naturals	There's A New Moon Over My Shoulder/Golden Slippers	
6651	Three Lapels (Rockford, IL)	Love Is A Wonderful Thing/Mitts Place	**Sara**
6661	Dave & Pancho	Riders In The Sky/Bottle Of Four Roses	
6661	Arty Minz & Ellie Shepherd	Which One Of Us Is To Blame/Just Another Name	
6662	Ellie Shepherd & Country Men	I Love You Only/Detour	
6674	Jerry Miller	Blue Destiny/Blue Side Of Life	**Sara**
6681	Bobby Hankins	Just Between The Two Of Us/Boy Oh Boy	
6690	Skeeter Osborne & Blue Jays	I'm So Lonesome I Could Cry/Beggar To A King	
66104	John Paul & Liberators	Midnite Hour/Rock 'n' Roll Music	
66121	Larry Morgan	Red Roses For A Blue Lady/You Win Again	
6711	Trodden Path	Don't Follow Me/Can't You See	**Night Owl**
6712	Skip 'n' Gail	Sweet Thang/That's All I Want From You	
6713	Skeeter Osborne & Westernaires	What Any Man Can Do/Tender Years	
6714	Rodney Moag	Fool Over You/Rachel Ann	
6723	June Klick	Fool They Called Me/How Can I Believe In You	

6731	Henchmen VI	All Of The Day/Is Love Real?	
6732	John Paul & Liberators	Around And Around/Somethin' Else	**Night Owl**
6733	Earl Hooker & Soul Thrillers	Dynamite/End Of The Blues	
6741	Hitchikers	Feel A Whole Lot Better/One Too Many Mornings	
6742	Jerry Miller & Cimarrons	Honky Tonk Song/Man Walks Among Us	
6744	Orbits	Don't/Goodbye My Lover Goodbye	
6745	Edgewater Ramblers	Born To Lose/Blackboard Of My Heart	
6746	Edgewater Ramblers	Get Off The Stool, You Silly Fool/Each Night At Nine	
6749	Paul Rushing & Nashville Sounds	Blue Guitar/The Gypsy	
67410	Tony Turner	Carefree/You're Telling Lies Again	
67412		I Stopped And Listened/Truckin'	
6750	Julie Durocher	You're Still On My Mind/Wild As A Wildcat	
6751	Kenny Bee & Plainsmen	This Broken Heart Of Mine/Frosted Window	
6752	Rog Winters & Plainsmen	When I See You/Shelly	
6753	Bobby Art & Plainsmen	You Can't Love Me/	
6754	Tommy Kay	Oh My Love/Hey There Mr. Lonely	**Sara**
6758	Jay Taylor	Turnaway/I Understand I Better Beware	
6759	Doc & Roundy	Not Your Kind/Pardon Me	
6761	Rob Kirk & The Word	Girl Talk/Summer Winds	
6766	Eastman Blues Band	I Found A New World/Before The Snow Falls	
6767	Mack & Sandy Ford	I Don't Love You Anymore/That Crazy Feeling	
6768	Chain Gang	Come On Up/Monkey Time '67	**Night Owl**
6769	Sandmen	World Full Of Dreams/You And I	**Night Owl**
6771	Wanderer's Rest	The Girl That I Love/The Boat That I Row	**Wright**
6772	Caliphs	Today, Tomorrow/Slow Down	**Sara**
6781	Fastells (Negaunee, MI)	Take You Away/So Much	**Night Owl**
6784	Bill Nehring	I Want To Know/Since You Left Me	
6785	Forgotten Tymes (Wauconda,IL)	Little Black Egg/Won't You Be With Me	**Night Owl**
6791	Jerry & the Continentals	I've Had It/A Heart Of Stone	**Night Owl**
6792	Ron Roberts	May You Never Be Alone/Joe Polka	
6794	Challengers	I Wanna Hold You/The Challengers Take A Ride On The Jefferson Airplane	**Night Owl**
67101	Wanderer's Rest	You'll Forget/Agripine III	**Wright**
67102	Rogues	The Secret/Pearl Girl	**Night Owl**
67114	Molly Fay	The Bottle Or Me/The Best Dressed	
67115	Gib Osmus	Bad Love/It's Been Rotten	
67116	Revens (Ft. Wayne.,IN)	For You/In The Rain	**Night Owl**
67119	Margie Dudeck	Prancer's Got Red Spots/	**Sara**
67121	Jerry Miller & Cimmeron	A Thing Called Sadness/Leah	**Sara**
67122	Mark & Sandy Ford	The Squeak Of The Old Rocking Chair/A Little Bit More Time	
67123	Exceptions	Candy/NittyGritty	
6811	Curley Fields & Kentuckians	Trouble, Sweet Trouble/Kansas City	**Top Gun**
6812	Sunstone Lollipop	Sunshine/People Of Today	**Kel**
6813	Wanderer's Rest	Temptation/Love Is A Beautiful Thing	**Wright**

6814	Millionaires	The Packer Backer/Patriotic Medley	
6815	Dick Hiorns	Cattle Call/Columbus Stockade Blues	
6816	Dick Hiorns	Every Time The Phone Rings/Two Of A Kind	
6821	(same as 6811)		
6828	Melo-D-Rays +Two (Grand Rapids)	Apples, Peaches, Pumpkin Pie/Ma Cher Amie	
6834	Merlin Nielsen	How Long Must I Wait/If You Only Knew	
6835	Scarlet Henchmen	Ring Dreams/Train 2:15	**Night Owl**
6836	Kiriae Crucible	The Salem Witch Trail (sic)/Complain	**Night Owl**
6837	Changing Tydes	Love Is A Beautiful Thing/You Don't Know Like I Know	**Night Owl**
6841	We Three	Our Graduation Song/For Ever More	
6844	Johnny Cherry	Oklahoma/Chequita	
6848	Fuzzy Moore & Tradewinds		
6861	Blue Feeling	Tell Her No/And My Baby's Gone	**Night Owl**
6863	Plague	Mr. White Collar Man/When I See That Girl Of Mine	**Wright**
6881	Silver Notes	The Girl That I Love the Most/Zip Code 54923	**Sara**
6882	Summertime Trio	Summertime/Black Bart	
6892		Hello Houston/Hell's Angels	
6894	Best People	Dreamin' (On A Sunday Afternoon)/Rainbow	
68101	Bobby Hodge	Blue Christmas/Sing A Song Of Christmas	
68102	Sound Department	(You're A Kind Of) Plain Girl/After My Horn	**Cite**
68111	Janet Kay (Oelwein, IA)	The Worst Is Yet To Come/Heaven Help The Working Girl	
68121	Del Rays (Madison)	I'll Feel A Whole Lot Better/Twelfth Of Never	
68122	Major & The Lieutenants	The Thing/Happy	**Night Owl**
6912	Willing Mind	Can I Get To Know You Better/Decide	
6913	Scarlet Henchmen	Crystal Palace/Melody For An Unknown Indian	**Night Owl**
6915	Johnny Cherry	The County Sheriff's Patrol/Big John's Coming To Town	
6939	All Heart	I Can Make You Happy/And We Love You	**Revolution**
6951	Sheer Coincidence	I Don't Lie/Shake	**Wright**
6952	Johnny Cherry	Biggest Clown In Town/Home On Parole	
6962	Dick Campbell	Train To Hollywood/Sugar	
6963	Mendelbaum	Try So Hard/Can't Be So Bad	**Smack**
6967	Hal Waze	Two Hearts Are Lonely Now/	
6972	Bud & Ginny Loy	Losing My Mind/The Angels Are Singing	
69711	East Moline Truckers	Grip On It/Don't Come Around	**Blue Hour**
6981	Coreys	Movin' Out/The Summer's Gone	
6982	6 Dimension	The 27th St. Off Ramp, Part 1/Part 2	
6992		Moon Struck/The Leprechaun	
6993	Axis	Somebody To Love/I Can't Wait	**Plastic Earth**
69103	Mavericks	Patty, Joanne, Christine/Don't Try To Cry	
69129	Gary Rasmussen (Oelwein, IA)	Closet Full Of Clothes/Oh Hear The Train	
7021	Big Jim & Country Clan (Zion, IL)	Country Girl/A Real Friend	(unk)
7022	Donnie Loew	Muleskinner Blues/Sweet Dreams	**Sara**

7514	Sound Hemisphere	Jam/Jones Boys	American
7403	Duke Davis	Kentucky Sunshine/Rodeo Man	
7721	Binders	You Don't Have To Cry Anymore/When We Were Young	Sara
7722	Binders	Mojo Hanna/When We Were Young	Sara
7772	Binders	Save The Last Dance For Me/	Ankh

LP's:

The vast majority of LP's released by Cuca were ethnic, old time music, polka, gospel, etc. The following are of interest in the pop/rock field. The number sequence is not chronological.

1100	Jim Langdon Trio	(same)	/63
1126	Franciscan Cords	Spiritual Troubadors	/70
2255	Pee Wee King	Country Western Hoedown	
3000	Doc De Haven	Dixieland Treasure	
3100	Doc De Haven	On Location	
3200	Doc De Haven	Doc Swings A Little	
3300	Doc De Haven	Just Off State Street	
3400	Doc De Haven	Erle Of Madison	
4000	Birdlegs	Birdlegs & Pauline	9/64
4100	Earl Hooker	The Genius Of Earl Hooker	4/65
4150	Corporation	Get On Our Swing	/69
4250	Corporation	Hassles In My Mind	/70
4500	Various Artists	Badger A Go Go	/70
5174	Parrish Brothers	Variety Of Songs	
7100	Fred Lowrey	Whistling In Heaven	

Contents of *Badger A Go Go* compilation LP (4500):

		(Original release #)
Betty Moore w/Esquires & 7 Sounds	Long Hot Summer	(1134, 1467)
Dave Kennedy & the Ambassadors	Zombie Jamboree	(1133)
Centurys	Her Love	(6344)
Chieftones	Do Lord	(1287)
Seven Sounds	Gettin' Down	previously unreleased
Grapes Of Wrath	Flower Lady	
Mule Skinners	Muleskinner Blues	
Rod Means	That's All Right	(1206)
War Lords	Sad Songs	(6816)
Jerry & the Continentals	I've Had It	(6791)
Esquires	You Don't Care	previously unreleased
(The above track probably also includes the Seven Sounds)		
Del Rays	Twelfth Of Never	(68121)
Robin Lee & the Lavenders	Aw Shucks	(1130)
Kiriae Crucible	Salem Witch Trial	(6836)
Voodoos	The Voodoo Walk	

White Label of Holland has issued the following compilation LP's as *The Cuca Records Story*:

8847 Volume 1

Dick Hiorns	I'm Movin' On	(1047)
Willie Tremain's Thunderbirds	Frankie's Rock	(1001)
Dave Kennedy & the Ambassadors	You Didn't Listen	(1036)
Six Shooters	Rotation	(1011)
"	Don't You Just Know It	(1011)
Don & the Dominos	Weary Blues	(1109)
Nigh Tranes	Rockin' Abe	(1012)
Larry Lee Phillipson	Miami Road	previously unreleased
Don & the Dominos	Just Let Me Be	(1088)
Willie Tremain's Thunderbirds	Midnight Express	(1001)
Rock-A-Fellers	Say Mama	(1039)
Dave Kennedy & the Ambassadors	Peepin' & Hidin'	(1107)
Montereys	Rockin' Fool	(1002)
Larry Lee Phillipson	If You Are A Coward	previously unreleased

8848 Volume 2

Bud Squires & the Teen's Men	Like Now	(1021)
Orbits	Orbit Rock	(1006)
Jimmy Sun & the Radiants	Molly And Ten Brooks	(1046)
Zakons	Wasted	(1033)
Night Hawks	Jitterbug Joe	(6311)
Steve Sperry	That Ain't So	(1021)
Teen's Men	Spin Out	(1021)
Dick Marshall & the Night Hawks	The Hawk	(6311)
Bob Mattice & the Phaetons	What's All This	(1016)
Zakons	Trackin'	(1033)
Larry Lee Phillipson	I'm Wondering Now	previously unreleased
Furys	This Way Out	(1010)
Ray Kannon & the Corals	Muleskinner	(1078)
Bob Mattice & the Phaetons	Safari	(1034)
Bob Mattice & the Phaetons	Kaw-Liga	(1016)
Furys	St. Louis Blues	(1010)

8849 Volume 3

Marv Blihovde & the Vanguards	Little Boy Blue		(1025)
"	Bye Bye Baby		previously unreleased
"	White Lightning		(1025)
"	Nobody's Darlin'	(alternate take)	(1023)
"	Sweet Little Wife	(alternate take)	(1023)
"	Sensation		previously unreleased

Vigilantes	Ramblin' On	(1042)
Badgers & the Royal Lancers	Badger Twist	(1072)
Dick Miller & the Wranglers	Cherokee Songs	(1049)
Teentones	Told Ya Little Baby	previously unreleased
"	Borderline	" "
Teen Kings	I Might Have Known	(6342)
Bobby Smith & the Neat Beats	St. Louis Twist	(1071)
Bobby Hodge	Sitting On Top Of The World	(1066)
Vibratones	Sidewinder	(1073)
Lavenders	White Lightnin' Effin'	(1152)
Catalinas	War Party	(1094)
Mule-Skinners	Rocky Road Blues	(1139)
Teentones	Sands Of Arabia	(1160)

Sources: Clee. <u>American 45 R.P.M. Records.</u>
Tourville. <u>Wisconsin . . . Discography.</u>
Jeff Naskrent, 1991
White Label LP jackets - courtesy Rick Schurk

Milwaukee

"There were a lot of local bands that were better than a lot the ones that had hits."
- Tom Lindemann (Starfires - Milwaukee), 3/12/94

"We never played much in the Milwaukee area. You guys always had that kind of locked up."
- Steve Sperry (Madison), 3/8/94

"It was just a really strange place to play. We played all over the country but nothing was quite like Milwaukee for some reason."
- Cub Tracy (Bowery Boys/Clicker - Madison), 5/2/93

"Adamany and Vilas Craig and Scotty Stuart had things kind of tied up in all the rest of the state except for Milwaukee. Milwaukee was kind of an entity in itself."
- Allen Bauman (Crossfires - Madison), 1/20/93

"We had more talent there than anybody realized and it's a shame that you had to go to the coast to get exposure."
- Rick Bieniewski (Baroques - Milwaukee), 3/9/94

"Milwaukee was just a hard market to break into."
- Ron Buchek (Matadors/Easy Street - East Troy/Palmyra), 5/22/94

"Milwaukee groups of the early 60's had a bit of magic. They were doing a style that was copied and became famous nationwide. I hope some day history records that."
- Jim Kirchstein (Cuca Records - Sauk City), 8/29/88

It was the land of the Braves, bubblers and beer depots[1]. Perhaps bands from the smaller towns were a bit intimidated to come to the big city. Maybe there were just too many good local groups for Milwaukee music fans to pay much attention to outside talent. Whatever the reason, Milwaukee seemed to favor its hometown groups. Even a few of the combos from the outlying suburbs found more employment in other parts of the state.

---

[1]For the uninitiated: Milwaukee Braves baseball team; a bubbler is a Milwaukee term for water fountain; a beer depot is a liquor store.

These are the Milwaukee artists on record in the 50's and 60's, presented in alphabetical order. Also see label discographies, especially Raynard and Teen Town (see Wisconsin Labels), for listings of those not covered separately.

Affluents

Ted Pfeffer - org (8/13/48; Racine)
Jim Morris - gtr   **George Shuput** - gtr (2/3/47; Wausau)
Tom Pilizak - kb   **Russ Engelwire** - org
Dan Carson - bs
Jeff Schmus - dr (8/12/49; Milwaukee)

Cuca		I Feel Free[1]/	/67
USA	901	Get Ready[2]/Tom's Song	/68

The Affluents were managed by Con Merten who handled the Robbs, Messengers and others. "Get Ready" was recorded in Chicago using members of a soon-to-be superstar group. "Chicago played horns on it, the three horn players," recalls Jeff Schmus, "We paid them $65 for the entire session." Schmus went on to record for Paramount in the early 70's with Apothecary.

Also see: Dynastys (George Shuput)
Sources: George Shuput telephone interview, 1/2/94
        Jeff Schmus telephone interview, 2/6/94
        Ted Pfeffer telephone interview, 4/16/94
        Tourville. Wisconsin . . . Discography.

All Heart

Revolution	6939	And We Love You/I Could Make You Happy	3/69

Label was owned by Jack Tadych of Jack & the Beanstalks.

Sources: Jack Tadych telephone interview, 6/29/94
        Tourville. Wisconsin . . . Discography.

Jimmy Allen

Cinch	102	At The DJ Convention/I'm Trading	/64

Source: Tourville. Wisconsin . . . Discography

---

[1]Cream - *Fresh Cream* LP, 1967
[2]Temptations, 1966; Rare Earth, 1970

Apollos

Bobby Ray (Reindorp) - ld gtr
Denny McCarthy - kb (8/19/40; Milwaukee)
Roland Stone (Oeller) - bs (3/17/41; Milwaukee)
Pete Miller - dr   **Duane Lundy** - dr

Cite   5006   For Pete's Sake/Good For A Laugh   /64

Known primarily as the backing group for Paul Stefan, then Danny Peil, the Apollos released this instrumental featuring drummer Pete Miller with a novelty on the flip side. Denny McCarthy is the brother of Patrick of the Corporation.

Also see: Roland Stone
        Skunks (Duane Lundy)
        Paul Stefan
        Corporation - On The Charts
        Danny Peil & the Apollos/Tigers
Unrelated Apollos: California, Cicadelic, Colossus, Delta, Galaxy, Harvard, Mercury,
        Montgomery, Orlyn
Sources: Dennis McCarthy telephone interview, 8/6/94
        Rick Schurk
        Clee. American 45 R.P.M. Records.
        Osborne-Brown. Rockin' Records.

Baroques

Jay Borkenhagen - ld gtr/mandolin/fl/kb (9/7/47; Milwaukee)
Jacques Hutchinson - rh gtr (2/8/46; Milwaukee)
Rick Baroque (Bieniewski) - bs (2/26/47; Milwaukee)
Dean Nimmer - dr (4/20/45; Milwaukee)

Chess   2001   Iowa, A Girl's Name/Mary Jane   6/67
Baroque   4554   I Will Not Touch You/Remember   4/68
LP's:
Chess   1516   The Baroques   7/67
(One cut, "Nothing Left To Do But Cry," reissued on Pebbles *Highs in the Mid 60's - Vol 15*)
Baroque   9005   The Baroques   /90

Career opportunities seemed to open very quickly for the Baroques when they signed with Chess Records after having played professionally for only a few months. Originating with a trio of friends from West Division High, the completed version of the band played their first club gig at the Galaxy in Cudahy August 29, 1966.

Apollos: Roland Stone, Denny McCarthy,
   Bobby Ray, Pete Miller, Paul Stefan

Baroques: (L, top-bottom) Rick Bieniewski,
Jacques Hutchinson, Jay Borkenhagen,
(R,top-bottom) Wayne Will (left before recording),
Dean Nimmer (courtesy Dean Nimmer)

Bonnevilles: Johnny Edwards, Paul Frederick,
   Larry Lynne, Rick Allen

Their reliance on original material didn't win a large following among club-goers who wanted to hear current hits, but it did impress an agent who got them an audition with Ralph Bass of Chess Records. They signed in January 1967, and the album was recorded at Ter-Mar studios (2120 S. Michigan Avenue, Chicago) in March.

The LP did well locally, reportedly selling second only to the Beatles *Sgt. Pepper* in some stores. The Baroques worked at the Avant Garde Coffeehouse, The Scene and Gallaghers, peppering their show with costumes, props and stunts, but still had some difficulty with audiences who wanted to hear the hits.

Eventually it seemed that Chess wanted to hear hits, too. The company turned down the songs submitted for a second album so the boys recorded a single on their own. The record stiffed and the gigs were dropping off. On Sunday, October 27, 1968, when the Avant Garde closed (their lease had expired), so did the Baroques.

"Part of the demise of the group was that Jay refused to do any of the songs that Chess brought to us," says Dean Nimmer, who eventually became head of the painting department at *Massachusetts College of Art*. Nimmer says Chess also brought Minnie Ripperton in to audition with the band. Ripperton went on to become part of Rotary Connection, a psychedelic-type group that apparently fulfilled the idea the company originally had in mind for the Baroques.

Rick Bieniewski, who went into the business of selling dental equipment, reminisces that, "The Baroques were such a high point, I couldn't imagine being in any other band. It's really weird to talk about because it was so magical."

Jacques Hutchinson worked with a few other bands before gaining his Ph.D. and going on to teach applied communication at a technical center in suburban Denver. Jay Borkenhagen worked with Major Arcana and Feather, two Milwaukee groups that recorded self produced albums in the 70's. He then relocated to Northern California where he continues to gig as Jay Blue.

Despite their short life span and the scattering of the members to Boston, Albuquerque, San Francisco and Denver, a new Baroques LP has appeared in the 90's. "This is a very bizarre thing that happened," explains Nimmer. "A member of a local (Boston) group called the Liars called and said, 'Love your music. A friend of mine is bootlegging the album in Europe and he's very interested to know if you have any tapes that could be made into another album.' So I called my brother in Milwaukee and he came up with some interesting, but God-awful, things that we recorded. This guy pressed 1000 copies of the album." With a CD in the works, the Baroques live on nearly 30 years after their demise.

Unrelated Baroques: Van Gogh
Unrelated Feather: Columbia, White Whale
Sources: Rick Bieniewski letter, 3/9/94
     Dean Nimmer telephone interview, 3/19/94

Jacques Hutchinson letter, 3/24/94
Jay Borkenhagen telephone interview, 3/30/94
Tourville. <u>Wisconsin . . . Discography.</u>
Bruckner, Bill. "Milwaukee's Music & Musicians." <u>Bugle American</u> 11/5/75: 145-149 -
     courtesy Peter Lewna and Jacques Hutchinson.
Clee. <u>American 45 R.P.M. Records.</u>
Osborne-Brown. <u>Rockin' Records.</u>

Willie Batchelor

Formula   101   I Need A Hit/I Know She Loves Me

Source: Tourville. <u>Wisconsin . . . Discography</u>

Bel-Airs

Wayne Demmer - voc (7/3/44; Milwaukee)
Dennis   - ld gtr
Dennis Gehrke - rh gtr
Bob Wickert - bs
Pete Miller - dr

Sara   6431   I'll Be Forever Loving You[1]/Hey Little Girl   3/64
Raynard   Treat Me Right/Don't Destroy Me[2]

Singer Wayne Demmer continued performing until 1990.

Also see: Apollos (Pete Miller)
Unrelated Bel-Aires (Belaires): Action, Arc, Arvee, Brut, Crown, Flip, Decca, Discotheque,
     Lewis, Lucky Token, M.Z., Nu Sound, Piv, Raft, Spartan, Times Square, Triumph
Sources: Wayne Demmer telephone interview, 8/17/94
     Tourville. <u>Wisconsin . . . Discography.</u>
     Osborne-Brown. <u>Rockin' Records.</u>

Bloomsbury People
(Waukesha)

Sigmund Snopek III - harpsichord/pno (10/25/50; Milwaukee)
Jon Wyderka - voc
Dennis Lanting - gtr

-----

[1]El Dorados, 1956
[2]Billy "Crash" Craddock, 1959

Greg Janick - org/sx   **Michael "Ding" Lorenz** - dr
Michael DuJardin - bs
Rick Harris - dr

Page	1109	Have You Seen Them Cry/Madeline	/69
MGM	14158	Gingerbread Man/Witch Helen	7/70
LP:			
MGM	2184	The Bloomsbury People	5/70

Sigmund Snopek III
Mountain Railroad

	105	Kathleen/New York Jumpers	/79
	107	If You Love Me Kill Yourself/Solalex	/81
Couth Youth	1003	Cookin' With A Wok In Milwaukee/	
		They're Coming To Take Me Away[1]	/83

LP's:

Water Street	1001	Virginia Wolf	/72
Akashic	1002	Trinity Seize, Sees, Seas	/74
Couth Youth	1001	Nobody To Dream	/75
Mt. Railroad	52709	Thinking Out Loud	/78
	52795	First Band On The Moon	/80
	8004	Roy Rogers Meets Albert Einstein	/82
Chameleon	20010	Wisconsinsane	/87
Beachwood	2511	Sigmund Snopek III Turnaround	/93

The Bloomsbury People was another young group that seemed to be off to a quick start. Formed in 1968 at the University of Wisconsin in Waukesha, the band cut their first single at Raynard. They got an early break while appearing at the Midwest Rock Festival II in West Allis in 1969. Elliott Abbott, manager of Jim Croce, the Carpenters, and Randy Newman, saw their show and took an interest.

The group turned down an offer from RCA and signed with MGM, recording an album at Audio Finishers in Chicago. The LP got a pick in Billboard and the Bloomsbury People did the 1970 Atlanta Rock Festival, but MGM was running into financial difficulties and the band was running into personality clashes.

After the breakup of the group, Sigmund Snopek went on to record several solo albums. Among the often bizarre titles one can find tunes that include the names "Milwaukee" and "Wisconsin," along with a cover of Napoleon XIV (Has anyone else ever done that?). He has recorded with many other artists (including the Violent Femmes), written for films and orchestra, and performed at Milwaukee's *Summerfest*. He appears on a 1993 CD, *Celebration Of Music*, to

---

[1]Napolean XIV, 1966

benefit the Waukesha Training Center. The Vangold Productions release includes the Night Beats, the BoDeans, and Les Paul.

Sources: Sigmund Snopek II letter and telephone interview, 10/93
         Bruckner. "Milwaukee's Music & Musicians." <u>Bugle American</u>

Bonnevilles

Larry Lynne (Ostricki) - gtr (12/14/40; Waukesha)
Pete Funck - sx   **Tony Kolp** - sx
Dennis Madigan - vibes (7/9/41; Milwaukee)   **Vince Megna** - gtr (8/24/44; Milwaukee)
Danny Edwards (Sesso) - pno   **Howard Wales** - org
John Cerniglia - bs   **Bob Merkt** - bs (8/28/44; Waukesha)
Teddy (Salvatore) Peplinski - dr (10/7/42; Milwaukee)

Fenway	7000	Sky Dive/Lazy Waters	(I/I)	2/60
Coral	62273	Johnny/Freeway U.S.A.	(I/I)	/61
Drum Boy	45101	Don't You Dare Let Me Down/Bacardi	(/I)	/62
		(Wendy Colby/Bonnevilles)		

LP:

Drum Boy	1001	Meet The Bonnevilles	/62

Occasionally an unusual instrument would spice up an early rock 'n' roll group, and the inclusion of Dennis Madigan's vibes made the Bonnevilles somewhat of a rarity. What stands out in retrospect, however, is the number of musicians involved during a three-year period, and the noteworthy later musical accomplishments of several of them.

The first two singles were recorded by the same basic line-up. The Coral 45 featured a solid, sax-led version of the old "When Johnny Comes Marching Home" with an effective minor-to-major key change. Shortly after that the personnel changed extensively.

Larry Lynne - gtr
Rick Allen (Sutherland) - pno (3/15/43; Los Angeles, CA)
Johnny Edwards - bs   **Tom Hahn** - bs (5/17/39; Tipton, IN)
Paul Frederick (Edwards) - dr (11/13/41; Springfield, IL)

While drummer Peplinski carried on in Milwaukee with a brand new line-up, guitarist Lynne put together another Bonnevilles to go on the road through Milwaukee's ACA (Artists Corporation of American, headed by Bill Rothe). Though this group never recorded, Lynne and Allen would later form the Skunks, a band that would eventually include Teddy Peplinski, who was then succeeded by Paul Edwards. Tom Hahn went on to record with the Mojo Men.

Rick Allen, after returning to his native Los Angeles, toured extensively with Bonnie Bramlett and has since performed and recorded with dozens of name artists, including Etta James, Dr.

John, Steve Cropper, Ringo Starr and many others. Allen was among the earliest to use the Hammond B-3 organ in a rock 'n' roll band. He has been credited by many Milwaukee area musicians as an important r&b/blues influence. (When a different Ricky Allen, a blues singer with many releases, was getting airplay on a record, Allen admits that "I learned the song and I fooled a lot of people and got gigs that way.") He went on to work as a studio musician in New Orleans for famed producer/songwriter Allen Toussaint.

Meanwhile, Peplinski's Bonnevilles recorded their album at Chicago's Universal Studios, employing the background vocals of the Esquires, who later hit with "Get On Up." The LP included a track by 12-year old singer Wendy Colby, who was not a member of the group.

Guitarist Vince Megna later recorded with jazz great Herb Ellis and other name artists, while Tony Kolp was another founding member of the Skunks. Organist Howard Wales toured with the Greenmen before going on to record with many name artists, most notably the Grateful Dead and Jerry Garcia. Peplinski continues in the 90's with Teddy & the Rough Riders. Danny Edwards (Sesso) worked as a piano single for many years in New York. Saxophonist Pete Funck reportedly worked extensively in Las Vegas. Bob Merkt still plays locally in the 90's. Larry Lynne and Rick Allen have reunited nearly every year to play at the Bayou Lacombe Crabfest in Louisiana.

Also see: Skunks (Larry Lynne, Paul Edwards, Teddy Peplinski, Rick Allen, Tony Kolp)
      Continentals (Vince Megna, Dennis Madigan)
      Larry Lynne Group
      Rock-A-Fellers, Mad Lads, Tom Collins & the Mixers (Bob Merkt)
      Green Men (Howard Wales)
      Darnells, Mojo Men (Tom Hahn)
Unrelated Bonnevilles: Barry, Capri, Collectables, Munich, Now, Pleason, Question Mark,
      Spotlight, Whitehall
Sources: Rick Schurk letter, 2/93
      Larry Lynne telephone interview, 1/30/93
      Bob Merkt telephone interview, 1/93
      Vince Megna letter, 5/17/93
      Rick Allen letter, 2/4/93
      Howard Wales letter, 9/93
      Teddy Peplinski telephone interview, 8/28/93
      Tourville. <u>Wisconsin . . . Discography.</u>
      Osborne-Brown. <u>Rockin' Records.</u>

Gary Brown

Venus	101	Lonely Summer/Cold Day In June	/66
USA	821	Lonely Summer/Cold Day In June	/66
Dynamic Sound	2005	Would You Laugh At Me/Oh My Love	/67

Sources: Tourville. <u>Wisconsin . . . Discography</u>
    Clee. <u>American 45 R.P.M. Records.</u>

Carousel

Terry Sweet - kb (1/31/51; Dallas, TX)
Will Pionke - ld gtr
John Schiefelbein -rh gtr
Tony Shinners - bs
Tim Poremba - dr

Teen Town	108	I've Been With You/What Will You Do For Me	/68
	114	I've Been With You/I Get Along Indefinitely	/69
	116	To Say Goodbye/I Get Along Indefinitely	/70

Related:

Blue Ribbon	101	(Go On Out To) California Tonight/Keep The Customer Satisfied[1]	
		(Sweet & Hirschi)	/72

Keyboardist Terry Sweet formed his own jingle company in 1972. He continues to write music for radio and television commercials.

Unrelated Carousel(s): ABC, Autumn, G.C., Gone, Guyden, Jaguar, Roulette, Spry, Vintage
Sources: Terry Sweet telephone interview, 3/19/94
        Tourville. <u>Wisconsin . . . Discography.</u>
        Osborne-Brown. <u>Rockin' Records.</u>

Challengers
(Waukesha)

John McCurdy - voc
Mike Hoolihan - gtr   **Chris Connors (John Dahlberg)** - gtr (10/2/46; Milwaukee)
Keith Pentler - org (dec: ca 1985)
Pat Clark - bs
John Beaster - dr (11/13/49; Waukesha)
David Wayne (Waehner) - org

Night Owl	6794	I Wanna Hold You/The Challengers Take A Ride	
		On The Jefferson Airplane	9/67
		(Side 2 reissued on Pebbles *Highs In The Mid 60's, Vol. 15*)	
	1457	Leave Me Be/It's Love (Challengers of "Who")	/69
Age Of Aquarius			
	1500	Hear My Message/I Wanna Hold You	/70

---

[1]Simon & Garfunkel - *Bridge Over Troubled Water* LP, 1970

Though based in the Milwaukee area, the Challengers did most of their work in other parts of the state, one exception being a steady Sunday-nighter at Gallagher's downtown (829 N. 3rd St.). The band never called themselves "Challengers of Who" as shown on their second release. "That was just someone's dumb idea for the record," says drummer John Beaster. (brother of Mike Beaster who drummed with Picture).

Guitarist Chris Connors left to join Underground Sunshine as they were about to do the Dick Clark Show with their hit "Birthday." When the Sunshine began to fade a few years later, some remaining members joined with some former members of the Challengers to form an unrecorded band called Eden Stone.

Also see: Underground Sunshine - On The Charts
Unrelated Challengers: Challenge, Chess, Fantasy, GNP Crescendo, Kix Int., Triodex, Tri Phi,
        Triumph, Vault
Sources: Chris Connors letter, 12/93
        John Beaster telephone interview, 12/18/93
        Clee. <u>American 45 R.P.M. Records.</u>
        Osborne-Brown. <u>Rockin' Records.</u>

Cheaters/Vic Pitts & the Cheaters

Vic Pitts - dr
Sharon Pitts - voc   **Julian**   - gtr
Omar Dupree - voc   **Beverly Pitts** - voc (7/9/36; Milwaukee)
Lee Brown - voc   **Bertha Downs** - voc
Van Patterson - gtr   **Al Vance** -bs
E.C. (Eric) Reynolds - tp   **Rollo Armstead** - sx
Ray Maxwell - bs   **Greg Browder** - tp

Raynard	10055	Satisfaction/When Johnny Comes Marching Home (with Beverly Pitts)	/66
	10056	You're Mine/Barefootin'	/66
Brewtown	009	Astrology Child/Why, Why, Why	/72
Jewel	846	Loose Boodie/Modern Crucifixition	/74

Vic Pitts left the Seven Sounds and formed this group with many of the same musicians. There was apparently a great deal of interaction between the two bands. The Cheaters backed former Esquire Sean Taylor on a Magic Touch release. Pitts now resides near Paris, France.

Also see: Harvey Scales & the Seven Sounds - On The Charts
        Esquires - On The Charts (Sean Taylor)
Unrelated Cheaters: Wax
Sources: Beverly Pitts telephone interview, 2/94

Al Vance telephone interview, 4/3/94
Brian Van Dusen telephone interview, 9/27/94
Tourville. <u>Wisconsin . . . Discography.</u>
Clee. <u>American 45 R.P.M. Records.</u>

Challengers: Keith Pentler, Dave Wayne, John Beaster, Mike Hoolihan, Chris Connors
(courtesy Chris Connors)

Vic Pitts & the Cheaters: (rear) Van Patterson, Al Vance, Vic Pitts, E.C. Reynolds, Rollo Armstead,
Greg Browder, (front) Lee Brown, Bertha Downs, Omar Dupree

Chevrons: Dave Zadra, Tom Olivas, Fred Herrmann, Ken Vanslett, Jim Woelfel (courtesy Tourville)

Citations: Tom Lamanchek, Ted Kasper, David Gustin, Joe Halser (courtesy Tom Tourville)

Chevrons

Dave Zadra - voc (6/21/44; Milwaukee)
Fred Herrmann - sx
Tom Olivas - gtr   **Tom Louchbaum** - org (7/11/48; Milwaukee)
Jim Woelfel - bs (dec: 2/93)
Ken Vanslett - dr

Sara	6381	Good Good Lovin'[1]/For Your Love[2]	8/63
	6462	Please Don't Make Me Cry/Still In Love With You	6/64

The Chevrons are surely tops in this book for longevity of original members. Organist Louchbaum was added in the mid 60's to expand the group to six pieces. When singer Dave Zadra left near the end of the decade, the remaining five continued with no further changes until the death of bassist Jim Woelfl. Then, after an absence of 25 years, Zadra rejoined and took over on bass (which he had never played before). 1994 marks the Chevrons' 34th year.

Unrelated Chevrons: Brent, Cuca, Fenton, Gait, Independence, Kiski, MMC, Time
Sources: Dave Zadra telephone interview, 11/28/93
        Tom Louchbaum letter, 1/94
        Tourville. <u>Wisconsin . . . Discography.</u>
        Osborne-Brown. <u>Rockin' Records.</u>

Citations

Ted Kasper - ld gtr
David Gustin - rh gtr (12/14/45; Milwaukee)   **Brad Meyers** - voc
Joe Halser - bs   **Kenny Stupek** - dr
Tom Lamanchek - dr   **Bob Sanderson** - bs
                                                      Plamen Sisters - voc
                                                      Rick - rh gtr
                                                      Dick - dr

Sara	3301	Moon Race/Slippin' & Slidin'[3]	4/63
Epic	9603	Moon Race/Slippin' & Slidin'	8/63
		(Side 1 reissued on *Surfin' In The Midwest, Vol 1*)	
Sara	101	I Don't Love Anymore/Just For You	3/64
		(Brad Meyers & the Citations)	

---

[1]Chubby Checker, 1961
[2]Ed Townsend, 1958
[3]Little Richard, 1956

A band formed in high school, the Citations garnered air play and a major label release on their first record. "We recorded in somebody's attic," explains David Gustin, "and put it on the radio because the drummer's sister worked for WOKY. They voted on it and I think we came in first."

At that point a manager stepped in, bought the tapes, put the record out on Sara and shopped for a deal that resulted in the Epic release. Things soured quickly, however, on a $2700 gig. "The band got $900, the manager got $900, and the silent partner got $900," claims Gustin, "but we weren't aware that there was a silent partner. So they think the manager took the other share."

Kasper and Gustin put together another lineup for a second record. Another version of the band existed for a while without Gustin and may have done some additional recording. Kasper eventually joined the Good Intentions. In the 90's, Gustin plays private parties and Sanderson has worked with an Elvis impersonator.

Unrelated Citations: Ballad, Canadian American, Don-El, Fraternity, Just, MGM, Mercury,
        Princess, Roulette, Swan, Vangee
Sources: David Gustin telephone interview, 9/26/93
        Osborne-Brown. Rockin' Records.

Coachmen

Ray Johnson - voc
Rick Preis - org   **Paul Strnad** - gtr
James Kaminski - gtr   **Jim Paolo** - bs
Jeff Greenthal - bs   **Byron Weiman** - 12 strg gtr
Leon Klekowski - dr (8/29/51; Milwaukee)

Target	1001	The News Is Out/Girl In The Window	3/69
	1009	Hey Bulldog/Just Knowing Her	/69

The Coachmen worked often in the Fox Valley where they hooked up with Appleton's Target label for their two releases. In the early 80's drummer Leon Klekowski worked with the One-Eyed Jacks, a band that backed Sly Stone on tour. In the 90's keyboardist Rick Preis works with a new version of the Wrest and Byron Weiman records in Germany.

Unrelated Coachmen: Bear, Capitol, Hi-Fi, Iona, MMC, Orbit, Pico, Roulette, SSS
        International, Trump, X
Also see: Wrest
Sources: Sue Klekowski telephone interview, 7/24/93
        Posniak, Alan. "Badger Beat." Milwaukee Journal, date unknown - courtesy Brian Lake
        Tourville. Wisconsin . . . Discography.

Osborne-Brown. <u>Rockin' Records.</u>

Tom Collins & the Mixers

Tom Collins - voc
Laurie Collins - pno
Pete Glystiein - gtr
Bob Merkt - gtr (8/28/44; Waukesha)
Ray - bs   Tony Kolp - sx
Gene Stoiber - dr (6/27/41; Milwaukee)

                    Mixers' Rock/Laurie Ann   /59

"I'd give $1000 right now for that record," says Bob Merkt, who no longer owns a copy. The session was done at Universal in Chicago. The Mixers played CYO and high school dances including one gig backing Bobby Rydell. "I'll never forget when we were playing at Pius High School and they turned the electricity off because they said our bass player was making 'Elvis Presley gyrations'," says Gene Stoiber. "We had more fun than any of them - and that's what it was all about."

Also see: Bonnevilles, Rock-A-Fellers, Mad Lads (Bob Merkt)
          Bonnevilles, Skunks (Tony Kolp)
Source: Bob Merkt telephone interview, 6/4/94
          Gene Stoiber telephone interview, 7/27/94

Comic Books/Ronnie Premier

Floyd Dorsey (2/1/40; Milwaukee)
Ronnie Premier (Barzyk) (8/11/38; Milwaukee) **James Pike**
Bill Dorsey (1942, Milwaukee)   **Greg Browder**
Lloyd Johnson   **"Bullet" Bob Barian** (10/13/42; Milwaukee)

New Phoenix	6199	Manuel/Black Magic And Witchcraft	/62
Citation	5001	Manuel/Black Magic And Witchcraft	3/62
Dynamic Sound			
	2005	Young Blood[1]/The First Time In My Life	/66

Related:

Sara	1020	Angel In My Eyes/So Loved Am I	12/60
Laurie	3091	Angel In My Eyes/So Loved Am I	3/61

                    (Above two as Ronnie Premier & the Royal Lancers)

---

[1]Coasters, 1957

Magic Touch 2004   The Bat-Mo/Way 'Cross The Sea   /66
                    (Bullet Bob Barian)
Ron-Ron   10595   You Don't Have To Be A Star[1]/My Merry Go Round[2]   /78
                    (Fun & Games)

Ronnie Premier seemed to have attained legendary status around Milwaukee by the mid-60's. A white r&b singer/songwriter with many of his tunes recorded by local groups, he has been cited as an influence by Paul Stefan and several others. From about 1955 to 1961 Premier sang with the Comic Books, a racially integrated vocal group."Excellent talent," says Cuca's Jim Kirchstein. "Ronnie grew up in a black district. Songwriter, performer, grew up with back kids, learned to sing like them - just a fantastic talent. I'm real sorry he didn't go further."

Royal Lancers guitarist Doug Tank recalls Premier's songwriting talents: "This guy could write songs as fast as you could read! I remember many times going over to his house and we'd sit down for four or five hours and we'd have 10 or 15 songs down. He was amazing."

Premier recalls the group taking part in the Continental Caravan, a show that was put together in various clubs. Other performers included Charlene Gibson (who eventually joined the Friends Of Distinction), Harvey Scales, the Esquires, and possibly Al Jarreau (though Jarreau doesn't recall being a part of this).

Brothers Floyd and Bill Dorsey were the constants throughout the history of the group, including a stint as the Belvedors, expanded to five pieces with the addition of Pike and Browder. (Browder also played trumpet and is one of the backing musicians on "Impossible" by Little Artie & the Pharaohs).

The name was changed back to the Comic Books when Bob Barian joined around 1966. The recordings for Dynamic Sound took place at that time. Barian eventually left to join a Las Vegas show group, the Swingin' Lads, in 1969-70. The release on Ron-Ron by Fun & Games was a duet that Barian recorded with his wife. He also worked with the Walking Sticks.

Floyd Dorsey recalls an ill-fated road trip hastening the end of the group. The car broke down, the guys were broke, and they never made the gig. It was time to get a real job.

Meanwhile, Premier had one of his compositions, "I'm No Romeo," placed on a Billy Stewart LP. When he began to experience some voice problems around 1966, he moved out of Milwaukee to Merton. Premier eventually resumed performing in 1977 in West Bend under the name Ron Bishop.

---

[1]Marilyn McCoo & Billy Davis, Jr., 1976
[2]Johnny Nash, 1973

In Nashville since 1984 and the owner of a successful commercial cabinet business, Premier says, "I haven't given it up. I still would love to put a gold one on the wall. I love the writing part of it. I've got a better voice now than I did then." With his cabinet company doing work for the likes of Barbara Mandrell and (publisher) Buddy Killen, Premier continues to submit songs. "That's how you do it," he says. "You can't really run through the front door here."

Also see: Royal Lancers (Premier)
          Walking Sticks (Barian)
          Cheaters (Greg Browder)
Sources: Bob Barian telephone letter and telephone interview, 9/93
          Ron Barzyk telephone interview, 10/93
          Floyd Dorsey telephone interview, 12/26/93
          Jim Kirchstein interview, 8/29/88
          Tourville. Wisconsin . . . Discography.
          Clee. American 45 R.P.M. Records.

Continentals

Rusty Harding - voc
Vince Megna - ld gtr (8/24/44; Milwaukee)
Roger Roessler - rh gtr
Ron Evans - bs
Dennis Madigan - vibes (7/9/41; Milwaukee)
Lee (LeRoy) Breest - dr

Cuca	1063	Tic Toc/Sue	12/61
Related:			
EMP	1001	Poinciana[1]/Red Vent (sic - should be "Red Vest")	/65
		(Herb Ellis & Vince Megna)	
Verdict	12455	Truth Is Irrelevant (In A Criminal Case)/I.R.S.B.S.	/81
		(Attorneys)	
	10404	I'm Gonna Sue You/Truth Is Irrelevant/The Pawnbroker	/90
		(Cassette produced by Daryl Stuermer)	
		(Vince & the Attorneys)	

The Continentals included both a former and a future Bonneville simultaneously. Vibist Dennis Madigan had left the Bonnevilles while guitarist Vince Megna would join a later version of the same group. Singer Rusty Harding later added guitar to his repertoire and worked with several other bands, including the Greenmen. He reportedly relocated to the East Coast to work with the Kalin Twins ("When," 1958). Drummer Lee Breest left to become a Royal Lancer.

---

[1]Bing Crosby, 1944; many others

After his Bonnevilles stint, Megna worked with Rick Allen's blues trio. Relocating to Los Angeles in 1964, he toiled with many name artists, from jazz greats Herb Ellis and Tommy Gumina to pop names Bobby Hart (Boyce & Hart), Teddy Randazzo, Ray Peterson, Larry Taylor (Canned Heat) and Moby Grape.

Back in Milwaukee, Megna, a practicing attorney since 1976, has recorded occasionally. His 1990 cassette release features the production and guitar work of Daryl Stuermer of Genesis/Phil Collins. Since 1982 Megna has been selling prints of his drawings of famous baseball players.

Also see: Bonnevilles (Dennis Madigan, Vince Megna)
      Royal Lancers (Lee Breest)
      Johnny Green & the Greenmen (Russ Harding)
      Bonnevilles
Unrelated Continentals: A-OK, Bolo, Candi, Cuca (1596), Davis, Epic, Era, Gaylo, Hunter, Key, Lifetime, Penguin, Port, Rama, Roulette, Union, Vandan, Virgo, Whirlin' Disc
Sources: Vince Megna letters, 5/17/93, 6/15/94
      Osborne-Brown. <u>Rockin' Records.</u>

Crystal Rain

Dynamic Sound	91101	You And Me/World On Fire	/67
Vangee	904100	Hey Ma Ma/Funeral At Dawn	

Source: Tourville. <u>Wisconsin . . . Discography</u>

Darnells/Denny & the Darnells

Denny King (Ottenbacher) - gtr (8/4/41; Milwaukee)
Tom Fabre - sx (11/15/40; Milwaukee)
Bruce Wells - kb   **Tom Hahn** - bs (5/17/39; Tipton, IN)
Gary Lane - voc (3/28/42; Sturgeon Bay)   **Mike Blattner** - dr
Norm Sherian (Basherian) - rh gtr   **Gary Myers** - dr (8/28/42; Milwaukee)
Jerry Sworske - dr (4/8/42; Milwaukee)

Sara	1055	Little Sheila[1]/Besame Mucho[2]	(/I)	11/61
	5016	Fate Of A Fool/Don't Talk Baby		/62
		(Denny King)		
Tide	1090	Spooner/Sleepy	(I/I)	9/63

---

[1]Gene Vincent LP
[2]Jimmy Dorsey, 1944; many others

Related:

Edit	2005	Poor Little Baby/If (You'd Only Be Mine) (Gary Myers)			11/63
Tide	2000	Surfin' Fat Man/Paula (Mojo Men)		(I/I)	2/64
Specialty	726	Bessie Mae/Go Down Moses (Denny King)			/72

LP:

Specialty	5003	Evil Wind Is Blowing (Denny King)	/72

Beginning about 1959, various musicians (including future Legend's drummer Jim Sessody) passed through the Darnells. Later the band also featured female vocalist Kim Marie. The line-up that included Gary Lane and Tom Fabre was the unit that went in to the Cuca studios to record the first single. Lane does the vocal on the A side with Fabre featured on the instrumental flip.

In September of 1962, down to just one night a week at the Spa (5th & Wisconsin), King accepted a full time gig with the Night Beats, the traveling band from Florida for which I played drums. Five months later King and I left the Night Beats, re-formed the Darnells with Tom Hahn on bass, and left for Southern California. Checking in at the Firehouse, a beer bar in Costa Mesa (where Hahn had worked the previous year with the Bonnevilles), we spent the summer of 1963 there and recorded for Tide/Edit in Los Angeles.

Not long after returning to Milwaukee that fall, Hahn and I left to join the Cashmeres, bringing an end to the Darnells. The Cashmeres metamorphosized into the Mojo Men. Hahn later left that group and did some work in Memphis with Ace Cannon ("Tuff," 1962) before leaving the music business.

After doing some club work with country singer Johnny Carver, Denny King returned to California in early 1964. There he teamed up with the Canadian Beadles and recorded one single as the Mojo Men. This has no connection with any other Mojo Men release. It seems that Tide Records, having had their only national chart appearance with a song called "Mojo Workout," tried to capitalize on the "Mojo" name in every possible way. This record came out at virtually the same time as the record by Tommy Hahn & the Mojo Men back in Milwaukee (see Mojo Men).

After one more trip to Milwaukee, King remained in California, eventually doing some session work for the Monkees and joining the Marketts for their final LP, "Batman Theme," which charted in 1966. King did much of the vocal work on the Marketts live gigs.

After his solo recording for Specialty in 1972, King moved to the Sacramento area and started a booking agency. Through a connection made while performing in Korea, he began importing medical supplies. That business has grown phenomenally and King is now the president of a multi-million dollar operation. His is a story that shows another side to the benefits music can bring.

"When I was young I was a hoodlum," King says. "I got in a lot of trouble and ended up in the Waukesha reform school. When I got out, my mom got me involved in doing an Elvis Presley mime thing on some local television station. So I did, and I happened to win the thing, so that's how I got into music. From there the music got more absorbing than the other. It certainly did turn my life around."

Also see: Bonnevilles (Tom Hahn)
     Mad Lads, Saints Five (Gary Lane, Norm Sherian)
     Mojo Men (Tom Hahn, Gary Myers)
     Junior & the Classics - On The Charts, Noblemen (Jerry Sworske)
Unrelated Darnells: Bana, Gordy, (Columbia, Vernon - Debbie & the Darnells)
Sources: Denny King telephone interviews, 1/93, 1/2/94
     Tom Fabre telephone interview, 1992
     Gary Lane telephone interview, 8/8/92
     Personal recollections
     Clee. American 45 R.P.M. Records.
     Osborne-Brown. Rockin' Records.

Danny Darren
(Dan Solberg)

Label	Number	Title	Date
Draeger	360	Road Side Rag/Tear Drop On A Rose	/66
	4561	Fool About You/Moon Over Naples	/66
Allan Dale	3063	Loneliness/Road Side Rag	/67
Silver Star	1039	Nothing To Write Home About/World Of Make Believe	/70
Coulee	141	Medals For Mother/Foggy Mountain Breakdown	/72
KL	KS10	Love Makes The World Go Round/Grand Old Opry Song	/72
Rainbow	201	Go Menasi/Beyond A Shadow Of A Doubt	/72
Pyramid	15	No Reason To Quit/Mansion On A Hill	/73
	18	Take These Chains/Hank And Lefty	/73

LP:

Label	Number	Title	
Maverick	1002	Country Time Music	
		(Various Artists)	

Primarily a country artist, Darren's earlier disks may be of interest to rockabilly collectors.

Sources: Tourville. Wisconsin . . . Discography

Darnells: Gary Myers, Denny King, Tom Hahn

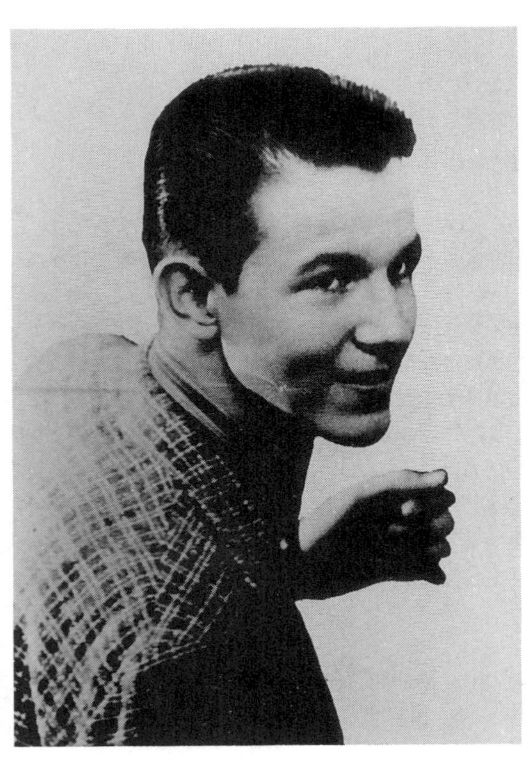

Bobby Dean

Destinations: Fred Hadler, Bruce Robertson, Rick Wolf, Sid Rice, Reed Kailing (courtesy Reed Kailing)

Bobby Dean
(Robert Bullock)

Chess	1673	Just Go Wild Over Rock & Roll/Dime Store Pony Tail		11/57
	1710	Go Mr. Dillon/I'm Ready		11/58
Profile	4006	It's A Fad, Ma/Just Between Teens		/59

Possibly related:
Scarlet Target 100 Amazon Dance/(Someone Special)
(Bobby Dean & the Amazons - flip by Nancy & the Amazons)

Bobby Dean, who recorded in Chicago, was reportedly from Brookfield. His releases would certainly place him among Milwaukee's early rock and rollers, however I was unable to find any musicians who remembered him. He apparently never worked enough around town to become known among the other musicians.

Sources: Mean Mountain Music, 1/29/94
     Tourville. Wisconsin . . . Discography.
     Bill Davis, 1/94

Destinations

Reed Kailing - ld gtr (7/23/47; Milwaukee)
Sid Rice - kb/gtr (3/15/49; Milwaukee)

Bruce Robertson - bs	**Bill Wilson** - bs
Fred Hadler - dr	**Rick "Boozer" Sorgel** - dr

Destination	638	Hello Girl/With You		9/67
Hardy Boys				
RCA	0228	Love And Let Love/Sink Or Swim	(#101)	9/69
LPs:				
RCA	4217	Here Come The Hardy Boys	(199)	10/69
	4315	Wheels		/70

Seeing the Destinations on the Destination label might give the impression that this was some producer's one-shot studio project, but there is much more to the story. First, the band and the label (a Chicago company) existed separately and met purely by coincidence. Secondly, guitarist Reed Kailing went on to an extensive and varied career.

There were several members that preceded the recorded line-up, including original lead singer Rick Wolf, who took the band's name out of the dictionary. WRIT DJ King Zbornik took the group to the record label. Zbornik produced the session after the Destinations won the *Milwaukee Sentinel Battle of the Bands* for Wisconsin and Michigan. The Robbs also helped on the record as both bands were handled by manager Con Merten.

To help promote the record, the Destinations drove to Chicago every week to do Art Roberts *Swinging Majority* show on WCIU-TV, Channel 26. Other guests included Traffic, the Grass Roots (who would figure prominently in Kailing's life a few years later), and a group of brothers from Indiana. "There was Michael Jackson when they were just coming out of Gary," recalls Kailing. "No dancing. He was about five years old and I remember old man Jackson used to cut a check for $50.00 to Art Roberts just to get them on."

Differences arose and the Destinations dwindled. Sid Rice did some work in the 70's with Stuffy Schmidt & the Frozen Parachute Band. He eventually went into the construction business near Lake Tahoe, Nevada. Rick Sorgel recorded with the Flying Machine about 1970. (Even though a British group by the same name was hitting with "Smile A Little Smile For Me"). Kailing left to work as *Reed In His Own Rite*. Then came a call from Jim Golden at Destination Records with a referral that led to the next step.

"They were doing a nationwide hunt for five kids that resembled what they wanted to form as the Hardy Boys, which was based on that old book series by S.W. Dixon," explains Kailing. "The Archies had such success with 'Sugar, Sugar' that they figured they'd do another one, but with a live group. It was a weird decision, but I decided I might learn something. I wasn't excited about being a cartoon character, but at least I'd get into another mode of the business. It was really a learning experience, really great. I saw a lot of places, we traveled first class." Oddly enough, another Milwaukee musician was also selected. Jeff Taylor of the Messengers was cast as the bass player, an instrument he had never played before. "Then reality set it," says Kailing. "We went into rehearsals and, oh, was that a nightmare!"

Kailing negotiated an early release from the two-year contract and moved to Los Angeles where he bought a house across the street from Warren Entner of the Grass Roots. One thing led to another and Kailing landed with the hit-making group in 1971. "I was lucky," he says. Though most of the group's biggest hits were behind them by that time, there was still a lot of life, a few more hits, and plenty of touring.

One trip brought them to a small airport in Louisiana at the same time as Jim Croce. With both acts headed in opposite directions and just one charter plane available, it came down to a flipping of a coin. "I just happened to have a quarter on me, I threw it to Richard, our road manager, and they flipped," says Kailing. We ended up with seven guys in a station wagon and I'm fiddling with the radio and all of a sudden I heard something about Jim Croce and found out the plane had just crashed."

That episode began to sour him on the touring and Kailing left the Grass Roots in 1975. (Another member, Dennis Provisor, moved to Stevens Point when he left the group in the early 80's. Provisor had no previous Wisconsin connection). The next opportunity was "a boyhood dream come true," as Kailing was one of the musicians on John Lennon's *Rock 'n' Roll* LP in 1975.

After taking a year off to build an airplane, Kailing became involved in another project that resulted in the hit group Player. Though he had exited by the time of the first album's release, he did co-write some of the songs. The LP charted at number 26 in early 1978.

Next came a stint with the Beatlemania Show in Boston, New York and Los Angeles; recording with Kiki Dee and writing with Don Johnson; then a return to Milwaukee in 1981. The 80's brought one last tour with a re-formed Badfinger shortly before keyboardist Tom Evans committed suicide, the second member of the group to do so.

Apart from occasional shows at *Summerfest* and a few others, Kailing has devoted his time to family and land development and treasuring his experience. "I've had a very interesting background," he reflects. "I had the advantage of being involved in a lot of different areas, meeting a totally incredible circle of different people. It's been great!"

Unrelated Destinations: AVI, Cameo, Fortune
Sources: Reed Kailing telephone interviews, 9/8/93, 9/19/93, 10/3/93
      Tourville. <u>Wisconsin . . . Discography.</u>
      Whitburn. <u>Record Research.</u>

Driftwoods

Pete Sorce - voc (6/22/44; Milwaukee)
Al Babicky - sx
Dick Aulbaencher - gtr   **Steve Olson** - dr
Mike Tezaloff - pno
Nick Fera - bs
Wayne Walters - dr

Leaf   8973   Have You Ever Had The Blues/For Your Precious Love[1]   /62

Also see: Pete Sorce
      Catalinas - Appleton/Fox Cities (Pete Sorce)
      Mad Lads (Al Babicky, Wayne Walters)
Unrelated Driftwoods: DBS
Sources: Pete Sorce telephone interview, 4/9/94
      Osborne-Brown. <u>Rockin' Records.</u>

Dynastys

George Shuput - gtr (2/3/47; Wausau)
Duane Schallitz - gtr (2/16/47; Milwaukee)   **Mark Ladish** - org

---

[1]Jerry Butler, 1958

Dave Maciolek - bs   **Jim Serrano** - ld gtr
Kenny Arnold - dr

Fan Jr.	9374	I'll Be Forever Loving You[1]/Mountain Of Love[2]		4/64
Coulee	108	Go Gorilla[3]/Birmingham	(/I)	9/64
Jerden	783	It's Been A Long, Long Time/Forever And A Day		/66

How did a teen age Milwaukee band land on Jerry Dennon's Seattle label? "We wanted to get out and play the West Coast," says guitarist George Shuput. Their manager Lindy Shannon arranged for a Portland agent to book them at the Longhorn there. "We were only 15, 16, 17, so we had to play and get to the back room. One day Jerry Dennon came in. We played him our records and some other tapes and he liked it. I think we were about the only group from the Midwest that he handled."

The band's previous two releases had come out of Madison and La Crosse. "'Mountain Of Love' really upset us because we sent that to bunch of record companies and, if you listen to it, it's exactly the same as the one Johnny Rivers came out with about four months later."

The Dynastys remake of "Go Gorilla" proved to be their most successful attempt. "In the Coulee region it was number one for six weeks in a row," claims Shuput. Covering a lot of ground for such a young group, the band got it to famed Buddy Holly producer Norman Petty in Clovis, New Mexico. Petty tried, unsuccessfully, to place it on a national label.

Almost immediately after returning from Oregon, Shuput accepted an offer from the Shades Of Blue in Chicago and participated in their national hit,"Oh How Happy" in the summer of 1966. Shuput left them to work with Conway Twitty, then back to Milwaukee for brief stints with the Affluents and the Gremlins before electing to leave the music business. He later formed a charter boat company. "There were so many bands and we had so many places to play," says Shuput. "It's not like that for kids today."

Drummer Ken Arnold helped form Short Stuff with Jim Liban. That group was active on record in the 70's and 80's. Duane Shallitz joined the Good Intentions in the 70's. The four original Dynastys reunited August 28, 1994 for a La Crosse show honoring Lindy Shannon.

Also see: Affluents
        Gremlins
        Thee Prophets - On The Charts (Dave Maciolek)
        La Crosse section (Lindy Shannon)
Unrelated Dynasty(s): Royal Court, Solar, Westchester

---

[1]Eldorados, 1956
[2]Harold Dorman, 1960; Johnny Rivers, 1964
[3]Ideals, 1963

Sources: George Shuput telephone interviews, 1/2/94, 2/13/94
       Tourville. Wisconsin . . . Discography.

Eastman Blues Band

Gerry Smith - ld gtr
John Kondos - rh gtr
James Hanns (Walner) - kb
Tom Jones - sx
Curt Vandenhuevel - sx
Nick Kondos - dr

Cuca   6766   I Found A New World/Before The Snow Falls   6/67

Also see: Corporation - On The Charts (Gerry Smith, John Kondos, Nick Kondos)
       James Hanns & the Soul Entertainers (Hanns, Tom Jones, Curt Vandenhuevel)
       John Kondos & the Galaxies
Sources: Gerry Scheulke telephone interview, 6/18/94
       Gene Recob telephone interview, 7/17/94
       Tourville. Wisconsin . . . Discography.

Ethics

Don Gruender - gtr
Mark Miller - bs   **Gene Peranich** - org (12/29/43; Milwaukee)
Mike Jablonski - dr

Dynamic Sound   2001   Confusion/Out Of My Mind   /67

"He was phenomenal," says Gene Peranich of guitarist Don Gruender. "He could play like Jimi Hendrix." The band impressed Dynamic Sound owner Lenny LaCour with their energy. After one record they became the Invasion.

Also see: Invasion
Unrelated Ethics: Golden Fleece, Phalanx, Vent
Sources: Gene Peranich telephone interview, 6/8/94
       Tourville. Wisconsin . . . Discography.
       Osborne-Brown. Rockin' Records.

Freddie & the Freeloaders

Fred Bliffert - voc
Tom McCutcheon - gtr
Jimmy Gaskill - bs
Peter Leshin - dr

Sam Friedman - gtr
Stan Kellicut - gtr
Barry Biehoff - bs
Jeff Irwin - org
Jack Felstein - sx/hca (4/22/44; Milwaukee)
Craig Colberg - sx
Warren Wiegratz - sx (5/5/48; Milwaukee)
Phil Stokes - bari sx
Charlie Betts - tp
Mike Betts - tp
Randy Byrd - tp
John Burgess - tp/fr horn
Pat Tilka - tb

A&M	1148	I Who Have Nothing[1]/Can't Forget About You	12/69
Related:			
Asylum	45388	Broken Man/No One Like My Baby	4/77
	45449	Elijah/I Want You To Dance	12/77
		(above two by Jelly)	
TK	1045	Tell Her/Trying To Live My Life Without You[2]	4/81
		(Freddy Henry & Betty Wright)	
LP's:			
Zero	1	You'll Like Bliffert	/72
		(Freddy Bliffert)	
Asylum	1096	A True Story	/77
		(Jelly)	
Clouds	8809	Get It Out In The Open	/79
		(Freddy Henry)	

The Bliffert Lumber Company was established in Milwaukee in the early 40's, but it was timbre rather than timber that attracted grandson Fred. He traces it back to the first time he heard "All Shook Up" on the radio.

Beginning as a quartet playing teen dances in 1963, the band grew to a large r&b horn group by the time the recording opportunity came six years later. "I Who Have Nothing" was an overly dramatic arrangement of the previously done song and the label showed the band name only as the Freeloaders. How did an unknown Milwaukee band get on Herb Alpert's A&M

---

[1]Ben E. King, 1963; Terry Knight, 1967; Tom Jones, 1970
[2]Otis Clay, 1972; Bob Seger, 1981

label? "It was all political," says Bliffert. "It was a series of favors owed. It had nothing to do with me being worthy of putting out a record." The record sank quickly, though Tom Jones would hit number 14 with the same song less than a year later.

After the break-up of the Freeloaders, Bliffert did a solo album (produced by Greg Jeresek of the Messengers), acted with a theater company, and co-hosted *Sunday Night Special* on Channel 6. A few years later he relocated to Los Angeles with an acoustic trio called Jelly. This group included Jesse Roe of the Messengers and future actress Amy Madigan. They recorded two LP's for Asylum while appearing frequently at the Bla Bla Cafe.

Bassist Barry Biehoff recorded for Hi in 1975 as a member of Hindsight. Saxophonist Warren Wiegratz (previously of the Mustard Men) went on to do several jazz/fusion albums with Sweet Bottom, Ocean and his own band, Street Life.

In 1979 Bliffert did an album produced by Al Kooper utilizing Al Green's back-up singers. Released as by Freddy Henry on a Miami label, it featured a duet with soul star Betty Wright which was later issued on a 45 (Bliffert himself was not aware of this single until our 1993 conversation). The flip side, "Trying To Live My Life Without You," was an Otis Clay song that Bob Seger took to the top five just a few months later.

"Even though none of my albums did very well, they were all just such a great experience to record," says Bliffert, who was finally ready for the family business in 1980. While working for the lumber company he still does occasional gigs, but for a different type of audience. "I sing for old ladies and retarded adults," he explains. "Once in a while I'll do a gig for normal people but it's just not as rewarding."

Also see: Mustard Men (Warren Wiegratz, Stan Kellicut)
        Messengers (Greg Jeresek, Jesse Roe)
Unrelated Freddie & the Freeloaders: Laurie, 1 And 1, Redd Hedd, 309
Sources: Fred Bliffert telephone interviews and letters, 4/93, 7/93
        Barry Biehoff telephone interview, 1/93
        Tourville. Wisconsin . . . Discography.
        Osborne-Brown. Rockin' Records.
        Clee. American 45 R.P.M. Records.

Freefall Three

Doug Tank - gtr
Roy Malvitz - bs
Lee (Leroy) Breest - dr

Cuca   1174   616/Walk On The Wild Side[1]   9/64

This is three former members of the Royal Lancers after the break-up of that band. 616 refers to a club in Green Bay owned by Roy Malvitz' uncle. The session was backed financially by Milwaukee DJ Bill McCullough.

Also see: Royal Lancers
Source: Doug Tank telephone interview, 6/19/94

Futuras

Jerry Mallon - gtr
Gary Josing - org
Jack Edwards (Strucel) - gtr
Gary Dee (Bareman) - bs
Al James - dr

Rampro   119   Signed, Sealed and Delivered[2]/Portrait Of A Fool[3]   /66

This band changed their name to *The Wind* in 1967. Organist Gary Josing later moved to Southern California and now teaches music in Chatsworth. Jack Strucel shifted to B3 organ and joined the Good Intentions in the 70's.

Also see: Mad Lads (Jerry Mallon)
          Walking Sticks (Gary Josing)
Unrelated Futuras: Arjay, Warwick
Sources: Gary Josing telephone interview, 1/93
          Tourville. Wisconsin . . . Discography.

Terry Gale
(Terry Galecki - 7/25/42; Milwaukee)

Las Vegas Strip	1001	Betty Jean/Think It Over[4]	/63
Larry Bee	1107	The Voodoo/Just 15	/65
Pro-Gress	3524	Midnight Woman/Child	/74
Water Street	504	Grin And Bear It/New Orleans On The River	/75

Terry Gale may have been Milwaukee's first rock 'n' roller to land a Las Vegas gig. "I had a

---

[1]Jimmy Smith, 1962, from film of same title
[2]James Brown, 1963
[3]Conway Twitty, 1962
[4]Buddy Holly & the Crickets, 1958

(courtesy Terry Gale)

go-go review in the early 60's at the Nevada Club on Fremont Street," he recalls. "Wayne Newton was working at the Fremont Hotel and Patsy Cline was working at the Mint." Actually more than a rock 'n' roller, Gale is an excellent guitarist with a strong jazz influence, and a dynamic performer who sings in a variety of styles, though he often gravitates to a Bill Medley sound-alike or a Wilson Pickett/Otis Redding scream.

Gale had initially worked around Milwaukee with the Zodiacs, then Terry Gale & the Storms. He traveled with *National Auto Shows*, and finally hooked up with the Gail McConkey Agency in Los Angeles before the Vegas opportunity. Back in Milwaukee he did a very brief stint as Sam McCue's replacement with the Legends. John Rondell, the next replacement in line, recalled Gale's vibrant stage presence: "All of a sudden this guitar player jumped up in the air and jumped to the front of the stage and I just sat there with my mouth open. I think if that guy had had his head on even half way straight, he could have definitely been somebody."

Gale returned to Los Angeles in the mid 60's. There he connected with producer H.B. Barnum and played on sessions for Lou Rawls, O.C. Smith, Don Ho and others. In the early 70's he did some club gigs with his younger brother Danny on bass and yours truly on drums. Unfortunately, he built his own road block by developing a penchant for arriving late every night.

Returning to Milwaukee, Gale did several radio commercials in the 70's and 80's. He also recorded 24 Buddy Holly tunes for a company that was releasing product under the titles *Old and Heavy Gold* and *Journey Into Yesterday*. It turned out that proper royalties were not being paid and the project disappeared. Gale continues to gig around town in the 90's.

Also see: Legends
        Pharaohs (Danny Gale)
Sources: Terry Gale telephone interview, 11/3/93
        Personal recollections

Girls Take Over

Pentagon   001   Hi Heel Sneekers[1] (sic)/Stardust Come Back   /69

Female quartet included three sisters.

Source: Prellberg, Mark. "Diggin' the Grooves." Lost and Found #2, 1993: 121

Grand Prix's
(Greendale)

Rick Berkanovic - ld gtr (7/8/46; Milwaukee)
Kenny Knoll - rh gtr   **Bruce Cole** - dr (5/11/47; Milwaukee)
Don Longhurst - bs
Jeff Hammer - dr
Sara   6354   Linda/San Jose[2]   5/63

Though he joined the Grand Prix's after their recording, this was the first group for Bruce Cole who went on to play for several other Milwaukee bands. The Legends' Jim Sessody helped him get the gig. "When I went and saw the Legends as a kid and I looked at the stage and then the crowd - bingo, that was it. I went out and bought a set of drums," says Cole. Rick Berkanovic has continued to perform and submit demos.

Also see: Invasion, Ricochettes, Savoys, Van-Tels, Triumphs (Bruce Cole)
Sources: Bruce Cole telephone interview, 7/27/94
        Rick Berkanovic telephone interview, 8/17/94
        Tourville. Wisconsin . . . Discography.

Tony Grecco
(Charles Anthony Olla - 10/22/40; Homestead, PA)

Fenway   The Day We Met/She's All Mine   /60
                        (Chuck Tyler & the Royal Lancers)

---

[1]Tommy Tucker, 1964; Jose Feliciano, 1968; many others
[2]Freddy King, 1961

Big Beat	1053	Say Mama/Some Tears Must Fall	/61
	100	Rockin' Pneumonia[1]/Something Else	/62
Buzz	101	Dreamin'[2]/Lonely Weekend[3]	/62

Though born in Pennsylvania, Tony Olla grew up in the same Milwaukee neighborhood with guitarist Doug Tank. Both musicians were in the first Royal Lancers group and Olla recalls a contest leading to their first release on Fenway. "We won the talent contest along with the Bonnevilles and we both were on that label," he says.

After leaving the Lancers and changing his stage name from Chuck Tyler to Tony Grecco, his next record was one of the earlier versions of "Say Mama." "Sam McCue (of the Legends) played on that," claims Olla, "and Ronnie Premier sang background." Having begun as strictly a vocalist, Olla was also playing bass by that time. He later went on the road with the Danny Monday Review. Monday was Danny Peil (later with the Apollos/Tigers) and the tour included Las Vegas and Hollywood.

Olla spelled his stage name with two c's, though the record labels may not have always conformed to that preference. With a decision to get off the road around 1969, he settled in Pittsburgh and works in the lumber business.

Also see: Royal Lancers
    "Say Mama"
Sources: Doug Tank telephone interview, 9/6/93
    Tony Olla telephone interview, 3/15/94
    Whitburn. <u>Record Research.</u>

Johnny Green & the Greenmen

Johnny Green (Pavlik) - bs (4/5/42; Sturgeon Bay)

Misty Masters (Joyce Bowers) - voc	**Mickey Moose (Dorin Miller)** - sx
Howard Wales - org	**Denny Lee (Sesso)** - gtr
Tommy Lee (Ziviloski) - gtr	**Eric Monn (Russ Harding)** - gtr
Bobby "Rabbi" Van (Van Holten) - dr	**John Frost (Trombatore)** - gtr
	Marilyn Winters - voc
	Dick Person - org, tp
	John Stratford, Jr. - dr
	George Eberdt - dr

---

[1]Huey Smith & the Clowns, 1957
[2]Johnny Burnette, 1960
[3]Charlie Rich, 1960

Kapp	619	I've Had It[1]/So Fine[2]	10/64
		(Greenmen)	
Emerald	2001	Something You Got/Green Thumb	/65
Ranwood	838	Poor Little Fat Girl/Stained Glass Lady	5/69
LP's:			
AVI		Seven Over From Mars	/67
Edmar	1140	When You're Green You're Clean	/74

This group originated in Minneapolis as Roscoe & His Little Green Men and, from 1959-1963, recorded for Pontiac, RGM, Four Winds, RSVP, and Golden Wing. The Wisconsin connection came through John Pavlik, aka Johnny Green, previously of the Royal Lancers. "The Green Men had been working and they broke up," explains Green. "The original drummer, Bobby Van Holten, had known of me because of the Royal Lancers and he called and asked if I could find him a keyboard player. They were looking to put the group together." Green picked up organist Howard Wales and they joined the band. There was a brief attempt to retain the "Roscoe" identity but Wales didn't care for the name. (Pavlik, who took over the group and changed his name to Johnny Green, is no connection with the John Pavlik who recorded as Johnny Powers.)

The Greenmen - with their green hair and a show that includes Green's fire eating act - went on to make appearances in 102 countries, the 1964 New York World's Fair, *Life* and *Esquire* magazines, and several episodes of the *Batman* TV show. In the 90's the band continues its road trek 49 weeks a year.

The musicians listed above include only those from the first few years under Green's leadership. Tommy Lee had previously recorded with the Orbits of St. Cloud, MN, on Space and Gaity. John Trombatore had been a later member of the Champs ("Tequila," 1958). Guitarist Denny Lee went on to work with many name artists and appeared on the 1970 chart LP *Lord Sutch & Heavy Friends* which included Jimmy Page, Jeff Beck and John Bonham. George Eberdt is rumored to have done some work with Janis Joplin. Howard Wales has worked and recorded with many name artists including the Grateful Dead. He is co-featured with Jerry Garcia on the LP *Hooteroll* which has been reissued on CD.

Also see: Royal Lancers (John Pavlik)
      Bonnevilles (Howard Wales)
      Ramrods - Around The State (Denny Lee)
      Continentals (Russ Harding)
      Dave Kennedy & the Ambassadors - Cuca (George Eberdt)
Sources: Johnny Green telephone interview, 6/25/94
      Denny Lee Edwards, 1993
      Clee. <u>American 45 R.P.M. Records.</u>

---

[1]Bell Notes, 1959
[2]Fiestas, 1959

Gremlins

Fred Regenfuss - ld gtr (5/16/49; Milwaukee)
Jim Eide - rh gtr/perc
Dale Pax - org   George Shuput - gtr
Tom Marach - bs
Robin Hauber - dr

| Teen Town | 101 | Have You Seen My Little Girl/Sometimes I Feel | /67 |

The Gremlins began in 1964 and disbanded in early 1969. Their single was the first release for Jon Hall's Teen Town label.

Also see: Dynastys (George Shuput)
Sources: Fred Regenfuss letter, 4/10/94
        Tourville. Wisconsin . . . Discography.

Tommy Gumina
(Thomas Joseph Gumina - 5/20/31; Milwaukee)

Continental	5615	Charmaine[1]/Without You[2]	/56
		All The Things You Are[3]/	/56
Decca	30265	Theme From Pagliacca/Cumana	6/57

Jazz accordionist Tommy Gumina is probably best known for the recordings he did with clarinetist Buddy DeFranco in the early 60's. The road leading to Gumina's greater recognition began with an appearance on the Arthur Godfrey Show at age 18. An important step came when band leader Harry James saw him playing at the Tic Toc in Milwaukee. The accordionist spent three years with James, then returned to Milwaukee and did his first solo recording.

The first two singles were on Gumina's own label. "That's what got me the Decca contract," he says, "'cause they made some noise." He worked extensively in Las Vegas with his own group through the rest of the 50's. After forming the quartet with Buddy DeFranco there was another LP for Decca, followed by several with Mercury. Gumina went on to record with artists such as Nelson Riddle and many others.

In 1968 he started the Polytone Company to manufacture his own design of amplifiers. The

---

[1]Guy Lombardo, 1927; Paul Weston, 1952; many others
[2]Frankie Carle, 1946
[3]Tommy Dorsey, Artie Shaw, 1940; many others

company has been very successful and spawned another record label for an LP with guitarist Joe Pass. Gumina still plays occasionally in the 90's.

Sources: Tommy Gumina telephone interviews, 11/20/93, 7/16/94
        Vince Megna, 1993
        Clee. American 45 R.P.M. Records.

Royce Hall & the Lucky Four

Royce Hall - rh gtr (4/1/39; Foulton, MS)
Billy Woods - ld gtr
Mark Sands - bs
Richard Kermesey - dr

Raynard	1068	That's My Life/One More Glass Of Wine	/67
Nu-Trayl	933	No Love Have I/Why Can't You	/77
		We Give Each Other Love/Anything That Suits You Baby	/78
		(w/Gloria Taylor)	

Larry Lynne (Bonnevilles, Skunks) credits Royce Hall as his first guitar teacher. Hall and his band played mostly country material and, though he now plays only occasionally, Hall still hopes to place some of his original songs.

Sources: Royce Hall telephone interview, 1/19/94
        Larry Ostricki telephone interview, 1/30/93
        Tourville. Wisconsin . . . Discography.

James Hanns & the Soul Entertainers

James Hanns (Walner) - voc/kb
Marty   - gtr
Patrick McCarthy - org (11/11/47; Milwaukee)
Tom Jones - sx
Gene "Yogi" Recob - sx (9/20/45; Milwaukee)
Curt Vandenhuevel - sx
Doc Mathias - tp
Tom Cody - bs
Dennis Reeves (Regowsky) - dr

Raynard	1004	It's A Fine Thing/I Found You	/66

Keyboard player Pat McCarthy (later of the Corporation) is the brother of Denny McCarthy of the Apollos. Gene Recob recorded as a session musician with several other bands.

Also see: Eastman Blues Band (James Hanns, Tom Jones, Curt Vandenhuevel, Pat McCarthy)
    Corporation - Wisconsin On The Charts, John Kondos & Galaxies (Pat McCarthy)
    Van-Tels (Gene Recob)
Sources: Gerry Sheulke telephone interview, 6/18/94
    Gene Recob telephone interview, 7/17/94
    Barry Biehoff telephone interview, 1/93
    Tourville. Wisconsin . . . Discography.

Impalas

Jeff Moretti - voc (3/3/47; Milwaukee)   **Chuck Loth** - rh gtr
Jerry Norcia - ld gtr   **Jerry Kueper** - voc
Ron Moen - rh gtr   **Jack Gebhardt** - bs
Gene Schiller - bs   **Steve Keppen** - dr
Mike Price - dr (4/21/46; Waukesha)   **Phil Shields** - kb (10/11/47; New Berlin)
                                               Donnie Roberts - dr (3/24/51; Watertown)
                                               Emmit Smith - bs

Feature	107	Spoonful[1]/Talkin' About You[2]	/66
		(Side 1 reissued on Pebbles *Highs In The Mid 60's, Vol. 15*)	
Elaart	3001	Great Pretender[3]/Mary Lou[4]	/75
Page	8083-26	Teenager In Love[5]/I'm Gonna Love You Too[6]	/77

The Impalas chose their name around 1962 despite the top hit record ("Sorry [I Ran All The Way Home]") by a group of the same just three years earlier. "The way we got the Impalas was Gene Schiller drove a '58 Impala," says Jeff Moretti, "never dawning that there was already an Impalas." Moretti had left by the time of the band's first record (produced by Sam McCue), but he came back and took over the name for two more releases in the 70's. Moretti moved to Florida in 1981 but has occasionally returned to Milwaukee for reunions of the Impalas.

Also see: Picture (Phil Shields)
Unrelated Impalas: Bunky, Bunny, Checker, Collectables, Cub, Hamilton, MGM, Red Boy,
    Rite-On, Steady, Sundown, 20th Fox
Sources: Jeff Moretti telephone interview, 4/9/94
    Mike Price telephone interview, 1993

---

[1]w: Willie Dixon
[2]Chuck Berry, 1962
[3]Platters, 1956
[4]Ronnie Hawkins, 1959
[5]Dion & the Belmonts, 1959
[6]Buddy Holly, 1958

Phil Shields telephone interview, 3/20/94
Donnie Roberts telephone interview, 3/20/94
Tourville. <u>Wisconsin . . . Discography.</u>
Osborne-Brown. <u>Rockin' Records.</u>

Inspirations

Clarence Campbell
William Miller
Willie Patterson

Midas   9003   I'll Take A Chance On You/Your Wish Is My Command   /67

A Soft-soul vocal group, these Inspirations were backed instrumentally by John Kondos' Galaxies on this record. The label is a subsidiary of One-derful Records in Chicago.

Also see: John Kondos & the Galaxies
Unrelated Inspirations: Al-Brite, Apollo, Beltone, Bim Bam Boom, Black Pearl, Breakthrough,
        Feature, Genie, Gone, Jamie, Lamp, PKC, Rondack, Sparkle, Sultan
Sources: Pruter, Robert. <u>Chicago Soul.</u> Chicago: University of Illinois Press, 1992
        Osborne-Brown. <u>Rockin' Records.</u>

Inspirations

John Draws - voc
Tom Bloom - gt
Ron Skaluta - kb
Dean Hottinger - sx (1/17/49; Milwaukee)
Steve Fuchs - sx
Dave Zylka - tp
Bill Tate (Tazinsky) - bs (1/21/49, Milwaukee)
Dale Streeter - dr

PKC   1012   Watermelon Man[1]/Tell Daddy[2]   /68
Related:
Sage   101   I Do[3]/Things I Could Be   (Monopoly)   /72

These Inspirations played mostly CYO dances and college functions before breaking up about 1969. Dean Hottinger and Bill Tate went on to record with Monopoly. Tate is now co-owner

---

[1]Mongo Santamaria Band, 1963; w: Herbie Hancock
[2]Ben E. King, 1963; Clarence Carter, 1967
[3]Marvelows, 1965

of clubs in Milwaukee and Scottsdale, Arizona.

Also see: Van-Tels (Dave Zylka)
Unrelated Inspirations: see other Inspirations above
Sources: Gene Recob telephone interview, 7/17/94
Dean Hottinger telephone interview, 7/17/94

Invasion

Gene Peranich - kb (12/29/43; Milwaukee)
Don Gruender - gtr
Mark Miller - bs
Mike Jablonski - dr

Tony Menotti - gtr
Bob McKenna - rh gtr (8/17/48; Milwaukee)
Rick Cier - org
P.T. Pedersen - bs (8/2/47; Milwaukee)
Gary Frey - bs
Bruce Cole - dr (5/11/47; Milwaukee)

| Dynamic Sound | 2004 | The Invasion Is Coming/I Want To Thank You | /67 |
| | 2009 | Do You Like What You See/same | /68 |

The Invasion had previously been known as the Ethics. The original line-up lasted about a year, followed by many personnel changes. After disbanding, Gene Peranich, Don Gruender and Mike Jablonski reunited to form Raw Meat and recorded for Blue Hour in the 70's. Both Invasion and Raw Meat opened shows for major groups including Cream, Mothers Of Invention, Spirit and others.

P.T. Pedersen has worked and recorded with noted bluesman Charlie Musselwhite and has gigged with many other name musicians from the 60's to the 90's. Peranich continues to play in a duo in the Fayetteville, Arkansas, area.

Also see: Ethics
Picture (Bob McKenna)
Grand Prix's, Ricochettes, Savoys, Van-Tels, Triumphs (Bruce Cole)
Sources: P.T. Pedersen telephone interview, 1/94
Bob McKenna telephone interview, 3/28/94
Gene Peranich telephone interview, 6/8/94
Tourville. Wisconsin . . . Discography.

Jack & the Beanstalks

Jack Tate (Tadych) - rh gtr (12/30/37; Milwaukee)
John Conrath - ld gtr (8/25/44; Milwaukee)
Robert Kennedy - bs
John Lyons - dr

Pat Glass - pno
Doug Werginz - dr
Jim Dietrich - dr

Le Ron	3601	Don't Bug Me/So Many Times	/66
		(both sides reissued on Pebbles *Highs In The Mid 60's, Vol. 10*)	
Revolution	2914	A Long Time Coming, A Long Time Gone/Mood For Hurt	/68

Jack Tadych started in country music and drummer Doug Werginz had sung in a review type show featuring the Bonnevilles circa 1960. Jack & the Beanstalks' Le Ron sides were recorded in Chicago. The Revolution label was owned by Tadych. The band also worked as the Thunderbirds at Gallagher's but never recorded under that name.

Tadych now presides over American Building Restoration of Oak Creek and plays occasionally for weddings. Jim Dietrich, who used to work with Tadych's business, now has a competing company. John Conrath continues to play occasional gigs. Doug Werginz was also with a band called the Noblemen, though it had no connection with the other Noblemen covered in this section. Werginz now has his own manufacturing business.

Also see: Revolution Records - Wisconsin Labels
       Legends (Pat Glass)
Sources: Rick Schurk telephone interviews, 2/4/93, 1/29/94
       John Conrath telephone interview, 1/29/94
       <u>Tourville. Wisconsin . . . Discography.</u>

Norb Kamin (courtesy Norbert Kaminski)

Norb Kamin
(Norbert J. Kaminski - 2/27/30; Kenosha)

Erro   203   Nite Rider/Pick 'n' Shuffle   (I/I)   /59
Mean Mountain 1421 Nite Rider/Pick 'n' Shuffle   (reissue)   /81

Though Norb Kaminsky's sole recording didn't make a great impact, his influence has come through hundreds of guitar players since then. "I've been teaching since 1959 and I'm still teaching," he says. "I think I had a guitar player in every other rock group in town.

Regarding his record, billed as an answer to "Rumble" (Link Wray, 1958), Kaminsky says, "I didn't do any promotion 'cause I was too busy teaching and the label was just too small. I got my own airplay on WRIT but WOKY wouldn't play it." Kaminsky worked with Tommy Sheridan's jazz group for five years.

Sources: Norb Kaminsky telephone interview, 7/16/94
        Tourville. Wisconsin . . . Discography.

John Kondos & the Galaxies

John Kondos - gtr
Mike Miller - sx   **Patrick McCarthy** - kb (11/11/47; Milwaukee)
Nick Kondos - dr

Galaxie   5009   Hip Snap/I Made A Change   /66

This record reportedly includes backing vocals by the Inspirations.

Also see: Corporation - On The Charts, Eastman Blues Band (John & Nick Kondos,
        Pat McCarthy)
    Inspirations, (on Midas), James Hanns & Soul Entertainers
Sources: Patrick McCarthy telephone interview, 8/8/94
        Clee. American 45 R.P.M. Records.

Kenny Kotwitz
(4/27/41; Milwaukee)

Cuca   1052   Wooden Heart[1]/Adelita   10/61
                3001   Skyliner[2]/C'est Magnifique[3]   11/61

---

[1]Joe Dowell, 1961; Elvis Presley - *G.I. Blues* LP, 1960
[2]Charlie Barnet, 1945

LP:
Kimberly Kreek 7039 Front Street   /92

In the 30 years between releases under his own name, Kenny Kotwitz has conducted for the Mills Brothers, toured France and Switzerland, and been a successful studio musician in Los Angeles. His accordion and keyboard work has been heard on motion picture soundtracks such as *The Natural* and *Who Framed Roger Rabbit?,* as well as television productions including *Moonlighting* and *A Woman Called Golda.*

Presented with an accordion at age five, Kotwitz was playing weddings and parties in his early teens. Before his high school graduation, he had made a guest appearance on the Lawrence Welk Show. One day at a music lesson, he was astounded by a record featuring the jazz accordion of Art Van Damme. The young student followed that course and eventually studied and recorded with Van Damme on the Pausa label.

Following his Army discharge, Kotwitz moved to Southern California to embark on his studio career. His 1992 CD, "Front Street," pays tribute to the so-named alley along the river in downtown Milwaukee where he absorbed the sounds of top jazz artists who appeared at the clubs there. The CD is dedicated to the memory of jazz trumpet player Dick Ruedebush, a long time attraction at Front Street's Tunnel Inn.

Also see: Dick Ruedebush
Sources: Kenny Kotwitz telephone interview and letter, 1/93, 2/93

Tommy Lane
(Thomas Wernsberger)

Erro   201   Teenager's Lament/My Baby Likes To Rock And Roll
                300   My Bobby Sox Queen/You're So Easy On The Eyes

The release on Erro 300 features backing by El Rey & the Night Beats. Guitarist Norb Kaminsky recalls the previous record using the Tommy Sheridan band for backing. "When Tommy's solo came for 24 bars of the rock 'n' roll solo it sounded like George Shearing was playing a jazz chorus," he laughs. "It stuck out like a sore thumb."

Also see: Night Beats
         Norb Kamin
Sources: Raymond Ojeda telephone interview, 2/93
         Norbert Kaminski telephone interview, 7/16/94
         Tourville. <u>Wisconsin . . . Discography.</u>

---

[3]From *Can Can* - Cole Porter

La-Sabers

Bill Meusy - ld gtr (9/18/45; Milwaukee)
Terry Lee Oman - rh gtr (dec)
Ken Erdeman - bs   **David Wenca** - org
Dennis Rinzel - dr (3/18/46; Pt. Washington)   **Richard Bucholz** - bs

Co-op   EP 1001   Goodbye Johnny[1]/ (others by the Echoes, Stoney Kilroy)   /64

This record is a real oddity. The La-Sabers recorded four re-makes and one original at Dave Kennedy Studios on April 16, 1964. Only the Chuck Berry tune was selected for release and the EP, which included two other artists, came out on a label out of Wolfe City, Texas.

Not long after that, an unrelated record by a different La Sabers came out of the Kennedy Studios (Raynard (10011). Dennis Rinzel of the former group recalls an incident involving the two bands. The *Sumthin' Else* TV show ran a promotion asking for fans to send in cards for their favorite bands. Those receiving the greatest response would be invited on the show. Rinzel's group had their friends bombard the station with cards but the producers called in the wrong La Sabers. Rinzel also believes the other band spelled it Le Sabers, however the Raynard release does not show it that way.

The La Sabers lasted from 1962-66. Rinzel went on to work with several unrecorded groups, including the Blu Mob and the LYFT. The latter band included former members of the Ricochettes and the Renegades.

Also see: Raynard discography - Wisconsin Labels (other La Sabers)
Sources: Bill Meusy telephone interview, 12/93
        Dennis Rinzel letters, 3/7/94, 6/15/94
        Deniel Edwards Scrapbook

Legends

Sam McCue - ld gtr (4/20/41; Milwaukee)
Larry Foster - rh gtr   **Denny Sachse** (sock'-see) - dr (dec)
Rich Radaj (rad'-eye) - rh gtr   **Jerry Schils** - bs (2/5/42; Sheboygan)
Dennis Bertrand - dr   **Jim Sessody** - dr
                                              Terry Gale (Galecki) (7/25/42) -gtr
                                              Billy Joe Burnette - voc
                                              John Rondell (Beilfuss) - gtr (3/9/45; Milwaukee)

---

[1]Chuck Berry, 1960

Key	1002	Lariat/Gail	(I/I)	/61
Ermine	39	Say Mama[1]/My Love For You		7/62
	41	Lariat/Late Train	(I/I)	9/62
	43	Bop-A-Lena[2]/I Wish I Knew[3]		10/62
	45	Marionette/Temptation[4]		1/63
Capitol	5014	Run To The Movies/Summertime Blues[5]		7/63
Flight	616	What To Do/Valley Of Tears[6]	(Sam McCue)	4/64
Warner Bro.	5457	Here Comes The Pain/Don't Be Ashamed		7/64
Parrot	45010	Just In Case[7]/If I Only Had Her Back		3/65
	45011	Alright[8]/How Can I Find Her		6/65
Thames	104	Raining In My Heart[9]/How Can I Find Her		5/66
Date	1521	Raining In My Heart/How Can I Find Her		6/66

LP's:

Ermine	101	The Legends Let Loose	3/63
Capitol	1925	The Legends Let Loose	5/63
Capitol Custom	--	Run To The Movies	7/63

Related:

Ermine	40	While You're Young/Diggety Doggety	8/62
		(Johnny Cooper - backing by the Legends)	

Crowfoot

Paramount	0029	California Rock And Roll/Maybe I Can Learn To Live	/70
	0074	Love Is Everywhere/Groove Along	/71
ABC	11315	Travel In Time/We're Doin' It Wrong	12/71

LP:

ABC	745	Find The Sun	/71

Our band arrived in Milwaukee on September 2, 1962 and checked into the Wisconsin Hotel. I unpacked my radio, clicked on WOKY, and out jumped the Legends' "Say Mama." I had not heard of the group or the song, but the excitement of the record engraved the moment into my mind. It had spirit, energy, strong vocals, and a stand-out guitar solo. Sam McCue's 12 bar excursion probably became as imitated around Milwaukee as Danny Cedrone's classic "Rock Around The Clock" ride with Bill Haley. And, as if to prove it was no fluke, McCue did it twice!

---

[1]Gene Vincent, 1959
[2]Ronnie Self, 1958
[3]w: Roland Stone (Oeller)
[4]Bing Crosby, 1934; Everly Brothers, 1961; many others
[5]Eddie Cochran, 1958
[6]Fats Domino, 1957
[7]Everly Bros. - *It's Everly Time!* LP, 1960
[8]Searchers - *Meet The Searchers* LP, 1964
[9]Buddy Holly; 1959

Over the years the Legends have pretty well lived up to their name, though it wasn't their original moniker. Starting as the Nomads circa 1959, they changed when they learned of another Nomads group in the area. It was the first Legends line-up, with no bass, that recorded their initial instrumental sides for the Key label. Though Sam McCue feels that Dennis Bertrand was the best drummer they had, a disagreement between Bertrand and Larry Foster resulted in the drummer's firing. "I never forgave him for it," laughs McCue. His replacement was Denny Sachse, who came from Sheboygan's Crown Jewels along with Jerry Schils. Sachse soon gave way to Jim Sessody and the classic Legends line-up was established.

When they learned "Say Mama," an obscure Gene Vincent tune, it became a heavily requested number at Muskego Beach Ballroom, where the boys had quickly become teen favorites. They headed for Chicago and recorded it for Ermine Records, a label owned by former saxophonist Bill Erman. (Erman also ran the Diamond Coal Co., the family business he had inherited).

The record became a huge local hit. It was followed by a newly recorded version of their earlier instrumental; then another obscure rockabilly remake ("Bop-A-Lena") and an album. The group also backed label-mate Johnny Cooper on one release. The Legends could do no wrong and major label interest was brewing. Capitol purchased the LP and brought in producer Jim Economides with a song titled "Run To The Movies," reportedly written for the Drifters. But the magic was missing. "I thought Little Artie & the Pharaohs should have recorded that song," says McCue.

Capitol put out another album of cover tunes but, though the Legends had high hopes for "I'll Be Forever Loving You," no more singles were released. "I didn't really want to sign with Capitol," claims McCue, "because we had a comparable offer from Columbia and a whole lot more interest in the band."

Meanwhile, the Legends had encountered various guest star acts at Muskego Beach. Among them were the Everly Brothers, who had been especially impressed with McCue. While the Legends were making the transition from a teen band to a club band and dealing with the recording disappointment, the Everly's were losing guitarist Don Peake to Ray Charles. The brothers offered the gig to McCue.

There was a brief interim period after flying to Los Angeles to meet with the Everly's. Back in Milwaukee sans the Legends, McCue did a gig at Layton Place with Junior & the Classics and cut a solo single (co-written by WOKY DJ Bill Taylor) using members of that band.

The Legends, meanwhile, expanded to five pieces with the addition of guitarist Terry Gale and singer Billy Joe Burnette. While both performers had great talent, no stage was large enough for both egos and Gale's stay was short lived. His replacement, young John Rondell, had been referred by Royal Lancers' guitarist Doug Tank.

"I was home skipping school when Larry Foster called," recalls Rondell. "I said, 'Hey look, I'm flattered that I'm even talking to you but I'm no Sam McCue. I've only been playing a couple years and I can't handle the gig.' He said, 'I really appreciate your being honest and not wasting our time.' About a week later he called and said, 'Look, your name has come up a bunch of times. Why don't you let us be the judge if you can cut the job?" Rondell figures he got it because he was "the only guy who was an OK guitar player, knew some of the material and didn't ask any questions!"

The band, believing that a change of scene was in order, headed for Miami, stopping in Roanoke, Virginia, long enough to record two unreleased songs. These were done under the sponsorship of Burnette's friend Doc Russo, reportedly at the same studio that had turned out Wilbert Harrison's immortal "Kansas City" five years earlier. Once in Florida there were three more additions: A manager: Steve Palmer, a keyboard player: Ronnie Davis, and an adjective: Thanks to Palmer, they became the Canadian Legends.

After singing lead on the Legends' first post-McCue record, Billy Joe Burnette left. During the sessions at Criteria Studios, the band also backed Burnette on a couple of his tunes which were never released. The Legends' "Here Comes The Pain" took off. "I would say within a week we were on the radio," recalls Rondell. "I was hearing the song every ten minutes on the beach; there was a plane flying down the beach with our name on it; it was pretty bizarre. I felt like, man, there was something happening!" The song also charted back in Milwaukee but, with the record's lead singer gone, there was no follow-up.

Rondell also recalls some of the fans' reactions: "Jerry was by far the most popular Legend in Florida. We used to come out on stage and I remember girls just falling down yelling 'Jerry, Jerry'."

Returning to Milwaukee in late 1964, the Legends let Rondell go and welcomed back McCue who, besides touring with the Everly Brothers, had been back in town working as Sam McCue & the Saints (Brad McKay - rh gtr, Phil Alagna - bs, Stu Moebus - dr). Along with reclaiming McCue, the band reclaimed their position on stage left at Muskego Beach. Foster refused to go on opposite the Renegades unless they were given the spot. The show came to a halt while all instruments were moved.

The Legends left for another Florida tour early in 1965 and two singles were released on Parrot during that summer. Then, back home in January of '66, Larry Foster received his draft notice. Sessody and Schils elected to continue enjoying Florida's climate and, with a final performance at *Beneath The Street* (3507 W. Burleigh), the classic Legends line-up bade goodbye.

While McCue carried on the name with new musicians, Sessody and Schils returned to Florida and secured a release on "Raining In My Heart," a Buddy Holly tune that the Legends had recorded during the 1965 tour. "They released it and sent me a contract," recalls McCue, "and I checked it over and I really didn't want anything to do with it. Sessody though I was crazy because they all thought it was a hit. I just wanted to dissociate."

> **Sammy McCue & the Legends:**
> **McCue** - ld gtr   **Pat Glass** - rh gtr
> **Brad McKay** - rh gtr   **Paul Chitwood** - bs
> **Pat Driscoll** - bs (3/17/39; Milwaukee)   **Terry Anderson** - dr
> **Rick Jaeger** - dr

McCue's new group recorded but nothing was released. McCue also teamed up with Madison musician Steve Sperry to produce records for many of Ken Adamany's bands at Cuca studios.

Epilogue:

Sam McCue: Upon the demise of his new Legends, McCue joined New Blues from about late 1966 to early 1968. He returned to the Everly Brothers about the same time that New Blues became A.B. Skhy and left for San Francisco. McCue moved to the Los Angeles area and resided in South Gate until 1978. In 1970-71 he recorded for ABC-Paramount with Crowfoot, a band that included drummer Rick Jaeger. Since his return to Milwaukee he has kept busy working with Rocket 88 and several other bands (some of them including his sons), recording, and doing custom guitar work.

Larry Foster: Foster took up residence in Tampa, Florida, after his military duty. He came back to Milwaukee for a time in 1980 to work with McCue in a country band called Dead or Alive. He then returned to the Tampa/St. Petersburg area where he has worked in commercial fishing, written and recorded a children's book, and now has a sculpture studio (Waterman Alley Art Gallery) in Clearwater.

Jerry Schils: In 1966, after a brief attempt to form a new Legends in Florida, Schils joined the Birdwatchers. That Miami band had good regional success with several releases on Laurie, Mala and Scott. Except for the Legends reunion (see below), Schils has been out of the music business since 1972. He now resides in St. Paul, Minnesota.

Jim Sessody: Sessody was involved with Schils in the 1966 short-lived new Legends endeavor. He then became a recording engineer at Criteria Studio and produced many local Miami bands.

These four "original" Legends reunited for a concert at Milwaukee's Eagles Club on Thanksgiving night, 1979, reportedly a resounding success. "It was the most fun I've had in 13 years,"[1] said Sessody. The band did two more shows at McCue's club, the *Lost Legends Saloon*, then went to Miami to record an album in May, 1980. The material was never released. Jerry Schils reports that he has been contacted in recent years about a possible release of the sessions. He was asked to sign away his rights, which he declined to do.

---

[1]Lemlich, Jeff. <u>Savage Lost.</u> Plantation, FL: Distinctive, 1992.

Billy Joe Burnette: Burnette went to California with another Milwaukee band, the Holidays, in late 1964, and again to work with the Mojo Men in late 1965. He recorded extensively on several labels and co-wrote "Teddy Bear" (not the Elvis tune), a country hit that crossed over to pop for Red Sovine during the CB craze in 1976.

Rick Jaeger: Jaeger had been in a Florida band, Beau Gentry, when he met McCue. Members of that group moved to Wisconsin and re-formed the band, booking through Ken Adamany. Beau Gentry recorded some unreleased material for Dunwich in Chicago and had one single on Adamany's label. The band's bass player, Doug Kilmer, joined Norman Greenbaum ("Spirit In The Sky," 1970). Jaeger joined New Blues, then left to work with Harvey Mandel and others in San Francisco. He also worked with Dave Mason, A.B. Skhy, and played on many hit records by the Pointer Sisters, Carly Simon, and others before returning to Milwaukee. Back in town since around 1987, he has worked often with McCue since then.

Paul Chitwood: Chitwood was from Janesville and had worked with Tim Davis and others prior to his brief Legends stint. He has remained in that area.

Terry Anderson: Anderson reportedly has recorded extensively in Canada.

Dennis Bertrand, Pat Driscoll: These two musicians continued working with many local groups through the following years.

John Rondell: Rondell joined the Mojo Men and went to California. He later returned to Milwaukee and worked with Pete Sorce in the Big Apple. He has continued to play as a single in the 90's. In retrospect he looks at his time with the Legends as a sideman hired to fill in temporarily for McCue, rather than as a full-fledged member. In fact, he was only given one day's notice at the end of the gig. Despite this he says, "I think of them often. They were a part of a very exciting and thrilling time of my life. I consider it a privilege that I got to tour with them."

Also see: Terry Gale
        Mojo Men (John Rondell)
        Robbs - On The Charts, Renegades (Denny Sachse)
Unrelated Legends: Caldwell, Columbia, CUR, Doc Holiday, Epic, Fenton, Frog, Hart-Van,
        Heart, Hull, Jamie, Melba, Railroad House, Up, White Cliffs (Canadian   Legends)
Unrelated Larry Foster: There are solo releases on by a Larry Foster but none of these are
        related to the Legends' Foster.
Sources: John Rondell telephone interview, 3/93
        Sam McCue telephone interview, 1/2/94
        Lemlich, Jeff. Savage Lost. Plantation, FL: Distinctive, 1992.
        Lemlich, Jeff. "A History Of the Legends." Blitz 5-6/80: 18-19
        Osborne-Brown. Rockin' Records.
        Personal recollections

Legends: Jerry Schils, Larry Foster,
Jim Sessody, Sam McCue
(courtesy Larry Foster)

Little Artie & the Pharaohs: Artie Herrera, Dick Baradic,
Mike Morgan, Phil Zinos, Jim Lombard

Legends: (top) Larry Foster, Jim Sessody, (bottom) Ronnie Davis, Jerry Shils, John Rondell

Little Artie & the Pharaohs

Artie Herrera - voc (Waco, TX)   **Dick Baradic** - dr
Mike Morgan - ld gtr (1/18/44; Nashville, TN)   **Chuck Matson** - dr
Pete Psiroupolis - rh gtr   **Tom Markin** - dr
Phil Zinos - sx   **Pat Short (Cibarrich)** - org
Jim Lombard - bs (2/7/43; Reedsburg)   **Al Herrera** - sx (3/17/41; Waco, TX)
Andy Bakiris - dr   **Danny Gale (Galecki)** (4/3/46; Milwaukee)

Cuca	1142	The Fox And The Hound/My Symphony	8/63
	1157	Impossible/It Puzzles Me	11/63
	1162	I'll Take Care Of You/Foxy Devil	3/64
Kane & Abel			
Destination	607	Break Down And Cry/Twist Is Back	/65
Red Bird	10-059	He Will Break Your Heart/Twist Is Back	5/66

This r&b band was one of Milwaukee's most popular groups in the early 60's. A stand-out among their Cuca singles is "Impossible," a Drifters-style tune written by Ronnie Premier. That recording also employed the services of Tony Kolp (Bonnevilles/Skunks) on sax and Greg Browder (Comic Books) on trumpet. Guitarist Mike Morgan (no connection with Michael Morgan of the Messengers) claims to be the uncredited co-writer of some of the Ronnie Premier tunes. "I provided the booze and the guitar," he laughs.

Around late 1964, Artie's brother Al came in from Texas to join the group. A chunky tenor sax player who sang a little background, Al began a metamorphosis when the Pharaohs began performing the Righteous Brothers' "You've Lost That Lovin' Feelin'." With Al doing the Bobby Hatfield part, the song became a favorite on their gigs. He began to sing more, dance more, and weigh less.

In 1965 Al and Artie recorded in Chicago as Kane & Abel. "Break Down And Cry," a Righteous Brothers-style tune, was written and produced by James Holvay and Gary Beisber. This proved to be the early stages of the Mob, a show group that included all of the above four as members. The Mob went on to much success on the Nevada circuit while placing two minor singles on Billboard's Hot 100 in 1971. Holvay and Beisber also co-wrote most of the Buckinghams' hits.

Artie dropped out of the Mob early and returned to Milwaukee. Al became the main front man for the band, looking and sounding like a different man than the Pharaohs sax player of a few years earlier. Jim Lombard worked with his cousin Jerry Lariden in Speedy & the Alka-Seltzers. He has also played steel guitar with many country bands and worked with Sam McCue in Dead Or Alive in the early 80's. Pat Short joined the Mojo Men in California in late 1965 and appears on one of their records. He later moved to Louisville, Kentucky, and is back in Milwaukee in the 90's.

After working briefly with the Mad Lads, Danny Gale moved to Southern California in 1967. He eventually relocated to Las Vegas where he has become a well-known local entertainer, perhaps fulfilling the promise abandoned by his brother Terry many years earlier. In the early 90's Al Herrera has been singing around Chicago. In September, 1992, Artie and Al reunited in a nostalgia show in Milwaukee. Since then Artie, Mike Morgan and Pat Short have again been working as the Pharaohs.

Also see: Speedy & the Alka-Seltzers (Jim Lombard)
      Mojo Men (Pat Short)
Unrelated Pharaohs: Capitol, Fascination, Flip, Pyramid, Scarab
Sources: Jim Lombard telephone interview, 1/5/94
      Danny Gale telephone interview, 1/12/94
      Al Herrera telephone interview, 7/30/93
      Clee. <u>American 45 R.P.M. Records.</u>

Larry Lynne Group

Larry Lynne (Ostricki) - gtr (12/14/40; Waukesha)
Tyler Famularo - gtr
Todd Famularo - pno
Val Dwyer - bs
Mike O'Krongly - dr

This was Larry Lynne's post-Skunks group from 1969-71. Tyler Famularo later had the Balloons who recorded for Blue Ribbon.

Water Street	8356	Till I'll Be there/Happiness Is	/69
Mammoth	101	Back On the Street Again[1]/Diamond Lady	/70
	103	Sudden Changes/Weeping Willow	/70

Also see: Bonnevilles, Skunks (Larry Lynne)
      Teen Town Records (Balloons on Blue Ribbon)
Sources: Larry Ostricki telephone interviews, 1/30/93, 5/22/94
      Tourville. <u>Wisconsin . . . Discography.</u>

Mad Lads/Gary Lane & the Mad Lads

Gary Lane (Von Vorous) - rh gtr (3/28/42; Sturgeon Bay)   **Wayne Walters** - dr
Larry Lynne (Ostricki) - ld gtr   **Jerry Mallon** - ld gtr
Norm Sherian (Basherian) - bs   **Al Babicky** - sx

---

[1]Sunshine Company, 1967

Paul Frederick - dr (11/13/41; Springfield, IL)   **Tom Fabre** - sx (11/15/40; Milwaukee)
Kenny Rogers - gtr (Kingsford, MI)
Stu Moebus - dr
John Grignon - bs (4/28/42; Marinette)
Mark Balzak - dr
Jimmy Civilotte - dr
Bob Merkt - gtr (8/28/44; Waukesha)
Danny Gale - bs
Rick O'Nash
Schervig Twins

Cuca	6494	Henrietta[1]/What Do You Do When (Gary Lane & the Mad Lads)	9/64
Raynard	10020	Rock Around The Clock[2]/Walkin' With My Angel[3] (Fabulous Mad Lads)	/65

Having started the Mad Lads as a teen dance band, Gary Lane elected to retain the name even when a group on the Volt label hit the r&b charts in 1965. "We had the name first," he claims, "so what happened there, I called them (Stax/Volt Records) and they had agreed to let me come in and I'd have been the first white guy to do a recording session there." Lane, who had recorded previously with the Darnells, never followed through to take advantage of that offer. As far as the name is concerned, there was a Mad Lads on record as early as 1957 (Frank Deaton & the Mad Lads on Bally).

The closest the Milwaukee Mad Lads came to a successful record was "Henrietta." "I was getting airplay on KOMA in Oklahoma City," Lane says. "I heard it coming home one night on WLAC in Nashville. I was impressed when I'd hear it, but the kids would go in the record store and it wasn't there."

After a stay at Monreal's (1566 W. National Ave.), Larry Lynne formed the Skunks and Lane joined the Saints Five. Next for Lane was a stint in country music with Bobby Nelson (who had three singles on Crescendo in the early 70's), then came a new incarnation of the Mad Lads. The latter group went up to eight pieces and had many personnel changes.

Eventually Lane decided to try the night club business from a different angle. He has owned the Sundazzle at 5012 W. Capitol Dr. since 1978.

Also see: Darnells (Gary Lane, Norm Sherian, Tom Fabre)
         Bonnevilles (Larry Lynne, Paul Edwards, Bob Merkt)

---

[1]Jimmy Dee, 1957
[2]Bill Haley, 1955
[3]Bobby Vee, 1962

Larry Lynne Group
Skunks (Larry Lynne, Paul Edwards)
Futuras (Jerry Mallon)
Driftwoods (Al Babicky, Wayne Walters)
Road Runners, (Kenny Rogers)
Saints 5 (Kenny Rogers, Stu Moebus, John Grignon)
Rock-A-Fellers, Tom Collins & the Mixers (Bob Merkt)
Unrelated Mad Lads: Bally, Capitol, IGL, K-Ark, Mark-Fi, Stax, Target, Volt
Sources: Gary Lane telephone interviews; 8/8/92, 8/8/93
    Osborne-Brown. <u>Rockin' Records.</u>

Toni Majestro

USA	My Boyfriend Charlie/	/60

Female singer backed by the Noblemen.

Also see: Noblemen
Sources: Brand Shank telephone interview; 6/20/93
    William Menor letter, 3/94

Jack Merlin
(1/1/33; Milwaukee)

New Phoenix	60-9210	Proverbs/Johnny And Stella	(with the Valiants)	/60
Dot	16332	Girl Of My Dreams/I Beat The Blues		3/62
Cameo	311	Drip Drop Sha La La Blues/My Debbie		4/64
Hickory	1296	Mechanical Man/One Song		1/65
	1322	Are You/Love Life Of Crime		7/65

The instrumental backing on Jack Merlin's first release was provided by the Valiants, a band that included singer Paul Stefan. "We were both like Elvis impersonators," he recalls, "and we tried to outdo each other all the time." Merlin left Milwaukee the following year and did all his subsequent recording in Nashville, where he has resided ever since. He has produced other artists, written commercials and had his own record label (Cor). He recorded for that label as a member of the Bluelights from 1972-78, and has worked with the County Line Band since then.

After retiring from the Nashville Police Department, Merlin formed his own company providing bodyguard service for many big name artists. He occasionally works as a movie extra and once turned down an offer for an A&R position with Columbia Records that would have required him to relocate. Though he never became a star, Merlin says, "As far as I'm concerned, I feel like I've been very successful in the music business."

Sources: Jack Merlin telephone interview, 4/9/94
         Paul Yopps telephone interview, 11/28/93
         Clee. American 45 R.P.M. Records.

Mad Lads: Norm Sherian, Paul Fredericks, Larry Lynne, Gary Lane

(courtesy Jack Merlin)

Johnny "Mad Man" Michaels

Michaels 1194/1195 Czarnina Kid (Lincoln Ave.)/Michaels Market (Kobasa Song)   /54
Raynard   8838 GWIAZDOP (sic)/   /55

Michaels was a WOKY DJ in the early and mid 50's. His first two sides poke fun at Polish dialect. The second release was probably intended to be GWAZIADOP (Gee, Was I a dope).

Sources: Reissue single
    Corenthal, Michael G. Illustrated History of Wisconsin Music.

Mid-Knighters

Jimmy Rosetti - voc   **Johnny Veer (Verbraken)** - elec pno
Keith Dreher - gtr (dec; circa 1972)   (12/25/43; Ft. Monmouth, NJ)
Charlie Lewondowski - kb
Bill Hakow - bs
Mel Lundie (Lewondowski) - dr (1/5/42; Milwaukee)

Key   1003 Baby My Heart[1]/More Than I Can Say[2]   /61
Paragon   814 Charlena[3]/Flower Of Love   /62
            (Side 1 reissued on Pebbles *Highs In The Mid 60's, Vol 15*)

The Mid-Knighters formed about 1960 and lasted for four years. The Key release was recorded in Chicago. Jimmy Rosetti reportedly later worked as a booking agent in Florida. John Verbraken remains in music as a school band director.

Also see: Trendells (John Verbraken)
    Renegades, Walking Sticks (Keith Dreher)
Sources: Rick Schurk, 1993
    John Verbraken telephone interview, 2/11/94
    Mel Lewondowski telephone interview, 3/6/94
    Whitburn. Record Research.

Mojo Men

Duane Smith - rh gtr/org   **John Rondell (Beilfuss)** - ld gtr (3/9/45; Milwaukee)
Doug Masters (Weiss) - ld gtr   **Phil Anthony (Alagna)** - bs (5/10/43; Milwaukee)

---

[1]Crickets, 1960
[2]Crickets, 1960; Bobby Vee, 1961; Leo Sayer, 1980
[3]Sevilles, 1961

Tom Hahn - bs (5/17/39; Tipton, IN)   **Pat Short (Cibarrich)** - org
Gary Myers - dr (8/28/42; Milwaukee)   **Paul Stefan (Stefaniak)** - voc (7/26/41; Milwaukee)

Tide	2001	Mojo Workout[1]/I Got A Woman[2]	5/64
		(Tommy Hahn & the Mojo Men)	

Related:

Dinamo	1001	Do You Love Another/You Are The One	/59
		(Doug Weiss, side 1 reissued on White Label LP *Swinging The Rock*)	
Tower	4261	Hiding From Myself/ (flip by different artist)	1/67
		(Paul & the Pack)	
		Devil's Angels[3]/ (flip by different artist)	6/67
		(Jerry & the Portraits)	

Portraits

Sidewalk	928	Let's Tell The World/A Million To One[4]	9/67
	935	Runaround Girl/Over The Rainbow[5]	12/67

LP's:

Tower	5053	Dr. Goldfoot And The Girl Bombs	1/67
		(Various Artists, including Paul & the Pack)	
	5074	Devil's Angels (#165)	6/67
		(Various Artists, including Jerry & the Portraits)	

The sole Milwaukee record for this band had several odd circumstances surrounding it:
1) The record, "Mojo Workout," came out on a small Los Angeles label though the group was playing full time in Milwaukee at the time.
2) The same label had a release by a different Mojo Men (also with a Milwaukee connection - see Darnells) at virtually the same time.
3) The record featured bassist Tom Hahn on lead vocal though Hahn sang lead on fewer songs than anyone else in the group. (Lead singer Doug Weiss was among the background vocals).
4) The name of the band was changed from Cashmeres to Mojo Men because of the record.
5) It was an r&b record that received some airplay on WAWA though the band was very "top-40" oriented.

The forerunner of the Mojo Men was the Cashmeres which, in late 1963, included Duane Smith and Phil Alagna. When an anonymous musician called the club where they were playing to tell the owner that Alagna was under age (apparently hoping to get the Cashmeres fired and create an opening for his own band), Smith had to let Alagna go. He decided to completely re-form the group.

---

[1]Larry Bright, 1960
[2]Ray Charles, 1955
[3]From 1967 motion picture
[4]Jimmy Charles, 1960
[5]From *The Wizard Of Oz*; Glen Miller, 1939; Dimensions, 1960; many others

Tom Hahn and I had recently returned from California where we recorded on Tide with the Darnells. We both accepted Smith's offer to join the Cashmeres. Smith also somehow found Doug Weiss, a singer/guitarist recently discharged from the armed forces. The new Cashmeres debuted backing Tommy Roe at Monreal's Sky Room on January 26, 1964. The band soon landed the full time gig downstairs.

Meanwhile back in L.A., Tide Records saw renewed interest in their copyright, "Mojo Workout," thanks to a Kingsmen cover version on the *Louie, Louie* LP. Believing Hahn's voice and style were appropriate for the song, they contacted him in Milwaukee to record it. For the session at Dave Kennedy Studios, the band was augmented by Larry Lynne, Rick Allen and Tony Kolp of the Skunks. The Cashmeres became the Mojo Men. Other than one show with Harvey Scales, it was back to normal at Monreal's where the band had the opportunity to back many name artists on weekend guest appearances.

The Mojo Men might have stayed at Monreal's forever if they hadn't gotten fired for selling tickets to another show that conflicted with one of their regular nights there. When the Beatles made their appearance at the Milwaukee Arena, a local promoter put on a show at the adjacent Auditorium in an attempt to take advantage of the excitement and the overflow crowd. The Mojo Men were on the bill, along with Harvey Scales & the Seven Sounds, Little Artie & the Pharaohs, and John Kondos & the Galaxies.

With the backing of advertising man John Reiss, the Mojo Men recorded four songs used as background music for a puppet show at the Manhattan Museum of Contemporary Crafts in 1964. Through an endorsement deal with locally based LoDuca Brothers Distributors, the band used Italian made Eko guitars and was depicted on the cover of an Italian music magazine.

In August 1965, after a personnel change that brought Phil Alagna back into the fold (now that he was over 21) along with John Rondell, the Mojo Men left for California. Their first gig there was at the Chatterbox in Garden Grove. Up the street about a mile was a club called Gold Street that featured the Skunks. It seems some of these Milwaukee bands kept running into each other no matter where they went!

When Doug Weiss left to join a Vegas-style review, Phil Alagna and John Rondell invited Billy Joe Burnette to fly out and join the group. He did so and fronted the band for a short time at Little Abner's in South Gate.

Another Milwaukean to turn up was Paul Stefan. In early 1966 Stefan replaced Burnette and the Mojo Men returned to Milwaukee that summer. After gigs at the Penthouse (formerly the Spa, 502 W. Wisconsin Ave.) and Mr. Roberts in Appleton, the band returned to California. The group did one record as Paul & the Pack (a name that was never used on stage), then chose the name Portraits. Stefan was drafted and replaced by Jerry Tawney from West Virginia. In 1968 the Portraits won a spot in the Schaefer Annual Talent Hunt and were flown to New York to do a beer commercial.

After many more personnel changes, the Portraits became a show group in the early 70's and Alagna continued the band as a full time club group until 1982. Doug Weiss (aka Doug Masters) moved to St. Paul, Minnesota, and continued playing clubs for many years. John Rondell landed in Eau Claire and has continued to play in the 90's. Duane Smith traveled with the Cee & Dee Review for several years before settling in Portland where he now owns a very successful rental business. I've continued playing part time since 1982.

Also see: Paul Stefan
        Crossfires (Phil Alagna)
        Legends (John Rondell, Billy Joe Burnette)
        Darnells (Tom Hahn, Gary Myers)
Unrelated Mojo Men: Autumn, GRT, Reprise, Tide (2000)
Sources: Personal recollections and record collection
        Osborne-Brown. Rockin' Records.

Betty Moore

(Betty Tori Moorer - 4/12/47; Milwaukee)

Cuca	1134	Long Hot Summer/Voo Doo Walk	6/63
	1467	Long Hot Summer/Voo Doo Walk	/69
		(Side 1 reissued on Cuca compilation LP *Badger A Go Go*)	
Wand	11202	It's My Thing[1]/Speed Up	6/69

Betty Moore is the sister of two of the principals in the Esquires and she was an early member of that vocal group. The Esquires are the background singers on her Cuca release. When her brothers signed with Wand, Moore also got on the label with "It's My Thing," an answer to the Isley Brothers' "It's Your Thing." A competing version of the song by Marva Whitney charted. Cuca apparently reissued her original single at that time. Shortly after that Moore relocated to Los Angeles where she continued singing until around 1990.

Also see: Esquires - On The Charts
Sources: Tori Moorer Jackson telephone interview, 7/28/94
        Clee. American 45 R.P.M. Records.

Mother's Worry

Rick Purcell - hca/voc
John Zaffiiro - gtr (9/12/51; Milwaukee)
Ernest Mathies - org (dec)
Keith Cravillion - bs
Peter Alioto - dr

---

[1]Marva Whitney, 1969

Look 5023/5024 Funky Good/Can't Seem To Come Down   /68
      5025/5039 It's A Long Way Back/Yesterday Where Is My Mind   /68

Mother's Worry may have been just that when they began in 1965, with the members still in high school. In 1967 the band spent a month touring in Tennessee (including gigs with the Box Tops) and recorded these sides in Nashville. Drummer Peter Alioto is from the family that owns several restaurants in Milwaukee. Rick Purcell does jingle work in Chicago. John Zaffiiro was with Montage Project for a self-produced LP in 1978, and he continues to play in the 90's.

Sources: Keith Cravillion telephone interview, 2/4/94
         John Zaffiiro telephone interview, 6/5/94

Mojo Men: (top) Phil Alagna, Doug Weiss,
Duane Smith, (bottom) Gary Myers, John Rondell

Betty Moore
(courtesy Tori Jackson)

Mustard Men

Keith Paplham - rh gtr
Warren Wiegratz - sx (5/5/48; Milwaukee)
Stan Kellicut - gtr
Jerry Wimmer - bs/sx
George Welik - dr

Raynard   10036 Another Day/I Lost My Baby   /65
                        (Side 2 reissued on Pebbles *Highs In The Mid 60's, Vol. 15*)

A two-time winner of WRIT's battle of the bands, the Mustard Men were playing high school and CYO dances at the time of their record In the contest the band managed to beat out Freddie & the Freeloaders, the group that both Warren Wiegratz and Stan Kellicut would later join. Wiegratz subsequently recorded with Family At Max and Sweet Bottom (a jazz/fusion group that featured the early efforts of guitarist Daryl Stuermer, who went on to great success with Jean Luc-Ponty and Genesis/Phil Collins). Next came Ocean and, in the 90's, his own group, Street Life .

Jerry Wimmer moved to San Francisco. George Welik went into the aerospace industry in California. Keith Paplham continued in lounge groups and relocated to the Quad Cities of Iowa. Stan Kellicut has a band in New Zealand.

Also see: Freddie & the Freeloaders (Warren Wiegratz, Stan Kellicut)
Sources: Warren Wiegratz telephone interview, 7/14/93
         Tourville. <u>Wisconsin . . . Discography.</u>

Next Five/Toy Factory

Steve Thomas - ld gtr
Eric Olson - rh gtr (1/8/49; Milwaukee)   **John Peter** - gtr
Mark Buscaglia - kb   **Gary Cooper** - dr
Gordon Wayne (Olski) - bs (Milwaukee)   **John Crook** - dr
Tom "Stewie" Stewart - dr

Destination   637   Little Black Egg[1] /He Stole My Love   /67
Wand   1170 Mama Said[2]/Talk To Me Girl   10/67
Jubilee   5668 Sunny Sunny Feeling/What's The Melody   7/69
                    (Toy Factory)

---

[1]Nightcrawlers, 1967
[2]Shirelles, 1961

Formed by students at Brookfield Central High, the Next Five achieved some local success with their first record, produced by WOKY DJ Paul Christy. Eric Olson says Christy asked them to become "Michael & the Messengers" when that fiasco began to happen (see Messengers - Wisconsin On The Charts). The Next Five was one of the bands in the stable of Con Merten, who got them on a national label with their second release. Although they were still the Next Five when they went in for the third record, some personnel had changed, and Jubilee Records renamed them the Toy Factory.

Gordy Olski later did some work in Las Vegas with 60's star Bobby Vee. Eric Olson moved to Los Angeles in 1977 and worked for the Robbs at Cherokee Studios before forming his own oldies band. The group, P.F. Flyer, has opened for the Mamas & Papas, Three Dog Night and the Righteous Brothers. "The 50's and 60's in Milwaukee, being in the heart of the Midwest," reflects Olson, "it was a whole different thing that could probably never happen again."

Unrelated Toy Factory: Avco Embassy
Sources: Gordon Olski telephone interview, 12/19/93
      Eric Olson telephone interview, 12/19/93
      Tourville. Wisconsin . . . Discography.
      Whitburn. Record Research.
      Clee. American 45 R.P.M. Records.
      Osborne-Brown. Rockin' Records.

Next Five: Eric Olson, Mark Buscaglia, Steve Thomas, Tom Stewart, Gordy Wayne (courtesy E. Olson)

Night Beats/El Rey & the Night Beats
(Waukesha)

Raymond "El Rey" Ojeda - sx (1/6/41; Green Bay)
Dick Whitstone - voc
Gerald "Rusty" Bartelmas - ld gtr   **Jack Staumbeil** - dr
Ron Kurtz - rh gtr   **Terry Thuemling** - gtr
Bruce "Ace" Rudan - bs   **Jack Gebhardt** - bs
Tom Montez - dr

Sound	100	Exotic/Cherry Pink And Apple Blossom White[1]	/60
Revive	103	My Secret/Come On Let's Go[2]	/63
		(El Ray & the Night Beats)	
Sound	101	Exotic/Midnight Walk	/65

The Night Beats qualify as one of the longest lasting rock bands around Milwaukee. They were also among the earliest if you go back to their original name as the Fendermen. "I had a letter from Leo Fender (owner of the Fender Guitar Co.) in California authorizing me to use their name in our name," explains Raymond Ojeda. "We were going along pretty good and then the 'Mule Skinner Blues' guys came out of Madison so we just decided to change it." The new name came from a closed down club on the East Side of Milwaukee.

The band did their first recording at Chess Studios in Chicago. Their update of "Cherry Pink And Apple Blossom White" was produced by Stu Glassman, owner of Radio Doctors Record Store in downtown Milwaukee. "I understood that the Harmonicats, who also recorded at Chess, ran across our version of that," says Ojeda. "They recorded the exact same arrangement and they had a big hit out of it."

Ojeda also recorded with the Noblemen and the Rollettes. In their 30+ years, the Night Beats have employed many musicians. Some of them got back together to record "La Bamba" for a CD in 1993 to benefit the Waukesha Training Center. The project, "Celebration Of Music" by Vangold Productions, also includes Les Paul, the BoDeans, and Sigmund Snopek III.

Also see: Noblemen (Raymond Ojeda, Ace Rudan)
     Rollettes Orchestra
     Tommy Lane
Unrelated Night Beats (Nightbeats, Nite Beats): Cuca, Tide, Zoom
Sources: Raymond Ojeda telephone interview, 2/93
     Tourville. <u>Wisconsin . . . Discography.</u>
     Osborne-Brown. <u>Rockin' Records.</u>

---

[1]Perez Prado, 1955; Jerry Murad's Harmonicats, 1961
[2]Ritchie Valens, 1958; Los Lobos, 1987

Noblemen

Brand Shank - ld gtr (8/19/40; Milwaukee)
Chuck Lalicata - rh gtr
Bob Stange - sx/accordion   **Bruce "Ace" Rudan** - bs
Jerry Sworske - dr (4/8/42; Milwaukee)   **Raymond Ojeda** - sx

USA	1213	Thunder Wagon/Dragon Walk	/58
	1222	Dirty Robber/Forever Lonely	/60
Proflie	4012	Dirty Robber/Forever Lonely	/60
		(Side 1 reissued on Pebbles *Highs In The Mid 60's, Vol. 10*)	

A local hit, the Noblemen's "Thunder Wagon" was one of Milwaukee's first rock 'n' roll recordings. The Night Beats' Raymond Ojeda plays sax on the disc. The Noblemen began at Washington High School and the band became an influence to many other teen musicians. ("They were the reason I started playing guitar," says Doug Tank of the Royal Lancers. Tank went on to spread the gospel while teaching at West Allis Music). The band also provided the backing for two other USA artists, Little Sir Ryland and Toni Majestro. (Oddly, another USA release shown as the Noblemen [#1215 - "Sleep Beauty Sleep"] has no connection with the group, according to leader Brand Shank.

Also see: Junior & the Classics - On The Charts (Brand Shank, Jerry Sworske)
     Night Beats (Raymond Ojeda, Bruce Rudan)
     Darnells (Jerry Sworske)
     Cheaters (Brand Shank)
     Toni Majestro
Unrelated Noblemen: Bee, CJL, Epic, Golden Gate, Kaleidoscope, Klik, Paris Tower, Prism,
     USA 1215
Sources: Brand Shank telephone interview, 6/20/93
     Raymond Ojeda telephone interview, 2/93
     Doug Tank telephone interview, 7/31/94
     Osborne-Brown. <u>Rockin' Records.</u>
     Tourville. <u>Wisconsin . . . Discography.</u>

Originals

Tom Spacek - ld gtr
Jim Nelner - org
Arthur Shore - tenor sx (7/30/51; Milwaukee)
Stanley Palkowitz - alto sx
Bob Radusta - tp
Steve Miscovey - bs
David Bruce - dr

Originals: (top) Mel Shore (mgr.), Bob Radusta,
Jim Nelner, David Bruce, Steve Miscovey,
(bottom) Stanley Palkowitz, Arthur Shore,
Tom Spacek (courtesy Mel Shore)

| Sara | 65125 Little Bit Of Everything/Watermelon Man | 12/65 |
| | 65126 Jive Samba/Taste Of Honey | 12/65 |

Unrelated Originals: Brunswick, Champ, Diamond, Fantasy, Jackpot, Motown, Original Sound,
　　　　Phase II, Raynard, Soul Stash
Sources: Mel Shore telephone interview, 8/16/94
　　　　Osborne-Brown. Rockin' Records.
　　　　Tourville. Wisconsin . . . Discography.

Otto & the Sensations

Probable member: Roy Turner

CTI　　　　2000　Girl, We Can Make It/Keep On Lovin' You

Source: Al Vance telephone interview, 7/31/94
　　　　Tourville. Wisconsin . . . Discography.

Danny Peil & the Apollos/Tigers

Danny Peil - voc
Denny McCarthy - org (9/18/40; Milwaukee)
Bobby Ray (Reindorp) - gtr
Roland Stone (Oeller) - bs (3/17/41; Milwaukee)　　　**Duane Lundy** - dr
Pete Miller - dr

Raynard	602	Jingle Jump/Flip Side	(Danny Peil & the Apollos)	/65
	602	Jingle Jump/Flip Side	(Danny Peil & the Tigers)	/65
Sumthin' Else	3929	She Calls Me Baby/I See The Light		/65
		(Tigers)		

Related:

| Curtis | -- | Four Ways To St. Paul/Snow Drifter | |
| | | (Danny Peil & the Sound Majority) | |

With his good voice and handsome, Elvis-like appearance, Danny Peil had been singing around town as Danny Monday when the opportunity came to replace Paul Stefan with the Apollos. The latter group was appearing at Claude's (5048 N. 35th) when Stefan decided to move to the West Coast. Not long after Peil joined, the Apollos took over as house band on *Sumthin' Else,* Channel 12's Bandstand-type show.

Robert Block, head of a local advertising agency, was managing the group and had them record "Jingle Jump" to promote a new product that his company was marketing. "This was right after the hula hoop," explains Denny McCarthy. "It was a gadget that you strapped around your ankle and there was a ball with a jingle bell on the end of it. You swung it around with one leg and you jumped over it with the other leg. They had TV spots with us playing and little girls jumping around." It was also Block's idea to change the band's name, resulting in the Raynard release coming out both ways.

The Tigers went to Los Angeles and did a TV pilot followed by work in Las Vegas and San Francisco. "It fell apart in San Francisco," says Roland Oeller, who left to join Moby Grape. "The whole music field seemed to be changing." With extensive revamps to the line-up, the group became the Danny Monday Review.

Peil eventually returned to Milwaukee and joined the newly formed Corporation. He is the cousin of Rick Colburn of the Titans (Minnesota band) and, before his Milwaukee involvement, he had sung with the Black Knights in Oskhosh. Peil reportedly suffered the tragedy of the death of his children in a mobile home fire.

Also see: Corporation, Karen Wells/Black Knights - Appleton/Fox Cities (Danny Peil)
        Roland Stone
        Apollos
Sources: Dennis McCarthy telephone interview, 8/6/94
        Roland Oeller telephone interview, 8/7/94
        Personal recollections
        Rick Schurk
        Tourville. <u>Wisconsin . . . Discography.</u>

Larry Lee Phillipson

Demo	1029	Bitter Feelings/While I Was Waiting For You	/64
Cinch	3858	Bitter Feelings/Talkin' To Myself	/64
Cuca	6541	Bitter Feelings/Talkin' To Myself	4/65
	6565	Milwaukee Road/Little Miss Teardrop	6/65
Raynard	770	Milwaukee Road/Greedy Lips	/65
	1053	Give Me Your Love For Christmas/Baby Sister's Christmas	12/65
Target	1010	Barney/Blackboards Of My Mind	/69
Phillipson	1002	Absent Minded You/A Few Kind Words	
	1004	First Night Back In Milwaukee/The Racing King	
	1005	Our Little Brother John/The Milwaukee Road	
	1006	Double Time Heart/A Corner In My Heart	
	2001	Charlene/Standing On The Corner	
	2004	Baby Sister's Christmas/Give Me Your Love	

Miami Road/ If You Are A Coward/ I'm Wondering Now

(The above are three otherwise unreleased tracks issued on *The Cuca Story, Vol 1 & 2*)

Larry Lee Phillipson may have worked at some country-western clubs in Milwaukee in the early 60's, possibly as Larry Lee. He was remembered by only a few other musicians from the era, however, and it seems he must have put more effort into recording than performing live. He apparently relocated to Eau Claire in the mid 60's and is believed to have since moved to Florida.

Sources: Tourville. <u>Wisconsin . . . Discography</u>
      White label LP jackets - courtesy Rick Schurk

Picture

Mick Milewski - gtr (2/17/49; Milwaukee)
Jim Milewski - rh gtr/bs (11/26/47; Milwaukee)   **Lon Omitt** - dr
Phil Shields - kb/sx (10/11/42; New Berlin)   **Bob McKenna** - voc (8/17/48; Milwaukee)
Wayne Babich - bs   **Michael Hoolihan** - bs
Mike Beaster - dr (3/1/47; Waukesha)   **Wayne LaPene** - dr
   Bill Aiken - gtr/org

Nasco	002	Reach Out[1]/Evolution	/68
WRN	101	Universal Soldier[2]/Dance Of Love[3]	/69

---

[1] aka "Reach Out I'll Be There" - Four Tops, 1966
[2] Glen Campbell, Donovan, 1965
[3] *This Is Tom Jones* LP, 1969; w: Charlie Rich

The Milewski brothers formed this group after the demise of the Ricochettes. WRIT DJ King Zbornik, who had done some production for the latter band, also produced Picture's Nasco release in Nashville. The WRN label was an enterprise of producer Wayne R. Novack.

Picture was involved in the shuffle of musicians between various groups. "There was a club in town called Gallagher's," says Bob McKenna, "and the bands that played there traded people every couple weeks. Somebody gets fired, somebody gets hired and six months later you change the name. There was a group of about 30 people that interchanged between about '67 and '72," says McKenna. A later line-up of Picture booked through Gary Van Zeeland and did much work around Madison.

Also see: Ricochettes (Mick & Jim Milewski)
      Impalas (Phil Shields)
      Challengers, Underground Sunshine (Mike Hoolihan)
      Invasion (Bob McKenna)
Sources: Phil Shields telephone interview, 3/20/94
      Bob McKenna telephone interview, 3/28/94
      Mick Milewski telephone interview, 4/10/94
      Tourville. Wisconsin . . . Discography.

Portraits

Emil Rakovich - voc
Peter Lewna - ld gtr (2/10/50; Milwaukee)
Bill Watson - kb (12/4/49; Milwaukee)
Greg Stupek - dr
Michael Szymborski - dr

Nike   --   It Had To Be You/That's My Time Of The Day[1]   /68

When the Mojo Men (for whom I played drums) moved to California and changed their name to the Portraits, we learned of another Milwaukee band by that name. 26 years later I have discovered that band.

It turns out that they had the name first. However, since they were a teen age band playing CYO dances when our group left Milwaukee, we had never heard of them. Guitarist Peter Lewna recalls the letter their manager received from us requesting that they change their name (which they, of course, ignored).

With members from Pulaski High and South Division High, the Portraits were a seven-man band

---

[1]Cowsills - *The Cowsills* LP, 1967

with two drummers when they played the UWM homecoming dance November 5, 1966. They had pared down to five pieces by the time of their recording the following year. "We got down to the RCA Studios in Chicago where the Monkees had previously been and we were just shaking," recalls keyboard player Bill Watson. "We rehearsed that song nine million times because we wanted to go in the studio and just go 'boom-boom' and get it done. We were totally intimidated."

The record, "It Had To Be You," is not the old standard from the 20's, but there is a connection. "The lead singer and keyboardist liked the words," says Lewna. "They decided to play with those words and put them to new music. It was kind of a psychedelic thing." The Portraits evolved into the band Omaha in the 70's.

Unrelated Portraits: Ariola, Capitol, RCA, Sidewalk, Tri-Disc
Sources: Peter Lewna telephone interview, 8/14/93
        Bill Watson telephone interview, 9/16/93
        Tourville. Wisconsin . . . Discography.
        Osborne-Brown. Rockin' Records.

Portraits: (top) Emil Rakovich, Bill Watson, (bottom) Gregroy Stupek, Peter Lewna, Mike Szymborski. Possibly the only time these guys wore ties! (courtesy Peter Lewna)

Renegades/Big Louie & the Renegades

"Big Louie" Friedman - voc (/42)
Micky Sommers (Slutzsky) - ld gtr (9/30/41; Milwaukee) **Paul Spencer (Rubitsky)** - dr
Dick Schurk - rh gtr (4/18/41; Milwaukee)   **Kurt Kronhelm** - sx (6/9/47; Milwaukee)
Denny Scheuneman - bs (10/42)   **Keith Dreher** - ld gtr (dec; circa 1972)
Denny Sachse - dr (dec)   **"Little Bob" Barian** - voc (10/13/42; Milw.)

Citation   5005   Istanbul[1]/Come On Out   2/63
                    (Side 1 reissued on *Surfin' In The Midwest, Vol. 2*)

A Four Lads hit from 1953 was an unlikely candidate to be turned into a surf-style instrumental, but that's what the Renegades did at the Cuca Studio on January 20, 1963. The record got no noticeable action and they continued the usual gigs until the end of that summer when they went to Tucson.

Upon their return the personnel began to change. About a year later Mickey Slutzsky joined the reserves to avoid the draft, and two other members quit. Down to just two musicians, Schurk switched to bass and recruited Bob Barian, Kurt Kronhelm and Keith Dreher. "We called that line-up the Renegades for about two months," Schurk explains, "then we lost a few gigs. People at Marty Zivko's and Muskego Beach got mad at us because they said we were misrepresenting the Renegades. They wanted Big Louie."

Slutzsky returned from an abbreviated military term and a brief fight for the name ensued. Schurk finally relented and renamed his band the Walking Sticks. Schurk later worked with the traveling version of the Bill Black Combo and with Troy Shondell ("This Time," 1961). He has resided in the Seattle area since the late 60's. Slutsky continued with the Renegades until about 1966. After a few years with other local bands, he left the music business in 1970.

Also see: Legends (Denny Sachse)
        Comic Books (Bob Barian)
        Mid-Knighters (Keith Dreher)
        Walking Sticks (Dick Schurk, Kurt Kronhelm, Keith Dreher)
Unrelated Renegades/Renegaids: American International, Chardo, Congress, Dorset, Dubonay,
        Garland, GNP Crescendo, Karate, Polaris
Sources: Rick Schurk telephone interview, 9/22/93
        Mickey Slutsky telephone interview, 7/10/94
        Osborne-Brown. <u>Rockin' Records.</u>

---

[1]Four Lads, 1953

Renegades: (top) Louie Friedman, Paul Rubitsky, Mickey Slutzky, (bottom) Dick Schurk, Denny Schueneman (courtesy Rick Schurk)

Ricochettes: (top) Herb Hohnke, Humpty Neuhofer, Mickey Milewski, (bottom) Ar Stevens, Jim Milewski, Jerry Wollenzien (courtesy Tom Tourville)

Ricochettes

Ar Stevens (Kriegel) - ld gtr (1/27/47; Milwaukee) **Bob "Humpty" Neuhofer** - dr
Jerry Wollenzien - rh gtr   **Mick Milewski** - gtr (2/17/49; Milw)
Herb Hohnke - bs/org   **Jim Milewski** - bs/tambourine (11/26/47; Milw)
John John Galobich - dr   **Bruce Cole** - dr (5/11/47; Milwaukee)

Raynard	10030	I'll Be Back[1]/Can I Be Sure	/65
Quill	102	Come In My Love (Out Of The Rain)/Losing You	/66
Destination	629	Find Another Boy/I Don't Want You	9/66
Continental	500	Find Another Boy/Don't Waste Your Time	/66
Mean Mountain	1424	Rock On/Carl's Rockabilly Roll	/82

(Ar & the Rockin' Ricochettes)

LP:

Ottertail	1235	Ain't Rock & Roll Pretty	4/85

(Ar Stevens & the Rockin' Ricochettes)

The unprecedented top 40 exposure of many Beatles' album tunes no doubt helped boost a few sound-alike cover versions onto the national singles charts (see Underground Sunshine). While the Ricochettes didn't achieve that status (with only 500 copies pressed), they were among the early wave of attempts. Recorded at Universal in Chicago, their version of "I'll Be Back" also helped cement their reputation as "Milwaukee's Beatles."

While hanging out at the Leilani on West Bluemound Rd., Ar Stevens had the opportunity to meet Roger Smith who was appearing there at the time. One thing led to another and the group got a 15 minute segment in his show. "I don't think we even got paid for that, and I don't think it really mattered to us if we did," says Stevens. "The final night he flew Ann Margaret in because he wanted to surprise her with the new part of his show, so that was a big event for all of us."

In his teens at the time, Stevens recalls being in awe of the Mojo Men during a show they shared at the Riverside Theater in October 1964. "We were playing this stuff that all these 10-year old kids are crazy about, and they were playing more rhythm and blues," he says. " The bass player had his guitar real low and then he'd flip the strap off his back and do something and then flip the damn thing back. I remember going home and trying that and it never worked, and I'd say, 'Geez, these guys got all the tricks!'"

The next record came about through WRIT DJ King Zbornik who somehow got hold of an unfinished Brian Hyland song. The Ricochettes worked it out and recorded it for Chicago's Quill label. The record did well locally but turned out to be "another one of those deals where the

---

[1]Beatles - *Beatles '65* LP, 1965

naive band gets screwed," claims Stevens. "They said we sold over 10,000 copies and we ended up not getting a penny."

A different sort of problem surrounded the next release. The Ricochettes "Find Another Boy" on Destination was followed by a release on Continental of the same song, also shown as the Ricochettes. According to Stevens, the Continental version had been previously recorded by the group Mickey, They and Them. That band consisted of brothers Mickey and Jim Milewski, Humpty Neuhofer and guitarist Burt Sinagub. All but Sinagub had joined the Ricochettes. Apparently someone connected with the label (probably King Zbornik who produced it) felt there was enough of a Ricochettes connection to justify using the name.

When three members left to join the Reserve, Stevens and the Milewski brothers formed Picture. Stevens was drafted in August 1968, and was not involved in any recording by that group.

In the 70's Stevens worked with the Music Company and later joined Rocket 88. After appearing with the latter band at the 1981 Buddy Holly Memorial Show, he formed the new Ricochettes for a return to the 1982 event. 60's star Bobby Vee heard the group there and made them an offer. The Ricochettes continue in the 90's as Vee's backup band.

Stevens overdubbed all the parts on "Carl's Rockabilly Roll" as a tribute to Carl Perkins. The LP on Ottertail was recorded live at the Valair Ballroom in Des Moines.

Also see: Picture
        Grand Prix's, Invasion, Savoys, Van-Tels, Triumphs (Bruce Cole)
Sources: Ar Stevens telephone interview, 8/21/93
        Mick Milewski telephone interview, 10/93
        Tourville. <u>Wisconsin . . . Discography.</u>
        Posniak, Alan. "Badger Beat." <u>Milwaukee Journal</u> date, unknown - courtesy Brian Lake
        Record photocopies - courtesy Jane Huyser
        Clee. <u>American 45 R.P.M. Records.</u>

Road Runners/Bogis Chimes

Road Runners:
Jimmy Dentici - gtr
Kenny Jablonski - voc   **Richie Rendzik** - dr
Rudy Villasenor - rh gtr   **Tom Fabre** - sx (11/15/40; Milwaukee)
Dave Frasheski - bs   **Kenny Rogers** - gtr (Kingsford, MI)
Mike Kowaleski - dr   **Doug "Rockin' Robin" Schanning** - voc (1/14/43; Milw)

Raynard	10031	It's So Hard/Do The Temptation	/65
Champ	3402	It's So Hard/Do The Temptation	/65

Bogis Chimes:
Jimmy Dentici - gtr
Glen "Stretch" Frank - voc
Rick Skow - org
Dave Frasheski - bs
Mike Kowaleski - dr

Champ   3403 I Think You'll Find/Please Don't Forget   /66

Bogis Chimes: Dave Frasheski, Rick Skow, Mike Kowaleski, Jimmy Dentici, Glen Frank
(courtesy Tom Kubanek)

"The Road Runners never got what we deserved as far as recognition," says their manager, Tom Kubanek. "We traveled with the Stones, Dave Clark Five, Herman's Hermits, Wayne Fontana & the Mindbenders. Bob Barry (WOKY DJ) was the only one who ever gave us credit for that. We did a lot of recording at RCA, Universal, Columbia and Chess/Checker. We did a lot of work with Jan Bradley and Phil Upchurch."

Formed around 1962, the band's only released recordings were two Ron Barzyk (Ronnie Premier) tunes. Then came personnel changes and the name switch to Bogis Chimes. Some of the band's material was recorded by Manifest Destiny who also appeared on the Champ label. The Road Runners re-formed in the early 70's with some of the same members.

Also see: Darnells, Mad Lads (Tom Fabre)
          Mad Lads, Saints Five, (Kenny Rogers)

Unrelated Road Runners: Challenge, Chan, Colossus, Commerce, Felsted, Footnote, London,
        Michigan Nickel, Miramar, Morocco, Reprise,
Sources: Tom Fabre telephone interview, 12/93
        Tom Kubanek telephone interview, 2/6/94
        Tourville. <u>Wisconsin . . . Discography.</u>
        Osborne-Brown. <u>Rockin' Records.</u>

Rock-A-Fellers

Bob Merkt - gtr (8/28/44; Waukesha)
Del Stralo - gtr
Miles Merkt - sx (9/28/40; Waukesha)
Ken Berdoll - bs (12/14/43; Milwaukee)
Jim Sessody - dr

Cuca   1039   Say Mama/Reaction   6/61
                    (Side 1 reissued on *The Cuca Story, Vol. 1*)

It may be the Rock-A-Fellers who got the first Wisconsin version of "Say Mama" on wax.
"Ours was real close to the Gene Vincent version," says Bob Merkt. An interesting sidelight is
the fact that future Legends' drummer Jim Sessody was on it. The record was financed by the
owner of This Old House, one of band's frequent gigs. The group, which lasted from about
1959-62, also played often at Wyler's.

Also see: Corporation (Ken Berdoll)
        Bonnevilles, Tom Collins & the Mixers, Mad Lads (Bob Merkt)
        Legends (Jim Sessody)
        "Say Mama"
Unrelated Rock-A-Fellas: ABC-Paramount, Devere, SCA, Southern Sound
Sources: Bob Merkt telephone interview, 6/4/94
        Ken Berdoll telephone interview, 1/93
        Osborne-Brown. <u>Rockin' Records.</u>

Rogues

John Castellano - voc
Larry Krzeminski - ld gtr
Rick Rebstock - B3, pno
Casey Dutcavich - bs
Ron Olenik - dr (8/3/48; Milwaukee)

Night Owl   67102 Pearl Girl/The Secret   10/67

"The Secret" side of this band's record was written by a school teacher who lived on the same block as drummer Ron Olenik. "This man claims adamantly - adamantly! - to have written 'I Left My Heart In San Francisco'," says Olenik. The composer claims his registered letter copyright was not accepted in court when he tried to sue. The Rogues lasted about five years playing mostly CYO dances and teen gigs.

Unrelated Rogues: Action, Audition, Bing, Columbia, Guyden, Kapan, La Louisiane, Mirage, Norman, Old Town, Peyton, Rogue, Thunderbird, Waverly, Welhaven
Sources: Ron Olenik telephone interview, 7/23/94
    Peter Lewna, 1993
    Osborne-Brown. Rockin' Records.
    Tourville. Wisconsin . . . Discography.

Rollettes Orchestra
(Waukesha)

Leroy Titzi - stl gtr
Floyd Jester - ld gtr (5/19/31; Wausau)   **Raymond Ojeda** - sx (1/6/41; Green Bay)
Leroy Titzi - rh gtr   **Gerry Bartelmas** - gtr
Ray Titzi - bs
Louis   - dr

Cinch	2025	Venus Rock/Back Off	(/I)	/58
		Satellite Boogie/	(I/)	/59

"When the records first came out, they came out as Roulettes," recalls Floyd Jester. "Somebody made a mistake. That was very exciting. They (Roulette Records) were out to sue us and everything." The Rollettes played gigs with just Jester and the three Titzi Brothers, adding the drummer and additional musicians for these recordings. Jester still teaches guitar in the 90's.

Also see: Night Beats (Raymond Ojeda)
Unrelated Rollettes: Class, Melker
Sources: Raymond Ojeda telephone interview, 2/93
    Floyd Jester telephone interview, 7/2/94
    Tourville. Wisconsin . . . Discography.
    Osborne-Brown. Rockin' Records.

Royal Lancers

Chuck Tyler (Olla) - voc (10/22/40; Homestead, PA)
Doug Tank - ld gtr (8/16/43; Binghamton, NY) **Lee Breest** - dr
John Pavlik - rh gtr (4/5/42; Sturgeon Bay)   **Hal Block** - sx
Roy Malvitz - bs   **Ronnie Premier (Barzyk)**-voc (8/11/38; Milwaukee)
Bob Casey - dr   **Paul Stefan** - voc (7/26/41; Milwaukee)

Chuck Tyler & the Royal Lancers
Fenway   The Day We Met/She's All Mine   /60
Ronnie Premier & the Royal Lancers
Sara   1020   Angel In My Eyes/So Loved Am I   12/60
Laurie   3091   Angel In My Eyes/So Loved Am I   3/61
Vilas Craig & the Royal Lancers/Badgers & the Royal Lancers:
Cuca   1072   Skinny Minnie Twist/Badgers Twist   3/62
                       (Side 2 reissued on *The Cuca Story, Vol 3*)
Paul Stefan (Stefen, Steffen) & the Royal Lancers
Citation   5003   I Fought The Law[1]/Say Mama   7/62
               5004   Angel In My Eyes/Baby I Don't Care[2]   10/62

Dodge introduced their Royal Lancer in 1957 and the Milwaukee version came out about a year later. In fall of 1962 the Lancers became the owners of the second biggest local hit of the early 60's. Oddly enough, it came precisely as the Legends were racking up the biggest one.

The band's first record, featuring Chuck Tyler, had come about because of a talent contest victory. The Lancers often backed the Comic Books on gigs and eventually Ronnie Premier left that group to work with the Royal Lancers. For a short time both Premier and Tyler were featured with the group. Tyler left to go solo as Tony Grecco.

Not long after the release featuring Premier, Vilas Craig, a singer from Richland Center, was in a serious auto accident while traveling with his band, the Viscounts. With one musician killed and most of remaining members out of action, Craig hired the Royal Lancers as his backing band in the winter of 1961.

It was the next edition of the group that achieved the most success. Paul Stefan took over on lead vocals, Lee Breest moved in on drums, and "I Fought The Law" became a hit. Guitarist Doug Tank thought it should have gone further. "We had a manager named Jay Albrent and he was a record distributor," explains Tank. "Laurie wanted to buy 'I Fought The Law' and he wouldn't let it go because he thought he'd be out in the cold. That's what put the kibosh on that band, because we had a chance to do something. 'I Fought The Law' was cooking along pretty well for a while."

The follow-up record, "Angel In My Eyes" was the same song they had recorded previously with the composer, Ronnie Premier. It was a total departure in style from their hit and it did not fare as well. The Royal Lancers broke up shortly after. "I had an offer to go on the road and back up Jimmy Velvet with Col. Tom Parker, and nobody in the group wanted to go," says leader John Pavlik, who then joined the Green Men out of Minneapolis. "I'm kind of a founder in Milwaukee," he adds, claiming involvement in the careers of the Skunks, Ken Adamany and

---

[1]Crickets LP, 1961; Bobby Fuller Four, 1966
[2]Elvis Presley - *A Date With Elvis* LP, 1959

many others.

Doug Tank recalls Pavlik's mind for business. "I think of the time Fabian came to town and John went out and rented that big Dodge trailer home. He picked him up at the airport and took him everywhere in that, just so that every picture taken was Fabian and the Royal Lancers."

Also see: Tony Grecco (Chuck Tyler)
       Paul Stefan
       "Say Mama"
       Mojo Men (Paul Stefan)
       Comic Books (Ronnie Premier)
       Cite/Citation Records (Jay Albrent)
       Greenmen (John Pavlik)
       Freefall Three (Doug Tank, Roy Malvitz, Lee Breest)
       Linda Hall - Eau Claire
       Vilas Craig - Around The State
Unrelated Royal Lancers: ABC-Paramount, Hi-Mar, Lawn
Sources: Doug Tank telephone interview, 9/6/93, 6/19/94
       Tony Olla telephone interview, 3/15/94
       Vilas Craig, 1993
       Personal recollections
       Osborne-Brown. <u>Rockin' Records.</u>

Saints Five

Santo (Santo) Cincotta - voc	**Gary Lane** - rh gtr (3/28/42; Sturgeon Bay)
Kenny Rogers - ld gtr (Kingsford, MI)	**Gordy Elliot** - gtr (1/22/46; Evergreen Park, IL)
Brad McKay - rh gtr	**John Grignon** - gtr (4/28/42; Marinette)
Jim Nowicki - bs	**Mike Fitzpatrick** - kb
Stu Moebus - dr	**John Dombeck** - dr

Pentagon   2001   Mercy, Mercy[1]/Have Love Will Travel   /66

The Saints Five replaced Danny Peil & the Tigers as the house band on Channel 12's *Sumthin' Else Show*.

Also see: Mad Lads (Gary Lane, Kenny Rogers, Stu Moebus)
       Road Runners, (Kenny Rogers)
       Legends (Brad McKay)
       Shags (Gordy Elliot)

---

[1]Don Covay, 1964

Sources: Gary Lane telephone interview, 8/8/93
         Gordy Elliott telephone interview, 12/93
         Ken Rogers telephone interview, 7/23/94
         Rick Schurk, Tom Fabre, Sam McCue, 1993
         Tourville. <u>Wisconsin . . . Discography.</u>

Royal Lancers: Bob Casey, Doug Tank, Hal Block, John Pavlik, (bottom) Roy Malvitz

Saints Five: Ken Rogers, Jimmy Nowicki,
Santo Cincotta, Gary Lane, Stu Moebus

Savoys: (top) Mike Minikel, Ron LaBode,
(bottom) Ron Faith, Bruce Cole
(courtesy Tom Tourville)

Savoys

Ron Faith - ld gtr
Mike Minikel - pno/gtr   **Bruce Cole** - dr (5/11/47; Milwaukee)
Ron LaBode - bs (5/2/44; Milwaukee)
Brad True - dr

Raynard   10019 Charlena/Pretty One   /65

In addition to their own release the Savoys, did some back up recording for Chicago's Ideals who had scored a regional hit with "The Gorilla" in 1963. The band also did shows with Peter & Gordon and the Dave Clark Five.

Also see: Ricochettes, Invasion, Grand Prix's, Van-Tels, Triumphs (Bruce Cole)
Unrelated Savoys: Bella, Catamount, Christy, Combo, NRM, PDQ, Savoy, Summit
Sources: Ron LaBode telephone interview, 11/28/93
        Bruce Cole telephone interview, 7/27/94
        Deniel Edwards scrapbook, 9/22/93
        Tourville. <u>Wisconsin . . . Discography.</u>
        Osborne-Brown. <u>Rockin' Records.</u>

"Say Mama"

Say Mama, can I go out tonight
Say Mama, would it be all right
They've got a rockin' party goin' down the street
*Say Mama, **DON'T YOU HEAR THAT BEAT***
        (Used by permission of Big D Music, Dallas, TX. Thanks to Jeanne Bullington)

For some reason this obscure Gene Vincent song became a favorite of Milwaukee bands, with no less than four recorded versions in the space of about a year. Co-written by Johnny Earl (real name: Earl Baughman) and guitarist Johnny Meeks, Vincent's original came out about a year after his final chart record. Best known for his 1956 hit, "Be-Bop-A-LuLa," Vincent died from an ulcer hemorrhage in 1971.

Meeks (4/16/37; Gaffney, SC) began working in Vincent's Blue Caps upon the departure of original guitarist Cliff Gallup. He later worked with the Champs and Jimmy Clanton, played on European tours and did years of club work in Southern California. He now lives back in South Carolina, not far from a restaurant owned by his old co-writer, Earl Baughman.

The Legends' Sam McCue reportedly played on Tony Grecco's version, and also filled in on some Rock-A-Fellers gigs around the time they recorded it. McCue says the Legends picked it up from Sheboygan's Crown Jewels. "They did it more like Gene Vincent's record because they had a horn player," he reports. "We just revved it up a little bit and used two guitars instead of horns." (The Crown Jewels never recorded but bassist Jerry Schils and drummer Denny Sachse both went from that group to the Legends). McCue actually blew a word in the tune, singing the line "I've got a notion what you're gonna say" as "I've gotta know just what you're gonna say." The local popularity of the song is part of what prompted me to adapt one of its lines as my title.

Gene Vincent	Capitol	4105	1/59
Rock-A-Fellers	Cuca	1039	6/61
Damon Lee & the Diablos (Minneapolis)	Soma	1181	/61
Tony Grecco	Big Beat	1053	10/61
Legends	Ermine	39	7/62
Paul Stefan & Royal Lancers	Citation	5003	8/62

Also see: Legends
        Trendells - Racine/Kenosha (Damon Lee)
Sources: Johnny Meeks telephone interview, 1993
        Sam McCue telephone interview, 1/2/94
        Whitburn. Record Research.
        Clee. American 45 R.P.M. Records.

Sevilles

Joe Zampach - gtr/bs
Jack Abuya - gtr/bs
Virgil " Butch" Herder - gtr (12/22/43; Milwaukee)
Jerry Crocker - sx
Ronnie Lalich - dr   **Charlie Lewondowski** - pno
                               Mel Lundie (Lewondowski) - dr (1/5/42; Milwaukee)

Ren-Co   1056   Burnell Blues/St. Louis Blues[1]   /61

One of Milwaukee's early rock 'n' roll bands, the Sevilles began around 1958 with three core members from Juneau High School. Their sole release was on their own label, though guitarist Virgil Herder claims they got airplay in New York on an unreleased demo. "Somebody grabbed it from the studio and they were pushing it on the East Coast," says Herder. The song was recorded at radio station WEMP as a promo for the play *Bye Bye Birdie*. "A disc-jockey that we were really close to, O.C. White, found out somehow that it was on a top-20 list in New York City," continues Herder, "and it kind of shocked us."

The band played one of their first club gigs at the College Inn on 27th and College. "The

---

[1]W.C. Handy, 1914; many others, 1916-53

Bonnevilles came in to catch our group and they all got thrown out because they were underage. I kind of enjoyed that," laughs Herder. The Sevilles spent three years at another College Inn in Racine and broke up around 1964.

Also see: Mid-Knighters (Mel Lundie. Charlie Lewondowski)
Unrelated Sevilles: Cal-Gold, Galaxy, J.C.
Sources: Mel Lewondowski telephone interview, 3/6/94
      Virgil Herder telephone interview, 3/12/94
      Osborne-Brown. Rockin' Records.
      Tourville. Wisconsin . . . Discography.

Shags

John Sahli - gtr   **Gordy Elliot** - ld gtr (1/22/46; Evergreen Park, IL)
Mike Lamers - rh gtr/ dr   **Ray McCall** - gtr
Don Luther - bs (6/23/43; Milwaukee)
Paul "Green" Greenwald - dr/fl/pno (5/13/40; Milwaukee)

Raynard	10034	Dance Woman/Cause I Love You	/66
Capitol	5995	Stop And Listen/Melissa	10/67
		(The Shag - Side 1 reissued on Pebbles *Highs In The Mid 60's, Vol. 10*)	

Related:

Just Sunshine	507	Heartbroken Heartbreaker/Abalone	8/73
		(Ducks)	

LP:

Just Sunshine		(Ducks)	/73

"We were sort of beatniks at art school," says Paul Greenwald. "The Beatles came along and we bought instruments - we had the hair already - and we just started teaching ourselves how to play. We started doing Stones-like stuff. We were almost an instant hit with the art people just because we were nuts and really energetic and danceable. We were terrible musically but easy to dance to, and we looked cool (laughs)."

Playing at O'Brad's (827 E. Locust) for over a year and a half, their reputation grew. Other club gigs included Le Bistro and the Scene. "It was amazing," Greenwald continues. "We became such a sensation and it was mainly because we had costumes and lights and explosions and smoke bombs and everything you could think of. So, record companies would come up and they'd say, 'Good God, we've got to get these guys.' So, we would go down to Chicago and record, and without the smoke bombs and the costumes and the whole thing, they listened to us said, 'Geez, these guys suck!'"

Capitol remained interested enough to release one single, an anti-drug song. The Shag opened for the Blues Project in New York and, in May 1968, the band moved to Marin County,

California. They did some gigs on the Coast, including the Whisky in Hollywood, but the members began to go their own ways.

Don Luther joined a band called Elixir, which included two former members of H.P. Lovecraft. Elixir was managed by Bill Graham but no recordings were released. Luther and Gordy Elliot then joined the Ducks, which included former members of Blue Cheer. The Ducks recorded for Just Sunshine in 1973.

Elliot also worked with Big Brother and the Holding Company after Janis Joplin's death. He has done a great deal of session work, had his own studio and has been playing with musicians from Van Morrison's old band. Among his Milwaukee memories he says, "Sam McCue (Legends) was one of my early heros."

Greenwald went back to Milwaukee as The Space Captain, a DJ at WQFM from 1973-78, then returned to Sonoma County, California. Mike Lamers opened Mom's Apple Grave (named after one of Shag's tunes), a clothing shop on San Francisco's famed Haight Street. The shop catered to Jimi Hendrix and many other stars.

All members except Ray McCall got together for a reunion party in 1992, and Greenwald and Luther still play together for their own enjoyment.

Also see: Saints Five (Gordy Elliot)
Unrelated Shags: Cameo, Capitol (Shaggs), Eagle, Golden Voice, Jo-Jo, Kayden, Laurie, Nutta,
  Palmer, Power, Rounder, Sammy, Taurus, Third World
 Sources: Paul Greenwald telephone interview, 9/19/93
  Don Luther telephone interview, 10/16/93
  Gordy Elliot telephone interview, 12/93
  Tourville. Wisconsin . . . Discography.
  Liner notes. Pebbles *Highs In The Mid Sixties, Vol. 10.*
  Clee. American 45 R.P.M. Records.
  Osborne-Brown. Rockin' Records.

Shaprels

Jimmy Meier - voc
Bob Sczweda - ld gtr
Tom Richards - rh gtr
Bob Mehring - bs/org (1/8/45; Milwaukee)
Don Hrnjak - dr (9/19/47; Milwaukee)

Feature	103	A Fool For Your Lies/You're Cheating On Me	/66
		(Side 1 reissued on Pebbles *Highs In The Mid 60's, Vol 15*)	
		Rock-A-Boo/Dare I Weep, Dare I Mourn	/67
Chess	1993	Rock-A-Boo/Dare I Weep, Dare I Mourn	/67

Tee Pee   39/40   Clara Bloomtree/Desert Maiden   12/67
PKC   1017   A Fool For Your Lies/You're Cheating On Me   /69

Shags: Mike Lamers, Paul Greenwald, Don Luther, John Sahli (courtesy Paul Greenwald)

Shaprels: Jim Meier, Bob Mehring, Tom Richards, Don Hrnjak, (horizontal) Bob Sczweda
   (courtesy Don Hrnjak)

The Shaprels began in 1964 with a dance at Whitnall High and went on to work clubs such as the Catalina (900 S. 16th). Despite the gigs and the number of record releases they had, the musicians were virtually unknown to their contemporaries around town, as they never mingled much.

For a short time it looked as if the Chess release they might bring recognition on a much larger scale. "We got some local action," says Bob Mehring, "but, unfortunately, our manager got greedy. He went in to Marshall Chess and he was demanding $30,000 to promote the group. Marshall Chess said, 'You don't need that, we're promoting the group.' He said, 'You don't understand them like I do.' Marshall Chess said, 'Well, you don't understand them at all, because they're shelved. We're going to pull the record,' and within a couple of days it was gone. We had a contract that had provisions in it for worldwide distribution and it was all down the tubes."

The members went their own ways around 1968. Singer Jimmy Meier is believed to be the only one who did additional recording, a 45 with the Kids From Wisconsin on Cuca. In a statement that may hit home many other bands, Mehring says, "We had a lot of fun, we had some tremendous opportunities, and it all went by the boards when some things happened that we had no control over."

Unrelated Shaprels: Bennett Ent.
Sources: Bob Mehring telephone interview, 7/25/94
        Doug Tank, 1993
        Tourville. <u>Wisconsin . . . Discography.</u>

Sidewalk Skipper Band

Brian Balestrieri - B3/pno/gtr
D.A. (Dave) McDowell - gtr/kb
Rick Novac - gtr   **Barry Biehoff** - bs
Joe Balestrieri - bs   **Tom Janovic** - gtr
Tom Youkam - dr

Capitol	2127	Strawberry Tuesday/Cynthia At The Garden	2/66
	2205	(Would You Believe) It's Raining Flowers In My House/	
		Seventeenth Summer	7/68
Teen Town	113	Sidewalk Skipper/Jeannie At The Circus	/69

A studio project rather than a gigging band, this group recorded an album's worth of material in 1968, "but internal changes at Capitol caused problems," says Brian Balestrieri. "For example, whose name was to get credit." The Balestrieri brothers went into the club business with *Humpin' Hanna's* and *The Stone Toad* in the 70's.

Sources: Brian Balestrieri letter, 12/30/93
Bob Metzger, 1993
Tourville. <u>Wisconsin . . . Discography.</u>
Clee. <u>American 45 R.P.M. Records.</u>

Skunks: Larry Lynne, Rick Allen, Duane Lundy, Tony Kolp

Skunks

Larry Lynne (Ostricki) - gtr (12/14/40; Waukesha)
Rick Allen (Sutherland) - kb ((3/15/43; Los Angeles, CA)
Tony Kolp - sx/org   **Randy Klein** - rh gtr (8/22/44; Chicago, IL)
Duane Lundy - dr   **Paul Edwards (Fredericks)** - dr (11/13/41; Springfield, IL)
Jack Tappy - bs
Teddy Peplinski - dr (10/7/42; Milwaukee)

Era	3155	Ring Rang Roo/There's A Little Bit Of Heaven (Unbelievables)	11/65
USA	865	Elvira/The Journey	1/67
Quill	120	Don't Ask Why/Do The Duck[1]	6/67
	121	Little Angel/It's Only Love[2]	/67

---

[1] Jackie Lee, 1965
[2] Beatles - *Rubber Soul* LP, 1965

Teen Town	103	I Recommend Her/I Need No One	/67
World Pacific	77889	I Recommend Her/I Need No One	/67
Teen Town	104	Crying[1]/By The Time I Get To Phoenix[2] (Randy)	/68
	106	Small Town Girl/You Better Hold On To Me	/68
	110	Doing Nothing/Listen To The News Today	5/69
White Whale	322	Doing Nothing/	8/69
	325	Doing Nothing/Listen To The News Today	9/69
Sheri	100	Heart Teaser/You, Me And Happiness	/70

EP:

WRIT	--	Small Town Girl/(others by Robbs, Tygers)	/68

LP:

Teen Town	101	Getting Started	/68

If the Legends were the Milwaukee 60's band Most-Expected-To-Make-It-But-Didn't, the Skunks may be the runners-up. It was spring, 1964, a time when bands began to look seriously for gimmicks. The Beatles had just exploded into the American consciousness with long hair and a funny name (Yes, that hair was considered long, and "Beatles" sounded funny back then). The four musicians assembled by guitarist Larry Lynne dyed their hair black with a white stripe down the side and picked an even funnier name. It got their picture in the Milwaukee Journal and they opened at Monreal's on 16th & National.

The Skunks recorded some demos in Chicago utilizing the services of famed bluesman Sonny Boy Williamson on harmonica. Despite Lynne's claim that "they were great. They came out powerful," nothing was released. Around this time Lynne, Rick Allen and Tony Kolp also played on a session with the Mojo Men (who would follow them into the Monreal's gig).

Allen and Duane Lundy left to be replaced by Jack Tappy and Teddy Peplinski, Kolp moved to organ, and the band moved out to Papa Joe's (16600 W. Bluemound, Brookfield). A little later, Randy Klein came in to replace Kolp and the band headed for Southern California. They spent most of the summer of 1965 at a club called Gold Street in Garden Grove. (In August, none other than the Mojo Men would show up to rival them at the Chatterbox a mile away.)

The band recorded for Era but label owner Herb Newman didn't believe in the name Skunks, so it was issued as the Unbelievables. Nothing happened there and another tune was cut at the famous Gold Star Studio, (site of many Phil Spector sessions). The result was a song that may have been 14 years too early. "Elvira" became famous by the Oak Ridge Boys in 1981, though the original by songwriter Dallas Frazier charted briefly in 1966. (Frazier also wrote "Alley Oop" - maybe you noticed the similarity). The Skunks had picked it up from yet a different source.

---

[1]Roy Orbison, 1961
[2]Glen Campbell, 1967

"I used to listen a lot to WLAC in Nashville," explains Lynne, "and a guy by the name of Baby Ray was a blues musician. It was done as a blues song. When Oak Ridge got a hold of it - there is absolutely nothing different other than shifting the bridge part to the middle instead of at the end, so that was kind of crazy. I'm still driving a '65 Buick and they're driving a 50-foot long limousine"(laughs).

The record was not released until after the Skunks returned to Milwaukee and hooked up with manager Jon Hall. It was about this time that drummer Peplinski left to be replaced by Lynne's old Bonnevilles mate, Paul Fredericks (aka Paul Edwards).

Ironically, the Skunks achieved their greatest success after Lynne, the last original member, left. Their first release on Teen Town was picked up by World Pacific (a division of Liberty) and became their biggest hit, though still falling short of national charts. "We were like a semi-national band at that point of time," says Paul Edwards. "We were big in the sun belt - we played the Nashville State Fair two consecutive years. We did a lot of national TV, we were in California, and we were in the Midwest. It was like we weren't local anymore, yet we weren't national. We were somewhere in the middle - no man's land."

The Skunks final release came out on Sheri, a new company formed by Edwards who then moved into that side of the business full time. The endeavor eventually developed into Trax 32, one of the largest studios in Wisconsin. Most of the other members have continued to play into the 90's.

Also see: Bonnevilles (Lynne, Edwards, Peplinski, Allen)
      Mad Lads (Lynne, Edwards)
      Larry Lynne Group
      Apollos (Randy Klein)
      Teen Town (Jon Hall)
Unrelated Skunks: Arvee, Mercury, Skunks
Sources: Larry Lynne telephone interview, 1/30/93
      Paul Edwards telephone interview, 5/9/93
      Personal recollections
      Randy Klein telephone interview, 3/94
      Clee. <u>American 45 R.P.M. Records.</u>
      Posniak, Alan. "Badger Beat." <u>Milwaukee Journal,</u> date unknown - courtesy Brian Lake

Pete Sorce
(6/22/44; Milwaukee)

Count   1002   I'm Too Young For Love/You Got It Good   /59

Leaf	8973	Have You Ever Had The Blues/For Your Precious Love[1]	/62
		(Driftwoods)	
Fan Jr.	5080	I'm Too Young To Love/Have You Ever Had The Blues	
		(Pete Source & the Driftwoods)	
Tee Pee	117/118	Dee Dee/Mojo Workin' (Golden Catalinas)	/67
Pro-Gress	503	Girl I Love You/Laugh And Smile (Big Apple)	/75

Pete Sorce started in the business early, winning on the *Ted Mack Original Amateur Hour* at the age of 10. His performance of Frankie Laine's "Shine" (1948) took first place in Milwaukee and earned him a trip to New York where he placed second. His first record came a few years later and Sorce says it attained some success locally and took him to "within two inches of the Dick Clark Show."

Sorce's subsequent recordings were done as a member of various bands, including one during a stint with Appleton's Golden Catalinas. The singer also worked with the Pharaohs when Little Artie left to join the Mob. He was with the Good Intentions and Big Apple in the early 70's.

Also see: Catalinas - Appleton/Fox Cities, Driftwoods
Sources: Pete Sorce telephone interviews, 2/13/94, 4/9/94

Starfires: Rick Sherman, Kip Maercklein, Mickey Abrams, Tom Lindemann, Bill Kucharek
(courtesy Tom Lindemann)

---

[1]Jerry Butler, 1958

Starfires/Tommy Lee & the Starfires

Tommy Lee (Lindemann) - gtr (3/7/45; Milwaukee)
Rick Sherman - gtr
Kip Maercklein - bs   **Bill Kucharek** - pno
Bill Orr - dr   **Mickey Abrams** - dr

Sara   6363   Nervous Breakdown[1]/Lost Love   6/63

"It was kind of exciting for me," says Tom Lindemann, "when I received the Local 8 Musician's Union membership roster and found my name right below Walter Liberace's. Heady stuff for a 17-year old kid." The Starfires lasted from about 1962-66 and Lindemann says their sole recording did well regionally, selling about 6,000 copies. Bassist Kip Maercklein reportedly went on to work with Elvin Bishop and Mike Bloomfield in the 70's.

Unrelated Starfires: Accent, Apt, Bargin, Big Sound, College, D&H, Decca, Duel, G.I.,
          LaBrea, Ohio, Pama, Round, Sonic, Triumph, Yardbird
Sources: Tom Lindemann telephone interview and letter, 3/12/94, 3/23/94
          Osborne-Brown. Rockin' Records.

Paul Stefan
(Paul Stefaniak - 7/26/41; Milwaukee)

New Phoenix   102   I Had A Dream/ (see Valiants)   /60
                            (Valiants)
Paul Stefen & the Royal Lancers
Citation   5003   I Fought The Law/Say Mama   7/62
                  5004   Angel In My Eyes/(You're So Square) Baby I Don't Care   11/62
Paul Steffen & the Apollos
Cite   5007   Hey Lonely One/Devil's Soul Is Black   10/63
Dot   16573   Hey Lonely One/Devil's Soul Is Black   1/64
Cite   5008   Cry Angel Cry/You   /64
Paul & the Pack
Tower   4261   Hiding From Myself/ (flip by the Mad Doctors)   1/67
LP:
Tower   5053   Dr. Goldfoot And The Girl Bombs   1/67
                  (Various artists including Paul & the Pack)

Possibly the best pure voice in pop music to come out of Milwaukee in the 60's, Paul Stefan started as a drummer for the Valiants. He sang lead on the 'B' side of their only release. Stefan

---

[1]Eddie Cochran LP

credits local singer/songwriter Ronnie Premier as an important early influence. Despite different spellings on record labels (Stefen, Steffen), the preferred spelling is Stefan.

In 1962, Stefan was working days at Radio Doctors (record store) in downtown Milwaukee and playing five or six nights a week at the 616 Club in Green Bay. This made for quite a hectic schedule but it was an incident at the day job that led to the record. "The Crickets had an album out of their own (after Buddy Holly's death)," Stefan explains, "and Gordy at Radio Doctors came to me and said, 'Do you know how many requests I'm getting for I Fought The Law?' In those days they didn't want to buy an album, they just wanted to buy a 45. I think it was in the thousands that wanted that song. He said, 'Why don't you take this album and play it for the guys and see what you can do with it?' So I took it to them and they all laughed. 'Oh, come, we don't want to do that. It's stupid.' So Jay (Albrent), our manager, stepped in and said, 'Well, let's give it a try. You never know."

The Lancers drove out to the Cuca Studios in Sauk City. Stefan first tried a Buddy Holly type vocal, which he thought sounded "like Johnny Mathis trying to sing rock 'n' roll." He then asked for the lights to be lowered for a better mood and the result was a Presley style vocal and a record that took off. "I Fought The Law" hit the top of the Mid-Western Top 40 chart September 17, 1962.

Many Milwaukee music fans will remember the magazine section of the Milwaukee Journal, Sunday, October 21, 1962. The front cover photo featured Paul Stefan & the Royal Lancers posed in the middle of downtown Wisconsin Avenue (the picture was taken at 4:00 a.m. on a Sunday). The Lancers and the Legends were the local stars of the day.

The follow-up record, "Angel In My Eyes," was the same song the Lancers had recorded previously with the writer, Ronnie Premier, on vocal. The Stefan-led version was a good doo-wop ballad and it got some play, but it was probably too different from the hit to capture the same audience. The group broke up shortly after.

A year later Stefan had another hit, this time with the Apollos. "Hey Lonely One" made the top five in town and got picked up nationally by Dot. Both sides were written by the group's bassist, Roland Stone. However, by the time the follow-up was released, Stefan had already decided to move to Southern California. A farewell party was held at Claude's (5048 N. 35th) June 11, 1964.

In late 1965 Stefan wandered into a club in Downey (suburban Los Angeles) to find Milwaukee's Mojo Men performing. Not long after that the group parted with lead singer Doug Weiss and, after a brief fling backing Billy Joe Burnette, hired Stefan. In early 1966 the Mojo Men signed with Mike Curb. The first recording was a filler tune for a movie soundtrack album. However, the San Francisco Mojo Men were starting to make some noise (they would later hit with "Sit Down I Think I Love You") and Curb wanted a new name. At a meeting in Curb's office the consensus was for Paul & the Pack, a name that was never used after that record.

The Mojo Men instead became the Portraits but, shortly after summertime gigs back in Milwaukee and Appleton, Stefan got drafted. At Fort Gordon, Georgia, he met and worked with former 50's teen star Frankie Lymon ("Why Do Fools Fall In Love," 1956) who was also fulfilling his military obligation. After his discharge, Stefan returned to the Portraits for a while. By the mid 70's he had left the music business and around 1990 he moved to the Yuma, Arizona, area.

Also see: Valiants
        Royal Lancers
        Apollos
        Roland Stone
        Comic Books (Ronnie Premier)
        Mojo Men
Sources: Paul Stefan interview, 1989
        Personal recollections

Roland Stone
(Roland Oeller - 3/17//41; Milwaukee)

USA   1212   Lost Love/Moanin' Soul   (I/)   /58

"I think I was the very first rock musician in Milwaukee to get on a label," says Roland Oeller, who claims Bobby Darin suggested his stage name. Oeller overdubbed all the instruments on "Lost Love." The tune was later recorded by the Legends on their first LP, re-titled as "Legendermaine." That same LP contains another of Oeller's tunes, "I Wish I Knew," which reportedly had once been considered by Buddy Holly. Oeller met Holly when the latter appeared at the Eagles Million Dollar Ballroom in Milwaukee. The young star expressed his interest in the song but the tragic plane crash came shortly after that.

A left-handed guitarist/bassist, Oeller joined the Royal Lancers as they were disintegrating and changed them into the Apollos. He wrote all of their recorded material. By the time the band landed in San Francisco around 1966 he had begun to grow disenchanted with changes in the music business. He left and became an early member of Moby Grape but departed that group before they did any recording. Moving to Arizona in the late 70's, Oeller had his own sign business and has since worked in commercial art.

Sources: Roland Oeller telephone interview, 8/7/94
        Grider, Edd. "Roland Stone - A Wisconsin Rocker." <u>Mean Mountain Music Magazine</u>
                date unknown.
        Personal recollections

Roland Stone, Paul Stefan
(courtesy Roland Oeller)

Tony's Tygers: (top) Fred Euler,
Dennis Duchrow, Tony Dancy,
(bottom) Craig Fairchild, Dave Kuck

Sammy Surf

Nu Sound   1023   Love That First Step/Don't Get Around Much Anymore   /62

Source: Tourville. <u>Wisconsin . . . Discography</u>

Bill Taylor

Citation   5002   Income Taxes And You/Lullaby To Carolyn   /62

WOKY DJ Bill Taylor also wrote the lyrics to Sam McCue's solo recording, "What To Do."
Taylor continued in radio in Los Angeles in the late 60's.

Unrelated Bill Taylor: Pen
Sources: Clee. <u>American 45 R.P.M. Records.</u>

Tony's Tygers

Tony Dancy - gtr (2/28/51; Milwaukee)
Dave Kuck - gtr   **Lanny Hale** - dr
Craig Fairchild - kb   **Donna**   - voc
Joe Turano - kb   **Gloria**   - voc

Fred Euler - bs
Dennis Duchrow - dr

Teen Town	102	Little By Little/Days And Nights	2/68
		(shown as Tonys Tygres on some pressings)	
A&M	921	Little By Little/Days And Nights	4/68
Teen Town	105	I Still Love Her/I Can't Believe	6/68
	107	Debbie On My Mind/I'll Know	/68
WRIT EP	--	Debbie On My Mind/ (2 by Robbs, 1 by Skunks)	/69
Jamie	1378	Sing It Together/Resurrection (Tygers)	/69

LP:

Teen Town	102	Little By Little	/68

Passion

Target	1014	Midnight In The Park/She's A Very Special Girl	12/70
Teen Town	121	Headaches And Heartaches/Castaway	/71

Though the Tygers and the Tigers both performed in Milwaukee about the same time, never the twain did meet. "I don't think they knew we existed," says Tony Dancy referring to Danny Peil & the Tigers. "I do every once in a while get asked about that and I'm usually not sure what they're talking about." Dancy's group was the younger one, just beginning their teen gigs about the time that Peil's band was changing their name (from the Apollos), and not really hitting their stride until after the older one had dissolved.

In the summer of 1967 the Tygers won an area battle of the bands and traveled to Boston where they came in second. "Little By Little," the band's first record, did well enough to earn a national release on A&M but, despite an album and three more singles, not much happened. "The other ones I kind of don't even consider," Dancy says. Finally, in an attempt to inject new life into the band, Dancy added two girl singers and changed the name to Passion. The resulting two singles are barely remembered even by Dancy.

With a move to Los Angeles in 1971, Dancy landed a gig as a staff writer composing music for Flintstones cartoons, the Brady Bunch and other television shows. He formed another band, Quiffy, along with Milwaukee keyboardist Doug West and tried for a record deal but none materialized. Dancy has since returned to Milwaukee and continues to play clubs. From the vantage point of 1994, the Tyger who made the biggest tracks is keyboard player Joe Turano, who works with superstar Michael Bolton.

Unrelated Tigers: Colpix, Roulette (Tony Sales & the Tigers)
Sources: Tony Dancy telephone interviews, 6/20/93, 7/17/93
      Tourville. Wisconsin . . . Discography.

Triumphs

Jim Peterson - gtr
Tom Runte - gtr
Jerry George - sx   **Tony Gazzana** - voc
Mike Prescott - bs   **Bruce Cole** - dr (5/11/47; Milwaukee)
Bob Hahm - dr

IFF   151   Susie In My History Class/Surfside Date   /63

Also see: Grand Prix's, Ricochettes, Invasion, Van-Tels, Savoys (Bruce Cole)
        Thee Prophets - On The Charts (Tony Gazzana, Jerry George)
Unrelated Triumphs: Barclay, Dante, Genuine, Joed, Kab, Okeh, Swan, Triumph, Verve, Volt
Sources: Gene Recob telephone interview, 7/17/94
        Tourville. <u>Wisconsin . . . Discography.</u>
        Osborne-Brown. <u>Rockin' Records.</u>

Uniques

Earl King - pno
Johnny Taylor - ld tenor
Charles Jordan - 2nd tenor
Leonard Garr - baritone
Bob Morland - bs/bass voc

Peacock   1677   Somewhere/Right Now   5/57
               1695   Picture Of My Baby/Mysterious   9/60

Originally Earl King & the Kingsmen, this r&b group began in early 1956. The first release was recorded in Chicago and label owner Don Robey changed their name to the Uniques. The group toured with other name acts from the Duke/Peacock stable, including Bobby Bland and Junior Parker. They also worked in bigger package tours with Brook Benton and the Coasters. The second record was done in Houston.

Johnny Taylor left in 1963 to join Stanley Morgan's Ink Spots. Taylor worked in Las Vegas with that group until 1986 when he returned to Milwaukee. In 1988 he formed Long Way Round, a group that includes Leonard Garr from the old Uniques. This new group has created a scholarship fund to help enable central city high school students to attend college.

Unrelated Uniques: Amber, Bangar, Capitol, Demand, Dot, End, Gone, Flippin', Lucky Four, Mr. Cee, Paramount, Paula, Pride, Roulette, 620, Tee Kay, United Southern Artists (Also, the above Earl King and Johnny Taylor have no connection with the more famous artists by those names.)

Sources: Grendysa, Peter. "Uniques Fans Were Adults During '50s R&B Era." <u>Record Collector's Monthly</u> 9/93: 11
Osborne-Brown. <u>Rockin' Records.</u>

Valiants

Jim Bing - rh gtr
Tony Kern - ld gtr
Gene Stankowski - sx
Ralph Stevens - pno/org
Paul Yopps - bs (1/18/36; Waukesha)
Paul Stefan (Stefaniak) - dr (7/26/41; Milwaukee)

New Phoenix 60-9150 Mutha/I Had A Dream   /60

"Mutha" features Jim Bing on lead vocal while the flip is the first Paul Stefan vocal on record. Paul Yopps later started his own label, Revive Records.

Also see: Paul Stefan
    Jack Merlin
    Revive Records - Wisconsin Labels
Unrelated Valiants: Amcan, Cortland, Destination, Dot, Fairlane, Imperial, Joy, KC, Keen, Roulette, Shar-Dee, Speck, Valor
Sources: Paul Stefan interview, 1989
    Paul Yopps telephone interview, 1993
    Tourville. <u>Wisconsin . . . Discography.</u>
    Osborne-Brown. <u>Rockin' Records.</u>

Van-Tels

Jerry Trado - voc
Joey Piccolo - ld gtr
Gary Jay - rh gtr
Chris King - bs
Skip Kamrath - dr

Bruce Cole - dr (5/11/47; Milwaukee)
Brad Craig - voc
Steve Fromm - voc
Bob Hershey - voc
Gene "Yogi" Recob - sx (9/20/45; Milwaukee)
Dennis Pleskeschek - bs/tb
Carl Biancuzzo - dr
Mike Balistrieri - kb/fl
Dave Zylka - tp

Cite   5009   Baby What You Want/Everybody But Me /64

Raynard   1085   Ain't Too Proud To Beg[1]/Stand By Me[2]   /68

Between their inception and the time of their second recording, the Van-Tels had gone through a complete change of personnel. That second record was done as a souvenir for the Whitefish Bay Post-Prom dance. The band continued for some time after that (with still more personnel changes) and became a very successful club group booking through Ken Adamany.

Also see: James Hanns & Soul Entertainers (Gene Recob)
         Grand Prix's, Invasion, Ricochettes, Savoys (Bruce Cole)
Sources: Brad Craig telephone interview 1993
         Gene Recob telephone interview, 7/17/94
         Tourville. <u>Wisconsin . . . Discography.</u>

Van-Tels: (rear) Joe Piccolo, Bruce Cole, Chris King, (front) Gary Jay, Steve Fromm (courtesy Bruce Cole)

Walking Sticks: Dick Schurk, Paul Rubitsky, Bob Barian, Keith Dreher, Kurt Kronhelm (courtesy Rick Schurk)

Chuck Velvet

USA   1224   Red Lipstick/Wonders Of Love   /60

Source: Tourville. <u>Wisconsin . . . Discography</u>

---

[1]Temptations, 1966
[2]Ben E. King, 1961; many others

Walking Sticks

"Little Bob" Barian - voc (10/13/42; Milwaukee)   **Gary Josing** - org
Keith Dreher - gtr (dec, ca: 1972)   **Mike Welch** - voc (12/30/43; Milwaukee)
Kurt Kronhelm - sx (6/9/47; Milwaukee)   **J.D. (Clarence) Harper** - ld gtr
Dick Schurk -bs (4/18/41; Milwaukee)   **Norm (Norbert) Drifka** - org
Paul Spencer (Rubitzky) - dr   **Denny Schuenemann** - bs

Raynard   10042 A Hundred Pounds Of Clay[1]/Why[2]   /65

The Walking Sticks rose from the remnants of the Renegades in late 1964. They, along with Dee Robb & the Starliners, opened the Dave Clark Five Show at the Arena December 15. "This was Dave Clark's 22nd birthday," says Rick Schurk, "and there were no less than 30 or 40 cakes backstage!"

By 1966 the line-up had changed extensively with only Paul Rubitzky and Kurt Kronhelm remaining. Mike Welch was the singer on their only recording. The band did a two-year engagement at Beneath The Street (3507 W. Burleigh) and eventually evolved into the Good Intentions in the 70's.

Bassist Dick Schurk (now known as Rick) left for California in 1965, later moving to the Seattle area. Mike Welch continues to sing around Milwaukee in the 90's. Kurt Kronhelm has remained at the helm the Good Intentions for over 20 years, employing many musicians during that time. The band recorded for Brewtown in the 70's, appeared at Harrah's Reno and Lake Tahoe, the Thunderbird in Las Vegas, and continues to be very popular in Milwaukee.

Also see: Comic Books (Bob Barian)
         Renegades
         Mid-Knighters (Keith Dreher)
Sources: Rick Schurk letters, 9/21/92, 6/30/94
         Kurt Kronhelm telephone interview, 12/19/93
         Mike Welch telephone interview, 6/14/94

Wanderer's Rest

Richard Podraza - ld gtr (1/9/48; Milwaukee)
Michael Podraza - rh gtr
Michael Milonczyk - bs
Stanley Starich - dr

---

[1]Gene McDaniels, 1961
[2]Lonnie Mack

Wright	6771	The Boat That I Row[1]/The Girl That I Love	7/67
		(Side 1 reissued on Pebbles *Highs In The Mid 60's - Vol 10*)	
	67101	You'll Forget[2]/Agripine III	10/67
		(Side 1 reissued on Pebbles *Highs In The Mid 60's - Vol 15*)	
	6813	Temptation[3]/Love Is A Beautiful Thing[4]	1/68

A young band playing mostly CYO and fraternity dances, Wanderer's Rest found a backer in West Bend DJ Ken Wright who put out their three records. "Mr. Wright really liked Neil Diamond," explains Richard Podraza. "We recorded 'The Boat That I Row' and it wasn't more than two or three weeks after we recorded it that Lulu released it (flip side of 'To Sir With Love')." When the draft claimed two of the members in 1969, the group disbanded.

Sources: Richard Podraza, 8/2/94
       Tourville. Wisconsin . . . Discography.

Wanted

Chuck Travis (Cherney) - gtr (8/1/41; Milwaukee)
Harry McCullough - gtr
Tony Wells - kb
Paul Leaken - bs
Paul Polizak - dr

Demo	1046	A Tribute To G.B./The Wanted	/66
Chuck Travis			
Round Up	24587	Don't Worry Baby/I Won't Say I Love You Anymore	/71
	3657	Sea Of Love[5]/I've Had It[6]	/73
Energy	105	Gone Too Soon/Tear Drop Blues	/75
Round Up	26401	Smile Now, Cry Later/Gimme A Sign	/76

The Green Bay Packers were big in the 60's, but the title "A Tribute To G.B." is not about the football team as one might guess. "It was just an initial," says Chuck Travis. "We thought we'd use an initial that might catch on." The Wanted stayed together about three years. Travis continues to perform oldies and country music in the 90's.

Unrelated Wanted: A&M, Detroit Sound

---

[1]Neil Diamond - *Just For You* LP, 1967
[2]Neil Diamond - *Just For You* LP, 1967
[3]Bing Crosby, 1934; Everly Brothers, 1961; many others
[4]Young Rascals - *Collections* LP, 1967
[5]Phil Phillips, 1959
[6]Bell Notes, 1959

Sources: Chuck Travis telephone interviews and letter, 1/20/94, 5/8/94
            Tourville. <u>Wisconsin . . . Discography.</u>

Sonny Williams

USA   900   Sweetest Little Girl In Town/You Didn't Find Her That Way   /68

Williams was a country artist who may have also done some earlier recording.

Sources: Johnny Carver telephone interview, 12/19/93
            Clee. <u>American 45 R.P.M. Records.</u>

Wrest

Bob Krause - voc (8/6/49; Milwaukee)
Tom Witter - gtr
Bob Sowinski - gtr
Carl Mussman - org
Ed Wegner - bs
Randy Fare - dr (8/9/49; Milwaukee)

Target	1003	Bet Your Sweet Bippy/Hatfield Junction	2/69
Tower	484	Bet Your Sweet Bippy/Hatfield Junction	3/69
Target	1013	The Two Of Us[1]/Old Joe[2]	11/70

"You bet your sweet bippy" ranked right up near "Sock it to me" as one of the popular phrases from *Rowan & Martin's Laugh-In* in the late 60's and, since the latter was made into a hit song by Mitch Ryder & the Detroit Wheels, someone figured "Bippy" could do it, too. In fact, the suggestion that the song might get them on the TV show helped convince the Wrest to put it on tape. "We reluctantly recorded the song but it wasn't our style of music," says Randy Fare.

With a battle-of-the-bands victory in 1968, the Wrest had won the opportunity to represent Wisconsin against 34 other bands in the national event at Steel Pier, NJ. After placing fourth and returning to Milwaukee, they recorded the song for Al Posniak's Target label. Despite making the Midwest top ten and going national on the Tower label, there was no follow-up. "That was that bubble-gum era," says singer Bob Krause. "We went into the studio and did a couple of other songs but it really wasn't the right time anymore for that stuff. Everything just wasn't turning out the way we wanted." Over a year had passed before a second Target single was finally released.

---

[1]Beatles - *Let It Be* LP, 1970
[2]Guess Who - *Canned Wheat* LP, 1969

The group's plans to cut "Celebrate," from the second Three Dog Night LP, were stymied when the latter band released their single. "We were on the way down to Chicago to record it when we heard it," says Krause.

Krause went on to sing in the 70's with Truc, a group that toured the country and had a national release on United Artists. He has owned Robert's restaurant/bar since 1978 and still does occasional gigs.

Some 17 years after their hit, the Wrest (minus Krause) decided to try a reunion concert in the form of a free party at Cudahy's Victory Hall. It went over so well that the band, expanded to 14 pieces, has continued to do yearly events to benefit charities such as *Midwest Athletes Against Childhood Cancer* and the *Muscular Dystrophy Association.*

Sources: Randy Fare telephone interview, 8/15/93
          Bob Krause telephone interview, 7/16/94
          Tourville. <u>Wisconsin . . . Discography.</u>
          Posniak, Alan. "Badger Beat." <u>Milwaukee Journal,</u> date unknown - courtesy Brian Lake.

Various Artists

Century   3313   Young America Rock 'n' Roll Songs   12/65
                       (Yorks, 7 Wonders, Coachmen, Shags, Destinations, Overtures,
                        Rogues, Fastbacks, Woodsmen, Ethics, Patriots, Radicals)

This album consists of live recordings of the entries in a Milwaukee Sentinel battle-of-the-bands contest.

Source: Tourville. <u>Wisconsin . . . Discography</u>

Historical and Relocated

Louie Bashell
(7/1/14; Milwaukee)

Accordionist Louie Bashell was probably Milwaukee's most popular polka band leader and even managed a couple of crossover pop hits. His "Messin' Around With Louie" and "Oklahoma Boogie" on RCA scored big locally in 1953 and early 1954 respectively. Both tunes were shuffle rhythm pieces, one instrumental, one with a vocal. They were, in fact, so similar as to be virtually the same tune, differing only by the added lyrics on "Boogie."

Bashell also recorded for Pfau, Mercury and King. In 1987 he became the first polka musician to receive the National Heritage Fellowship of the National Endowment for the Arts.

Sources: Louie Bashell letter, 6/22/93
         Corenthal. Wisconsin Music.

Lew Burdette
(Selva Lewis Burdette - 11/22/26; Nitro, WV)

Pitcher Lew Burdette was not really a Wisconsinite, nor much of a recording artist, but he was important to the Milwaukee Braves - and he did have a record out. He pitched for the Braves from 1953-63. His baseball record: 18 years in the majors with a 203-144 won-lost record and an E.R.A. of 3.66. His musical record:

Dot   15672 Three Strikes And You're Out/Mary Lou   12/57

Sources: Reichler, Joseph L. The Baseball Encyclopedia. New York: Macmillan, 1984
         Clee. American 45 R.P.M. Records.

Johnny Carver
(John David Carver - 11/24/38; Jackson, MS)

Johnny Carver moved from Mississippi to Milwaukee in 1957. He became one of the most popular local country acts of the early 60's before seeking recording opportunities in Los Angeles. "The reason that I went out there as opposed to Nashville," he explains, "was that I knew that there were more night clubs, and I knew that I could make a living out there easier than Nashville." Not long after his arrival in Southern California, Carver was leading the house band at the famous Palomino Club in North Hollywood.

Heading straight for the major labels, Carver secured his initial release on Dot, followed by Imperial in 1966. Over the next 25 years, he placed 28 records on Billboard's Country Singles chart, appearing on Imperial, United Artists, Epic, ABC, ABC-Dot, Equity, Tanglewood and Monument. Though he never crossed over to the pop charts, two of his biggest hits were covers of pop tunes.

Biggest Chart Hits:

Tie A Yellow Ribbon Round The Old Oak Tree[1]	#5 C	/73
You Really Haven't Changed	6 C	/73
Don't Tell (That Sweet Ole Lady Of Mine)	10 C	/74
Afternoon Delight[2]	9 C	/76

Sources: Johnny Carver telephone interview, 12/19/93
       Fred Masotti, 1993
       Whitburn. Record Research.
       Clee. American 45 R.P.M. Records.

Duane Dee
(Duane DeRosia -Hartford)

Though Freddy Fender made his breakthrough with "Before The Next Teardrop Falls" in 1975, it was Duane Dee who first charted the tune over seven years earlier. Dee, who had started out in clubs in the Milwaukee area, made the country charts six times while recording for Capitol, Cartwheel and ABC. None received any pop action but his most successful record was a Bee Gees cover.

Biggest Chart Hits:

Before The Next Teardrop Falls[3]	#44 C	/67
How Can You Mend A Broken Heart[4]	36 C	/71

Sources: Fred Masotti, 1993
       Clee. American 45 R.P.M. Records.
       Whitburn. Record Research.

Lee Maye
(12/11/34; Tuscaloosa, AL)

Though he recorded extensively, Lee Maye's biggest hits came on the baseball diamond rather than over the airwaves. As with Lew Burdette, the reason for Maye's inclusion here is his association with the Milwaukee Braves, however Maye was as serious about singing as he was

---

[1]Dawn, 1973
[2]Starland Vocal Band, 1976
[3]Freddy Fender, 1975
[4]Bee Gees, 1971

about baseball.

Beginning in 1954 with Modern Records and including releases as Arthur Lee Maye & the Crowns, Maye has a large discography with many high value items of interest to r&b collectors. He also recorded for RPM, Specialty, Dig, Cash, Flip, Imperial, Lakeside, Lenox, Jamie, Tower, Pacemaker, ABC and Antrell. Only one release appeared briefly on Billboard's Soul chart. The record, "Forgetting Someone," came out as the Country Boys & City Girls on Happy Fox in 1976. It slid in safely at number 99 for two weeks.

From 1959-1965 Maye hit .304 as an outfielder with the Braves before going on to play for Houston, Washington, Cleveland and Chicago in his 12-year major league career.

Sources: Reichler. Baseball Encyclopedia.
        Osborne-Brown. Rockin' Records.
        Whitburn. Record Research.

Gene Puerling
(3/31/29; Milwaukee)

Gene Puerling was the originator of the highly esteemed modern harmony vocal group, the Hi-Lo's, followed later by Singers Unlimited. Puerling had three unrecorded groups in Milwaukee - the Double-Daters, (who did a week with Horace Heidt), the Four Shades, and the Honeybees. The singer worked locally as a DJ for about a year and half before relocating to Los Angeles in 1950.

The Hi-Lo's began in April 1953, and had releases on Trend, Starlite, Kapp, Tiara, Omega, Sutton, DRG, Columbia and Reprise. They received additional notoriety for their work with Rosemary Clooney. Singers Unlimited recorded several LP's for MPS between 1967-1980. They reunited in 1993 to sing on Gloria Estefan's Christmas album.

Biggest Chart Hits (Hi-Lo's):

My Baby Just Cares For Me[1]	#29	/54
LP's:		
Suddenly It's The Hi-Lo's	13	/57
Ring Around Rosie (w/Rosemary Clooney)	14	/57
Now Hear This	19	/57

Sources: Gene Puerling telephone interview, 1993
        Clee. American 45 R.P.M. Records.
        Bob Flanigan interview. "Ray Breim Show." KABC, Los Angeles, date unknown.

---

[1]Ted Weems, 1930

Champ
CHAMP RECORDS, INC. MIL., WIS.
IT'S SO HARD
(Ronnie Barczak)
3402
Barczak-BMI
ZTSC-125521
Time: 2:02
Produced By
Tori Kleonik
ROAD RUNNERS

Citation
J-5004
Pub: James E.
Kirschstein
- BMI
ZTSC 88082
ANGEL IN MY EYES
(R. Barzyk)
PAUL STEFEN
AND THE ROYAL LANCERS

HEY
LONELY ONE
(Roland Deller)
CITE
J-5007
Side 1
Time: 2:30
Ken Rose
Music - BMI
ZTSC-94272
PAUL STEFFEN
and THE APOLLOS

Marten Music, BMI
Arranged By U. S.
Produced By U. S.
2:42
100-A
"BIRTHDAY"
(Lennon — Mc Cartney)
UNDERGROUND SUNSHINE
MFG. BY CUCA RECORDS, SAUK CITY, WIS.

ERRO
Records INC.
MFG. IN U.S.A.
PRESSED BY COLUMBIA REC.
BADGER MUSIC CO.
(ASCAP)
TIME: 4:15
INSTRUMENTAL
#400
ZTEC-83582
"RUNNING WILD"
and
"MID-KNIGHT WALK"
By
THE MID-KNIGHTS

"BROADWAY FREEZE"
(Harvey Scales-Lennie LaCour)
magic touch
records
MTA-16001
MT-007-PL
Pub., East-
Lennie LaCour
Music BMI
Time: 2:55
HARVEY SCALES &
THE SEVEN SOUNDS
Produced by Lennie LaCour
Dist. By VOLT RECORDS - 926 East McLemore, Memphis, Tenn.

Raynard
RS-10039
843K-1039
SK4M-4840
Renrel: BMI
Time: 2:19
"PRETEND IT'S ALL RIGHT"
(Daniel J. Helland)
"THE ORIGINALS"
DAVE KENNEDY RECORDING STUDIOS • MILWAUKEE, WISCONSIN

Tee Pee
RECORDS
T45-29
ALPD Music
2:40
UK4M-2611
834T-4529
Produced by
Alan Pasnick
Engineered by
Marty Jensen
TO BE WITH YOU
(M. Sortino)
Arranged by T. Gazzana
THEE PROPHET
A Subsidiary of Target Records, Appleton, Wis.

TEEN TOWN
Jab Music BMI
Time: 2:46
Side 1
Prod. By
Jon Hall
No. 102-A
LITTLE BY LITTLE
(Dancy & Duchrow)
TONY'S TYGRES

Wisconsin Record Labels

"I always thought Wisconsin had so much interesting and good music. It was never really given the credit for what was going on there."
- Tom Gress (Pro-Gress Records), 5/94

Somewhere between Cuca's prolific output and the many one-shot private labels lies a vast array of Wisconsin record companies. Often it was strictly a business proposition - the band paid all the expenses; the company delivered the product. Sometimes, however, the label owner and the artist shared the same dream.

Big Sound/Northland
(Wausau - Duke Wright)

Wausau is probably not the place one would guess to be the site of Wisconsin's first rock 'n' roll recording session. However, all signs suggest that Duke Wright's Northland Studio (531 3rd Street) holds that honor.

While still in his early teens, Wright had his own polka band. In 1956 he started the Northland label to record the band in the studio above his parents' music store. That label remained mostly for polka type material, with more rock 'n' roll coming on Big Sound a few years later. A new studio was built at 2401 3rd Street.

Wright also got into radio while still in his teens. The family purchased WSAU and transformed it into WRIG, the first top 40 format in the area. Wright went on to become one of the most powerful independent radio station owners in the Midwest, with stations in Green Bay, Des Moines (KIOA), and Lincoln, Nebraska.

Northland

7002	White Caps	Rock 'n' Roll Saddles/Why'd You Leave Me	1/57
7003	Roger Winston & the Plaids	I Want To Be Love By You//Ever Ever True	/58
7005	Teddy Boys	She Rocked With Me/Jody	/58
	(27 additional releases are all polka-type material)		

Big Sound

6427	Randy & Candy Men	Little Sister/The Girl Can't Help It	2/64
300	Robin Lee	Barbara Jo/Carnival Of Love	/65
301	Starfires	I'll Be Your Man/Please Go Away	/65
302	Robin Lee	Feet Of Clay/Medal Of Honor	
303	Spacemen	Retro/Modman	3/66
304	Orbits	Fuzzy/Make Me Feel Good	/66
305	Rejects	Hey Girl/Find Your Man	/66
306	Benders	Can't Tame Me/Got Me Down	5/66
307	Robin Lee	Little Boy Blue/Blue Water	/66
308	Corals	Blue Moon/Everyday	/66
309	Spacemen	Same Old Grind/Retro	9/66
310			
311	Corals	Baby My Heart/Stand By Me	/67

Unrelated Big Sound: Iowa label with Pawnbrokers, Church Keys, others
Unrelated Northland: Minnesota label with releases by Darkhood
Sources: Tourville. <u>Wisconsin . . . Discography.</u>
    Dave Pilz, 1994
    Prellberg, Mark. "Spacemen." <u>Lost and Found</u> #2, 1993: 102

Blue Hour
(Milwaukee - Richard Paul Thomas/Susan Marie Lindner/James Podlich)

Richard Thomas and his wife-to-be Susan Lindner were fans and performers of acoustic and folk music. Their label was active primarily in the early 70's.

69711	East Moline Truckers	Grip On It/Don't Come Around	7/69
12161	Raw Meat	Stand By Girl/Out In The Country	
1007	Kind	Travel On/Words	
--	Woodbine (LP)	Roots	

Source: Bruckner, Bill. "Night Flights And Folk Music." <u>Bugle American</u> 11/5/75: 153
    Tourville. <u>Wisconsin . . . Discography.</u>

Champ
(Milwaukee - Bernice "Bernie Champ" Ziblicki)

3402	Road Runners	It's So Hard/Do The Temptation	/65
	(Above also released on Raynard 10031)		
3403	Bogis Chimes	I Think You'll Find/Please Don't Forget	/66
3404	Manifest Destiny	Silly Me/Reminds Me Of You	/66
3405	Manifest Destiny	I Hear Bells/Christmas Toy Shop	12/66
3406	John T. & Bobby Manz	Here I Am/Be On Your Way	/67

12148 Wendi   You're So Fine/The Right Way   /67

Unrelated Champ: There is a different Champ label from 1959
Sources: Tom Kubanek, 1994
        Tourville. <u>Wisconsin . . . Discography.</u>

Cinch
(Milwaukee)
(see Jimmy Allen, Larry Lee Phillipson, Rollettes)

Cine Vista
(Dick Campbell)

A recording artist, producer and manager, Dick Campbell was from Monroe. For additional releases on Cine Vista see Jules Blattner (Appleton/Fox Cities), Easy St. (Around The State).

LP   Tayles   Who Are These Guys   /72
                                  (recorded live at Nitty Gritty Bar, Madison)

Also see: Dick Campbell (Around The State)
Sources: Phil Holzbauer, 1994
        Tourville. <u>Wisconsin . . . Discography.</u>

Citation/Cite
James "Jay" Albrent (10/18/25; Wausau)

Jay Albrent formed his own label after some early involvement at Cuca with releases by Ronnie Premier and Dave Kennedy. "I had to change it from Citation to Cite because Decca had (Citation) reserved for oldies-but-goodies," Albrent explains, "and they never used it." A few of the records did well locally but Albrent left to work for MGM and later for GRT. He moved to Arizona in 1977.

Citation
5001	Comic Books	Manuel/Black Magic And Witchcraft	3/62
5002	Bill Taylor	Income Taxes And You/Lullaby To Carolyn	/62
5003	Paul Stefan & Royal Lancers	I Fought The Law/Say Mama	7/62
5004	Paul Stefan & Royal Lancers	Angel In My Eyes/(You're So Square) Baby I Don't Care	10/62
5005	Renegades	Istanbul/Come On Out	2/63

Cite
| 5006 | Apollos | Good For A Laugh/For Pete's Sake | /63 |
| 5007 | Paul Stefan & Apollos | Hey Lonely One/Devil's Soul Is Black | 10/63 |

(Above also released on Dot 16573)

5008	Paul Stefan & Apollos	Cry Angel Cry/You	/64
5009	Van-Tels	Baby What You Want/Everybody But Me	/64
5010	Launchers	Space Cowboy/The Puppet	/64
5011	Robin Lee	Marie And The Stranger/I See Her Face	/64
68102	Sound Dept. (Waukegan, IL)	(You're A Kind Of)Plain Girl/After My Horn	10/68

Unrelated Citation: There is a 1000 series Citation label from 1959.
Sources: Jay Albrent telephone interview, 1/12/94
     Clee. <u>American 45 R.P.M. Records.</u>

Claremont
(Lake Geneva)

5590	Chieftones	Rang-Dang-Do/Indian Moon	
5596	Chieftones	Steal Away/A Closer Walk	
661	Tommy King & Starlites	I'm Gonna Knock On Your Door/ Bop Diddle In The Jungle	
662	Intruders	Bringin' Me Down/World You've Created	/67
LP 672	Night Pastor & Seven Friends	Music To Lure Pigeons By (includes Dick Ruedebush)	/67

Source: Tourville. <u>Wisconsin . . . Discography</u>
     Corenthal. <u>Wisconsin Music.</u>

Coulee/Transaction
(La Crosse - Bill Grafft [4/1/28 - 7/1/82])

Bill Graft had been a television technician for NBC in New York and a musician. He was working as a troubleshooter for a nuclear plant when he formed his own recording company. Named for the Coulee valley, the label's releases were not prolific but continued for nine years. "There were times when he wanted to quit his regular job because it was hard to keep up both," relates the former Mrs. Grafft, now Lucine Engstad, "but insurance-wise and benefits-wise, it was wise for him to stay with his regular job."

The company produced a variety of music, usually pressed initially in quantities of 500. At least two releases were picked up by major labels. Engstad recalls Buddah buying the Unchained Mynds local hit when they heard it over the telephone.

Coulee

101	Jerry & Way-Outs	Castaway Of Love/That's Why I'm Happy Now	8/63
102	Johnny Waleen	Mystery Train/Now Is The Hour	3/64
103	Twi-Lites	(not released)	
104	Jerry & Silvertones	Ce'ny/Moonlight Bay	5/64
105	Terry Coshart	Why/I'm Walking	6/64

106	Chessmen	Baby Weemus/Dark Eyes	6/64
107	Shelly & Kim	We Love Them All/Where's It Gonna Get Me	8/64
108	Dynasty's	Go Gorilla/Birmingham	9/64
109	Dee Jay & the Runaways	Love Bug Crawl/The Pickup	11/64
110	Marauders	I Can Tell/Hi-Di Hi-Di	12/64
111	Dude Rhomberg	Your Broken Heart's Starting To Show/	1/65
112	Torkays	Linda, I'm Worried So/You Don't Know About Love	2/65
113	Showmen with Bobby Lee	Alright/Dawning	2/65
114	Jesters III	Pledge Of Love/Say That I'm The One	4/65
115	(Boom) Exchequers	Greensleeves/Is There Some Girl	10/65
116	Limeys	Silly Little Girl/Sweet Sweet Love	12/65
117	Walton Ofstedahl & Loretta See Kamp	Unlock Your Heart/Dear God	5/66
118	London Fog	Mr. Baldi/Maudie	1/67
119	Sheri Lynn	Deep Purple/Yes Sir, That's My Baby	4/67
120	Sheri Lynn	You're Nobody/Caravan	5/67
121	Polka Knights	Musette Polka/Pennsylvania Polka	1/68
122	Rubber Band	Baby Left Me/Five Foot	5/68
123	New World Congregation	My World Is Empty Without You/Day Tripper	5/68
		(Above also on Atco 6667)	
124	Al Souchek & 5 Yanks	Laendler #3/Banjo Polka	6/68
125	Tiny Coshart	Double Life/Time To Bum Again	7/68
126	Buddy Quinn	I Need An Angel/Rivertown	5/68
127	Don Thompson & Westchester Singers	Try To Remember/The Girls In Their Summer Dresses	8/68
128	Jim Bee Quartet		10/68
129	Sev & Fred	Girl, You'll Be A Woman, Soon/By Bye Love	
130	Country Gents/Tom McCormick	I Turned And Walked Slowly/I'd Meet Me Leaving	
131	Touchstone	Sweet 'n' Tender/The Intruder	
132	Kitty & Kats	Windy/Tell Me Pretty Baby	
133	7th Day Creation	She Is My Reason/Evil On Your Mind	
134	The Hope	Where Do You Want To Go/One Man	/71
135	Jack Hefti & Rusty	My Wife Is Happy/Tick Tock Polka	
136	Lenny Ray	I'll Be Home Honey/Man's Destruction	
137	Atlantic Ocean	I Thought A Lot Today/Sunday Morning	
138	Village Rovers	Don't Take Away My Home/I Couldn't Answer	
139	Tschann & Burnham	Everything I Do/Lord, Take Me Where I'm Going	
140	Bill Kernan	A Traveling Song/Happy Thoughts	
141	Danny Darren	Medals For Mother/Foggy Mountain Breakdown	/72
142	Studebaker 7	One Fine Day/Come Go With Me	
143	Marv Dennis	The Great Drinkin' Bout/No No On Her Lips	/72
144	Music Tymes	Lonely Man/Oh Evil Woman	
145	Vickie Jean	My Wish For You/You're My Star	

LP's:

1001	Dave Kennedy & Ambassadors	Breaking Up Is Hard To Do	/64
1002	Marv Dennis IV	The Marv Dennis IV	/72
1003	- 1008 (gospel)		
1009	Townsmen	I Believe	
4949	**(Boom)** Five Chords	Wild Are The Five Chords	

Knight

100	Denny Noie & the Catalinas	Dee Dee/It Ain't No Big Thing	/65
101	Golden Catalinas	Yakety Sax Express/Come To Me	/65

Transaction

701	Fax	Her Love/I Can Only Give You Everything	/66
702	Fax with Alex Campbell	Just Walking/Not Too Long Ago	8/66
703	Ladds	Wild Angels Theme/Keep On Running	/67
704	Fax/Lost & Founds	I'll Go Crazy/If I Needed Someone	/67
705	Unchained Mynds	We Can't Go On This Way/Goin' Back To Miami	1/69
	(Above also on Teen Town 109 and Buddah 111)		
706			
707	Unchained Mynds	Hole In My Show/Warm Smoke	4/69
708	Touchstone	The Show/Last Laugh	/69
709	Molly Maguires	First Spring Rain/But It's All Right	/69
710	Division	Not Fade Away/Please Please Me	
711	Last Draft	It's Been A Long Time/Lovely To See You	
712	Stone Flour	Till We Kissed/Help	
713	Molly Maguires	Our Favorite Melodies/You Can All Join In	/70
714	Changing Times	Diana/We Got To Live Together	/70
715	Flying Free	You Can Do/Your Day	

Source: Lucine Engstad letters and telephone interview, 1/18/93, 6/20/93, 8/14/93

Demo

(Milwaukee - Angelo Ferlano)

Owner Angelo Ferlano reportedly passed away in the 60's. See Wanted, Larry Lee Phillipson.

Sources: Chuck Travis, 1994
Tourville. <u>Wisconsin . . . Discography.</u>

Earth/Plastic Earth

(Madison - Jonathan Little [Whirry])

Madison radio personality Jonathan Little formed the Earth label to release Underground Sunshine's "Birthday." Due to the existence of another Earth label, the Plastic Earth name was also used. Little used the label for occasional releases over a period of some 20 years.

100	Underground Sunshine	Birthday/All I Want Is You	4/69
6993	Axis	I Can't Wait/Somebody To Love (**Plastic Earth**)	9/69
5001	Paraphernalia	Quicksand/It Came Out Of The Sky	
5002 - 5003			
5004	Jim Gregory	Friends/I Do Love You	
5005	Benedict	Back It Up/Gonna Have A Good Time	/72
5006	Jim Gregory	Love Song/If It's Love	/76
5007	Jim Gregory	Linus & Lucy/I Do Love You	
5008	Sonrize	Feeling/Sonrize	

Sources: Jonathan Little, 1993, 94
       Tourville. <u>Wisconsin . . . Discography.</u>

Enterprise 13
(Racine/Milwaukee - Dr. Louis Maxey, John Braun)
(see Sultans Five - Racine)

Erro
(Bob Stevens - Milwaukee)

Owner Bob Stevens was a big band leader in the 40's.

111	Gene Tello & Doo Doos	Take A Tip From The Lord/
201	Tommy Lane	Teenager's Lament/My Baby Likes To Rock 'n' Roll
203	Norb Kamin	Nite Rider/Pick 'n' Shuffle
300	Tommy Lane	My Bobby Sox Queen/You're So Easy On The Eyes
400	Mid-Knights	Running Wild/Mid-Knight Walk

Sources: Tourville. <u>Wisconsin . . . Discography.</u>
       John Cooke, 1994

Fan Jr.
(Madison- Skip Nelson)

The name of this Madison label comes from the initials of Fred Arthur Nelson, Jr., better known as Skip. Nelson was a paraplegic who owned the Music City record store in Westwood Mall. He reportedly went into the jewelry business in California.

1000	Corvettes & Toddettes (Shane Todd)	Jeri/Johnny Goes To Philly	2/61
1001	Nite-Caps (also on #6007)	Poinciana/Flying Sinner (I/I)	/61
1002			
1003	Marrell's Marauders	I Wanta Do It/The Marauder	
1003	Robin & the Three Hoods	I Wanta Do It/The Marauder	

1706	Vilas Craig	Little Miss Brown Eyes/Poor Loser	/61
1992	Jimmy Dawson	Playboy/Double Bug Rag	
4729	Vilas Craig	Walkin' Down The Avenue/Don't Sweetheart Me	/62
9374	Dynastys	I'll Be Forever Loving You/Mountain Of Love	4/64
5080	Pete Source & Driftwoods	I'm Too Young To Love/Have You Ever Had The Blues	
5504	Cannons	Sweet Georgia Brown/Lonesome	/65
5678	Robin & the Three Hoods	We The Living/A Day You'll Never Forget	
5680	Robin & the Three Hoods	I Wanna Do I/That's Tuff	

Sources: Tourville. <u>Wisconsin . . . Discography.</u>

Feature/Rampro
(Madison/Janesville - Ken Adamany [3/25/early 40's; Janesville])

These were the labels formed by Ken Adamany to help promote the acts he booked. Many of these records were produced by Sam McCue (of the Legends) and/or Steve Sperry. "We used to crank records out like cookies up there," says McCue of his work at Cuca Studio. Adamany also had the Third Coast label later in the 70's.

Feature

501	Speedy	Donna/Stop The World	/65
1001	Casuals	Come On (Pretty One)/Angel On My Shoulder	/65
101	Voyagers	Can't Save This Heart/	/65
102	Those lil' ole music makers - Us	Summertime/Hitchike	/65
103	Shaprels	A Fool For Your Lies/You're Cheating On Me	/66

(Above also on PKC 1017. Side 1 reissued on Pebbles *Highs In The Mid 60's, Vol. 15*)

104	Komons (Rockford)	Caught In The Trap/Why	/66
105	Madadors	Girl Don't Leave Me/Alright	/66
106			
107	Impalas	Spoonful/Talking About You	/66

(Side 1 reissued on Pebbles *Highs In The Mid 60's, Vol. 15*)

108	Intrigues	I'll Sigh Over You/I Don't Care	
109	Matadors	You're A Better Man Than I/Bright Lights, Big City	
110	Inspirations	That Girl/Baby Please Come Home	
111	Voyagers	Away/I'm So Lonely	
112	The Society	One Way Ride/For Me	/66
	Shaprels	Dare I Weep, Dare I Mourn/Rock-A-Boo	/66

(Above also on Chess 1993)

Rampro (Ram Productions)

115	Talismen	Glitter & Gold/She Belongs To Me	10/66
116	Union Jacks	I Gotta Go/No One But You	
117	Converts	A Guy Without A Girl/Don't Leave Me	
118	Why Four	Hard Life/Not Fade Away	/66
119	Futuras	Signed, Sealed & Delivered/Portrait Of A Fool	/66

120 - 121
122   Paegens (Rockford)   Good Day Sunshine/I Can Only Give You Everything   /67
Feature
201   Esquires (Belvidere, IL)   Am I to Blame/Pretty Little Blue Girl
202   Beau Gentry   Just In Case/Dream Girl   /67
203   Heard (Peoria, IL)   Stop It Girl/Take It On Home   /67
              (Above also on Phillips 40454 as by the Wyld Heard)
9427   Disciples (Norman, OK)   (It's) Over/Respect

Also see: Legends - Milwaukee (Sam McCue)
         Steve Sperry - On The Charts
         Nigh Tranes -Madison/Janesville (Ken Adamany)
Sources: Sam McCue, 1994
         Ken Adamany, 7/94
         Tourville. Wisconsin . . . Discography.

Gold Star
(Appleton)

This label was probably owned by WAPL DJ Bob Falkner. See the Montereys and Dick Miller.

Sources: Don Pinnow telephone interview, 7/4/94
         Tourville. Wisconsin . . . Discography.

International Artists/Rif
(Richland Center - Vilas Craig)

Vilas Craig created these two labels for his own productions. Other than Craig's own releases, only the following has turned up:

2121   Steve Mutimer & Rhythm Kings   Stuck On Me/Don't Sweat The Small Stuff /60
              (Group is from Rockford, IL)

Also see: Vilas Craig
Unrelated International Artists: This label has no connection with the better known company
         noted mostly for Bubble Puppy and the 13th Floor Elevators.
Sources: Vilas Craig, 1993
         Tourville. Wisconsin . . . Discography.

Kel
(Oshkosh)
(Kelly Diciani - 7/3/29; Chicago)

Kelly Diciani played with a trio in the Fox Valley and taught music. As a sideline he recorded a few Oshkosh area bands, primarily Sunstone Lollipop, which included two of his sons.

Diciani was also involved as writer/producer of two Cuca releases with Raylene & the Blue Angels/Dairylanders. "We got a little notoriety but we didn't make a lot of money." he says. The Dairylanders' record was Cuca 1141, perhaps the reason Diciani chose that number for his first Kel issue.

1141	Karl Fields & Sands of Time	Just Like That/I Was Wrong	/63
1000	Nomads	You Come Around/Don't Come Running To Me	/65
8515	Sunstone Lollipop	People Of Today/Sunshine	/68
8516	Sunstone Lollipop	Never Sad/Forever Be In Doubt	/68
8518	Sunstone Lollipop	Mr. Keat/My Day Of Dream	/68

Sources: Kelly Diciani telephone interview, 4/2/94
         Tourville. Wisconsin . . . Discography.

Key

1002	Legends	Lariat/Gail
1003	Mid-Knighters	Baby My Heart/More Than I Can Say
5804	Mel-O-Tones	Little Bit More/When Love
15131	Counts	All Night/Sittin' Here Wonderin'

Source: Tourville. Wisconsin . . . Discography

Leaf
(Herb Hugunen - 10/29/20 - 7/31/94; Janesville)

Beginning with a wire recorder, Herb Hugunen taught himself the ins and outs of recording. He converted an old barn on his farm into a studio and recorded and released many area bands. Hugunen eventually switched from farming to the construction business while continuing to record into the mid-70's.

8973	Driftwoods	Have You Ever Had The Blues/For Your Precious Love	/62
6238	Ace Bauman/ Crossfires	All American Twister/This Should Go On Forever	3/62
6467	Tim Davis & Chordairs	Wine, Wine, Wine/Workout	6/64
LP 6475	P.J. Murphy	P.J. Murphy	7/64
852	Steve Mills	New York City/Nothing To Do With Love	/64
6581	Squires	Dear Jan/On Probation	8/65

6670	Cavemen	No Reply/	7/66
6684	Henchmen (Rockford,IL)	Love Till The End Of Time/Last Monday Blues	8/66
667	Primates	Girl Don't Tell Me/I'll Feel A Whole Lot Better	/66

Lindy
(La Crosse - Lindy Shannon)

DJ Lindy Shannon is the godfather of rock 'n' roll in the Coulee Valley region. Instrumental in bringing the first top 40 format to area radio at WKBH, Shannon also produced, recorded, booked and managed bands, and ran a record shop. Besides his own label, Shannon worked with groups on Cuca and Coulee/Transaction.

On August 30, 1992, Shannon, in failing health at the time, was honored with a tribute concert featuring reunions of many of the 60's bands with whom he had worked. A repeat performance on August 28, 1994 found Shannon in better condition.

740	TJ's	Party, Party/Take My Love	/57
741	TJ's	I got A Baby/Live It Up	/57
1113	Marv Blihovde	Dearest Darling/Cigarettes And Coffee Blues	/58
1124	TJ's	Baby Doll/Broken Hearted Prayer	/58
1551	Marv Blihovde	Sweet Little Wife/Pickles	/59
101	Super-Phonics with Dave Kennedy	B-L-U-E/Me Neither	/60
102	Super-Phonics	Teen-Age Partner/My Love For You	/60

Source: Tourville. <u>Wisconsin . . . Discography.</u>

Lompri
(Racine - Jim Lombardo, Tim Prideaux)

Comprising only two releases, this label was owned by Jim Lombardo and Tim Prideaux. The two high school boys got together to promote shows, taking their first big shot with a Byrds concert on April 29, 1967. Prideaux soon left to be replaced by Dave Nimmer. Lombardo now runs Bell Ambulance Service. See Line's End and Little Gregory & the Concepts.

Source: Jim Lombardo telephone interview, 3/12/94

Magic Touch/Dynamic Sound
(Milwaukee)
(Lenny LaCour - 4/27/32; New Orleans)

Among other things, Lenny LaCour claims:
(1) He worked as a musician with Elvis in Presley's early years.
(2) The movie *King Creole* is based on his life.

(3) He began in the record business as an engineer for Leonard Chess and his own company was bigger than Chess (!).
(4) He believes he was the first in Milwaukee to do anything for the local talent.

One thing we do know is that LaCour had several labels in Chicago before moving to Milwaukee around 1966 and starting Dynamic Sound (for rock) and Magic Touch (for soul). Some groups appeared on both labels and some releases were still by Chicago acts. The confusion of the numbers is a discographer's nightmare. "My numbering system got fouled up for a while," says LaCour. "I was doing so many things at the time. Several times the manufacturer called me and said, 'Give me a number,' and I said, 'Make up your own!"

The labels include an odd mix of artists, ranging from Harvey Scales (with his national chart hit) to groups that weren't even known around town. "I scouted the clubs," LaCour explains, "and they came to me a lot because I had another business (Magic Color Plastics, an interior design company) going at the time. I was advertising a lot on the radio and O.C. White and Dr. Bop (of WAWA) were big fans of mine. I'd get a lot of kids pop in and want to know if I'd help them out."

Dynamic Sound

2001	Marvelle & the Blue Match	The Dance Called The Motion/Mellow Man	
2001	Ethics	Confusion/Out Of My Mind	
2003	Hugh Barrett (Chicago)	Moonlight Down By The River/Another Lonely Soldier Boy	
2004	Invasion	The Invasion Is Coming/I Want To Thank You	
2005	Comic Books	Young Blood/First Time In My Life	/67
2006	Young Savages (Chicago)	The Invaders Are Coming/A Very Special Day	
	(Side 1 above reissued on Pebbles *Highs In The Mid 60's, Vol. 10*)		
2007	Young Savages	I Love You Oh So Much/Welcome To My World	
2008	Friday & the Weekends (Rockford, IL)	You Baby/I Need Her	
2009	Invasion	Do You Like What You See/	
1002	Filet of Soul	Sweet Lovin'/Do Your Thing	
91101	Crystal Rain	You And Me/World On Fire	

Magic Touch

2001	Swinging Hearts (Chicago)	You Speak Of Love/I Got It	/67
2001	Junior & the Classics	Wise Up/Stock Blues In D	/67
2003	Sean (Mr. Esquire) Taylor (with Vic Pitts & Cheaters)		/67
		Never Do I Worry (About You)/Funky Soul Dance	/67
2003	Junior & Classics	Wise Up/Mix Up A Go Go	/67
2004	Bullet Bob Barian	The Bat-Mo/Way 'Cross The Sea	/67
2005	Gary Brown	Would You Laugh At Me/Oh My Love	/67
2006	Evelyn Smith	Don't Make Me No Promises/You Don't Mean A Thing To Me	
2007	Harvey Scales & Seven Sounds	Get Down/Love-Itis	10/67
2008	Junior & Classics	Mix Up (A Go Go)/Marching Around Your Heart	
2008	Sean Taylor	Put Me Down Easy/Too Late To Turn Back Now	11/67
2009	Attila & Huns	Hula Shake/Hurry Back	11/67

2009	Junior & Classics	Kill The Pain/Please Make Love To Me	12/67
2010		Funky Way	
16001	Harvey Scales & Seven Sounds	Broadway Freeze/I Can't Cry No More	1/68
007	Herman Griffin & Boys in the Band	Are You For Me Or Against Me/Gettin' Better	
2069	Harvey Scales & Seven Sounds	Love Is A Gas/Too Good To Be True	4/69
2070	Huns of Time	Walking In The Vineyards/Here's Where I Get Off	
2071	Attila & Huns	The Vineyards Of My Time/Here's Where I Get Off	
2072	Harvey Scales & Seven Sounds	Don't You Ever Let It End/ The Sound Of Soul	
2075	Sonny Freeze & Unchained (Chicago)		11/69
		White Snowflake-Blue Christmas/Ain't Getting Nothing For Christmas	
2076	Marvelle & Blue Match	Don't End Up Like Me/A Man Ain't Nothing	/69
	(Marvelle is Marvelle Love)	Till A Woman Takes His Name	
2077	Harvey Scales & Seven Sounds	Welcome Home/Trackdown	/69
2078	Filet of Soul	Proud Mary/We Want Peace	
3002	Harvey Scales & Seven Sounds	Bump Your Thing/Trying To Survive	/69
3002	B.B. Jones (Chicago)	Stoop Down (Way, Way Down)/The Real Thing	
7006	Harvey Scales	Groove On Sexy Lady/Rock The World	/75
8002	Harvey Scales	Groove On Sexy Lady/Rock The World	5/76
9001	Lenny LaCour	Mona Lisa/Simple Life	
9002	Krystal	False Alarm/Body Dance	
9003	Harvey Scales	Follow The Disco Crowd/Love Thief	/76

LaCour then returned to Chicago and continued the Magic Touch label there.

Also see: Harvey Scales
      Junior & the Classics
      Esquires (Sean Taylor)
      Comic Books
Sources: Lenny LaCour telephone interview, 4/2/94
      Robert Pruter, 1994
      Clee. <u>American 45 R.P.M. Records.</u>

Lenny LaCour (courtesy Lenny LaCour)

MMC
(Madison - Scott Cameron [11/20/38; Madison])

The Monona Music Company (Monona is both a lake and a suburb of Madison) was originally owned by Welton Firehammer who recorded pop/easy listening music. Singer Scott Cameron (aka Scotty "Honey" Stuart) purchased the label and publishing company. Cameron left music for a few years while working in the hotel/motel business. He later reactivated the label in Omaha, Nebraska where it enjoyed substantial success with the Coachmen. See Honey & the Dew Drops for the only two known Wisconsin releases. All later releases are from the Nebraska era of the company.

Source: Scott Cameron, 1993

New Phoenix
(Hartland - John Dolan)

John Dolan also worked for the Chicago-based Stacy label.

9150	Valiants	Mutha/I Had A Dream	/60
9210	Jack Merlin	Proverbs/Johnny And Stella	/60
6110	Jim Bing/Don Heinze	St. Patrick Polka/St. Patrick Polka (/I)	/61
6190	Chico Holiday	God, Country And My Baby/Fools	9/61
	(above also on Coral 62291)		
6198	Renee Roberts (Chicago)	I Want To Love You (So Much It Hurts Me)/Aching Heart	1/62
6199	Comic Books	Manuel/Black Magic And Witchcraft	/62
6200	Renee Roberts	I Need You/(Dear One) Let Me Love You	/62

Sources: John Dolan, 1993
         Paul Yopps, 1993
         Tourville. Wisconsin . . . Discography.

Odessa

307	June Bateman	I Still Love Him/I Don't Wanta
2001	Jimmy Russell	Come Here My Love/Soft Feeling
4658	Medius	Let Me Show You/Your Love

Source: Tourville. Wisconsin . . . Discography.

Owl
(Hoot Roberts - Wausau)

Label owner Hoot Roberts was a country singer. See Denny Lee (Wausau/Stevens Point).

740501	Load	Wow, We'll Say We Tried/She Calls My Name

Pfau
(Harold Pfau; Milwaukee)

Pfau was one of Milwaukee's earliest labels, dating back to 1952. The material consists of mostly old-time and country-western music. The owner, an electrician, died of complications resulting from a fall through a floor while working at his trade. Cuca's Jim Kirchstein later purchased the library of 300 acetates from Pfau's widow. See Robin Lee and Ken Davis.

Source: Jim Kirchstein telephone interview, 4/94

PKC
(Phil Klinger)

Phil Klinger was a white DJ on r&b station WAWA.

1011	Dr. Crudley's Prescription	Losing You/Bye Bye	/68
1012	Inspirations	Watermelon Man/Tell Daddy	/68
1013	Zoo	Gonna Miss Me/Sometimes	/68
1014 - 1015			
1016	New Breed	It's Got to Be Somethin'/Please Give Me A Chance	/69
1017	Shaprels	A Fool For Your Lies/You're Cheating On Me	/69
		(Above also on Feature 103)	
2280	Dr. Crudley's Prescription	Hey, What's The Matter/Eyes Of A Wonderer	

Sources: Bill Tate telephone interview, 8/11/94
Tourville. <u>Wisconsin . . . Discography.</u>

Pro-Gress/Water Street
(Milwaukee - Tom Gress - 7/19/41)

Tom Gress played bass with Jim Sundquist's Muleskinners after the breakup of the Fendermen. He moved to Milwaukee and continued performing with various bands, gradually shifting behind the scenes. He is the uncredited (and almost unpaid, he claims) producer of Underground Sunshine's "Birthday." Gress worked in sales and promotion for both Liberty and Capitol before starting his own label. He now resides in Tucson, Arizona, where he does wildlife paintings.

Water Street

8356	Larry Lynne Group	Till I'll Be There/Happiness Is	/69
8596	Muleskinners	Muleskinner Blues/Whiskey	/70
8826	Cypher	Ballad Of The U.S./Woman	/70
504	Terry Gale	Grin And Bear It/New Orleans On The River	/75

Pro-Gress

0529	Rory Slick & Roadsters	Runaway/At The Hop	
8357	Robin Lee & Royal Host	Sure I Will/Your Whole World Is Falling Down	/69
8893	D.C. Mudd	Once Hey/Rocket 88	/71
8940	Zebra	A Better Way/That Kind Of Man	/72
3524	Terry Gale	Midnight Woman/Child	/74
503	Big Apple	Laugh 'n' Smile/Girl I Love You	/75

LP's:

Pro-Gress

2204	Robin Lee	Robin Lee	/69
2468	Bon-Aires	La Versatile (Live at the Ram's Head Inn)	/69
	Silver		

(Above band also recorded for United Artists but is not related to the group on Arista.)

Water Street

| 1001 | Sigmund Snopek III | Virginia Wolf | /72 |

Sources: Tom Gress telephone interview, 5/94
        Tourville. <u>Wisconsin . . . Discography.</u>

Raynard/Page
(Milwaukee - Dave Kennedy 7/17/25; Wales -6/1/89; Milwaukee)

"Dave never was given the credit he deserved," believes Kennedy's wife, Lottie. The Kennedy recording operation was probably the most prolific in the state after Cuca's. Beginning in 1956 at Bayshore, moving to 3rd & Meineke, 3rd & Center, and downtown, it was the most important studio in Milwaukee in the 60's. The Raynard label initially was used by Dave Kennedy for his own releases. The studio carries on in the 90's with Kennedy's son Darrell.

EP 10065	Chico	What Did I Do/Just Because You're You/Calypso Song/Riddle Song	/58
014	Statesmen	Teen Theme/Roo-Buh-Doo-Buh-Doo	/65
602	Danny Peil & Apollos	Jingle Jump/Flip Side	/65
602	Danny Peil & Tigers	Jingle Jump/Flip Side	/65
770	Larry Lee Phillipson	Milwaukee Road/Greedy Lips	
10011	La Sabers	Lonely Days/Mix Up	
10012 - 10018			
10019	Blue Echoes	Moonride/What I Say	/65
10019	Savoys	Charlena/Pretty One	/65
10020	Fabulous Mad Lads	Rock Around The Clock/Walking With My Angel	/65

10021			
10022	Al Jarreau	I'm Not Afraid/Ska-Bobbi	/65
10023			
10024	Al Jarreau	Shake Up/Room Boom	/65
10025 - 10026			
10027	Billy Real	Foolish Me/The Girl I Love	/65
10028 - 10029			
10030	Ricochettes	I'll Be Back/Can I Be Sure	/65
10031	Road Runners	It's So Hard/Do The Temptation	/65
10032	Vibratones	Eventually/Little Egypt	5/65
10033	Dale Anderson	Tattoo For Rosalie/Working All Day	/65
10034	Shags	Dance Woman/'Cause I Love You	/65
10035			
10036	Mustard Men	Another Day/I Lost My Baby	/65
10037			
10038	Bryds	Your Lies/Why Did You Have To Break My Heart	
10039	Originals	Now's The Time/Pretend It's Alright	/65
10040 - 10041			
10042	Walking Sticks	100 Pounds Of Clay/Why	/65
10043	Moody Walkers	We Never Loved Before/Barbara	/65
10044	Vibratones	I Remember Yesterday/Screaming Mimi	/65
10045 - 10046			
10047	Secrets	I Don't Know/I Know It's You	/65
10048 - 10051			
10052	Sultans Five	Tonight Is The Night/With You	/65
10053	Sultans Five	Daisy/Life Is Like A River	/65
10054			
10055	Cheaters	Satisfaction/When Johnny Comes Marching Home	
10056	Cheaters	You're Mine/Barefootin'	/66
10057 - 10064			
10065	Tomorrow's Children	Midnight Hour/I Can Only Give You Everything	
10066 - 10068			
10069	Cheri Thomas	Glory Girl/You Can Count On Me Babe	
10070 - 10071			
10072	Chapters	Without You/If You Can't Love Me-Pity Me	
10073 - 10078			
10079	FSQ	A Girl Named Mae/Sweet Talkin' Hanna	
233	Flash & Blue Sky Ramblers	Milwaukee Stomp/Why Do I Think Of You Tonight	
1001	Dave Kennedy	Some Sweet Tomorrow/I Put My Last Nickel	
1002	Dave Kennedy	That Ring On Your Finger/Woochee Woochee Woo	
1003			

1004	James Hanns & Soul Entertainers	It's A Fine Thing/I Found You	
1005 - 1013			
1014	Rose DuBats	Wonder The Boys Go/Signals From Saturn	/66
1015	Mike Denett	Why Wait For Winter/Ghost Of Your Love	/66
		(Above also on Stacy 955)	
1045	Invaders	Mickey Finn/Dedication To Her	/66
1046	Deverons	On The Road Again/Unnoticed	/66
		(Side 1 reissued on Pebbles *Highs In The Mid 60's, Vol. 10*)	
1047 - 1052			
1053	Larry Lee Phillipson	Give Me Your Love For Christmas/Baby Sitters Christmas	/66
1054 - 1057			
1058	Coves	You're All Right/a Love Like That	
1059 - 1060			
1061	Moses & 10 Commandments	Monkey Time/Son Of Monkey Time	/67
1062 - 1067			
1068	Royce Hall & Lucky Four	That's My Life/On More Glass Of Wine	/67
1069 - 1084			
1085	Van-Tels	Ain't Too Proud To Beg/Stand By Me	/68
1086			
1087	Kracker-Barrel-Komplex	My World/Different Than Me	**Page** /68
1107	Bennie Cole & Soul Brothers	Love You Till I Die/I Don't Want To Cry	/69
1108			
1109	Bloomsbury People	Have You Seen Them Cry/Madeline	**Page** /69
1110 - 1120			
1121	Renaissance	I Need You, I Need You/Keep On Pushing	**Page**
2001	Tony Tucker	Jane/Redeemed	**Page**
4101	John Patachek	Bartender/Frankie	**Page**
6289	Peasants	Big Boss Man/The People Are Wrong	
8796	Rat Pack	I Need You/Frosty Rudolph With Bells	
Page			
20014	Flash & Blue Sky Ramblers	Milwaukee Stomp/Why Do I Think Of You Tonight	
		(also see Raynard 233)	
20027	Barbara Benson	Wishing My Time Away/Truth	
8083-26	Impalas	Teenager In Love/I'm Gonna Love You Too	/77
810029	J. Harrison B.	Leavin' You/Travelin' Down	

Sources: Lottie Kennedy telephone interview, 5/22/94
      Tourville. <u>Wisconsin . . . Discography.</u>

Revive
(Waukesha - Paul Yopps [1/18/36; Waukesha])

Paul Yopps was a member of the Valiants who recorded for John Dolan's New Phoenix label.
Yopps went on to work closely with Dolan in various facets of recording and publishing.

101   Nocturnals w/Chico Vance (Phoenix, AZ) The Twister's Stomp/My Linda Jo /63
102
103   El Rey & the Night Beats   My Secret/Come On Let's Go   /63

Also see: Valiants (Paul Yopps)
Source: Paul Yopps, 1993

Revolution
(Jack Tadych - 12/30/37; Milwaukee)

Jack Tadych was the leader of Jack & the Beanstalks. Now busy with his American Building Restoration Company, Tadych says he would have to do much digging to find information on the Revolution label. "Many groups came in and out of there back in the 60's," he says. "We probably did a lot of stuff at my studio that never even got released."

See Jack & the Beanstalks and All Heart (Milwaukee).

Sources: Jack Tadych telephone interview, 6/29/94
        Tourville. Wisconsin . . . Discography.

Sonic/Hodag
(Rhinelander - Michael Kuehl 1/10/46; Rhinelander)

The Hodag label is named after a mythical beast invented by one of the city fathers of Rhinelander. Michael Kuehl worked in radio and television at WOBT and WAEO-TV in Rhinelander and WXMT in Merrill. He later served as business and promotion manager for Full Compass Studios in Madison. Back in Rhinelander, he has reactivated his studio for the 90's.

Audio Unlimited
1000	Illusions	The Outcast/Now That It's Over	/66
826A6359	David Yonker	A Song/Prettier	/67

Hodag
0540	Gord's Horde	I Don't Care/Please Tell Me	6/66
		(Side 1 reissued on Pebbles *Highs In The Mid 60's, Vol. 15*)	
6932	Rebounds	Summertime/Don't Throw Your Love Away	/66

Sonic
2746	Sons of May	Tossin' & Turnin'/Morning Dew	/67
4626	Lexington Project	She Looks Much Older/It Looks A Lot Like Rain	/67
5476	Midnight Sun	I'll Find A Way/You Keep Me Hangin' On	/67

Unrelated Sonic: There was a Sonic label in Minneapolis. There may also be others.
Sources: Michael Kuehl telephone interview, 4/3/94
        Tourville. Wisconsin . . . Discography.

Sound
(Milwaukee - Stu Glassman)

Stu Glassman was the owner of Radio Doctors, a record store located in downtown Milwaukee at the time. There apparently were only two releases on this label. See the Night Beats.

Source: Raymond Ojeda, 1993

Starlight
(Racine - Harry Smith)
(see Ken Davis - Racine)

Target/Tee Pee
(Appleton - Al Posniak)

Al Posniak was the leader/founder of Appleton's Catalinas (later the Golden Catalinas). As his entrepreneurial talents grew, Posniak left the band to form Target Productions (Tee Pee). Dan Liebhauser was also an important part of the company. The recording sessions often used some of Appleton's top musicians and some of them, such as drummer Tom Gebheim and keyboardist Wilbur Vandenburgt, also did engineering and production work. Jim Kelly of the Catalinas also joined the company a bit later.

Besides the two releases that were picked up by national labels, many productions were placed directly with the majors, including Buddah, Mercury, MGM, RCA and Stax. Target ceased operations in July 1972, after Posniak was diagnosed with a brain tumor. He recovered and has been involved in various entertainment related activities since (see the Catalinas story). Dan Liebhauser has continued in the business as producer/booker of shows featuring name acts.

Most of these releases use different numbers on either side.

Target

10/11	13th Hour	Alright And About Time/Badger Beat	10/66
101/102	Golden Catalinas	Varsity Club Song/Can Your Monkey Do The Dog	11/66
103/104	Faros	I'm Calling You Back/I'm Crying	11/66
		(Side 2 reissued on Pebbles *Highs In The Mid 60's, Vol 10*)	
105/106	The Drifter	Show Me The Road To Heaven/Why Didn't You Wait	12/66
107/108	Lord Beverly Moss & the Mossmen		
		Please, Please What's The Matter/the Kids Are Alright	1/67
		(Side 1 reissued on Pebbles *Highs In The Mid 60's, Vol. 10*)	
109/110	Private Property Of Digil	Look At Me (the Mantelpiece Marter)(sic)/	
		To My Friends	2/67
111/112			

Tee Pee

113/114	Couriers	Would You Still Be Loving Me/You Honey Baby	3/67

115/116	Private Property Of Digil	Destination Nowhere/The Patch Of Brick	5/67
117/118	Golden Catalinas	Dee Dee/Mojo Workin'	/67
15/16	New Raging Storm	Cry Girl/Monkey Time	/67
17/18	Ricky & Raylene	It Must Be Love/Light Of Day	/67
19/20	Jules Blattner	Pledging My Love/Summertime Blues	/67
21/22	Don The Drifter	Christine/Three Steps	/67
23/24	Private Property Of Digil	Sunshine Flames/Princess	/67
25/26	Sertified Sound	Love Is Strange/Everyday	/67
27/28			
29/30	Thee Prophets	To Be With You/If You Would Leave Me	/67
31/32			
33/34	Capt. Hershel Gober	Pictures Of A Man/Her Am I	11/67
35/36	Private Property Of Digil	Jewelry Lady/I'm Looking At You	11/67
37/38	Bloos Phase	Will You Love Me/The Basic Works Of Father Timothy	12/67
39/40	Shaprels	Clara Bloomtree/Desert Maiden	12/67
41/42			
43/44	Torquays	I'll Never Forget/Even The Wind	1/68
45/46	Syndicate	Next 21st Of May/My Baby Kicked The Bucket	2/68
47/48	Speedy & the Alka Seltzers	Cathy Lost Her Love Today/I Wonder What She's Doing Tonight	3/68
49/50	Love Society	Do You Wanna Dance/Without You	4/68

(Above also on Scepter 12223)

51/52	No Names	Take It From Me/I Never Realized	5/68
53/54	(**Baroque**) Baroques	I Will Not Touch You/Remember	5/68
55/56	Knights Of Day	Mr. Pitiful/Then There's You	6/68
57/58	Journeymen	You're A Better Man Than I/Realities In Life	6/68
59/60	Mark IV	Rollin' Stone/The Wayward Wind	7/68
61/62	Susan Marie	The Moon Won't Tell/Warm In The Wintertime	/68
63/64			
65/66			
67/68	Robin Lee	To Hell With Love/The Urge For Going	/68
69/70	People	I Can't Stand It/Ode To Billy Joe	10/68
71/72	Country Rogues	Somebody Else Is Taking My Place/Just Because	11/68
73/74	Individual Activity	Ten O'clock/Don't Let The Sun Catch You Cryin'	11/68
75/76	Hinge	Come On Up/The Idols Of Your Mind	12/68

(Side 1 reissued on Pebbles *Highs In The Mid 60's, Vol. 10*)

101	Hot Ice	I'm Your Fool/Last To Die	1/69
1002	K&D Bootery Co.	Birthday/Don't Let The Sun Catch You Cryin'	1/69
1003			
1004	Gene Ski	To Hell With Love/The Urge For Going	1/69
1005			
106	Beast	Live Your Life/Anything You Want	1/69
200/201	Timothy (Calumet, IL)	What Good Will Crying Do Me Now/Life Once	/69

201	DJ's	Stuck On You/Happy Anniversary	2/69
1001	Tumbleweeds	Truck Driver's Wife/Another Fool Is On The Way	

Target

1001	Coachmen	The News Is Out/Girl In The Window	3/69
1002	Loyal Opposition	Telling Lies/Love Has Come Your Way	3/69
1003	Wrest	Bet Your Sweet Bippy/Hatfield Junction	3/69
	(Above also on Tower 1003)		
1004	Glass Candle	Light The Glass Candle/Keep Right On Living	4/69
1005	Soup	Big Boss Man/Veronica	4/69
1006	Love Society	Let's Pretend (We're Making Love)/You Know How I Feel (And Why)	5/69
1007	Phase III	I'm Not A Fool Anymore/Back In The USA	/69
1008	Phase III	Taxman/Working In A Coal Mine	/69
1009	Coachmen	Hey Bulldog/Just Knowing Her	/69
1010	Larry Lee Phillipson	Barney/The Blackboards Of My Mind	
1011	Gentle Thud	On The Road Again/Good Time Music	
1012	Bare Blue Water	In The Midnight Hour/My Giant Cork	
1013	Wrest	Old Joe/Two Of Us	11/70
1014	Passion	Midnight In The Park/She's A Very Special Girl	12/70
2000	Jules Blattner	Fannie Mae/School Days	
2001	Father Time	I'm Gonna Get You/Yesterday Will Never Come	
2002	Ron Besaw & Mojo Men	I'm Sorry/I'm Sorry (/I)	/71
2003	Redstone	Looking Through A Glass Darkly/I Fought For Sloopy	
2004			
2005	Bungi	Tuck's Squad/Six Days On The Road	
2006			
2007	Will Zeamer & Northerly Winds	What's The Game (You're Playing With My Heart)/Lenny Doesn't Live Here Anymore	/72

Also see: Catalinas (Al Posniak)
   Lord Beverly Moss & the Mossmen (Tom Gebheim)
Unrelated Target: This company had no connection with an early 70's Target label releasing country music for Alice Creech, Jacky Ward and many other artists.
Sources: Tourville. <u>Wisconsin . . . Discography.</u>
   Prellberg. "Target/Tee Pee Records." <u>Lost and Found.</u>
   Dean Nimmer letter, 5/20/94

Teen Town/Blue Ribbon
(Jon Hall - 8/27/40; Thiensville)

Jon Hall's teen center, *Teensville in Thiensville,* and his *Teen Artists* management/booking company formed the basis for his early success. These enterprises led to a record label, which generated greater fortune for many of the area's bands. In the early 70's, Hall formed a second label, Blue Ribbon. Also a musician, Hall played drums and accordion.

Teen Town

101	Gremlins	Have You Seen My Little Girl/Sometimes I Feel	/67
102	Tony's Tygers	Little By Little/Days And Nights	2/68
	(Above also on A&M 921)		
103	Skunks	I Recommend Her/I Need No One	/68
	(Above also on World Pacific 77889)		
104	Randy	By The Time I Get To Phoenix/I Still Love Her	/68
105	Tony's Tygers	I Can't Believe/I Still Love Her	5/68
106	Skunks	Smalltown Girl/You Better Hold On To Me	/68
107	Tony's Tygers	Debbie On My Mind/I'll Know	/68
108	Carousel	I've Been With You/What Will You Do For Me	/68
109	Unchained Mynds	We Can't Go On This Way/Going Back To Miami	2/69
	(Above also on Buddah 111)		
110	Skunks	Doing Nothing/Listen To The News Today	5/69
	(Above also on White Whale 322 & 325)		
111	American Express	You're Going To Be The One/You And Me	/69
4789/4790	Ladds	Bring Back The Days/Goodness Gracious Baby	10/69
113	Sidewalk Skipper Band	Sidewalk Skipper/Jeannie At The Circus	/69
114	Carousel	I've Been With You/I Get Along Indefinitely	/69
115	Silver Bullets	The Lone Ranger/No Name Boogie	/70
116	Carousel	To Say Goodbye/I Get Along Indefinitely	/70
117	Pandemonium Shadow Show	Sunshine Summer Day/Tender Is The Girl	/70
118	Today's Tomorrow	You've Gone Away/Wanton Forest	/71
119	Family	I Wanna Do It/A Song	/71
	(Side 1 reissued on Pebbles *Highs In The Mid 60's, Vol. 15*)		
120	Avatar	Off Your Feet/It's All Right	/71
121	Passion	Headaches And Heartaches/Castaway	/71
122	Jon Hall & Lemon Drop Band	Twist Of Lemon/Lemon Drop Polka	/72
123	Jon Hall & Lemon Drop Band	Lemon-Aid/Chubby Mind	/72
124	Brethren	Can This Be Real/Happy Feeling	/72
125	Today's Tomorrow	Lifeless/Smile Away	12/72
1001	Fourth Generation	I'm So Happy/Revolution	

USA

The better known USA label of the mid and late 60's was a Chicago company with well over 100 releases and major chart action with the Buckinghams. However, the earlier USA was a Milwaukee based company. Whereas the Chicago company uses a 700 through 900 numbering system with an additional brief 100 series, the Milwaukee releases appear on a 1200 series. DJ's Lee Rothman (WRIT) and "Coffeehead" Larson (WEMP) were initial investors in the company, but dropped out after the first two releases due to possible conflict of interest. The names Bill Farrell and Phil Foster have also been mentioned as possible principals with the company. It is not clear if there was any connection between the two labels.

The early USA releases may have all been recorded in Chicago but the artists seem to have been primarily Milwaukee based. (There were also several Wisconsin artists on the later Chicago label and its affiliate, Destination).

1212	Roland Stone	Lost Love/Moanin' Soul	/59
1213	Noblemen	Thunder Wagon/Dragon Walk	/59
1214	Little Sir Ryland	My Worried Lover/	
		(with the Noblemen)	
1215	Noblemen	Sleep Beauty Sleep/	
	Toni Majestro	My Boyfriend Charlie/	
		(with the Noblemen)	
1216 - 1220			
1221	Von Gayels	Twirl/Loneliness	
1222	Noblemen	Dirty Robber/Forever Lonely	

(Above also on Profile 4012. Side 1 reissued on Pebbles *Highs In The Mid 60's, Vol 10*)

1223			
1224	Chuck Velvet	Red Lipstick/Wonders Of Love	
1311	John Frigo	Rock Em Sock Em/Bear Down	

Sources: Lee Rothman telephone interview, 6/4/94
       Brand Shank telephone interview, 6/20/93
       Clee. American 45 R.P.M. Records.
       Robert Pruter letter, 1994
       William C. Menor, 3/94
       Tourville. Wisconsin . . . Discography.

Window
(Sheboygan)

1009	Don Ragon	Jungle Rock/After Love	/59
1115	Gingersnaps	Bald Headed Papa/There's A Little Rock	
1116	Northernaire Serenaders	Well, Oh Well/My Reverie	

Source: Tourville. Wisconsin . . . Discography.

Wright
(Ken Wright)

Ken Wright was the radio name of a DJ who worked on a West Bend station. "His dream was to find a group to record and get the thing going," recalls Richard Podraza of Wanderer's Rest. Steve Turner of the Trodden Path remembers Wright having worked as a high school P.E. teacher. The company appears to have been run as a custom label of Cuca. See Cuca 6771, 67101, 6813, 6863, 6951, 7241 and Wanderer's Rest (Milwaukee).

Source: Richard Podraza telephone interview, 8/2/94
    Tourville. <u>Wisconsin . . . Discography.</u>

Cross Reference

For:	**See:**
Audio Unlimited	Sonic
Boom	Coulee
Dynamic Sound	Magic Touch
Hodag	Sonic
Knight	Coulee
Northland	Big Sound
Page	Raynard
Rampro	Feature
Rif	International Artists
Transaction	Coulee
Water Street	Pro-Gress

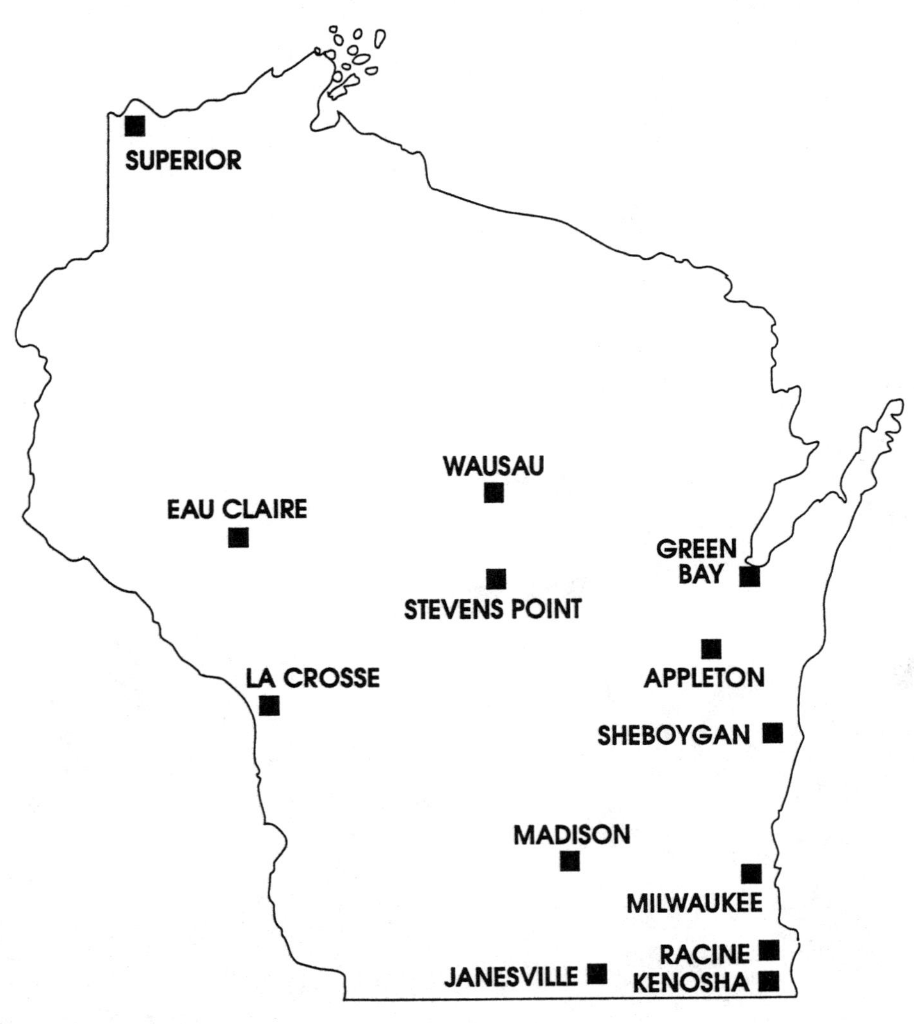
SUPERIOR
WAUSAU
EAU CLAIRE
GREEN
BAY
STEVENS POINT
APPLETON
LA CROSSE
SHEBOYGAN
MADISON
MILWAUKEE
RACINE
JANESVILLE
KENOSHA

All Over This Land

"It was a terrific time for bands in Wisconsin. We had all those beer bars, a lot of teen places to play, a lot of CYO dances and things like that. It was fun teaching guitar back in those days, too. Heck, you could teach kids 'Gloria' and 'Louie, Louie' and all those kinds of songs and within three or four months they could put a little band together."
  - Rick Gustafson (Loyal Opposition - Sheboygan), 6/14/94

And many of those little bands went on to record. This is an attempt to document as many of them as possible, subdivided by area as follows:

Appleton/Fox Cities	Sheboygan
Green Bay	Superior
Madison/Janesville	Eau Claire
La Crosse	Stevens Point/Wausau
Racine	Around The State

Also see label discographies for listings on many other artists for whom not enough information was found to justify an individual listing.

Appleton/Fox Cities

"Fox Valley might have been a bigger breeding ground for rock 'n' roll in Wisconsin than even Milwaukee or Madison, involving the 50's"
  - John Cooke (various bands), 2/20/94

An atypical ingredient in the Wisconsin scene was the existence of teen beer bars. Eighteen was the legal age for drinking beer outside Milwaukee county, and the locations that engaged in that trade provided a great outlet for young bands. The Fox Cities (Appleton and its surrounding suburbs, so named for their location in the Fox River Valley) and nearby Green Bay were the home of many such bars. The Prom, the Quarry, the Starlite and others were a hotbed of rock 'n' roll. The agency of Gary Van Zeeland, prominent in booking bands throughout the state, was also based in the area. Oshkosh bands are included in this section. Several area bands have reunited in recent years for an annual park dance known as *Applesock*. Proceeds go to benefit a local CYO.

Jules Blattner
(2/8/41; St. Louis)

Bobbin	105	Rock & Roll Blues/Gamblin' Man	3/59
	113	Green Stuff/Teen Town	7/59
K-Ark	609	Till I'm With You/Lonesome	/60
	612	Lover Doll/One More Time	/60
Norman	509	Slip 'n' Slide/Heartbeat	/61
	512	Do You Love Me/St. James Infirmary[1]	/61
Gaslight	400	Butterscotch Twist/Liszt Twist	/62
Norman	533	500 Pound Canary/I'm So Blue	/62
	538	Lover Doll/One More Time	/63
Coral	62437	The Thing/No Money Down	1/65
Norman	557	Crazy Stockings/Goodbye Baby	/65
Tee Pee	19/20	Pledging My Love[2]/Summertime Blues[3]	/67
DMA	101	That Ain't Love, That's Emotion/Tell Me About Hard Times	/69
Cine Vista	5	Unreal People/2001: A Soul Odyssey	/69
Target	2000	Fannie Mae[4]/School Days[5]	/71
Buddah	245	Down Bound Train/What You Gonna Do When I'm Gone	8/71
MGM	14396	Back On The Road Again/Backwater Blue	6/72
Metromedia	0105	Goin' Back On The Road Again/Backwater Blue	/73
Blue Ribbon	102	I Love You Mary Hartman/Jump In, Get Some	/76
Norman	1020	New Orleans[6]/Island Song	/89

LP's:

Buddah	5080	Call Me Man	/71
MGM	4808	The Mishtabula, Maine, Marching Band & Soil Salvation Society (Seluj Renttalb)	/72
Mountain	5624	Live (with Warren Groovy All-Stars)	/74
Desmond	A210	Back To The Basics	/79
Bon Air	2004	Jump On This	/92

Transplanted St. Louis rocker Jules Blattner made himself part of the Wisconsin scene when he moved to the Appleton area in the late 60's. During that time he wrote, recorded and produced at Target Productions.

Blattner started the Teen Tones at age 15, with his mother driving him to the gigs. The group's

---

[1]Louis Armstrong, 1929; many others
[2]Johnny Ace, 1955
[3]Eddie Cochran, 1958; Blue Cheer, 1968; Who, 1970
[4]Buster Brown, 1960
[5]Chuck Berry, 1957
[6]Gary U.S. Bonds, 1960

first record, "Rock 'n' Roll Blues"/"Gamblin' Man" in 1959, remains the most successful of his career. He claims that he and his band provided the backing for Chuck Berry on the *Chuck Berry In London* LP (Chess 1495) from 1965. (That album - apparently not done in London after all - included a chart single, "Dear Dad").

The singer/guitarist first made the Wisconsin scene working with a trio (Darrell Meister - bs, Paul Spencer - dr) and later hooked up with Warren Groovy's All-Star Band. His work at Target resulted in his first album, released on Buddah in 1971, and a second LP on MGM the following year. The MGM platter featured "Back On The Road Again," a single that got some action. Back in St. Louis and still cranking it out, Blattner won an award as the best local rock 'n' roll artist in December 1992.

Also see: Chosen Few - Stevens Point/Wausau (Warren Groovy)
Sources: Jules Blattner letter and telephone interviews, 3/93-4/93
     Tourville. <u>Wisconsin . . . Discography.</u>
     Clee. <u>American 45 R.P.M. Records.</u>

Jules Blattner (courtesy Jules Blattner)

Catalinas: Denny Noie, Harry Wheelock, Bob Dix, (bottom) Jim Kelly (courtesy Denny Noie)

Catalinas/Golden Catalinas

Al Posniak - gtr   **Roger Loos** - sx (11/28/40; Oshkosh)
Harry Wheelock - ld gtr (dec: 1988)   **Pete Sorce** - voc (6/22/44; Milwaukee)
Bob Dix - bs (1947-1987)   **Judy Lee (Reeths)** - voc
Jim Kelly - dr   **Denny Noie** - gtr (10/10/40; Little Chute)

Cuca	1094	War Party/Crazy Twistin' Baby		6/62
		(Side 1 reissued on *The Cuca Story, Vol.3)*		
Mundo	1000	Hey Little Girl/Forever And A Day		/63
Sara	6392	By My Window/Wo Wo		9/63
Knight	100	Dee Dee/It Ain't No Big Thing	(Denny Noie & the Catalinas)	/65
Knight	101	Come To Me/Yakety Sax Express		/65
Target	101/102	Varsity Club Song/Can Your Monkey Do The Dog[1]		11/66
Tee Pee	117/118	Dee Dee/Mojo Workin'		/67
Mean Mt.	1422	Dee Dee/It Ain't No Big Thing	(reissue)	/82

A typical name and a fairly typical beginning for this band but, with the entrepreneurship of Al Posniak, the story of the Catalinas goes beyond the ordinary. Starting with Posniak, two inexperienced guitarists, and borrowed drummers, the band survived on pure enthusiasm for the first few months. "There are no words to describe how bad we were," says Posniak, "but we went over."[2] The addition of drummer Jim Kelly from the Phaetons helped to solidify things.

Bob Mattice, who had previously fronted the Phaetons, was considered one of the best rock 'n' roll singers in the area. Upon his discharge from the armed forces, he was hired as a frequent guest with the Catalinas. The band's reputation grew. The Quarry, the hottest local teen bar, became known as the home of the Catalinas. They signed with Chess Records, though nothing was released.

The band's most successful record was their first release, "War Party." Their "Varsity Club Song" four years later was written about, and financed by, the well-known club in La Crosse. The Catalinas became the Golden Catalinas with gold suits, gold shoes and gold hair. They graduated from teen bars to night clubs. A few other lead singers and musicians went through the band over the next several years.

Posniak eventually began to shift into other aspects of the business. He was writing the *Badger Beat* column for the *Milwaukee Journal* and *Rockin' 'Round The Valley* for the *Appleton Post-Crescent*. In late 1966 he formed his record company, Target Productions. He closed it in 1972 when he was diagnosed with a brain tumor. He moved to Chicago and lived with a sister during his recovery.

---

[1]Rufus Thomas, 1964
[2]Milwaukee Journal, date unknown - courtesy Al Posniak

In the 80's he returned to the entertainment field, working for Talent International, an agency active in 10 states booking child talent. The company ran into some problems and became the subject of an expose on *Inside Edition*, bringing a rapid conclusion to that venture. Though Posniak says he was one who blew the whistle, it wasn't the type of national publicity he had once hoped for.

Drummer Jim Kelly had also become involved working with Target Productions. After the company's closing, he relocated to Las Vegas where he worked in an agency along with ex-Louis Prima drummer Bobby Morris. With a return to Appleton a few years later, he worked in a similar capacity with Gary Van Zeeland. Kelly also played in revival bands in the late 70's and now deals in rare antiques.

In 1985 the original Catalinas reunited for a performance at a 25-year class reunion. Sadly, before another three years had passed, both Bob Dix and Harry Wheelock had died, Dix of lung cancer and Wheelock from complications of diabetes. In 1991 Posniak returned to live performing as a single in Des Plaines, Illinois.

Also see: Denny Noie & the 4th of Never
        New Raging Storm, Raylene & the Blue Angels (Roger Loos)
        Judy Lee & the Playboys - Green Bay
        Bob Mattice - Cuca
        Pete Sorce - Milwaukee
Unrelated Catalinas: Backbeat, Catalinas, Crystal Ball, Dee Jay, Dial, Dominant, Fortune, Glory, Little, Original Sound, Pagoda, Ric, Rita, Scepter, S.E.I., Sims, Sugarbush, Summertime Sounds, 20th Century, Zebra
Sources: Al Posniak letters and telephone interview, 3/23/93, 8/28/93
        Bob Mattice telephone interview, 7/93
        Denny Noie telephone interview, 8/15/93
        Tourville. <u>Wisconsin . . . Discography.</u>
        Prellberg, Mark. "Golden Catalinas." <u>Lost and Found</u> #2 1993: 41-45

Cobblers/Syndicate
(Oshkosh)

Ron Spanbauer - voc
Pat Nugent - ld gtr (9/26/48; Oshkosh)
Mike Meidl - rh gtr   **Nick Christas** - gtr
Bob Weisapple - bs
Bob Misky - dr (2/6/48; Oshkosh)

Studio City   1060   Smokin' At The Half Note/Maybe I Love You   /66
                        (Cobblers)

Tee Pee   45/46   Next 21st Of May[1]/My Baby Kicked The Bucket   2/68
                     (Syndicate)

On the referral of a friend, the Cobblers traveled to Minneapolis for their sole recording on the Studio City label. After changing their name to the Syndicate of Sound, they were dismayed to see a California group by that name hit the national charts ("Little Girl," 1966). With the name shortened to Syndicate, they recorded at Target in Appleton.

Pat Nugent also recorded in the 70's with Blue Tail Fly on the Chief Oshkosh label. Bob Misky worked with Skip Arne & the Dukes out of Chicago. Nick Christas is reportedly playing blues gigs in San Francisco.

Unrelated Syndicate: Dore, Dot, Ebb Tide
Sources: Pat Nugent telephone interview, 4/2/94
         Bob Misky telephone interview, 6/5/94
         Tourville. <u>Wisconsin . . . Discography.</u>

Faros

Gary Daily - ld gtr (3/7/48; Neenah)
Steve Berg - rh gtr/kb (10/29/47; Appleton)
Chris Wyman - bs (8/14/47; Menasha)   **Bill "Wilbur" Vandenburgt** - kb (10/6/46; Appleton)
Dan Meredith - dr (11/23/47; Appleton)

Target   103/104   I'm Calling You Back/I'm Crying[2]   11/66
                      (Side 2 reissued on Pebbles *Highs In The Mid-60's, Vol 10*)

In addition to this release, some of the Faros were involved in other Target/Tee Pee recordings. Guitarist Gary Daily was a studio musician on the Lord Beverly Moss & the Mossmen single, as was Wilbur Vandenburgt, who took part in many of the company's sessions. "On the original Tee Pee label of 'Do You Wanna Dance' (by Love Society) it says 'Produced by Wilbur'," he explains. "Then, when it went national and it was pressed by Scepter, it says 'Produced by Al Posniak'. That's always been a bit of a sore spot with me." The Faros have appeared regularly in the annual *AppleSock* park dance.

Also see: Lord Beverly Moss & the Mossmen
          13th Hour (Wilbur Vandenburgt)
Sources: Gary Daily letter, 11/8/93
         Tourville. <u>Wisconsin . . . Discography.</u>

---

[1]w: Rick Smolinski
[2]Animals, 1964

Karl Fields & the Sands of Time
(Oshkosh)

Karl Fields (Nuenfeld) - 12 strg gtr

Kel   1141   Just Like That/I Was Wrong   /63

Karl Nuenfeld was working as a single at the Pioneer Restaurant on Lake Winnebago where he was seen by label owner Kelly Diciani. Nuenfeld later moved to Canada.

Source: Kelly Diciani telephone interview, 5/8/94

Kenny King & the Be Bops

Kenny King (Jaeger) - voc (8/22/41; New London)
Ken Kleist - gtr
Dan Derfus - gtr   **Rick Leigh (Smolinski)** - gtr (1/10/42; Appleton)
Tom Leininger - bs
Darryl Jaeger -dr (8/18/43; New London)

Cuca   1101   You're Alright/I'm Gonna Love You   7/62

Guitarist Rick Smolinski wrote both songs that this band recorded and joined the group when Tom Derfus left. Singer Kenny and drummer Darryl are brothers.

Also see: Denny Noie & the In-Crowd (Darryl Jaeger, Rick Smolinski)
       White Caps, Ricky & Raylene, Temptations (Smolinski)
Sources: Rick Smolinski telephone interview, 2/13/94
       Darryl Jaeger letter, 2/28/94
       Clee. American 45 R.P.M. Records.

Lord Beverly Moss & the Mossmen

Lord Beverly Moss - voc
Bob Timmers - ld gtr/bs
Gary Laabs - gtr (3/5/39; Appleton)
Vic Wendt - kb/bs
Tom Gebheim - dr

Target   107/108   Please, Please, What's The Matter/The Kids Are Alright 1/67
                           (Side 1 reissued on Pebbles *Highs In The Mid 60's, Vol. 10)*

"He was kind of Eric Burdon type guy, kind of hard to control," says Bob Timmers of this group's British singer. Since the English sound was big, these guys decided to go for the real thing by advertising in England's *New Music News* for a singer. "He came in on a visitor's visa and played with us for a while," says Timmers. "then he went to go on the road a little bit before the feds caught up with him and took him to Canada."

Though the Mossmen had just one release, the musicians all played in many area bands and Timmers has many happy memories. "People like myself, we turned on the radio and there was Elvis and we had to go out and buy a guitar and try to do it," he says. "I had the good fortune of growing up right with it. I was the first electric bass player in the area. We had to go order one out. There was no such animal available. You just saw them on TV or something."

Timmers added guitar to his arsenal by watching Gene Vincent's lead man, Johnny Meeks. "He was my idol in those days. We saw Vincent play around here and I'd just stand there and watch his hands for four hours. I'd get all kinds of free guitar lessons."

Also see: Say Mama - Milwaukee (Johnny Meeks)
      Target/Tee Pee Records - Wisconsin Labels (Tom Gebheim)
Sources: Bob Timmers telephone interviews and letter, 3/25/93, 4/3/93, 7/17/93
      Gary Laabs telephone interview, 2/13/94

Memories

Tom Noffke - ld gtr
Chuck Posniak - elec pno   **George Baer** - ld gtr
Bob Fusfeld - rh gtr   **Kip Kruse** - ld gtr
Dennis Becker - bs   **Frank Criclear** - bs
Charles Reitzner - dr

K.O.   107852   Mercy Mercy[1]/That's How Strong My Love Is[2]   /66

"As a band, the Memories were terrible," says former member Bob Fusfeld. "They were never in tune and the harmonies were lacking, but the fans loved them." Formed in 1965, this band may have been more noted for controversy than music.

As the first long-hair, non-uniformed band in the area, they became the first documented case of hair discrimination in the Appleton Public School System. They were the subject of articles in many newspapers around the state. Al Posniak (leader of the Catalinas, brother of keyboardist Chuck, and on the verge of forming Target Productions) exploited this situation to publicize the group and billed them as "Wisconsin's Own Rolling Stones."

------

[1]Don Covay, 1964; Rolling Stones - *Out Of Our Heads* LP, 1965
[2]Otis Redding, 1965; Rolling Stones - *Out Of Out Heads* LP, 1965

Fusfeld recalls the "Memoriesmania" incidents that followed: "Generally, these took place in Green Bay, where their clothes were ripped off, jealous boyfriends threatened band members, tires were slashed, Catholic authorities were outraged at their scruffy appearance, and parents overreacted."

The band played at WBAY auditorium dances and opened for the Turtles, Byrds, B.J. Thomas and Bobby Sherman at the Knight in Green Bay. They also provided some of the first stage experience to Doug Yankus who sat in on drums Monday nights at Clyde Schumacher's Highway 96 Beer Bar. (Yankus went on to work with Private Property and Soup and later with many name artists). The Memories' sole vinyl effort, recorded at a bar in Kaukauna, was one of Al Posniak's earliest productions.

A venture into the world of night clubs proved to be a visit to an alien planet. The Memories played their final gig in Rhinelander late in the summer of 1967. Drummer Chuck Reitzner later worked with the Velvet Whip, an unrecorded Milwaukee band circa 1969.

"The Memories were really the transition group in the valley," claims Fusfeld. "Do not allow anyone to understate this. They gave rise to many groups who emulated them."

Also see: Private Property of Digil (Chuck Posniak)
      Catalinas, Target/Tee Records - Wisconsin Labels (Al Posniak)
Unrelated Memories: Old Sound, Times Square, Way-Lin
Sources: Bob Fusfeld telephone interview and letter, 4/10/93, 5/7/93
      Tourville. <u>Wisconsin . . . Discography.</u>
      Osborne-Brown. <u>Rockin' Records.</u>

Montereys
(Winneconne)

Kenny Loehrke - voc
Wes Phillips - ld gtr   **Jimmy Thiele** - pno/org
Orville Luebke - rh gtr
Rudd Hoger - bs
Don "Pudge" Pinnow - dr (4/21/39; Winneconne)

Cuca	1002	Rockin' Fool/Rocker	(/I)	/59
		(Side 1 reissued on *The Cuca Story - Vol 1*)		
Gold Star	1001	Whiplash/Swamp Girl	(I/)	/62

The Montereys had an early Cuca release. Their second record was produced by WAPL DJ Bob Falkner who also owned the Gold Nugget in Appleton, where the band frequently appeared. The group broke up around 1966 and Don Pinnow worked with the Nashville Sounds for 17 years.

Unrelated Montereys: Arwin, Blast, Dee Jay, Dominion, East West, GNP Crescendo, Impala,
        Nestor, Prince, Rose, Saturn, Teenage, Trans American
Sources: Don Pinnow telephone interview, 7/4/94
        Tourville. <u>Wisconsin . . . Discography.</u>
        Osborne-Brown. <u>Rockin' Records.</u>

New Raging Storm/Ron Besaw & The Mojo Men

New Raging Storm:

Ron Besaw - gtr (4/19/46; Gresham)	**Roger Loos** - sx (11/28/40; Oshkosh)
Dick Schelk - gtr/kb	**Bob Anderson** - bs
Rollie Ritchie - bs	**Denny Noie** - gtr (10/10/40; Little Chute)

Tee Pee   15/16 Cry Girl/Monkey Time[1]   /67

Ron Besaw/Fuller was not aware of the previous Raging Storms from Toledo ("The Dribble,"
1961) when he chose the same name for his band. Perhaps someone at the record company was,
which would explain why the label modified it to New Raging Storm, something that Fuller
himself did not understand at the time.

The musicians in the right-hand column (above) did not work in the band with Fuller. It is not
clear whether Dick Schelk or Rollie Ritchie may have continued the band with various personnel
changes, or whether the others may have simply taken over the name.

Fuller readily acknowledges the source of the name of his later band. When I expressed my
curiosity because of my own membership in Milwaukee's Mojo Men, he said, "That's where
I got the name!" Oddly enough, this was apparently after San Francisco's Mojo Men had hit the
national charts, causing our group to abandon the title.

Ron Besaw & the Mojo Men:
Ron Besaw (Fuller) - gtr
Jesse Vasquez - kb/bs
Bobby Borlee - dr

Target   2002   I'm Sorry/I'm Sorry   (/I)   /71

Although the group was only a trio, Fuller says he used an orchestra on their recording session.
"I hired the Green Bay Symphony," he explains. "It cost me a fortune!" He also played on a
record by Kitty & the Kats (on Coulee) in 1970 before heading to Las Vegas and attracting the
attention of Tanya Tucker's manager. Making the name change from Besaw to Fuller, he
recorded an album that he feels could have put him in the big time, but medical problems took

---

[1]Major Lance, 1963

over and it was never promoted. Having filed a multimillion dollar malpractice lawsuit, Fuller is back with a Las Vegas show in 1994 and he expects to be recording again.

Ronnie Fuller

ECR		We All Play The Same Guitar
ECR	LP 392	The Only Way Back Home Is My Guitar

Also see: Coulee Records - Wisconsin Labels (Kitty & the Kats)
      Karen Wells/Black Knights (Bob Anderson)
Sources: Ron Fuller telephone interview, 12/12/93
      Tourville. Wisconsin . . . Discography.

Denny Noie & the In Crowd/4th of Never

Denny Noie - rh gtr (10/10/40; Little Chute)
Ricky Lee (Smolinski) - ld gtr (1/10/42; Appleton)
Dave Hermson - bs (5/29/40; Appleton)
Darryl Jaeger - dr (8/13/43; New London)   **Dave Yokam** - dr

Knight	101	Dee Dee/It Ain't No Big Thing	/65
		(Denny Noie & the Catalinas)	
Tener	150/151	Dee Dee/Don't Follow Me	/67

Denny Noie & 4th of Never: Dave Yokam, Dave Hermson, Denny Noie, Ricky Leigh (courtesy D. Noie)

Denny Noie goes back nearly to the beginning of the Fox Valley rock 'n' roll scene, having worked with both the White Caps and Jerry Williams & the Rockets. He formed the In Crowd in 1962 and worked clubs in Wisconsin, Minnesota, Illinois and Ohio. It was during a brief hiatus from that band that Noie worked with the Catalinas and recorded his first version of "Dee Dee."

In 1965, while visiting his estranged wife in Florida, Noie made a contact with the Orlando-based Tener label. It was this connection that resulted in the Appleton band, recording in Sauk City, securing a release on the obscure Florida label, even though the group never worked in that state. The second oddity is the fact that the record was released two different ways, one credit showing the In Crowd, the other the 4th of Never. Apparently Noie had decided to change the name because of a better-known In Crowd. (There was a minor chart record by the In Crowd on Viva and a top 20 hit by Jon & Robin & the In Crowd on Abnak. However, both appear to have been after Noie's record). After this second version of Dee Dee came out, the Catalinas also re-recorded the song with Pete Sorce on vocal.

In the years since, Noie has worked as a folk/Christian single, played with a 50's revival group and a blues band, and spent 12 years out of music. In the 90's he is a member of the Full Moon Blues Band.

Also see: White Caps, Ricky & Raylene, Temptations (Ricky Lee)
        Kenny King & the Be Bops (Darryl Jaeger, Ricky Lee)
        Jerry Williams & the Rockets (Denny Noie)
Sources: Denny Noie telephone interview, 8/15/93
        Dave Hermson telephone interview, 12/12/93
        Lemlich, Jeff. <u>Savage Lost</u>. Plantation, FL: Distinctive, 1992.

Nomads
(Oshkosh)

Jack Litjens - gtr
Mike Yanke - elec pno
Joe Litjens - bs
Larry Wolfe - dr (11/10/46; Oshkosh)

Kel   1000   You Come Around/Don't Come Running To Me   /65

The Nomads included a pair of identical twins from Holland on guitar and bass. Drummer Larry Wolfe later joined the Friends who had a 1970 release on Night Owl.

Unrelated Nomads: ABC, Balboa, Damon, Derby, Discotek, Genie, J&S, Josie, Mo-Groov,
        Northern, Orbit, Pharos, Prelude, Rust, Samter, Soft, Spotlight, Stark, Tornado
Sources: Larry Wolfe telephone interview, 4/2/94
        Tourville. <u>Wisconsin . . . Discography.</u>
        Osborne-Brown. <u>Rockin' Records.</u>

Private Property (of Digil)

Doug Yankus - gtr (11/20/50; Orange, NJ - 9/24/82; Long Beach, CA)
Chuck Posniak - kb (10/7/44; Appleton)   **Gary Schibilski** - kb/rh gtr
Dan Jacklyn - bs   **Dave Faas** - bs
Steve Gertch - dr

Target	109/110	Look At Me (The Mantelpiece Marter)(sic)/To My Friends	2/67
Tee Pee	115/116	Destination Nowhere/The Patch Of Brick	5/67
	23/24	Sunshine Flames/Princess	/67
	35/36	Jewelry Lady/I'm Looking At You	11/67

"It had something to do with the streets we lived on," says Dan Jacklyn, attempting to explain what "Digil" means. "It was just kind of nonsense and it stuck with us." Keyboardist Chuck Posniak is the brother of the Catalinas' Al Posniak. The most noteworthy member of the band was Doug Yankus, already an accomplished songwriter and guitarist. Yankus formed the power trio Soup, then graduated to working with several name artists before his death at age 31.

Also see: Memories (Chuck Posniak)
      Soup (Doug Yankus, Dave Faas)
Sources: Chuck Posniak telephone interview, 7/93
      Dan Jacklyn telephone interview, 10/24/93
      Prellberg. "Private Property Of Digil." _Lost and Found_
      Tourville. _Wisconsin . . . Discography._

Raylene & the Blue Angels/Dairylanders
(Oshkosh)

Raylene Loos - voc (1/10/38; Winneconne)
Roger Loos - sx (11/28/40; Oshkosh)
Tom Loos - gtr
Tom Reischl - bs
Don   - dr

Cuca	1141	Sentenced/This Is The Last Time	8/63
		(Raylene & the Dairylanders)	
	6633	Shakin' All Over[1]/Canadian Sunset[2]	3/66
		(Raylene & the Blue Angels)	

---

[1]Guess Who, 1965
[2]Hugo Winterhalter, Andy Williams, 1956

Raylene Loos was the wife of Tom Loos who is the brother of Roger. Producer Kelly Diciani, also owner of the Kel label, says the choice of group name on the first release was Cuca's idea. Cuca head Jim Kirchstein apparently thought "Dairylanders" was appropriate to the polka feel of the record. Raylene later moved to Milwaukee and sang in country-western clubs until 1975.

Also see: Ricky & Raylene
        Bob Mattice (Tom & Roger Loos, Tom Reischl)
        Kel Records - Wisconsin Labels
Sources: Raylene (Loos) Bartel telephone interview, 5/28/94
        Kelly Diciani telephone interview, 4/2/94
        Tourville. <u>Wisconsin . . . Discography.</u>

Ricky & Raylene

Ricky Lee/Leigh (Smolinski) - gtr (1/10/42; Appleton)
Raylene Loos - voc (1/10/38; Winneconne)
Roger Loos - sx (11/28/40; Oshkosh)
Tom Loos - gtr

Tee Pee 4517/4518 It Must Be Love/Light Of Day   /67

"There was another excellent player around here who should have made it and never did," says Bob Timmers (of Lord Beverly Moss & the Mossmen and other bands). "It was Ricky Lee Smolinski. The guy was fantastic. In 10th grade he was showing all the teachers how to play. The guy was a super talent who should have gone somewhere but just didn't have the breaks, I guess."

Lee, who used alternate spellings of his stage name, worked with many area bands, recorded with several and wrote a great deal of material. He is the lead guitarist and songwriter on both sides of Wisconsin's first rock 'n' roll record by the White Caps. He and Raylene Loos did not actually work together as a duo. This record was their only joint venture, though they do share the same birthday.

Smolinski later joined California Earthquake, a group fronted by Lana Bogan. Bogan was the daughter of Marcia Day who was involved in the management of Seals & Crofts. California Earthquake had previously recorded for World Pacific in their namesake state. The group had disbanded when Bogan and her husband came to Wisconsin to attend school. The new incarnation of the band, including Smolinski, returned to the West Coast and opened many shows for Seals & Crofts and other name acts.

Smolinski never recorded with that band, opting instead to return to Wisconsin to get his degree at Lawrence University. Now a computer analyst, he played until 1980 when carpal tunnel surgery forced a stop. Informed of the complimentary comments of his early peers, he replied, "I appreciate that. It's nice of them to still remember."

Also see: Denny Noie & the In Crowd
        Kenny King & the BeBops
        Raylene & the Blue Angels/Dairylanders
        Temptations
        13th Hour
        White Caps
        Bob Mattice & the Phaetons - Cuca (Roger Loos, Tom Loos)
Sources: Bob Timmers telephone interview, 4/3/93
        Rick Smolinski telephone interview, 2/13/94
        Photocopy of Whitecaps record - courtesy Allen Bauman
        Tourville. Wisconsin . . . Discography.

Soup

Doug Yankus - gtr (11/20/50; Orange, NJ - 9/24/82; Long Beach, CA)
Dave Faas - bs
Rob Griffith -dr (dec)   **Roger Jerry** - bs (2/6/48; Green Bay)

Target	1005	Big Boss Man[1]/Veronica	4/69
LP's:			
Arf Arf	1	Soup	12/69
Big Tree	2007	The Soup Album	/71

"Soup formed in May of 1968," explained Doug Yankus in a 1975 interview.[2] "That was when Cream was happening and Jimi Hendrix and that whole trip, so were a quote-unquote power trio. That was the only side of the band that ever really got exposed, but we were into other things, too. It was always a schizophrenic band." Yankus and Dave Faas had both come from Private Property of Digil.

"The first (LP) came out in December '69. We had done some demo tapes for Elektra down in Ohio and when we left the session we got a rough copy of the mix. They ended up turning us down but we really liked the tapes so we released them, just the raw copies that we had. The flip side somebody recorded on a little home machine at a concert we did at the University of Whitewater."

The band began to gain notoriety with a performance at the Fillmore East, a review in Rolling Stone and an album on a national label, but there were disappointments. The sessions for the Big Tree LP were rushed because of a small budget. Regarding the New York appearance, Yankus said, "Everybody was building us up for all the big things and all this big money, and nothing

------

[1]Jimmy Reed, 1961; Charlie Rich, 1963; Elvis Presley, 1967
[2]Bruckner, Bill. "Milwaukee's Music & Musicians." Bugle American 11/5/75: 152

came of it, so we came back here. When we got together we were young, in our teens, and I had those stars for a long time. When things started getting too realistic and I realized all the things that were coming down, I sort of flipped out. Things fell apart and I got sick of the whole mess."

Soup became an off-and-on enterprise for a few years. Yankus recorded in Nashville with White Duck on Uni, then came back and re-formed the band. About 1974 Yankus left again and played on John Hiatt's first LP. What was probably the final edition of Soup included Roger Jerry on bass, due to an auto accident injury to Dave Faas. Jerry also recalls another drummer doing some of the gigs.

Yankus went on to work with Tracy Nelson and Jimmy Buffet. He moved to Hollywood where he continued music studies and did studio work. He died at age 31 of insulin shock syndrome after a prolonged diabetes illness.

Also see: Private Property of Digil
        People, Society - Green Bay (Roger Jerry)
Sources: Roger Jerry telephone interview, 12/13/93
        Bruckner, Bill. "Milwaukee's Music & Musicians." <u>Bugle American</u> 11/5/75: 152 -
            courtesy Peter Lewna and Jacques Hutchinson.
        Tourville. <u>Wisconsin . . . Discography.</u>
        Clee. <u>American 45 R.P.M. Records.</u>
        Osborne-Brown. <u>Rockin' Records.</u>
        Prellberg. "Private Property ..." <u>Lost and Found.</u>

Sunstone Lollipop
(Oshkosh)

Keith Diciani - bs/kb (9/17/51; Oshkosh)
David Diciani - gtr/kb (5/26/53; Oshkosh)
Tom Hansen - dr (9/30/52; Oshkosh)

Kel			
	8515	People Of Today/Sunshine	/67
	8516	Never Sad/Forever Be In Doubt	/68
	8518	Mr. Keat/My Day Of Dream	/69

The Diciani brothers are the sons of label owner Kelly Diciani. They later worked as a duo. David continues in the music business in Sacramento, California. Tom Hansen recorded as a member of Blue Tail Fly in the 70's.

Also see: Kel Records - Wisconsin Labels
Sources: Kelly Diciani telephone interviews, 4/2/94, 5/8/94
        Tourville. <u>Wisconsin . . . Discography.</u>

Temptations

Ricky Lee (Smolinski) - gtr (1/10/42; Appleton)
Roger Loos - sx (11/28/40; Oshkosh)

Cuca   1094   Call Of The Wind/Bluer Blue   6/62

This is an earlier effort of noted Appleton guitarist Rick Smolinski.

Also see: Denny Noie & the In Crowd
        Kenny King & the Be Bops
        Ricky & Raylene
        13th Hour
        White Caps
        Bob Mattice & the Phaetons - Cuca (Roger Loos)
Unrelated Temptations: No other Temptations records are related to this group.
Sources: Rick Smolinski telephone interview, 2/13/94
        Roger Loos telephone interview, 3/94

13th Hour

Ricky Lee (Smolinski) - gtr (1/10/42; Appleton)
Bill "Wilbur" Vandenburgt - bs (10/6/46; Appleton)
Jimmy Joe Van Hoof - dr (dec)

Target   10/11 All Right And About Time/Badger Beat   10/66

This initial release for the Target label, described by *Lost And Found* Magazine as "crude
'She's About A Mover' style garage," was a studio project, rather a working band. Rick
Smolinski praises drummer Jimmy Joe Van Hoof as very talented young musician who also
played keyboard and harmonica. Van Hoof reportedly committed suicide.

Also see: Denny Noie & the 4th of Never
        Kenny King & the Be Bops
        Ricky & Raylene
        Temptations
        White Caps
        Faros (Wilbur Vandenburgt)
Sources: Rick Smolinski telephone interview, 2/13/94
        Prellberg. "Target/Tee Pee Records." <u>Lost and Found.</u>

Torquays

Jim Chase - gtr
Paul Smith - kb
Alan Ives - bs
Tom Guenther - dr (9/27/51; Oshkosh)

Tee Pee   43/44 I'll Never Forget/Even The Wind   1/68

With a name sounding more like 1958 than 1968, the Torquays were formed by a group of friends that came out of the Webster Stanley Jr. High Pep Band. A few years later they won a battle-of-the-bands in Oshkosh. The victory earned them the right to compete in the finals in Milwaukee where they lost to Tony's Tygers.

The Torquays were strong on group vocals, performing Four Seasons and Beach Boys material. After they recorded "Even The Wind," bassist Alan Ives did an arrangement of it for the Oshkosh High band and chorus. When drummer Larry Wolfe of the Nomads joined, the group evolved into the Friends who had a 1970 release on Night Owl. Tom Guenther and Jim Chase continue to work with the Friends in 1994.

Unrelated Torquays: Aertaun, Colpix, Gee Gee Cee, Gypsy, Holly, Original Sound, Punch,
        Rock-It, Whirl
Unrelated Friends: MGM, Oblivion
Sources: Larry Wolfe telephone interview, 4/2/94
        Tom Guenther telephone interview, 4/27/94
        Tourville. Wisconsin . . . Discography.
        Osborne-Brown. Rockin' Records.

Karen Wells - "The Winemaker's Daughter"
(Karen Sohm - 3/19/42; Oshkosh)

Cuca   1035   Believe Him/Never Gonna Let Him Go   5/61

Black Knights (backing band for Karen Wells)
Jerry Gehrke - ld gtr
Stan Siebold - rh gtr
Bob Anderson - bs
Jerry Kowall - dr

"My dad was a winemaker and he wrote a book about making wine when I was 16. That's why he wanted me to bill myself as the Winemaker's Daughter on the record," explains Karen Sohm. "Believe Him" is a country ballad with a Connie Francis touch while the flip is typical 12-bar teen rocker. Sohm did a demo in Nashville for Faron Young but nothing came of it. 30 years later, still sounding good and preferring pop-standard material, music remains her first love.

Karen Wells w/Temptations: Bob Anderson, Tom Reischl, Clyde Cox, Karen Wells, Jerry Gehrke
(courtesy Karen Wynveen)

Black Knights: Jerry Gehrke, Stan Siebold, Jim Kelly, Danny Peil, Bob Anderson,
guitarist in front right unidentified (courtesy Karen Wynveen)

The Black Knights and other area bands often played Sundays at the Kurve Inn, a beer bar outside Omro. Earlier members of the band included drummer Jim Kelly, who subsequently joined Bob Mattice's Phaetons and the Catalinas, and singer Danny Peil, later with Milwaukee's Apollos/Tigers and the Corporation.

Also see: New Raging Storm (Bob Anderson)
Source: Jerry Kowall telephone interview, 5/23/94
        Karen Sohm telephone interview, 6/4/94
        Clee. American 45 R.P.M. Records.

White Caps/Johnny Edwards & the White Caps

✳ **Wisconsin's earliest known rock 'n' roll recording session**

Johnny Edwards - voc (dec)
Ricky Lee (Smolinski) - ld gtr (1/10/42; Appleton)
Jerry Stengl - kb   **Denny Noie** - gtr (10/10/40; Little Chute)
Jack Gardner - rh gtr
    (Duke Wright - bs)

Northland   7002   Rock 'N' Roll Saddles/Why'd You Leave Me   1/57

Not Milwaukee, not even Madison, but a teen-age Appleton band recording in Wausau, of all places. This, as far as we know, is Wisconsin's first rock 'n' roll recording. Reportedly getting good regional chart action, the first 500 copies were pressed as the White Caps on a white label, the next 500 as Johnny Edwards & the White Caps on the same label, then 2000 as the White Caps on a maroon label. Wausau musician John Cooke recalls the record being played on *American Bandstand's* record rating segment.

With no bass player in the band, label owner and polka band leader Duke Wright filled in. The White Caps' previous drummer, Jerry Van Dynhoven, missed out by quitting the group the day before the recording session. As Jerry Williams, he then formed the Rockets. Rhythm guitarist Jack Gardner was an Appleton radio personality. "Jack was one of the DJ's - he and Johnny Coy from WAPL - that took our band over and put us on the circuit at the Casino and places like that," explains Rick (Lee) Smolinski. "They changed their format of record hops to having live bands and they were one of the first to promote that in this area."

Smolinski, who wrote both sides of the record, went on to work with many area bands. Singer Johnny Edwards died some years ago. "He was one of the finest people that I've ever known," says Smolinski. "He has touched my life in many ways. He is sorely missed."

Also see: Big Sound/Northland Records
        Denny Noie & the In Crowd; Kenny King & the BeBops; Ricky & Raylene
            Temptations; 13th Hour (Smolinski)

Unrelated White Caps: Blue River
Sources: Rick Smolinski telephone interview, 5/93
    Tourville. <u>Wisconsin . . . Discography.</u>
    Allen Bauman, 1993
    Osborne-Brown. <u>Rockin' Records.</u>

Rockets: (top) Roger Loos, Jerry Williams, (bottom) Cliff Peranto, Denny Noie, Larry Russell, Bill Pable
(courtesy Denny Noie)

Jerry Williams & the Rockets

Jerry Williams (Van Dynhoven) - dr/sx
Cliff Peranto - ld gtr   **Donnie Williams (Van Dynhoven)** - dr
Larry Russell - gtr   **Carol Williams (Van Dynhoven)** - voc
Denny Noie - gtr (10/10/40; Little Chute) **Denny Hymmerman** - bs
Bill Pable - pno   **Bob Timmers** - ld gtr
Roger Loos - sx   **Jerry Cole** - gtr (9/23/39; Green Bay)

Rocket   001   Blueberry Lane[1]/A Boy Like You[2]   (I/)   6/62

---

[1]Actually "Blueberry Hill" - Glen Miller, 1940; Fats Domino, 1957; many others
[2]"A Girl Like You" - Gary Stites, 1959

Perhaps it's appropriate that Jerry William's Rockets follow the White Caps in our alphabetical listing. Williams (Jerry Van Dynhoven) played drums for the White Caps until the day before their historic recording session. "WAPL was handling us (White Caps) at that time," Van Dynhoven says, "and they were really throwing the shaft to us because we were all young kids - like making $60 when they made $1,000 - so I broke away."

"They went on to head-on competition with the White Caps," says later member Bob Timmers. "The White Caps just stood there and played. The Rockets had uniforms, we had Chuck Berry stuff, we were flying all over the stage, we were doing the showman stuff, so the band was a little more popular."

The Rockets first line-up included no less than three guitar players. "All there was, was stand up bass in those days, so we played with rhythm guitars," laughs Van Dynhoven. He had apparently made amends with WAPL by 1962, as it was Bob Falkner, a DJ from the station, who produced their sole recording. The record couples a re-titled instrumental version of "Blueberry Hill" with the leader's wife singing the female version of a song charted three years earlier by Gary Stites.

Also see: White Caps
        Denny Noie & the In Crowd, Catalinas (Denny Noie)
        Lord Beverly Moss & the Mossmen (Bob Timmers)
        Jerry Cole - On The Charts
        Temptations (Roger Loos)
Sources: Bob Timmers telephone interview, 4/3/93
        Jerry Van Dynhoven telephone interviews, 6/20/93, 7/24/93

Green Bay

As the smallest city to have its own NFL franchise, Green Bay is well known for the Packers. But, with shows at the Riverside Theater, clubs like the Piccadilly (on Main Bl.) and the 616 (616 Lime Kiln Rd.), and some of the previously mentioned teen bars, the town had plenty of musical action, too.

Centurys

Phil Cornelisen - sx
Jim Morrison - ld gtr (6/24/45; Oconto) **Eddie Farah** - gtr
Paul Willems - rh gtr   **Dave Parpovich** - gtr
Donne Cornell - bs   **Mark Helniak** - bs
David K. (Pilz) - dr (8/21/45; Green Bay) **James Copeland (Scovell)** - kb

Micro	6344	Her Love/Wayward Wind[1]		4/63
		(Side 1 reissued on *Badger A Go Go* LP)		
Markus	LP1003	Centurys Live	(recorded at 1000 Club, Marinette)	/72
SSP	DK-019	Together/Liza, Liza	(2nd Century)	/77

Related:
James Copeland

| SSP EP | DK-004 | Super Star/Part Of You/Get It On/ | /75 |

Together since 1961 and still containing two original members, the Centurys/2nd Century is one of the longest running bands in the state. They are into their fourth decade, if not their 2nd Century, the new name they adopted in 1975. Though not as obvious as some, the initial title is one of those good old car names, the Buick Century. All five original members were students at Premontre High School.

Though drummer Dave Pilz is one of the remaining original members, he also moonlighted briefly with the Dupries in 1965. Pilz has been running his own studio, *Studio Sound Productions*, since the 70's, along with working for Henri's Music.

Also see: Dupries (Dave Pilz, Dave Parpovich)
      Rhythm Royals (Phil Cornelisen)
      Originals (Jim Morrison)
Unrelated Centurys/Centuries: Bangar, Carlton, Cleopatra, Dooto, Fortune, Life, Mark C,
      Renco, Rich, Spectra Sound, Swan, Times Square, Veltone
Sources: Dave Pilz telephone interview, 2/28/94
      Osborne-Brown. Rockin' Records.

---

[1]Gogi Grant, Tex Ritter, 1956

Dupries/Candy & the Corals

Dick Schulz - gtr/bs (10/7/46; Plymouth)
Annie Duprey Schulz - bs (11/7/46; Green Bay)
Joanie Duprey Rousseau - voc
Carol Duprey - voc   **Dave Parpovich** - ld gtr
Dave Pilz - dr (8/21/45; Green Bay)

Test	100	Baby Doll/Kissy Face	5/65
Thunderbird	106	Baby Doll/Kissy Face	6/65
Test	110	I Should Have Loved You More/I Know[1]	/66
		(Candy & the Corals)	
Dyn-O-Mite	012	More Today Than Yesterday[2]/If You Love Me[3]	/76
		(Candy & Co.)	

With a name derived from an altered spelling of the three sisters' surname, the Dupries hit the number 2 spot locally on WDUZ. Being produced by a DJ from the station probably didn't hurt any on its way to becoming a two-sided hit. Producer Dick Hoff, known on the air as Dick Holiday, also co-wrote the "Baby Doll" side. Test was a St. Paul, Minnesota, label. The subsequent Thunderbird release came out of Buffalo, New York.

The group evolved into Candy & the Corals, then Candy & Co. Schulz continues in the 90's, having resurrected the name of a 60's band from another part of Wisconsin, the Shy Guys.

Also see: Centurys (Dave Pilz, Dave Parpovich)
        Rhythm Royals (Dick Hoff)
        Jerry Dee & the Intruders - Eau Claire (Dick Hoff)
Sources: Dave Pilz telephone interview, 2/28/93
        Dick Schulz telephone interview, 3/3/94
        Tourville. <u>Wisconsin . . . Discography.</u>

Grease

Jim Krueger - gtr (9/24/49; Manitowoc - 3/29/93; Green Bay)
Junior Olson - gtr   **Paul Kowalski** - gtr
Larry Byrne - kb   **Mike Larsheid** - bs (6/3/44; Green Bay)
Jim Denk - bs   **Mark La Que** - dr
Andy Pigeon - dr

---

[1]Barbara George, 1962
[2]Spiral Staircase, 1969
[3]Kay Starr, 1954

Centurys: Donne Cornell, Paul Willems, Dave Pilz, Phil Cornelisen, Jim Morrison (courtesy Dave Pilz)

Grease: Paul Kowalski, Jim Krueger, Jim Denk, Mark La Coque, (bottom) Larry Byrne
(courtesy Richie Krueger)

USA   921   Spoonful[1]/Shimmick   /68

Grease is significant primarily for leader Jim Krueger who later worked with Dave Mason and noted pop-jazz flautist Tim Weisberg. Krueger wrote Mason's only major hit, "We Just Disagree," a song revived by country artist Billy Dean in 1993. Bassist Mike Larsheid worked with many Wisconsin acts and went to San Francisco to join the Denny Geyer Band (post A.B. Skhy), followed by Elvin Bishop. It was through some of these connections that Krueger landed in California and worked with the name acts. He recorded his own LP, "Sweet Salvation," for Columbia in 1978.

Back in Green Bay in more recent years, Krueger formed the Normal Adults. The band was slated to do the 1993 Milwaukee *Summerfest* when, sadly and suddenly, Krueger died while hospitalized March 29.

Also see: Judy Lee & the Playboys, The People (Mike Larsheid)
Unrelated Grease: Lion
Sources: Richie Krueger telephone interview, 8/14/93
         Erickson, Brenda. "Normal Adults satisfied being rock's local rebels." <u>Bay Beat</u> 7/1/92
             - courtesy Roger Jerry
         Osborne-Brown. <u>Rockin' Records.</u>

Invaders

Dave Dobry - voc
Mark "Squirrel" Paulick - ld gtr (3/4/51; Green Bay)
Pete Polzak - kb
Jim Sawyer - bs
John Sawyer - dr

Cuca	--	My One Love (unreleased acetate)		/68
Calendar		I Won't Be Lanly (sic)/A Song For Squirrel	(/I)	/68
USA	902	Flower Song/Without A Tear		/68
Capitol	2292	California Sun/Love And Hate		11/68

It looked as though this group of high school musicians was off to a great start when they got airplay on an unreleased acetate they had recorded at Cuca. "The radio stations all played it and got gangbuster response," claims Mark Paulick. "A producer who was in town from Chicago happened to hear it and said, 'I want to redo this,' so we redid it."

---

[1]w: Willie Dixon

In the process, the song changed from "My One Love" to "I Won't Be Lonely." Perhaps the misspelling of "Lonely" on the label was the first indication that things might not be so great after all. The Invaders did eventually land a contract with Capitol but, after one release, they decided the deal was too one-sided and the band broke up.

Paulick had originally formed the Journeymen but left that band before their recording. In the 90's, he plays with another band with 60's roots, 2nd Century.

Also see: Journeymen (Mark Paulick)
        Originals (Pete Polzak)
Unrelated Invaders: Bamboo, El Toro, Instro, Justice, Mohawk, Musitone, OO, Phillips, Raynard, Vaughn Ltd., Whingding
Sources: Mark Paulick telephone interview, 2/26/94
        Tourville. Wisconsin . . . Discography.
        Clee. American 45 R.P.M. Records.
        "Rogues Gallery." Lost and Found.
        Osborne-Brown. Rockin' Records.

Journeymen

Dennis Pharis - voc
Tom Halfpap - gtr
Mike Giese - kb
Tobin "Toby" Kraft - bs
Donald "Buzz" Eastman - dr

Tee Pee   57/58 You're A Better Man Than I[1]/Realities In Life   6/68

Formed in 1966 (including guitarist Mark Paulick), the Journeymen went through a series of personnel changes, bringing an entirely revamped line-up to the Target Studios in 1968. The session came about as a result of winning a battle-of-the-bands sponsored by Henri's Music in Green Bay. The group disbanded about a year later.

Also see: Invaders (Mark Paulick)
Unrelated Journeymen: Amy, Capitol, Iona
Sources: Prellberg & Tom Halfpap. "Journeymen." Lost and Found.
        Osborne-Brown. Rockin' Records.

---

[1]Yardbirds -*"Having A Rave Up With The Yardbirds"* LP, 1966

Judy Lee & the Playboys

Judy Lee (Reeths) - voc
Pat Reeths - gtr   **Dave Parpovich** - gtr
Dan Helland - gtr (8/18/37; Brooklyn, NY)   **Mike Larsheid** - bs (6/3/44; Green Bay)
Jim Jandrain - bs (7/12/44; Green Bay)
Tim Polzak - dr (1/25/42; Madison)

Darly   6382   I Wonder Could It Be You/Low Voltage   8/63

This is the same Judy Lee who worked with the Golden Catalinas. Brother Pat Reeths led the
Playboys as a separate entity before she joined.

Also see: Originals (Helland, Jandrain, Polzak)
          Dupries, Centurys (Dave Parpovich)
          Grease, The People (Mike Larsheid)
          Randy & the Candymen (Jim Jandrain)
          Catalinas - Appleton
Unrelated Playboys: This band has no connection with any other Playboys' recordings.
Sources: Jim Morrison telephone interview, 3/19/94
         Eddie Farah telephone interview, 3/27/94
         Dave Pilz letter, 3/12/94
         Dan Helland telephone interview, 4/94
         Jim Jandrain telephone interview, 6/12/94

Night Owls/Dick Allen & the Fairlanes
(Oconto Falls)

Dick Allen

Cuca   1075 Waitin' By The School/Please Don't   (Night Owls)   4/62
                  63114 Dreamin'/Night Twist   (Dick Allen & the Fairlanes)   11/63

Source: Cuca ledger cards - courtesy Jim Kirchstein

Originals

Dan Helland - ld gtr (8/18/37; Brooklyn, NY)
Jim Morrison - rh gtr (6/24/45; Oconto)
Pete Polzak - kb
Jim Jandrain - bs (7/12/44; Green Bay)
Tim Polzak - dr (1/25/42; Madison)

Raynard   10039 Pretend It's Alright/Now's The Time   /65

Though certainly not an original name, this band was started by three "original" members of Judy Lee & the Playboys and was in existence for just over a year. Dan Helland went on to work with Dan Riley, well known as an opening act for many name country entertainers. Helland then became a photographer in Nashville and has photographed Roy Clark and other top artists. Pete Polzak performs in hotels and lounges in the Chicago area.

Also see: Judy Lee & the Playboys (Dan Helland, Jim Jandrain, Pete Polzak)
　　　　　Centurys (Jim Morrison)
　　　　　Invaders (Pete Polzak)
　　　　　Randy & the Candymen (Jim Jandrain)
Unrelated Originals: Brunswick, Champ, Diamond, Fantasy, Jackpot, Motown, Original Sound,
　　　　　Phase II, Sara, Soul, Stash
Sources: Jim Morrison telephone interview, 3/19/94
　　　　　Dave Pilz letter, 3/12/94
　　　　　Dan Helland telephone interview, 4/94
　　　　　Osborne-Brown. Rockin' Records.

The People

Frank Ellefson - gtr
Michael Maltby - sx
Bob Vandersteen - tp/org/gtr/bs
Roger Jerry - tp/org (2/6/48; Green Bay)
Mike Larsheid - bs (6/3/44; Green Bay)
John McVane - dr

Tee Pee　　　　69/70 I Can't Stand It[1]/Ode To Billy Joe[2]　　　　　　　　10/68

An odd choice of name for this band, since the group People had a #14 national hit earlier that same year ("I Love You"). Roger Jerry says it's "The" that makes the difference in the name.

Also see: Soup - Appleton, Society, (Roger Jerry)
　　　　　Grease, Judy Lee & the Playboys (Mike Larsheid)
　　　　　Ventrills, Nigh Tranes - Madison/Janesville (Frank Ellefson)
Unrelated People: Capitol, Paramount, Polydor, Zebra
Sources: Roger Jerry phone interview, 12/12/93
　　　　　Tourville. Wisconsin . . . Discography.
　　　　　Osborne-Brown. Rockin' Records.

---

[1]Chambers Bros. - *The Time Has Come* LP, 1968
[2]Bobbie Gentry, 1967

Randy & the Candymen

Randy Rybicki - voc
Eddie Farah - gtr (7/1/47; Green Bay)
Jim Hanna - sx
Jim Jandrain - bs (7/12/44; Green Bay)
Andy Pigeon - dr

Big Sound   6427   Little Sister[1]/The Girl Can't Help It[2]   2/64

Father Cornell, an unlikely combination of priest and booking agent, booked this band to open shows locally. "He brought all the big acts in," says Eddie Farah, "and we were his favorite group." The band lasted from about 1963-66 and opened for the Byrds and many others.

Also see: Centurys (Eddie Farah)
          Judy Lee & the Playboys (Farah, Jim Jandrain)
          Originals (Jandrain)
Sources: Dave Pilz letter, 3/94
          Eddie Farah telephone interview, 3/27/94
          Jim Jandrain telephone interview, 6/12/44

Rhythm Royals
(Oconto)

Roger Sohrweide - ld gtr
Phil Cornelisen - sx   **Roger Pagel**
Dennis Swaer - bs   **Dave Swaer** - dr
Mark Thompson - dr (11/17/40; Manitowoc)

Test   103   Out Of My Mind/Near To You   /65
Sahara   109   I Don't Wanna Go Back To School/Loneliest Man In The World /65

The Rhythm Royals existed from about 1960 to 1970. Both records were produced by WDUZ DJ Dick Holiday (Dick Hoff) who, oddly enough, placed them with labels in St. Paul and Buffalo, New York. Mark Thompson recalled that the Buffalo label, Sahara, was supposed to have some connection with the company for which Del Shannon recorded. (Shannon was on Amy at the time). Unfortunately, the tapes sat on someone's desk until the subject matter (returning to school) was no longer timely. All four songs were written by Phil Cornelisen, who claims the first release made top 40 charts in 40 states.

---

[1]Elvis Presley, 1961
[2]Little Richard, 1957 (from film starring Jayne Mansfield)

Also see: Centurys (Phil Cornelisen)
        Dupries (Dick Hoff)
        Jerry Dee & the Intruders - Eau Claire (Dick Hoff)
Sources: Mark Thompson telephone interview, 4/10/94
        Dick Schulz telephone interview, 3/3/94
        Phil Cornelisen letter, 4/94
        Tourville. <u>Wisconsin . . . Discography.</u>

Secrets

Larry Fenlon - rh gtr
Pat Noel - ld gtr
Tom Bertrand - kb (4/13/49; Green Bay)
Bob Pitton - bs
Dave Krieger - dr (dec)

Raynard   10047 I Don't Know/I Know It's You   /65

Unrelated Secrets: Decca, DCP, Omen, Phillips, Quality/RFC, Swan, Wand
Sources: Tom Bertrand telephone interview, 6/11/94
        Tourville. <u>Wisconsin . . . Discography.</u>
        Osborne-Brown. <u>Rockin' Records.</u>

Society

Kevin Kohl - ld gtr
Roger Jerry - Farfisa org (2/6/48; Green Bay)
Mike Dennis - rh gtr
Kenny Rogers - bs
John Blarjeske - dr

Feature   112   One Way Ride/For Me   /66

Society's only release was produced by Sam McCue of Milwaukee's Legends.

Also see: The People (Roger Jerry)
      Soup - Appleton (Jerry)
Unrelated Society: Mark VII
Sources: Roger Jerry phone interview, 7/10/93
      Tourville. <u>Wisconsin . . . Discography.</u>
      Osborne-Brown. <u>Rockin' Records.</u>

Vibratones

Jim Maas - gtr   **Bob Ellis** - dr
Jerry Schroeder - gtr
Roger Bader - kb (2/20/40; Green Bay)
Reggie Roznowski - sx
Dickie Leigh - bs
Gary Van Sistine - dr

Cuca	1073	Money[1]/Sidewinder	3/62
		(Side 2 reissued on *The Cuca Story, Vol. 3*)	
Raynard	10032	Eventually/Little Egypt[2]	5/65
	10044	I Remember Yesterday/Screamin' Mimi	/65

The Vibratones began in 1958 and continued for 35 years with only a few personnel changes. They enjoyed a hit in some areas with their version of "Money." "That was the heyday," says Roger Bader, "when we were traveling all over Wisconsin and Upper Michigan, sold lots of records. I don't know how we did it!"

A Milwaukee musician who frequently worked in Green Bay recalled when "the Vibratones bass player kicked in all the Royal Lancers equipment on the stage at Jack's Point Tavern, because they thought the Lancers were moving in on their popularity - and they were! I can still see the foot marks in the Showman amps!" Bader, though admitting the bass player had a temper, does not remember this incident, saying, "We were all well behaved." Doug Tank of the Royal Lancers also claims no recollection of the episode.

With most of the members working their way through college, the group evolved into a club band, mixing comedy and show tunes with rock 'n' roll. Maas, Roznowski and Bader all earned degrees in music. Bader now works in the travel business and serves as a church music director.

Unrelated Vibratones: Mastertone
Sources: Roger Bader telephone interview, 2/20/94
      Tourville. <u>Wisconsin . . . Discography.</u>

---

[1]Barret Strong, 1960; Kingsmen, 1964
[2]Coasters, 1961

Vibratones: (top) Jim Maas, Roger Bader, Reg Roznowski, (bottom) Dick Leigh, Gary Van Sistine, Jerry Schroeder (courtesy Roger Bader)

Madison/Janesville

At a distance of about 30 miles, these two cities are close geographically but their musical proximity probably owes a lot to Ken Adamany. Beginning with his own Nigh Tranes and going on to major success managing Cheap Trick, Adamany must have booked nearly every band in the state at some point. He was born in Janesville and still maintains a Madison office in the 90's.

There were plenty of live music opportunities for college functions, and the Shuffle Inn was one of the popular clubs in town for many years. Many Illinois bands, especially from Rockford, also worked in the area and booked through Adamany. Except for possible listings in label discographies, those bands are not included in this book.

Bowery Boys/Baby Grand/Clicker

Dick Wiegel - gtr   **Jim Kelly** - tp
Ron Page - kb   **T.J. Wimperman** - tp
Ken Heim - gtr   **Greg Clemons** - voc
Jeff Amundson - fl   **George Cash** - sx
Don Richardson - tp   **Mar Everest** - gtr
Steve Tracy - bs   **Mike Briggs (Briganadello)** - gtr/bs
Cub Tracy - dr   **Bob Schmitke** - gtr
                                         Ron Sprous

Bowery Boys
Hemisphere   102   It's For You/Duck   /69
Baby Grand
Hemisphere   1604   Twelve Bars Of Blues/Nature's Way[1]   /72
               5009   Lucy Cain/Cockeyed Doodle Blues   /72
Clicker
Hemisphere   105   Keep On Tryin'/So Sharp   /73
Clicker   101   Tailspin/So Sharp   /73
               102   Toto Comes Home/Bottles   /74
               103   You Say Goodbye/Thinking About You   /75
LP's:
Hemisphere   5180   Clicker   /73
Clicker   1975   Harde Har Har   /75

Though this band came to its fruition as Clicker in the 70's, they qualify for our 60's coverage in their original incarnation as the Bowery Boys. The common thread is the Tracy brothers, Steve and Cub, who first began to play in teen-age bands around Platteville and Belmont.

Relocated to Madison, with horns added, the Bowery Boys did their first demos under the production of radio personality Jonathan Little, whom Cub Tracy holds in high regard. Hemisphere was the label of the band's management and the first release was recorded at Milwaukee's Kennedy Studios. The name was changed to Baby Grand after a couple of years and various personnel changes, but the final designation of Clicker was adopted soon after that.

"We traveled our brains out," says Cub Tracy, referring to 10 years of 275-300 one-nighters a year. Working with such names as Cheap Trick, Ides Of March, REO Speedwagon, Steve Miller, B.B. King and many more, the band was run on a very professional level. "We were trying to compete with the big groups," says Tracy, "and in order to do that you had to have good sound equipment, good lighting equipment, and you had to have the big time clothes, so we just loaded up and went to New York and got them."

---

[1]Spirit - *Twelve Dreams Of Dr. Sardonicus* LP, 1970

"Keep On Tryin'" was Clicker's most successful single, reaching the top five in Madison. Member Mike Briganadello (aka Memphis Johnny) went on to become a successful studio musician in Nashville and he appeared on the first two Amy Grant LP's. Later Clicker singer Greg Clemons (not on any of the recordings) had a solo release on Nemporer.

"(We were) trying to do anything that we could do to get to the pot of gold," Tracy says. "Almost got there a few times and, by golly, for one reason or another we just never got to stick our toe into it." Tracy and former members of the band's road crew bought into the Good Music Company in Madison. Drop in, he may divulge his real name.

Unrelated Baby Grand: Arista
Sources: Cub Tracy telephone interviews, 5/2/93, 6/20/93
       Phil Nee Show, WRCO, 10/92 - courtesy Phil Nee
       Tourville. __Wisconsin . . . Discography.__

Cannons

Lee Larson - voc (1/13/48; Madison)
Mike Keilhofer - gtr (6/28/47; Madison)
Pete Loeb - sx
Jerry Cratzenberg - bs   **Jim Perkins** - bs
Mike Turk - dr

Fan Jr.	5504	Sweet Georgia Brown[1]/Lonesome	/66
Night Owl	1312	Day To Day/Love Little Girl	2/67
		(Side 1 reissued on Pebbles *Highs in the Mid 60's - Vol 15* as "Days Go By")	

The Cannons began in 1965 and lasted about five years, playing around Wisconsin, Illinois and Michigan. Their first release was recorded while the band was appearing at the Satellite Lounge. The Night Owl sides, described on the Pebbles LP jacket as having a strong Beau Brummels influence, came during an engagement at the Gun Club. Lee Larson says the Cannons had discussed recording "I Wanna Do It" but felt it would be considered too suggestive to get airplay. The song then became an area hit for Robin & the Three Hoods.

Unrelated Cannons: Compleat, London, Mercury
Sources: Mike Keilhofer telephone interview, 8/16/94
       Lee Larson telephone interview, 8/21/94
       Tourville. __Wisconsin . . . Discography.__
       Osborne-Brown. __Rockin' Records.__

---

[1]Ben Bernie, 1925; Bing Crosby, 1932; many others (Harlem Globetrotters theme)

Crucibles/Kiriae Crucible
(Madison)

Ed Erickson - gtr (1/31/47; Dodgeville)
Greg Kimmerly - gtr   **John Edland** - voc
Treble Lysenko - gtr   **David Brownley** - kb
Bruce Hull - bs   **Rod Butler** - bs
Tom Fisher - dr   **Fred Elwakil** - dr

Madtown	401	You Know I Do/Beware Of Birds	/66
Night Owl	6836	The Salem Witch Trail (sic)/Complain	3/68
		(Kiriae Crucible) (Side 1 reissued on *Badger A Go Go* LP)	

This band seemed to be plagued by spelling problems. Their name was Crucible - singular - with the plural added by mistake on the record label. The record, which was financed by WISM newscaster Tom Rogers, also shortened the song title from its original "Beware Of Low Flying Birds."

In high school at the time, the group broke up when some of the members went their own ways after graduation. However, it wasn't long before another group of high school musicians approached Ed Erickson about putting another band together. A new incarnation of Crucible was born, a second recording was done, but the spelling problem was even worse. Trial was misspelled as trail on the label. The name change, however, was the band's idea. Ed Edland had been reading about Eric the Crucible and the Salem witch trials. Ed Erickson chose Eairik as a spelling of Eric (more odd spelling!), then reversed it (pronounced ki-ray). The spelling of the song title was finally corrected on the Cuca compilation LP *Badger A Go Go*.

Sources: Ed Erickson telephone interview, 3/94
        Prellberg. <u>Lost and Found.</u>

Jimmy Dawson/Dixie Drifter

County Fair	711	Mean Woman Blues/Big Black Bug Boogie	
Fan Jr.	1992	Playboy/Double Bug Rag	
Cuca	1186	Little Hero/Rings On My Fingers, Bells On My Toes	10/64

"He was a great guy," says Roger Brotherhood of Jim Dawson. "He used to have a show on WMAD and he featured a lot of local musicians. He always did a whole lot to help local groups. He was active in the scene right up until his death (of cancer) helping younger musicians." (Brotherhood is a well-known Madison guitarist who worked with the White Trash Blues Band in the late 60's. That band did some unreleased recording for Dunwich).

Sources: Roger Brotherhood telephone interview, 7/4/94
        Tourville. <u>Wisconsin . . . Discography.</u>

Fugitives

Dick Moulder - kb
Mike McCluskey - ld gtr

Trend   101   You're The Kind Of Girl/Come On And Clap   /66
                        (Side 2 reissued on Pebbles *Highs in the Mid 60's - Vol 15*)

Unrelated Fugitives: Arvee, Cleveland, Columbia, D-Town, Fenton, Hideout, Justice, Mala,
       Midnight, Roulette, Shoestring, Sims, Westchester
Source: Tourville. <u>Wisconsin . . . Discography.</u>
       Osborne-Brown. <u>Rockin' Records.</u>

Gentlemen: Bruce Shaw, David Kenison, Shane Todd, Jon St. John, Bob Kenison,
(courtesy Ken Adamany)

Gentlemen

Shane Todd - voc (6/21/43; St. Albans, WV)
Bob Kenison - ld gtr (2/1/46; Madison)
Robert Cardwell - rh gtr   **Bruce (Brewster) Shaw** - rh gtr (5/16/45; Cass City, MI)
David Kenison - bs(2/7/42; Madison)   **Chuck Scalia** - dr
Jon St. John - dr (12/30/45; Madison)

Spirit   5791   I Really Love You/Elephants   /65

The Gentlemen may be the only recorded band to feature a future astronaut as a member. Bruce Shaw joined the Air Force after graduating from UW and was chosen by NASA in January 1978. He was a pilot on the Spacelab 1 Mission in 1983 and commander on Mission 61-B two years later.

The Gentlemen became known for their tight show and appearance. "These guys had a show from start to finish on a set," recalls Oshkosh musician Jerry Kowall. "They were the first ones around here that were really that professional. They appeared in colonial uniforms and hats, just very attractive, professional costumes. And Shane Todd was like a DJ - a real big buildup on each song and he just kept it going and going. The whole thing was a real tight set." Though Todd had done other recording, he got drafted before this band's studio opportunity.

Bob Kenison later worked with Dr. Bop & the Headliners. Jon St. John continues in the entertainment business as a booking agent since 1968. The Spirit label was owned by Paul Logergren and Bob Olson who had also written and produced "I Want The Beatles For Christmas" by Jackie & Jill on Cuca.

Also see: Speedy & the Alka Seltzers (Bob Kenison)
        Shane Todd
Unrelated Gentlemen: Apollo, Vandan
Sources: Jon St. John telephone interview, 3/94
        Shane Todd telephone interview, 8/3/94
        Bob Kenison telephone interview, 8/7/94
        Jerry Kowall telephone interview, 5/23/94 (see Karen Wells)
        Cassutt, Michael. Who's Who In Space - The First 25 Years. Boston: G.K. Hall & Co.,
            1978
        Tourville. Wisconsin . . . Discography.

Honey & the Dew Drops/Scotty Stuart

Scotty "Honey" Stuart (Cameron) (11/20/38; Madison)
Sandy Stuart (Cameron) (2/1/41)
Jack Bach (Bieulisbach) (6/27/41)
Tip Topp (Walter Roberts) (11/28/40)
Frank Zitske

MMC   005   Come On My Little Baby/Confucius Say   /60
               006   Little Rocker/It Was A Nightmare   /60
                        (Scotty Stuart)

Honey, the lead singer of this vocal group, was actually a baby-faced young man, 21-year old Scott Cameron aka Scotty Stuart. Cameron's sister Sandy was also in the group and their father played piano and got together a group of musicians to back them on their first record. The second release, Scotty's solo effort, employed backing by Allen "Ace" Bauman, Leo Weidenfeld and Harry Jay (Johnson) of the Crossfires, along with Jim Krug on piano. The sessions were done at radio station WTTN in Watertown.

Cameron purchased the MMC label but deactivated it when he moved to Nebraska. He left the music business to run a motel in Omaha but was inspired to resurrect the label when the Beach-Niks, five musicians with their hair sprayed silver, checked into the establishment one day. The band recorded a remake of his tune "It Was A Nightmare."

From 1969-1973 Cameron worked for an agency in Chicago booking name big bands. In 1973 he began handling Muddy Waters. Relocated to Burbank, California in 1989, Cameron's management now handles Buddy Guy, Billy Cobham and others, while still taking care of business for the late Muddy Waters' family. Cameron is also very active in artists' rights and works to obtain funds that have been unfairly withheld from many older recording artists.

Recalling an early involvement with Ken Adamany, Cameron says, "His very first promotion was at, I think, an Elks Club in Janesville. Honey & the Dew Drops were his act. The top 40 DJ was Bill Dyke, who went on to be mayor (of Madison)."

Also see: MMC Records
        Crossfires
Sources: Allen Bauman, 1993
        Scott Cameron telephone interview, 4/27/94

Johnson Brothers

Cliff Johnson (Brizendine) - ld gtr
Chuck Johnson   **John Cooke** - dr (7/11/40; Green Bay)

Cuca   1024   Like Rachel/Julie Dear   (I/)   1/61

Chuck Johnson and Cliff Brizendine met in Greenland while serving in the Air Force. Brizendine later worked with country singer Bobby Hodge and with the Muleskinners, Jim Sundquist's post-Fendermen group. "We called him Cliff 'Guitar' Johnson," says Sundquist. "He was just absolutely fabulous." Drummer John Cooke (brother of Curley Cooke) was on the record though not actually a band member. John still plays in the 90's.

Also see: Fendermen - On The Charts
Unrelated Johnson Brothers: London, Valor
Sources: John Cooke letter, 3/94
        Jim Sundquist telephone interview, 7/3/94

Nigh Tranes

Ken Adamany - kb (3/25/"early 40's"; Janesville)   **Ron Boyer** - dr
Jerry Chase - gtr   **Denny Berg** - gtr
Bob Shebesta - sx   **Frank Ellefson** - gtr
Lloyd   - dr   **Steve Miller** - gtr
                                 Boz Scaggs - bs (6/8/44; Canton, OH)
                                 Tim Davis - dr (11/27/44; Janesville - 9/20/88; Las Vegas)
                                 Ben Sidran - kb (8/14/43; Chicago)

Cuca   1012   Hangover (Swamp Fever)/Rockin' Abe   9/60
                        (Side 2 reissued on *The Cuca Story, Vol 1*)

Ken Adamany's track to worldwide success managing Cheap Trick began on a Nigh Trane. The group's only record was produced by Vilas Craig. The Nigh Tranes were working steadily as Adamany was attending school. "The band became so popular that I ended up booking my friends' bands because I couldn't handle all the work," he says. This was the beginning of what was probably the largest agency in the state. "We were virtually THE clearing house for bands in the area," he continues. "At one time we had 112 bands."

The Nigh Tranes used many fill-in musicians on gigs, including Boz Scaggs and Steve Miller. Keyboardist Ben Sidran also went on to much success, primarily in the jazz field. After some session work for Miller and several others, Sidran's first recording as a leader was for Capitol in 1971. He later appeared on Blue Thumb, Arista, A&M, Polystar, Island, Madrigal, Windham Hill and Go Jazz. Sidran is a published author and has done record, radio and television production involving many name artists. He has worked with the Rolling Stones, Eric Clapton, Al Jarreau and many others.

In 1967 Adamany began to handle a group out of Rockford called the Grim Reapers. The band was scheduled to open for Otis Redding one night at the Factory in Madison. It was the night when the closing act didn't show up. Redding's plane crashed on Lake Monona December 12. Grim Reaper became Fuse and released an album on Epic. They broke up and reformed as Cheap Trick in about 1973 and first charted in 1977.

In the 90's, after a bout with cancer, Adamany maintains an office in Madison and continues to manage Cheap Trick.

Also see: The People - Green Bay, Ventrills (Frank Ellefson)
        Feature/Rampro Records - Wisconsin Labels (Ken Adamany)
        Tim Davis - On The Charts
        Boz Scaggs - On The Charts/Relocated
        Steve Miller - On The Charts/Relocated
Sources: Ken Adamany telephone interview, 6/7/94
        Ben Sidran letter, 7/10/93

P.J. Murphy

Kathy McBroom - voc
         - ld gtr
Gary Sagamiller - rh gtr   **Andy Duvall** - ld gtr (7/6/45; Milwaukee)
Ron Hileman - bs
Jim Kasdorf - dr

Leaf   LP   6475   P.J. Murphy   7/64

Legend has it that Sigma Alpha Epsilon fraternity member Paddy Murphy was "pinned" to three girls simultaneously and, upon their discovery of that fact, he drank himself to death. At an annual party in his honor, the fraternity would hold a parade down Madison's State Street. The event included the opportunity to lie in the coffin and be carried down the street by robed bearers in return for a pledge.

Such is the story behind the name of this band, made up of U.W. students. The group played two or three times each weekend and, "We used to sell a ton of them (LP's) at every gig," says Andy Duvall. "We were very popular, not only on our campus, but most of the Big Ten campuses. It was great, great fun."

Sources: Andy Duvall letter, 4/23/94
         Tourville. <u>Wisconsin . . . Discography.</u>

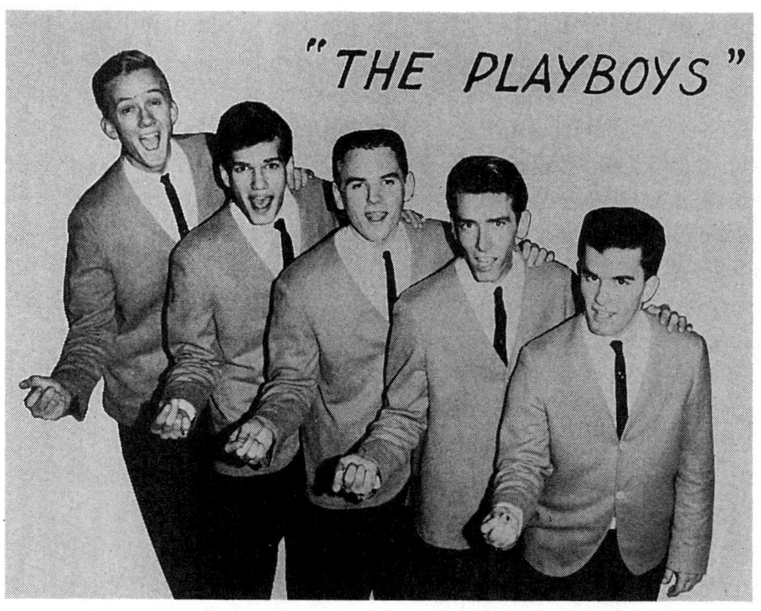

Playboys: Paul Zoerb, Jim Peterman, Bill Patterson, Rick Kludt, Nels Christiansen (courtesy Rick Kludt)

Playboys

Jim Peterman - voc (8/26/44; Milwaukee)   **Wayne Champion** - voc
Rick Kludt - ld gtr (3/24/45; Milwaukee)   **Kevin Peterman** - bs
Rick Bruhn - rh gtr   **Nels Christiansen** - dr (7/17/44; Milwaukee)
Paul Zoerb - bs   **Steve Sperry** - gtr (10/3/41; Ft. Atkinson)
Bill Patterson -dr   **Mike Warner** - dr

Cuca   6371   Look At Me[1]/Shout[2]   7/63

There were probably several thousand bands called the Playboys (I was in one, weren't you?), but the membership of Jim Peterman makes this one notable. Peterman went on to play keyboard on the first two Steve Miller albums, also appearing on record with Chuck Berry, bluesman James Cotton and others.

Though the Playboys started in the Milwaukee suburb of Wauwatosa, the band shifted to Madison as the members attended college there. Booking through Ken Adamany and rooming with Tim Davis, Peterman fell in with the Adamany clan of musicians, which included Boz Scaggs and Steve Miller. "There was a group of musicians that would play in one combination and be one name, and in another combination and be another name," says Peterman. "Sometimes Ken would play with the Chordairs (Tim Davis' band) and it would be the Nigh Tranes."

Peterman also worked with New Blues/A.B. Skhy before leaving for the West Coast to join Miller in 1967. "Steve Miller could be very difficult to get along with and there were some rough times," says Peterman, "but I have no regrets about either playing in the band or leaving when I did."[3] The keyboardist has been back in the Janesville area since the early 70's and he plays with the Gospel Bells.

Also see: A.B. Skhy (Jim Peterman)
        Easy Street (Nels Christiansen)
        Crossfires - Cuca, Steve Sperry - On The Charts (Steve Sperry)
        Robin & the Three Hoods (Mike Warner)
Unrelated Playboys: All of them - even two others on Cuca!
Sources: Jim Peterman letter and telephone interview, 5/10/93, 12/30/93
        Nels Christiansen telephone interview, 5/7/94
        Milam, Stan. "Area Rock Legends Reached For Top During The 1960s." Janesville
            Gazette 10/17/91: 1C - courtesy Stan Milam, 4/93.

---

[1]Buddy Holly
[2]Isley Bros., 1959; Joey Dee, 1962
[3]Milam, Stan. "Janesville's Rock 'n' Roll Roots." Janesville Gazette 10/17/91: 1C

Bobby G. Rice
(7/11/44; Boscobel)

Pre-1970 releases:

Jo-Cur		Break The News/Under The Midnight Lovelight	/68
		Every Moment, Every Hour/Butterfly Woman	/69

LP:

Jo-Cur	1000	Bobby's Best	/68

Beginning with the family band, Bobby G. Rice progressed into substantial success on the country charts in the 70's. Rice was only five years old when he first performed on the family's live radio show on WRCO in Richland Center. He also sang on some of his sister's recordings on Cuca. Rice went to Nashville to record his first LP from which a few tunes were released locally back in Madison. In 1970 his first national release became his first hit and he made the permanent move to the Music City the following year.

Though he never crossed over to the pop charts, his first five hits were all covers of earlier rock tunes, starting with "Sugar Shack" (with extensive lyric changes). His biggest success, his own composition "You Lay So Easy On My Mind," has also been covered by many pop artists, including Andy Williams, Pat Boone and Roy Orbison.

Rice has recorded for Royal American, Metromedia Country, GRT, Sunset, Sunbird, Chart, and Door Knob, while charting over 30 singles.

Sources: Bobby G. Rice telephone interview, 6/19/94
      Phil Nee, 1993
      Darold Beier telephone interview, 8/14/93

Robin & the Three Hoods/Marrell's Marauders

Dave Reed - gtr
Jim Schwartz - rh gtr
Bob Bernhagen -bs
Bruce Benson - dr   **Mike Warner** - dr

Fan Jr.	1003	I Wanta Do It[1]/The Marauder	(Marrell's Marauders)
	1003	I Wanta Do It/The Marauder	(Robin & the Three Hoods)
Hollywood	1110	I Wanna Do It/That's Tuff	
Fan Jr.	5680	I Wanna Do It/That's Tuff	
	5678	We The Living/A Day You'll Never Forget	

---

[1]Bobby Comstock, 1963 (flip of "Let's Stomp")

Possibly related:
Robin & the Batmen
Sara   6614   Batskinner/Louie Louie[1]   1/66
DJ   670   The Riddler/

This band was very popular as they toured throughout the state in their Robin Hood costumes. Their oft-released, and sometimes covered, version of "I Wanna Do It" became well known in the area. It's a logical guess that the Robin & the Batmen records are connected with the former Robin, but that may be a false assumption. The Batmen release on Sara had the involvement of a Greg Martin.

Also see: Playboys (Mike Warner)
         Speedy & the Alka Seltzers, Shane Todd (Bruce Benson)
Sources: Bob Gugel telephone interview, 8/12/94
         Tourville. Wisconsin . . . Discography.
         Dale Luther, 1994
         Dick Stark, 1994

Scarlet Henchmen
(Janesville)

Carl "Chark" Trieloff - rh gtr/sx/kb (6/10/47; Wauwatosa)
Jim Johnson - ld gtr
James Gardner - bs
John Schaller - dr

Night Owl   6835   Train 2:15/Ring Dreams   3/68
              6913   Crystal Palace/Melody For An Unknown Indian   1/69

Though a band called the Henchmen recorded right in the hometown of the Scarlet Henchmen, there is no connection with between the two. The former group was from Rockford, Illinois. There is also no connection with the Henchmen VI, who were from Ontonagon, Michigan.

The Scarlet Henchmen evolved out of an unrecorded band called the Motleys and toured around Wisconsin and Illinois between 1966-1968. Carl Trieloff, who wrote all four of the recorded songs, picked up the nickname "Chark" as a combination of Charlie, Chuck and Carl. Trieloff now resides in Kentucky. Guitarist Jim Johnson later worked in a duo with his wife.

Sources: Carl Trieloff letters, 4/12/94, 6/12/94
         Tourville. Wisconsin . . . Discography.

---

[1]Kingsmen, 1963; many others; w: Richard Berry

Scarlet Henchmen: Carl Trieloff, John Schaller, Jim Gardner (courtesy Carl Trieloff)

Talismen: John Javorsky, Dave, Paul Beneke, Bill Sherek, Russ Loniello (courtesy Russ Loniello)

Speedy & The Alka Seltzers

Jerry Lakes (Lariden) - gtr/bs (12/28/43; Reedsburg)	**Jim Donovan** - dr
Bob Kenison - bs/gtr	**Butch Moore** - gtr/bs (1942-1989)
Bruce Benson - dr	**Jim Bisbee** - dr (2/5/39; Portage)
	Bob Bellard - dr
	Jim Lombard - bs (2/7/43; Reedsburg)
	Lance Massey - ld gtr

Feature	501	Donna[1]/Stop The World	(Speedy)	/65
Tee Pee	3302	Cathy Lost Her Love Today/I Wonder What She's Doing Tonight[2]		/68

Related:

DBL Enterprise	LP 3001	All I Ever Need Is You	(April Walker & Jerry Lakes)	/74

"Everybody thought Butch Moore was Speedy because he was the lead guitarist," says Jerry Lariden, "but that wasn't the way it was. I was Speedy originally." It's interesting that Moore seemed to figuratively take Lariden's place as the "Speedy" entity. A few years earlier, Moore had taken Lariden's place on a Madison TV show. Lariden had appeared on Teen Time (with future country star Bobby G. Rice) and Moore was his replacement when he left to form the Alka Seltzers.

The band was threatened with a lawsuit by Alka Seltzer®, resulting in a brief name change. When they failed to draw much of a crowd under the name Double Image they went back to the previous title. "We said, 'Let them sue us," says Jim Bisbee. "It would be the best publicity we ever had." No legal action took place.

Guitarist Lance Massey also worked with Beau Gentry. Later Alka-Seltzers member Jim Lombard is Lariden's cousin. Lariden returned to TV in the 70's on the Glen Cass Show on WFRV, channel 5 in Green Bay. He and cast member April Walker recorded a Christmas album with Cass. Eventually Lariden and Walker took over the show and released their own album.

Also see: Ventrills (Bob Bellard)
      Gentlemen (Bob Kenison)
      Robin & the Three Hoods, Shane Todd (Bruce Benson)
      Shane Todd (Jim Bisbee)
      Little Artie & the Pharaohs -Milwaukee (Jim Lombard)
Sources: Bob Bellard telephone interview, 2/14/93
      Jerry Lariden telephone interview, 12/11/93
      Jim Lombard telephone interview, 1/5/94
      Jim Bisbee telephone interview, 8/12/94

---

[1]Ritchie Valens 1958
[2]Tommy Boyce & Bobby Hart, 1967

Talismen

Paul "Rabbit" Beneke - gtr
Bill Sherek - bs/gtr (3/10/46; Spartanburg, SC)
John Javorsky - bs
Russ Loniello - dr (5/24/45; Madison)

Rampro   115   Glitter And Gold/She Belongs To Me[1]   10/66

"We had good music, good booze and good women," laughs Russ Loniello, who had only been with the Talismen a few days when they cut their record. The session was produced by Dick Campbell who also played guitar on it. "Glitter And Gold" placed in WISM's top ten for the entire month of October 1966. Loniello is now a singer specializing in Italian festivals.

Also see: Tikis (Bill Sherek)
          Dick Campbell - Around The State
Unrelated Talismen: American Arts, Blue Star, Dot, Hideout, Prestige
Sources: Bill Sherek telephone interview, 8/22/94
         Russ Loniello telephone interview, 8/30/94

Teddy Boys

Don Uglow - voc
Leo Weidenfeld - gtr (2/18/40; Milford)
Allen "Ace" Bauman - gtr (7/9/40; Lake Mills)
Glen Zastrow - pno
Ron Bass - dr

Northland   7005   She Rocked With Me/Jody   /58

Formed in the summer of 1957, the Teddy Boys are responsible for one of Wisconsin's early rock 'n' roll releases. Allen Bauman, who wrote both sides, formed the Crossfires and was involved with a few other early rockers on record in the area.

Also see: Crossfires (Allen Bauman, Leo Weidenfeld)
Unrelated Teddy Boys: Cameo, Ricky Dog, MGM
Source: Allen Bauman letters, 1/93, 3/93
        Osborne-Brown. Rockin' Records.

---

[1]Bob Dylan - *Bringing It All back Home* LP, 1965

Tikis

Hugh Pearl - ld gtr
Dale   - rh gtr
Bill Sherek - bs (3/10/46; Spartanburg, SC)

Cuca	6641	We're On The Move/Rick-O-Shay	(/I)	4/66
Related:				
Mercury	73631	Roadie Song/Yellow Truck		11/74
		(Road Crew)		

You never know what might turn up when you search for members of an obscure rock 'n' roll band of nearly three decades past.

Bill Sherek began doing session work as a saxophonist at Cuca Studios while still in high school. He formed the Tikis at the beginning of his sophomore year at college and the band did well playing fraternity gigs. Sometime after the release of the record, Sherek formed a second band, the Talismen, who recorded on Rampro. After playing with other touring groups, he worked as a booking agent. In 1969 he was involved in the management of the band Axis (Plastic Earth 6993) for whom he also wrote songs.

After another year of college Sherek started a sound company and worked with Bachman-Turner Overdrive. Writing a song about the experience, he got a deal with Mercury Records. "So I put together a band - one last stab at rock 'n' roll stardom," he relates, "and opened for some of my sound company clients which, by that time, included Bob Seger, Kiss and Ted Nugent." The label didn't pick up the option for an LP and Sherek moved on. "One of the problems I had with Mercury was that all the executives assumed that Randy Bachman (of BTO) really wrote the song," he explains. By the second half of the 70's Sherek had become tour manager for Angel, a heavy metal band that charted six albums on Casablanca.

After an attempt to launch his own record label, Sherek ran Applewood Studios in Denver. Next came employment with a former road manager who was working as a television account executive. In 1983 Sherek became a project manager and, in the next three years, was involved in the start-up of five TV stations, including Madison's Fox affiliate, Channel 47. He then earned his MBA from Northwestern University in Chicago and, in 1990, joined Fox Television where he created their cable network.

After Fox's Barry Diller took over QVC in 1993, Sherek joined that company as Executive Vice President of broadcast operations and engineering. He was promptly put in charge of starting up operations in Great Britain and Mexico. In February 1994, Sherek became President of QVC's International Division, a long way from his days as a Wisconsin rock 'n' roller.

Also see: Talismen
Unrelated Tikis: Ascot, Autumn, Dial, Minaret, W.B.

Sources: Bill Sherek telephone interview, 8/22/94
      Cuca ledger cards - courtesy Jim Kirchstein
      Osborne-Brown. <u>Rockin' Records.</u>

Shane Todd/Corvettes
(David Todd - 6/21/43; St. Albans, WV)

Corvettes:
Shane Todd - voc
Tom Van Maren -gtr
Bob Gugel - org (11/29/44; Madison)
Gene Clifford - sx
George Moll - bs   **Jim Bisbee** - dr (2/5/39; Portage)
Bruce Benson - dr

Fan Jr.	1000	Jeri/Johnny goes To Philly	2/61
		(Corvettes with the Toddettes)	
Dutch	1061	Today/Lonely For You[1]	11/61

Shane Todd & the Shane Gang: Jon St. John, Shane Todd, Jerry Raimer, Darrell Meister

---

[1]Gary Stites, 1959

Shane Todd did a local Madison TV show around the time of his two recordings. Cuca's Jim Kirchstein describes him as a "Sal Mineo type," while his release on Dutch (a Cuca custom label) has a bit of a Paul Anka sound. Todd later joined the Gentlemen but was drafted before their recording. After his discharge he formed the Shane Gang. Though that band went into the studio several times, nothing was ever released. (The Shane Gang is not to be confused with Sheboygan's Chain Gang).

After disbanding the Shane Gang in 1976, Todd went into concert promotion at a club called Headliners. "We were one of those clubs across America that got in on some of the acts that are superstars today - like U2 and Police," he says, "so it was probably the best job I ever had."

Also see: Gentlemen (Shane Todd)
          Robin & the Three Hoods, Speedy & the Alka Seltzers (Bruce Benson)
Unrelated Corvettes: Corvette, Dot, Duncan, Sheraton
Sources: Shane Todd telephone interview, 8/3/94
          Jim Bisbee telephone interview, 8/12/94
          Tourville. Wisconsin . . . Discography.

Ventrills
(Janesville)

Frank Vale (Ellefson) - gtr (10/6/42; Janesville - 11/1/87; Green Bay)
Jan Hassman - org/sx (5/31/43; Chicago)   **Tommy Lee** - gtr
Dave Lexington (Hansen) - org   **Donnie Ray (Roush)** - bs
Bob Bellard - dr

Little Fort	1929	Don't Say No/Do The Jerk Waltz		/65
	1940	Tough Times/Let Me Love You		/65
Tower	298	Santa Claus Is Stuck In The Chimney/Tambourine Jingle (Little Kids)		12/66
Ivanhoe	5000	Alone In The Night/Confusion		2/67
Parkway	141	Alone In The Night/Confusion		4/67
Little Fort	833L-3	After My Horn, Part 1/After My Horn, Part 2	(/I)	/67

"I just made that up," says Bob Bellard, explaining the origin of the name Ventrills in 1964. "I sort of got it from the name ventriloquist and we couldn't think of anything else at the time, so it just stuck."

Guitarist Frank Ellefson has been called Janesville's father of rock 'n' roll. Playing guitar was part of the therapy to help him recover from the polio that struck him at age seven, and he eventually formed the town's first rock 'n' roll band. The group was named the Shamrockers for the Shamrock soda shop where Ellefson hung out and absorbed the sounds from the jukebox. Ellefson added Clarence Heath, a black singer to the group, a progressive move for this small town in the late 50's.

Multi-instrumentalist Jan Hassman came up from Rockford, where he had recorded as a member of Tony & the White Knights. He had also been working at Neilsen's Music where he taught the owner's son, Rick, his first guitar licks. Rick Neilsen later went on to fame and fortune with Cheap Trick.

The Ventrill's first record may have been the only teen dance tune done as a jazz waltz. "We were kind of looking for something that was different," explains Bellard. "Everybody had a dance that they were trying to originate, so Jan Hassman wrote 'Do The Jerk Waltz'. It was sort of done like 'Gravy Waltz' (Steve Allen, 1963). It wasn't really a rock 'n' roll type song. It was sort of done in a contemporary - well, it was just totally different. (laughs) We were searching, trying to do something that nobody else had done."

The Ventrills had the opportunity to open for the Kinks and Moody Blues at Chicago's McCormick Place June 21, 1965. The following year the band obtained a national release when they recorded a Christmas novelty tune as the Little Kids. The song was written by Eddie Mascari and Dutch Wenzloff, and Bellard recalls it being played on Dick Clark's show the week before Christmas. (Eddie and Dutch went on to chart with their own novelty hit, "My Wife The Dancer," in 1970).

In early 1967 it looked as if the Ventrills might break through with "Alone In The Night," written and produced by Mascari and Wenzloff. A group vocal, Bellard says Phillips Records turned it down because it sounded too much like the Four Seasons. The record charted on WLS in Chicago and WABC in New York. Next came a return to Al Schultz's Little Fort label with some material written by Hassman, who had also penned most of the previous releases.

Ellefson moved to Green Bay where he continued to play and teach, despite the onset of bone cancer. Finally, during a gig in 1987, Ellefson's arm snapped as he picked up his Gibson Les Paul. He was hospitalized and died nine weeks later. Ellefson is remembered with great fondness by his many friends and fellow musicians for the emotion in his music and for his big-hearted personality.

Hassman joined a road band that needed a replacement for departing musician Denny Zager. Zager was returning to his native Nebraska to work with Rick Evans and the duo subsequently had the huge worldwide hit "In The Year 2525." The band that Hassman joined became the Sound Department, a Waukegan-based group with one release on Milwaukee's Cite label. Hassman later worked with the Shy Guys, Changing Times, and Sunny & Her Guys. He did jingle work in Minneapolis and a Las Vegas lounge gig as a piano single. He has since relocated to Palm Springs, where he has returned to the music business after working in real estate.

Also see: Speedy & the Alka Seltzers (Bob Bellard)
      Nigh Tranes (Frank Ellefson)
      Shy Guys - La Crosse

Sources: Bob Bellard letter and telephone interview, 1/31/93, 2/14/93
      Jan Hassman telephone interview, 5/28/94
      Milam, Stan. "The heart of rock 'n' roll." <u>Janesville Gazette</u> 10/17/91 - courtesy Stan
        Milam
      Tourville. <u>Wisconsin . . . Discography.</u>
      Clee. <u>American 45 R.P.M. Records.</u>

Lonnie Walker

Cuca	1111	I Slipped, I Stumbled, I Fell[1]/Let's Talk About Us	11/62
Original Sound	108	They Gave Us Rock 'n' Roll/Ooh, Shucks Baby	/74
		(L.A. Walker)	

Lonnie Walker was a black Elvis sound-alike who was backed by Dave Kennedy's Ambassadors on his Cuca release. His own later band, the Hustlers, included guitarist Denny Geyer. Once rumored to have died in a train wreck in the late 60's, Walker reportedly worked briefly in recent years as a James Brown impersonator in a Las Vegas superstar tribute show.

Also see: A.B. Skhy (Denny Geyer)
Sources: Clee. <u>American 45 R.P.M. Records.</u>
      Paul Poletti - Original Sound Records, 1993

Zakons: Bob Bierd, Billy Lee King,
Tom Kropp, Bill Alexander
(courtesy Bob Bierd)

[1]Elvis Presley - *Something For Everyone* LP, 1961

Zakons

Babe Austin (Larry Krecowski) - voc
Bill Joswick - ld gtr   **Billy Lee King** - voc
Tom Kropp - rh gtr   **Bill Anderson** - bs
Ronnie Pagel - bs   **Bob Bierd** - dr (1/12/43; Madison)

Cuca   1033   Trackin'/Wasted   /61
                      (Both sides reissued on *The Cuca Story, Vol 2*)

Drummer Bob Bierd joined the Zakons shortly after their sole recording. He became the leader and the band went through several later personnel changes. Bierd hired an entire new group in 1963 after a long term engagement at Green Bay's Piccadilly Club.

Also see: Millionaires - Cuca (Bob Bierd)
Sources: Bob Bierd telephone interview, 7/30/94

La Crosse

The most important single ingredient in the development of the pop/rock music scene in the La Crosse area was surely Lindy Shannon. Shannon was instrumental in bringing the first top 40 format to local radio at WKBH. He managed and produced bands in the area for many years. Many of those bands reunited for a concert in his honor on August 30, 1992. The line-up included Marv Dennis, Fax, Linda Hall, Dave Kennedy & the Ambassadors, Marauders, Molly Maguires, Shy Guys, Super-Phonics, TJ's, Today's Tomorrow, and Unchained Mynds. A repeat performance on August 28, 1994, adds the Exchequers, Shelly & Kim, Touchstone, and Johnny Waleen. A few bands from out of the immediate area, but who worked locally, have also participated.

Marv Blihovde/Marv Dennis /Minnesota Marv
(11/16/34; Chaseburg)

Marv Blihovde (blee-ohv'-dee)
Lindy   1113   Dearest Darling/Cigarettes & Coffee Blues   /59
              1551   Sweet Little Wife/Pickles   /59
Kay Bee   6001   You're My Everything/Been Away Too Long   8/60

Minnesota Marv & the Vanguards
Cuca	1023	Nobody's Darling But Mine/Sweet Little Wife	1/61

(Alternate takes of both sides issued on *The Cuca Story, Vol. 3*)

Minnesota Marv & Ed Cree
	1025	White Lightning[1]/Little Boy Blue	1/61

(Both sides reissued on *The Cuca Story, Vol. 3*)

Marv Dennis/Marv Dennis Four
Bagdad	1962	The Girl With The Lollipop/You Build Me Up	/62
Film	1020	Sing Little Bird/Love Is Something	/65
Bear	1975	Honeycomb[2]/The Hurt Will Go Away	/65
Coulee	143	The Great Drinkin' Bout/No No On Her Lips	/72

LP's:
D&C		The Nashville Sounds of Dennis & Cree	/62
Garpax		Marv Dennis' Greatest Hits - We Hope	/65
Coulee	1002	Caught In The Act	/72

Marv Dennis Four: **Marv Dennis** - rh gtr
Ed Cree - ld gtr/banjo (2/15/34; Garards Fort, PA)
Leo Breidel - Cordovox (dec)
Terry Meale - dr (dec)

Besides the above names, Marv Dennis also did some of his early work as Mark Trance. Dennis and Ed Cree began incorporating comedy into their act by creating bits around novelty tunes such as "Alley Oop" and "Please, Mr. Custer." In 1962, relocating to California, they signed with the management company that handled Jimmie Rodgers and Miyoshi Umecki. The release on the Film label was financed by Gene Autry and Dennis' remake of "Honeycomb" was produced by Gary Paxton (Skip & Flip, Hollywood Argyles, others).

Eventually, with the comedy coming to the forefront, Dennis & Cree did a Garry Marshall television series titled *Who's Watching The Kids*. The show ran for three months on NBC in late 1978 and starred Scott Baio and Jim Belushi.

In 1979 Dennis opened his booking agency in Nashville. Marv Dennis & Associates has booked such names as Tanya Tucker, Dolly Parton, Alabama and many others. Ed Cree became a building contractor in Ridgetop, Tennessee.

Sources: Marv Dennis telephone interview and letter, 1/93, 4/22/94
    Ed Cree telephone interview, 7/24/94
    Tourville. <u>Wisconsin . . . Discography.</u>

---

[1]George Jones, 1959; w: J.P. Richardson (Big Bopper)
[2]Jimmie Rodgers, 1957

Exchequers

Arnie Bacon - ld gtr
Tom Hake - ld gtr
Rick Blomquist - bs
Dan Woodard - dr

Boom   115   Greensleeves/Is There Some Girl   10/65

This record was pressed on green vinyl. Boom is a custom label of Coulee.

Sources: Tari Tovsen letter, 6/7/94
         Tourville. <u>Wisconsin . . . Discography.</u>

Fax

Mike Palmer - gtr
Greg Fritsch - ld gtr
Steve Noffke - bs (9/1/49; La Crosse)
Greg Haskell - dr

Transaction   701   I Can Only Give You Everything/Her Love   /66
               702   Just Walking In The Rain[1]/Not Too Long Ago[2]   8/66
                          (with Alex Campbell)
               704   I'll Go Crazy[3]/(flip: see Lost & Found)   /67

As a word that we all recognize in the 90's, Fax is curious name for a mid-60's band. "We played some as the Gentrys," explains Steve Noffke, "and then the Gentrys came out with 'Keep On Dancing'. Lindy (Shannon) just came up with the name and put it on the label so we got named without even knowing it." The group worked often in the Appleton/Green Bay area and broke up around 1967. Mike Palmer remained in music. Steve Noffke has been involved in photography and racing sports cars.

Also see: Alex Campbell
          Lost & Found
Sources: Tari Tovsen letter, 4/1/94
         Tourville. <u>Wisconsin . . . Discography.</u>

---

[1]Johnny Ray, 1956
[2]Uniques, 1965
[3]James Brown, 1960, 1966

Linda Hall (courtesy Linda Kuehl)

Linda Hall
(4/25/43; La Crosse)

Cuca	1044	You Don't Have A Wooden Heart/Treat Me Nice[1]	8/61
	1070	Almost Always True[2]/G.I. Guy	2/62

Linda Hall was another Lindy Shannon act. Most of her gigs were done as a guest with various bands. "I remember one time I sang with a group in Madison," she relates, "and they had a murder right in the building, and my mother went wild. She didn't even want me to go there in the first place. I was 18 years old. Oh, she went wild!"

Hall's first release was an answer to "Wooden Heart," as Cuca tried to get back a little of what they lost by missing out on the original hit (see Dave Kennedy & the Ambassadors - Cuca). Dave Kennedy's Ambassadors backed her on the record. The follow-up features backing by Milwaukee's Royal Lancers. Hall has worked for the Trane Co. (mfg. of air conditioners) since shortly after high school, relocating to Tyler, Texas, in the late 80's. She has continued her singing at nursing homes, day care camps, and churches.

Also see: Royal Lancers - Milwaukee
Unrelated Linda Hall: Artcraft, Columbia
Sources: Linda Hall Kuehl telephone interview, 7/21/94
        Clee. <u>American 45 R.P.M. Records.</u>

---

[1]Elvis Presley, 1957
[2]Elvis Presley - *Blue Hawaii* LP, 1961

Jerry & the Silvertones

Jerry Grosskopf - rh gtr (9/5/42; La Crosse)
Rollie Grosskopf - ld gtr (10/5/44; La Crosse)   **Tom Perry** - dr
Calvin Grosskopf - bs (5/12/32; La Crosse)   **Jerry Oliver** - bs
Richard Krause - dr

Coulee   104   Ce'ny/Moonlight Bay[1]   (I/)   5/64

This band's instrumental "Ce'ny" was named for Lucine, the wife of label owner Bill Grafft. Rollie Grosskopf also recorded with Johnny Waleen and later with the Townsmen who did a country LP on Coulee. Jerry & the Silvertones existed for about six years.

Also see: Dave Kennedy & the Ambassadors - Cuca (Jerry Oliver)
       Johnny Waleen (related material)
Sources: Rollie Grosskopf telephone interview, 7/27/94
       Tourville. <u>Wisconsin . . . Discography.</u>

Jesters III

Wayne McKibbin - gtr (11/29/45; Bainbridge, MD)
Jim Burkhardt - bs
Tom Eisenman - dr

Coulee   114   Pledge Of Love[2]/Say That I'm The One   4/65

The Jesters III existed from 1963-69. Wayne McKibbin then helped form the group Hope, which recorded for Coulee and A&M in the 70's. That band also included Jeff Cozy of Lost & Found.

Also See: Dave Kennedy & the Ambassadors (Tom Eisenman)
Sources: Wayne McKibbin letter and telephone interview, 2/6/94, 5/1/94

Lost & Found

Larry Leach - ld gtr
Mark Heller - rh gtr
Eric Severson - bs
Jeff Cozy - dr (6/22/50; La Crosse)

---

[1]American Quartet, 1912; Bing & Gary Crosby, 1951; Drifters, 1958
[2]aka "Pledging My Love" Johnny Ace, 1955

Transaction	704	If I Needed Someone[1]/ (see Fax)		/67
Hope				
Coulee	134	Where Do You Want To Go/One Man		/71
A&M	1355	Where Do You Want To Go/Little Things		4/72
		(The A&M version is a re-recording)		
Related:				
New Style	--	Wild Ideas/Night On The Town		/75
		(Cozy & the Mercury Men)		

Teenage band Lost & Found did only one side of a record, but drummer Jeff Cozy continued in music. After traveling to the West Coast as a member of Hope, he remained in the Los Angeles area for a few years, doing session work for the Robbs.

"There were always people coming in and giving us feedback, I was learning from their second engineers," Cozy explains. "They were showing me a lot of the ropes of what they were doing on the boards. Now and then, probably unbeknownst to the Robbs, when people like Fleetwood Mac or Rod Stewart were in there, I'd go in and look at their mike setups and EQ's and stuff and take notes. I learned a lot from them." Since returning to Wisconsin, Cozy has applied those lessons and formed his own multi media production company, *Bright Ideas*.

Unrelated Lost & Found: International Artists, Tempo
Sources: Jeff Cozy telephone interviews, 10/93, 7/94
      Tourville. <u>Wisconsin . . . Discography.</u>
      Osborne-Brown. <u>Rockin' Records.</u>

Marauders/Satisfactions

Rick Pervisky (Przywojski) - rh gtr (7/7/48; La Crosse)
Rick Miller - ld gtr
Jim Young - bs (Milwaukee)
Terry Gardner - dr (dec)

Coulee	110	I Can Tell/Hi-Di Hi-Di		12/64
Twin Town	714	Bad Times[2]/Girl Don't Tell Me[3]	(Satisfactions)	/65

The name of this band was changed by producer Dave Garrett who had previously hit with the Trashmen's "Surfin' Bird" on his own label. "We were all against the name change," says Rick Przywojski. "The reason that they took the name was because 'I Can't Get No Satisfaction' was real hot right at that time."

---

[1]Beatles - *Yesterday And Today* LP, 1966
[2]w: Jeff Barry-P.F. Sloan
[3]Beach Boys - *Summer Days (And Summer Nights)* LP, 1965

The Marauders began in late 1963 and Pervisky cites Milwaukee's Legends as one of his early idols. The band's first record was issued by Coulee on blue vinyl. The Marauders had been "tearing up the Midwest" according to Przywojski, including a gig opening for the Dave Clark Five at Chicago's McCormick Place. The group broke up around the end of 1966. Rick Miller went on to become very successful as the owner of Harley Davidson Apparel.

Unrelated Marauders: Almo, FR, Hawk, Laurie, Lee, Skyview
Unrelated Satisfactions: Chesapeake, Imperial, Lionel, 1-2-3, Smash
Sources: Tari Tovsen letter, 4/1/94
      Rick Przywojski telephone interview, 6/11/94
      Tourville. Wisconsin . . . Discography.

Molly Maguires

Art McClure - gtr (6/26/50; Pittsburgh, PA)
Jim Davison - kb   **Tom Franzini** - gtr
Dirk Weber - bs   **Steve Kunes** - gtr
Eric Hartwig - dr (2/11/50; La Crosse)   **Neil Wang** - bs

| Transaction | 709 | First Spring Rain/But It's All Right[1] | /69 |
| | 713 | Our Favorite Melodies/You Can All Join In | /70 |

What's a Molly Maguire? "That's from history class, junior year of high school," says Art McClure. "The Molly Maguires were a group of rebel Irishmen in the coal mining county of Appalachia." It does make for a unique band name. The modern day Molly Maguires began about 1965 with the final line-up disbanding about 1973.

Working mostly in or near La Crosse, the Maguires served as the house band at the Varsity Club after the members were of age. They opened once for Archie Bell & the Drells and once for the Gentrys. With a nearly complete personnel change, drummer Eric Hartwig is the only common link between the group's two releases.

The 1992 reunion concert brought happy memories for Hartwig. "It was just amazing to see guys that we haven't seen in years," he says. "You think about the way you got started and the jobs that you played, it was just phenomenal. Very good times. It was really fun to relive them. Playing in a band in those days was really a significant part of your life."

Sources: Art McClure telephone interview, 5/6/94
      Eric Hartwig telephone interview, 5/7/94
      Tourville. Wisconsin . . . Discography.

---

[1] J.J. Jackson, 1966, 1969

Marauders: Rick Miller, Jim Young, Terry Gardner, Rick Pervisky (courtesy Tom Tourville)

Molly Maguires: (top) Jim Davison,
Dirk Weber, Eric Hartwig, Art McClure
(courtesy Eric Hartwig)

Lance O'Neal

Norko   1113   I'm Twistin' Alone/That's What I Would Do

O'Neal is backed by Dave Kennedy's Ambassadors on this release.

Also see: Dave Kennedy & the Ambassadors - Cuca
Source: Dave Kennedy, 1993

Shelly & Kim

Shelly Hutchins
Kim Statler (10/29/50; La Crosse)

Coulee   107   We Love Them All/Where's It Gonna Get Me[1]   8/64

These two preteens made up a song about the Beatles while spending the night in a back yard tent. "The next morning we said, 'Oh, Mom and Dad, look what we did'," relates Kim Statler. "They thought it was wonderful, of course. They took off with it and pushed us a little bit." The record became a local hit and the team continued singing together, often appearing at Pepsi Parties for teens at the Mary Sawyer Auditorium. Their reunion performance for the 1994 Lindy Shannon Show marks the first time they've seen each other in 30 years. "We had a good time and we met a lot of great people. We owe that to him."

Source: Kim Statler Wagner telephone interview, 7/27/94

Shy Guys/Johnny & the Shy Guys

John Bernadot - ld gtr (3/1/45; Winona, MN)
Rudy Von Ruden - rh gtr   **Hal Atkinson** - sx/kb (5/7/45; Laurel, MS)
Larry Ball (Gaulke) - bs   **Tari Tovsen** - ld gtr(10/25/42; La Crosse)
Les King - dr   **Jan Hassman** - sx/kb (5/31/43; Chicago, IL)
                                        Danny Baker - dr

Johnny & the Shy Guys
Cuca   1145   Moon Dawg[2]/Born To Be With You[3]   9/63
Cascade   1001   Pretty Baby/Till The End Of Time   /64

---

[1]Shelley Fabares - *Shelley!* LP, 1962
[2]Gamblers, 1960
[3]Chordettes, 1956

Ma	101	Shorty's Shack/From Me To You[4]		/64
Regal West	200	What'd I Say-Pt.1/What'd I Say-Pt.2[2]		/64
Shy Guys				
Little Fort	9663	Rockin' Pneumonia[3]/You Are My Sunshine[4]		9/67
Uni	55035	Rockin' Pneumonia & Boogaloo Flu/You Are My Sunshine		11/67
Shamley	44001	Payin' My Dues/No Flowers On My Mind		/68
Related:				
UA	50970	That's Happy/Midnight Is Golden		/69
		(Sunny Bernadette & Her Fabulous Guys)		
Ivanhoe	503	The Spider & The Fly/Judy	(Von Ruden)	5/70
Love Day	101	Kathy Believe Me[5]/Pork Belly	(Hal Atkinson)	/72

Though not an original member of the Shy Guys, Hal Atkinson has become the most visible member to pass through the band, thanks to his move into acting and a role in Disney's *The Mighty Ducks*. For Atkinson it was a long trip from Mississippi to Hollywood, via Oregon, Wisconsin and England, but the story of the Shy Guys begins in Winona, Minnesota.

John Bernadot formed the group and headed for La Crosse because "it was more of a music city than Winona was." Lindy Shannon took over management and their first release on Cuca consisted of remakes, a practice the Shy Guys would often repeat in future recordings.

The band traveled constantly and it was while touring the Northwest with Paul Revere & the Raiders (while the latter was still a regional act) that they released a live version of "What'd I Say." It was also during this tour that Atkinson first heard the group at the Chateau Club in Salem, Oregon. "I came back the next night and I brought my saxophone and they wouldn't let me in," he recalls. "I remembered that she had turned her back when I went in (the previous night). I've always gotten such a great big kick out the fact that, if that woman's back had not been turned, I would never have come back to that club. I would never have met my first wife. I would never have done any of the things - a woman turned her back one night and I can pivot that moment to incredible importance in my whole life."

Expanded to five pieces, the band returned to Shorty's Shack in La Crosse. The club on Irish Hill was owned by Ma Shorty, a woman "who was sort of legendary in that area," says Atkinson. The Shy Guys probably contributed to the legend by writing new lyrics to Jimmy Gilmer's "Sugar Shack" and releasing "Shorty's Shack" on the Ma label.

---

[1]Beatles, 1964
[2]Ray Charles, 1959
[3]Huey Smith & the Clowns, 1957; Johnny Rivers, 1973
[4]traditional - Bing Crosby, 1941; Ray Charles, 1962; many others
[5]from the motion picture *Just Be There*

Johnny & the Shy Guys: Larry Ball, Les King, John Bernadot, Rudy Von Ruden (courtesy T. Tourville)

Super-Phonics with Gene Vincent: George Eberdt, Ronnie Hanson, Vincent, Gary Wolf, Al Banasik

Rudy Von Ruden left for military service and Johnny Bernadot left to form a new group with his wife, Sunny. Tari Tovsen, formerly with Dave Kennedy & the Ambassadors, came into the band and it was this line-up that got the most action on any single record. Their remake of "Rockin' Pneumonia" was recorded for Al Schultz's Little Fort label and picked up nationally by Uni.

When the Shy Guys eventually called it quits, Atkinson and Les King joined Buddy & the Citations, a Chicago band that included Milwaukee guitarist Bob Penney. (That band later became the Second Coming on Mercury, though Atkinson had left by that time). Tovsen formed the Changing Times who recorded in the 70's.

Jan Hassman worked with Bernadot's new group on a weekly La Crosse TV show. That band, Sunny & Her Guys, featured Bernadot's wife on vocals. Eventually Sunny left to go on the road in a duo with Hassman. John Bernadot and Jan Hassman literally exchanged ex-wives when each married the other's former partner.

When Hal Atkinson returned to his home state of Mississippi, he ran into an old school friend, singer Nannette Workman. Workman was prospering in England and urged Atkinson to visit the U.K. He did, and while there he managed to hook up with the Brotherhood of Man, a studio vocal group who was coming off their major hit, "United We Stand." Atkinson's voice is on many of their later records, including their second biggest hit, "Save Your Kisses For Me."

After returning to La Crosse in 1972 Atkinson was doing commercials when he received a call from Dale Menten (writer of Gestures 1964 hit, "Run, Run, Run") in Minneapolis. The call led to a movie theme and on-camera work for corporate videos. It also led to a major change in Atkinson's career.

"He called me one day and he said, 'I want you to come out and do the lead in a Neil Simon play.' My heart started beating and I said, 'You want me to act?' So for about a month before we began rehearsing, I was just terrified every second of my life. But within 15 minutes of our first rehearsal I knew I was at home."

Rudy Von Ruden had a solo release and worked as a single through most of the 80's. Bernadot continues to perform with Bernadot & Griggs, and Tari Tovsen's guitar remains active in the 90's. Green Bay agent/musician Dick Schulz has resurrected the Shy Guys name for the 90's, but there is no connection with this band.

Also see: Dave Kennedy & the Ambassadors (Tari Tovsen)
        Ventrills (Jan Hassman)
Unrelated Shy Guys: Burger, Canusa, Hideout, Mu, Palmer, Panik, Reprise, Trump
Sources: Hal Atkinson interview, 5/20/93
        Rudy Von Ruden telephone interview, 1/93
        John Bernadot telephone interview, 8/7/93
        Jan Hassman telephone interview, 5/28/94

Clee. <u>American 45 R.P.M. Records.</u>
Osborne-Brown. <u>Rockin' Records.</u>
Tourville. <u>Wisconsin . . . Discography.</u>

Super-Phonics

Ronnie Hanson - gtr
Pete Larkin - bs   **Al Banasik** - ld gtr
George Eberdt - dr   **Gary Wolfe** - bs

Lindy	101	B-L-U-E/Me Neither	(/I)	/60
		(with Dave Kennedy)		
	102	Teenage Partner/My Love For You		/60
Mean Mt.	1425	Teenage Partner/Interview With Gene Vincent		

Lindy Shannon used this young band to back up Dave Kennedy's first recording, with their own instrumental on the flip. The A-side of their second record was reissued over 20 years later as the B-side to a 1958 Gene Vincent interview. George Eberdt later joined Dave Kennedy's Ambassadors and the touring Greenmen.

Also see: Dave Kennedy & the Ambassadors (George Eberdt, Al Banasik)
        Greenmen - Milwaukee (George Eberdt)
Sources: Ron Hanson letter, 7/5/94
        Tourville. <u>Wisconsin . . . Discography.</u>

TJ's/Caravans

Tom Terry - ld gtr/dr
Jack Roubik - rh gtr
Duane Schroeder - bs/rh gtr (4/29/39; La Crosse)   **Ronnie Hagaland** - dr
Bill Weigel - dr   **Guy Buchalou** - rh gtr/bs

Lindy	740	Party Party[1]/Take My Love	/57
	741	I Got A Baby/Live It Up	/57
	1124	Baby Doll/Broken Hearted Prayer	/58
Caravans:			
Cuca	1017	Rock & Roll Christmas/Caravan[2]	12/60

---

[1]Dean Beard, 1957
[2]Duke Ellington, 1937; Ralph Marterie, 1953; Santo & Johnny, 1960; many others

"We were the first rock 'n' roll recording group at the Kay Bank Studio," claims Duane Schroeder. As one of the earliest such bands in Wisconsin, the TJ's narrowly missed out on having the state's first rock 'n' roll record. "I guess they (Appleton's White Caps) were the first ones to come out with a record," he continues. "It was in February and ours didn't come out until April, so we missed it by that much."

Prior to the recording, Schroeder and Bill Wiegel were preceded by two musicians named Jerry and Jim. When that line-up appeared at a show in Winona, Minnesota, "they told the emcee to introduce the group as the JT's (for Jerry, Jim, Jack and Tom)," recalls Schroeder (who was on the same show as a separate act). "He went out on stage and introduced it as the TJ's."

"Baby Doll," the band's third release began to get action in Iowa at the beginning of 1959. After receiving many calls to play the record, DJ Dale Wood of KOLE in Olewein called the band and acted as their agent. "We could have sold 'Baby Doll' to Chess," claims Schroeder, who wrote both sides. "We had the contract, all we had to do was sign it. We had this high rating in Billboard Magazine and we got a phone call from Hawaii - about 4:00 in the morning because of the time change - stating that Liberty was interested. Chess was, I guess you could say, a Volkswagen compared to a Cadillac when you were talking about Liberty, so we gambled and went for the Liberty thing.

"While we were in Iowa some guy came to La Crosse from Fargo, ND, and wanted us to back him up. Then of course, Buddy Holly, Big Bopper and Ritchie Valens got killed only about 15 miles from where we were. We saw the plane in the corn field the next morning. We later found out that Liberty had chosen a song called 'Suzie Baby'. That, of course, was Bobby Vee, the guy who came from Fargo. So, it was a nice try."

The TJ's metamorphosized into the Caravans and tried one more record before breaking up. Jack Roubik later did some work with the Canadian Sweethearts. Tom Terry publishes *Plastic Figure & Playset Collector*, a toy collector's magazine, and Schroeder continues part time in music with his band, Country Pride.

Also see: Ramrods (Dale Wood)
Unrelated Caravans: TJ(!), Tornado, Vee Jay
Sources: Duane Schroeder telephone interview, 11/3/93
       Tourville. <u>Wisconsin . . . Discography.</u>
       Osborne-Brown. <u>Rockin' Records.</u>

Today's Tomorrow/Ladds

Chuck Holzer - voc
Alex Campbell - kb (6/23/52; La Crosse)
Ralph Russell - gtr   **Randy Taylor** - bs
Eric Melby - bs   **Clare Troyanek** - bs
Mark Melby - dr

Ladds

Transaction	703	Keep On Running/Wild Angel's Theme[1]		/67
UA	706	Survival/I Found A Girl		10/68
Teen Town				
	4789/4790	Goodness Gracious Baby/Bring Back The Days		10/69
	115	The Lone Ranger/No Name Boogie	(I/I)	/70
		(Silver Bullets)		

Today's Tomorrow

Bang	577	Witchi Tai To[2]/Bring Back The Days	4/70
Teen Town	118	Wanton Forest/You've Gone Away	/71
	125	Smile Away/Lifeless	12/72

Alex Campbell first recorded when Lindy Shannon produced him after seeing him in a talent contest. Shannon used a popular local group, the Fax, to back Campbell on that session. The Ladds were born shortly after that. The band's third release, a bubblegum style tune titled "Bring Back The Days," put them in the La Crosse top 10.

Teen Town label owner Jon Hall placed the next record, "Witchi Tai To," on Bang, a national label. "I think he just played it over the telephone to Eileen from Bang Records and that was it," says Campbell. "We actually had a full page ad in Billboard and we saw that and we said, 'Oh God! This is it, we're on our way!"

Most of the members were still in high school, traveling to gigs every weekend. "It was number one in Milwaukee for four weeks straight on WOKY," recalls Campbell, "so we really thought we were going to make the big time. We just never really got the break on the air on the big AM, WLS in Chicago."

Along with an instrumental as the Silver Bullets, Today's Tomorrow tried two more releases on Teen Town before splitting up. Campbell left music to attend college, returning in the 70's with the Changing Times. Eric Melby worked in the 70's with Ice and Flying Free. (Eric and Mark Melby are not brothers). Since 1986 Campbell has been with WLAX-TV in La Crosse, taking over as national sales manager in 1992.

Also see: Fax (Alex Campbell)
    Unchained Mynds - On The Charts (Clare Troyanek)
Sources: Alex Campbell telephone interview, 7/17/93
    Tourville. <u>Wisconsin . . . Discography.</u>

---

[1]Davie Allan & the Arrows, 1966
[2]Everything Is Everything, 1969

Touchstone

Janet Evans - voc
Tom Schmidt - voc
Dave Schwandt - 12 strg gtr (1/28/51; Manitowoc)
Bill Menke - rh gt
George Swan -bs

Transaction	708	The Show/Last Laugh	/69
Coulee	131	Sweet 'N' Tender/The Intruder	/69

"It was kind of a Peter, Paul & Mary instrumentation, but we tried to do a little more intricate things in the harmonization," says Dave Schwandt of Touchstone. Music remains an avocation for Schwandt, and Janet Evans moved into classical music after moving to Chicago.

Unrelated Touchstone: Sound Machine, U.A.
Sources: Dave Schwandt telephone interview, 7/20/94
        Tourville. Wisconsin . . . Discography.
        Osborne-Brown. Rockin' Records.

Johnny Waleen (Wallin)
(10/24/40; Cumberland)

Soma	1120	The Road Of Heartaches/Mandy	/59
Coulee	102	Mystery Train[1]/Now Is The Hour[2]	3/64

Johnny Wallin moved to Minneapolis and recorded his Soma sides while attending Oxford College there. After a change of studies to broadcasting, he returned to La Crosse and spent four years on WKTY in the time slot opposite Lindy Shannon. "I really would have liked to get into a band but it was really impossible because I worked every night," he says. Instead he did record hops on his nights off, sometimes taking along his guitar.

Wallin got to be good friends with Bill Grafft, owner of Coulee Records. "I would go over there after I got off the air at midnight," he says. "It was only about a mile from the station, which was out south of town, down in the swamps there. Rollie Grosskopf accompanied me on 'Mystery Train' and 'Now Is The Hour'. There was just the two of us on the record - and 'Mystery Train' was just a one-take-bang, there it was. It was kind of incredible."

Wallin later attended graduate school at UW Madison, where he worked at WISM. He now owns Wallin's West, a western store in Rochester, Minneosta.

---

[1]Elvis Presley, 1956
[2]Bing Crosby, 1948; many others

Also see: Jerry & the Silvertones (Rollie Grosskopf)
Sources: Johnny Wallin telephone interview, 7/20/94
      Tourville. <u>Wisconsin . . . Discography.</u>

Racine/Kenosha

Ray Allen & the Trendells

Ray Allen (Harbach) - bs/gtr   **John Verbraken** - kb (12/25/43; Monmouth, NJ)
Danny Riccio - ld gtr (4/5/45; Racine)   **Ted Riccio** - dr (12/24/34; Racine)
Larry Rongsvoog - bs/gtr   **Duane Gauger** - rh gtr
Dick Simon - dr   **Damon Lee** - gtr/hca

Cuca	63104	Who's Gonna Cry/Go On And Play Your Game	10/63
	6544	Look At Me/I Love You	4/65
	6562	Shake A Tail Feather[1]/I'm So Glad	6/65

Though this band's recordings were done with Ray Allen, they continued as the Trendells long after Allen had left for military service. Damon Lee, though not on any of these releases, had recorded previously in his home state of Minnesota. Danny Riccio describes Lee as a wild, blues-oriented entertainer who played in a Stevie Ray Vaughn style. "The guy was ahead of his time," says Riccio, whose brother Ted also joined the band. (Their uncle Frank had recorded two albums with his Cordovox-led trio.

Also see: Say Mama (Damon Lee)
    Mid-Knighters (John Verbraken)
Unrelated Trendells: Capitol, Jam, Sound Stage 7, Southtown, Tilt.
Sources: Ted Riccio telephone interview, 8/28/93
    Danny Riccio telephone interview, 2/6/94
    John Verbraken telephone interview, 2/11/94
    Tourville. <u>Wisconsin . . . Discography.</u>

Casuals

Albee (Albert) Clausen - ld gtr
Keith Bener - rh gtr
Steve Acklam - bs
Mike Morales - dr

---

[1]Five Dutones, 1963; James & Bobby Purify, 1967

Cuca	64121	Come On Pretty One/Angel On My Shoulder[1]	12/64
Feature	1001	Come On Pretty One/Angel On My Shoulder	/65
Destination	609	You're The Kind Of Girl/Good Things	/65
		(Albee & the Casuals)	

Unrelated Casuals: ABC, Back Beat, Black Hawk, Dot, Minaret, Monument, Scotty,
    Sound Stage 7, Toltec
Sources: Allen Clausen telephone interview, 12/11/93
    Tourville. Wisconsin . . . Discography.
    Osborne-Brown. Rockin' Records.

Ken Davis
(2/23/36; Racine)

Pfau	3507	Sittin' Pretty/Bundle Of Lovin'		/58
		(Ken Davis with the Honeybees)		
Starlight	1002	Uh Huh, That's Right/Without Her Love		/58
	1006	Shook Shake/Echo Rock		/59
Badger	250	Shook Shake/Echo Rock		/59
	251	Oh So Blue/Gone Again		/59
Singing Blue	--	The Next Little Town/Because I'm Blue		/62
Kay Dee	031	Play Ginger Play/What Would I Do Without Dreams	(I/I)	/67
Mean Mountain	1419	Shook Shake/Echo Rock	(reissue)	/82

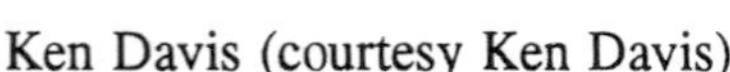
Ken Davis (courtesy Ken Davis)

---

[1]Shelby Flint, 1960

Makes me feel so good, don't know what to think
Of the clever little song that could have put me in the pink
But it just so happens I never made a dime
Off a song that's clearly passed the test of time
Guess It's just my luck and I'll never make a buck
Well, I'm SHOOK SHAKE like a big mix cake

Ken Davis added that 1991 verse to his 1959 song when he learned that his recording of "Shook Shake" had been included on a bootleg LP in France. "Wow! To think people are still listening to me sing a song I wrote and recorded over 30 years ago!" he says. "Sort of makes me feel like I've accomplished at least one creative milestone in my life. Actually, it's mind-boggling."

Davis began to play guitar shortly after his 1954 high school graduation, incorporating the influences of Hank Williams, Johnny Cash, Buddy Holly and Elvis. His first gig was playing bass with Buddy Nelson's Country Gentlemen, but he soon left to go solo. He added the Honeybees, Judy and Nancy, to his act and paid for his own session at Milwaukee's Pfau label. He recalls a Milwaukee country DJ playing "Sittin' Pretty" and commenting that "It might just be a hit if it were done at a quality studio."

Harry Smith, owner of Racine's Starlight label, liked it enough to produce a follow-up. "Uh Huh, That's Right" got a good review in Billboard and substantial airplay on WRJN. It didn't generate enough excitement for Smith to produce a second release, however, so Davis again tried on his own.

Having learned the importance of a catchy phrase in songwriting, Davis picked up on an odd one spouted frequently by his cousin's boyfriend - "Shook shake, like a big mix cake." The song that he created around it was recorded late one night at a garage studio, while the neighbors complained and called the police. Intended as the B-side to "Echo Rock," it came out on Starlight. Davis then signed with a manager, a local juke box operator, who released it on his Badger label. The record received favorable reviews in the trades and made some regional charts, including a number one placing on one Minnesota station. That's when Davis got drafted.

At Fort Sill, Oklahoma, Davis picked up where he left off, recording in Oklahoma City at the studio owned by Gene Sullivan (writer of "Blue Moon Of Kentucky"). While the previous records had a Buddy Knox type of sound, the new one, "Oh So Blue" was a more pop ballad with a Jack Scott flavor. Davis was interviewed on a Lawton radio station and it seemed as if something were beginning to happen. He received a call from ABC-Paramount expressing interest in all of the Badger masters. Davis turned it over to his manager and "nothing ever came of it," he says. "I was never able to contact anyone at ABC-Paramount and within months my so-called manager moved out of Racine and I never heard from him again."

After his military discharge, Davis continued to gig around Racine and released two more records. He retired from music in the mid 70's. "I have attended many, many live performances of entertainers over the past years and I have often regretted dropping out of music altogether," he says. "A few years back, when a publisher in England was interested in re-releasing two of my records, a booking agent there sent me an offer of an all-expense-paid trip to England to play several live gigs. Out of music too long, I turned it down."

Unrelated Ken Davis: Dot
Sources: Ken Davis letters, 3/13/93, 4/6/93
         Tourville. Wisconsin . . . Discography.

Line's End

Steve Harkus - ld gtr
Pat James - rh gtr
Rocky Rockwell - org (1/18/52; Lincoln, NE)
Mike Tebeau - bs
Bob Lakas - dr

Lompri   90599 Hey Little Girl/Miss Illusion   /68

Probably the most popular teen band in Racine for a time, this group did their sole recording after winning a local battle-of-the-bands contest. They did gigs with several of Milwaukee's better known bands and had the opportunity to open one show for the Byrds. Rocky Rockwell (yes, it's his real name) continued playing until 1986, Steve Harkus still plays in Madison, and Bob Lakas is believed to have remained active in music.

Sources: Rocky Rockwell telephone interview, 2/9/94
         Tourville. Wisconsin . . . Discography.

Little Gregory & the Concepts

Lompri   270   Go Away/Look And You'll See   /69

Label owner Jim Lombard recalls this as an 11-piece black group that had appeared on the Channel 18 show *Grapevine*. He believes the group consisted initially of neighborhood friends and acquaintances put together by a manager to provide positive activities and goals.

Sources: Jim Lombard telephone interview, 3/12/94

Marksmen

Dick Neu - ld gtr
Ken Locke - gtr   **Dan Vance** - rh gtr
Bob Allen (Humpa) - bs   **Jerry Bellamy**- voc
Ed Porcaro - dr (10/13/45; Racine)

| Sara | 65128 Black Pepper/Sharon | 12/65 |

The Marksmen went through several later personnel changes over an eight-year period beginning in 1962. The band did one show with the Kingsmen. Ed Porcaro was subsequently involved with drum and bugle corps instruction for many years.

Unrelated Marksmen: Blue Horizon, Dearborn, Westco
Sources: Ed Porcaro telephone interview, 8/17/94
      Cuca ledger cards - courtesy Jim Kirchstein
      Osborne-Brown. Rockin' Records.

Revels/Trafalgar Square

Tim Eifler - gtr
Steve Grim - gtr (7/16/50; Moline, IL)
John Marshall (Marselli) - bs

| USA | 890 | Til The End Of The Day/It's A Shame Girl | 10/67 |
| | | (Trafalgar Square) | |

"I looked at a model box one day and it said 'Revel'," explains Steve Grim regarding the name of this band. Unfortunately, after building that name up around Racine, they were unable to use it on record, due the existence of another Revels in Chicago. Their only single came out as Trafalgar Square.

Grim's father attended the Methodist church with Don Rowe, who brought in name acts to Racine to perform at YMCA dances. "He gave us countless openings," says Grim, recalling shows with the Association, Buffalo Springfield, McCoys, Buckinghams and many others. "I remember this in awe. It was wonderful," he says. Grim and John Marshall went on to work with Bad Boy, a Milwaukee 70's band that recorded for United Artists.

Unrelated Revels: This band never used the Revels name on record. A Revels group that backed Robin Lee on USA is also unrelated, and may have been the reason for this group's name change.
Sources: Steve Grim telephone interview, 4/21/94
      Clee. American 45 R.P.M. Records.

Sensations

Ray Plauske - ld gtr (dec)
Harry Voss - rh gtr   **Pete Ruffalo** - dr
Dave Villo - bs
Jeff Gertanbach - dr

Draeger   01   Wildcat 401/Bent Tappets   (I/I)   /63

Also see: Sultans Five (Ray Plauske)
Unrelated Sensations: Argo, Atco, Chess, Junior, King Co., River, Tollie, Way Out
Source: Vic Weinfurter letters, 5/11/94, 5/17/94

Starboys
(Kenosha)

John Sieger - gtr
Gregg Kishline - kb/bs   **Mike Sieger** - voc
Frank Niccolai - kb
Phil Clark - sx
Ken Vanderpoel - bs
Cy Costabile (cos-tah'-blee) - dr (10/19/49; Kenosha)

Dish   EP   Hey Mama/Coughing Up Blood/Good Old Blues/
                                          Hay In The Needlestack   /69
Criminal   822   Pennies In A Jar/Labor Pains   /75

The Starboys lasted for close to 10 years, including some time in Canada. Greg Kishline left in 1970 and recorded with the Studebaker Brothers on Little Fort. John Sieger and Cy Costabile later formed the R&B Cadets. In the 90's Costabile has recorded as a member of Ashcan School, whose LP features an appearance by Victor DeLorenzo of the Violent Femmes.

Sources: Mike Sieger letter, 6/30/94
        Cy Costabile telephone interview, 7/17/94
        Tourville. <u>Wisconsin . . . Discography.</u>

Starfires
(Kenosha)

Joe Santilli (Santiloni) - voc
Henry Rice - ld gtr (9/28/42; Kenosha)
Pete Tabili - gtr
Stan "Stosh" Wojtym - bs (dec)
Ronnie "Duke" Barret - dr

Sonic   7163   Handful Of Blood/Re-Entry   (I/I)   /63

"On WLIP, the local station, we were number one for five weeks," says Henry Rice. "We were the first local group to ever cut a record. It was getting airplay every day until some of the upper class people by the lake said that the title was 'unfit for young ears to hear'." Rice continues to write and record in the 90's.

Also see: Warlock (Henry Rice)
Unrelated Starfires: Accent, Apt, Bargin, Bernice, Big Sound, College, D&H, Decca, Duel,
    G.I., LaBrea, Ohio, Pace, Pama, Round, Sara, Triumph, Yardbird
Sources: Henry Rice telephone interview, 7/17/94
    Osborne-Brown. Rockin' Records.

Sultans Five

Ray Plauske - ld gtr (dec)
Len Juliano - rh gtr   **Tom Zager** - bs
Ken Allen - Farfisa org   **Butch Kieffer** org
Tim Michna - bs
Vic Weinfurter, Jr. - dr (4/2/42; Wisconsin Rapids)

RAL	1754-03	Tonight Is The Night/Hey Little Girl	5/64
	7934	Walk With Me/Who's At Fault	10/64
Raynard	10052	Tonight Is The Night/With You	7/65
	10053	Daisy/Life Is Like A River	8/65
Enterprise 13	1066	You Know, You Know/Calico	2/67

The Sultans Five began as just three, playing at Raymond Heights Country Club in early 1963.
Drummer Vic Weinfurter acknowledges the influence of the previous house band, Milwaukee's
Mad Lads. Guitarist Ray Plauske was an early addition and Ken Allen came aboard a little later
to complete the quintet.

The Sultans began to gain popularity at both night clubs and teen clubs. With their original tune,
"Tonight Is The Night," going over well with fans, they decided to record it. The follow-up got
enough local action to catch the ear of a Milwaukee producer, leading to more recordings.
"Daisy" received airplay on WOKY, WRIT, and WLS. Their fifth and final release, "Calico"
got a pick in Cash Box February 18, 1967 and, according to Weinfurter, "was even noticed by
several radio stations and spawned fan clubs from as far away as Pennsylvania."

The Sultans Five disbanded in 1968. Later member Tom Zager joined a group in San Francisco
and Weinfurter has recently returned to playing around Racine.

Also see: Sensations
Sources: Vic Weinfurter letter, 5/11/94
    Tourville. Wisconsin . . . Discography.
    Frank Merrill letter, 1994

Voyagers

Joey Gonzales - voc
Jay Seger - ld gtr
Steve Porter - gtr
Lance Davenport - bs
Dave King - dr

Feature	101	Can't Save This Heart	/65
	111	Away/I'm So Lonely	/66

Unrelated Voyagers: Ensign
Sources: Steve Grim, 1994
      Charlie Offer, 1994
      Tourville. Wisconsin . . . Discography.
      Osborne-Brown. Rockin' Records.

Sultans Five: Len Juliano, Ray Plauske,
Butch Kieffer, Tom Zager, (seated) Vic Weinfurter
(courtesy Vic Weinfurter)

Warlock: Frank Pederson, Bob Lawler, Larry
Threadgill, (bottom) Hank Rice
(courtesy Henry Rice)

Warlock
(Kenosha)

Henry Rice - ld gtr (9/28/42; Kenosha)
Bob Lawler - rh gtr
Frank Pederson - bs (Waukegan)
Larry Threadgill - dr

Ex-Plo   009   In A Dream/Feel A Whole Lot Better   /69

Frank Peterson carried on the name of this band for many years with various personnel changes. The Ex-Plo label was connected with the Al Schultz Agency in Waukegan.

Also see: Starfires (Henry Rice)
Unrelated Warlock(s): Ara, Decca, Mercury, Music Merchant, Washington Square
Sources: Henry Rice telephone interview, 7/17/94
          Osborne-Brown. Rockin' Records.

Sheboygan

Known as the nation's bratwurst capitol, Sheboygan was also the home of a surprising number of recorded bands in the 60's.

Blue Feeling

Ross Baldock - ld gtr
Steve Feudner - rh gtr
Jack Westfall - bs
Tommy Raml - dr (7/29/49; Sheboygan)

Night Owl   6861   Tell Her No[1]/And My Baby's Gone[2]   6/68

Also see: Matadors (Tommy Raml)
Source: Tom Raml telephone interview, 8/24/94
          Cuca ledger cards - courtesy Jim Kirchstein

---

[1]Zombies, 1965
[2]Moody Blues, 1965

Chain Gang

Joe Newman - ld gtr
John Kondreck - rh gtr   **Mike Butzen** - dr
Tom Hulbert - org
Steve Dotz - bs
Darrell Mand - dr (2/5/44; Fond du Lac)

Night Owl   6768   Come On Up[1]/Monkey Time '67[2]   6/67

Drummer Darrell Mand was involved with many Sheboygan bands. This group is not to be confused with Shane Todd's Shane Gang, which had no released recordings.

Also see: Teen Kings (Darrell Mand)
Sources: Darrell Mand telephone interview, 5/9/94
        Tourville. Wisconsin . . . Discography.

Chantels

Wes Jerving - voc (6/27/45; Long Island, NY)
Tom Frank - ld gtr
Bob Kampmann - rh gtr
Joel Grollmus - bs
Chuck Hertini - dr

Bryan   100   Time Slips Out The Window /Runaway[3]   /64

The Chantels were apparently unaware of the hit female vocal group of a few years earlier when they chose their name. Of course, that group's last real hit, "Well I Told You," came in late 1961, and three years is a long time when you're 16. At any rate, Sheboygan's Chantels are remembered in high regard by other musicians who knew them. Singer Wes Jerving says, "Yeah, we were probably the best band in Sheboygan," laughingly adding, "I don't know if that's saying much." Jerving continues to sing in the 90's.

Unrelated Chantels: ABC, Carlton, End, Eric, Lana, Ludix, MW, RCA, Roulette, TCF, Verve
Sources: Wes Jerving telephone interview, 4/24/94
        Mike Dellger, 1994
        Tourville. Wisconsin . . . Discography.

---

[1]Young Rascals, 1966
[2]Major Lance, 1963
[3]Del Shannon, 1961

Furys
(Sheboygan)

Wally Henel - ld gtr
Steve Getschou - rh gtr
Dennis Radloff - bs (dec)
Joel Jetzer - dr

Cuca	1010	St. Louis Blues[1]/This Way Out	9/60
		(Both sides reissued on *The Cuca Story, Vol. 2)*	

Not to be confused with the Stevens Point-based Furys, this band's only record was produced by Vilas Craig. Bassist Dennis Radloff then joined Craig's Viscounts and was killed when a drunk driver collided with the band's vehicle in 1961.

Also see: Vilas Craig
Unrelated Furys: Aura, Dee Jay, Diamond, Fleetwood, Laurie, Lavender, Liberty, Mack IV,
      Manor, World Pacific
Sources: Wes Jerving telephone interview, 4/94
      Tom Kuck telephone interview, 6/12/94

Gingersnaps

Window	1115	Bald Headed Papa/There's A Little Rock	/59
Jupiter	305	Remembering/A 150 Guys	
Possibly related:			
Kapp	226	Lenny, Lenny/Gingerbread	/58

Source: Tourville. <u>Wisconsin . . . Discography.</u>
    Clee. <u>American 45 R.P.M. Records.</u>

Loyal Opposition

Carl Weinberger - gtr (7/7/49; Sheboygan)
Rick Gustafson - gtr (5/30/48; Sheboygan)
Greg Rakun - org
Mike Eubank - bs (4/8/49; Louisville, KY)
Steve Hofschield - dr

---

[1]Prince's Orchestra, 1916 (I didn't realize Prince had been recording that long!);
Louis Armstrong, 1930; many others; w: W.C. Handy

Target   1002   Telling Lies/Love Has Come Your Way   3/69

"'Telling Lies' was originally called 'Pondering'," says Carl Weinberger. "But Al Posniak said, 'We'll record you guys for nothing if you let me change the words' - and he made me sing with an English accent. We just said, 'OK, sure'." Weinberger wound up purchasing most of Target's recording equipment when the company went out of business a few years later. He has remained in with music, both in management/booking and performing.

Also see: Primates (Mike Eubank)
Sources: Carl Weinberger telephone interview, 5/8/94
          Rick Gustafson telephone interview, 6/14/94
          Tourville. <u>Wisconsin . . . Discography.</u>

Loyal Opposition: Carl Weinberger, Greg Rakun, Steve Hofschield, Rick Gustafson, Mike Eubank (courtesy Rick Gustafson)

Matadors
(Sheboygan Falls)

Ronnie Thone - voc (9/16/45; Sheboygan)
Roman "Romy" Brotz - ld gtr
Greg Busch - rh gtr
Lee McGlade - bs (2/18/49; Rice Lake)
Tommy Raml - dr

Feature   109   You're A Better Man Than I[1]/Bright Lights - Big City[2]   /66

This band is not related to the Madadors from Palmyra, who appeared on the same label just four releases earlier. Neither group had any knowledge of the other. The Matadors started in high school circa 1962 and lasted till about 1967, playing often in the Fox Valley area. Ronnie Thone was later with Yazz (no related to the 80's British group), featured on a 1982 WAPL Battle Of The Bands LP, *Apple Cellar Tapes.*

Matadors: unidentified, Ron Thone, Tom Raml (drums), Lee McGlade, Greg Bush, Romy Brotz (courtesy Ron Thone)

Unrelated Matadors: Chart Maker, Colpix, Feature (Madadors), Forbes, Keith, Sue
Sources: Wes Jerving telephone interview, 4/24/94
          Lee McGlade telephone interview, 6/5/94
          Ronnie Thone telephone interview, 6/6/94
          Tourville. Wisconsin . . . Discography.

---

[1]Yardbirds - *Having A Rave Up With The Yardbirds* LP, 1965
[2]Jimmy Reed, 1961

Primates

Mike Eubank - gtr (4/8/49; Louisville. KY)
Tom Schilder - gtr
Clark Wessel - kb (8/12/50; Sheboygan)
Gary Hildebrand - bs
John Doll - dr

Leaf   667   Girl Don't Tell Me/I'll Feel A Whole Lot Better[1]   /66

"There was a music store in town, Goodell Music, that was kind of the central place where all the members from different bands would go," says Clark Wessel. It was there that this teen age band heard about the Cuca studios and the Leaf label and headed out to record. Having started with high school dances in 1966, the Primates landed gigs as far away as Green Bay and Milwaukee before their breakup two years later.

Mike Eubanks later returned to his hometown in Kentucky and worked with Leroy Parker & the Whiskey Mountain Band. They won a Seagram's Seven Battle Of The Bands in Louisville, and had a release on Seagram's record label. Later, back in Wisconsin, Eubanks worked with Tom "Grizzly" Adams & the Lazy Bones before leaving the music business and opening his jewelry store. He now plays for church functions.

Also see: Loyal Opposition (Mike Eubanks)
Unrelated Primates: Marko, Voxx
Sources: Carl Weinberger telephone interview, 5/8/94
        Rick Gustafson telephone interview, 6/14/94
        Mike Eubanks telephone interview, 7/25/94

Don Ragon

Window   1009   Jungle Rock/After Love   /59

Source: Tourville. <u>Wisconsin . . . Discography.</u>

Teen Kings

Tom Shills - ld gtr   **Wayne Ehler** - bs
Richie Ehler - rh gtr (11/15/46; Sheboygan)   **Bob Castellan** - voc
Mike Mellenhoeft - bs   **Tom "Kookie" Kuck** - dr (4/29/45; Sheboygan)
Darrell Mand - dr (2/5/44; Fond du Lac)

---

[1]Byrds - *Mr. Tambourine Man* LP, 1965

Sara   6342   It's Too Late[1]/I Might Have Known[2]   4/63
                     (Side reissued on *The Cuca Story, Vol. 3*)

"'It's Too Late' became number one over in Germany for a while," claims Tom Kuck. It's difficult to imagine how Cuca's distribution could have accomplished that, but he adds, "That's what we were told. We never really got any money out of it." Kuck was the drummer on the record, replacing Darrell Mand, who worked with many other area bands. Kuck also worked with several groups, including his own Kookie & the Premiers, who remained unrecorded. Now living in Virginia, he plays with a blues band. Guitarist Tom Shills is the brother of the Legends' Jerry Shills.

Also see: Chain Gang (Darrell Mand)
Unrelated Teen Kings: Bee, Je-wel, Rago, Willett
Sources: Darrell Mand telephone interview, 5/9/94
       Richard Ehler telephone interview, 5/27/94
       Tom Kuck telephone interview, 6/12/94
       Tourville. Wisconsin . . . Discography.
       Osborne-Brown. Rockin' Records.

Vikings

Leon Halverson - voc
Cliff Hanson - ld gtr
Carl Hintz - rh gtr
Bob Hinze - bs (dec)
Tom Stubler - dr (12/21/44; Sheboygan)

Cuca   1096   Rave On[3]/Rawhide[4]   (/I)   7/62

Unrelated Vikings: Athens, Del Mann, Salem, Viking
Sources: Tom Stubler telephone interview, 12/11/93
       Tourville. Wisconsin . . . Discography.
       Osborne-Brown. Rockin' Records.

---

[1]Chuck Willis, 1956
[2]w: Joe South
[3]Buddy Holly, 1958
[4]Link Wray, 1959

Superior

"Difficult to separate the Superior music scene from the Duluth/Minneapolis music scene but, on the whole, Superior musicians were louder, raunchier, played more original music, had much longer hair and, on occasion, could be quite territorial. They have generally rebelled against dressing alike, or even dressing up, for gigs.

"Nickelson's Music Store (1327 Banks Ave.) was intimately involved with the bands from this era and area. Len (Nickelson) loaned, rented, and sometimes repossessed equipment, taught, philosophized, scolded, even assaulted, and occasionally made a buck off us. Many, many musicians were kept from absolutely starving to death by teaching at Nickelson's. Without Len the Superior music scene of the 50's and 60's would not have been near as rich as it was."
  - Bill Forseth (Grassfire), 5/24/94

Dynamics: (top) Jack Rygg, Bob Tungsthal,
Bobby Price, Droop McPhearson,
Oliver Kennedy, Ken Mason,
Bill McCollough (producer), Perry Lee,
(bottom) Dick Ford, Don Anderson,
John Thompson (courtesy Richard Ford)

Dynamics/Bobby Price & the New Dynamics

Bobby Price - voc
Don Anderson - gtr
Dick Ford - kb (2/8/42; Superior)
John Thompson - bs   **John Murray** - voc
Jack Rygg - dr   **Dennis Murphy** - sx

Cuca   1081   Come Go With Me[1]/Money Honey[2]   4/62
                   1095   Oh, I Like It Like That/Is It True   7/62
                               (Bobby Price & the New Dynamics)

This group existed in three basic different versions from 1961-65, first with Price as the featured singer, then Murray, then as a harmony group without a featured lead. The second release consisted of two original tunes and included five additional background singers; Oliver Kennedy, Ken Mason, Droop McPhearson, Perry Lee and Bob Tungstahl. the record was produced by WEBC DJ Bill McCollough. Rygg and Ford also did a session for Len Gale that was released on Studio City (1006). Ford eventually became a high school music teacher.

Unrelated Dynamics: Arc, Big Top, Black Gold, Bolo, Capri, Cindy, Cotillion, Decca, Delta, Do-Kay-Lo, Douglas, Dynamic, Farrall, Guaranteed, Herald, Impala, Jerden, LaVere, Liban, Liberty, Penguin, Reprise, Seafair, Seeco, Top Ten, USA, Warner, Wingate
Unrelated Dick Ford: Soma
Sources: Dick Ford letter, 3/94
         Osborne-Brown. _Rockin' Records._

Dynasty

Jack Casper - ld gtr (6/4/48; Superior)
Mark Casper - rh gtr (9/15/50; Superior)
Ken Clark - kb   **Dan Egnash** - kb
Fred Anderson - bs   **Mike Polaski** - kb
Don Beetcher - dr

Royal Court   262   I've Gotta Shout/I'm Crying[3]   /66
Westchester   1156   Flying On The Ground Is Wrong[4]/Soul Kitchen   /68

Highlights for the Dynasty included opening for Tommy James & the Shondells at the Duluth Arena, and a show with the Electric Prunes. The band also worked often around Ashland and Ironwood. Guitarist Jack Casper has filled in with many other groups in the Superior-Duluth area since the wrap-up of Dynasty. He recorded with the Original Swift Brothers in Minneapolis in 1971 and worked for 14 years in a group called Vegas. Brother Mark Casper worked many years at Nickelson Music, a gathering spot for the local musicians. (Len Nickelson, owner of the store, had worked as a musician in Hollywood in previous decades).

---

[1]Dell Vikings, 1957
[2]Drifters, 1953
[3]Animals, 1964
[4]_Buffalo Springfield_ LP, 1967; w: Neil Young

Also see: Emotionals (Mike Polaski)
Unrelated Dynasty(s): Coulee, Fan Jr., Jerden, Solar
Sources: Jack Casper telephone interview, 2/14/94
        Tourville. <u>Wisconsin . . . Discography.</u>
        Oldsberg, Jim & Mark Prellberg. "Who, What, Then, Where, Now." <u>Lost and Found</u>

Emotionals: Jim Van Puymbrouck, Mike Polaski, Bob Davern, Dick Shaul, Rick Davern
(courtesy Jim Van Puymbrouck)

Emotionals

Mike Polaski - voc
Jim Van Puymbrouck - ld gtr (3/18/50; Superior)
Bob Davern - rh gtr
Rick Davern - bs   **Dick Shaul** - dr
Skip Anderson - dr

Robin   189   Misirlou[1]/Out Of Sight, Out Of Mind[2]   (I/)   1/67

The Emotionals were winners of WEBC's Battle Of The Bands in September 1966, and their
recording session took place in December. The surf standard Misirlou, chosen on the way to

---

        [1]Harry James, 1941; Dick Dale, 1962; many others
        [2]Astronauts LP, 1965

Dove Studios in Minneapolis, was the intended B-side. It ended up being the more popular one, though little airplay resulted. The label was named after the Davern brothers' younger sister.

Singer Mike Polaski later played keyboard for Dynasty and recorded with Atlantis in 1972. Dick Shaul recorded with Darkhood in 1970. In 1994 Jim Van Puymbrouck, still favoring the Ventures and Fireballs, returned to the stage as a member of a 50's band.

Also see: Dynasty (Mike Polaski)
Sources: Jim Van Puymbrouck letter, 2/94
      Jack Casper telephone interview, 2/14/94

Grassfire

Jerry Edwards - voc
Bill Forseth - ld gtr (6/21/50; Chicago, IL)
Gary Lynn - org
Roger Lynn - bs
Ed Gallagher - dr

Steamboat   48250 Aunt Morley's Wheatcakes/Smell Of Incense   /69
Related:
(label unknown)   Rock Bottom/   (Gusto Flash)   /71

Recorded in Minneapolis at Sound 80, this record was produced by Dave Zimmerman, the brother of Bob Dylan. "I don't know if Dave Zimmerman was totally unimpressed with us, or where he was at in his own career at that time," says Bill Forseth, "but his input was minimal. We had no contact with him after this. Nor did we want to, after hearing the final product." In fact, production credit on the label goes to Ed Gallagher and R. & G. Lynn.

"Outdoor concerts were the most fun for some of us musicians, as the hope was we'd get to play louder than anyone had ever played before," says Forseth. "Occasionally things got so loud that Duluth residents across the bay would call the police to shut us down, as we'd borrowed and rented every speaker and amplifier in town."

Grassfire opened local shows for the Animals, Guess Who, Zombies and others. Forseth and singer Jerry Edwards later formed Gusto Flash. Drummer Ed Gallagher had previously recorded with Seagram Quintet, a Minnesota band. In 1970 Gallagher joined with Don Harrich and Ken Smith to form D-E-K, a company that booked and recorded bands.

Sources: Bill Forseth letter, 5/24/94
      Ed Gallagher telephone interview, 6/22/94
      Tourville. <u>Wisconsin . . . Discography.</u>

Johnny Jay
(John Jerome Huhta - 10/9/34; Duluth)

Mercury	71232	Tears/Sugar Doll		10/57
	71267	I'm Gonna Keep It/Send Me Love		5/58
Play	1006	I Like (About Love)/Let Me Keep You Company		/58
Stop	115	Buck 2.80/Rosy Glow		6/67
	133	Reasonable Facsimile/One Way Ticket		1/68
D-E-K	101	Tears/The Bartender Song	(Johnny Huhta)	5/70

Out of the depths of Northern Wisconsin, Johnny Huhta managed to land his first releases on a major label. "I went to Nashville and knocked on doors," he says. "Cut an independent session and the masters were leased to Mercury."

Huhta toured extensively, working shows with Johnny Cash, Jim Reeves, Joe South, Brenda Lee, Marvin Rainwater and many others. In 1970 he reissued that first session on D-E-K. His one taste of chart action came in 1973 when he co-wrote Dave Dudley's top 40 country hit, "It Takes Time." Huhta continues to write and record demos while enjoying his hobbies of fishing and painting.

Sources: John Huhta letters, 4/5/93, 5/3/93
       Tourville. Wisconsin . . . Discography.

Vic Martinson
(8/27/40; Tony)

Cuca	1083	Boo On You/So Lonely Tonight	6/62

Martinson plays guitar, steel guitar, and fiddle. He continues to do country gigs.

Source: Mrs. Vic Martinson telephone interview, 3/94

Chet Orr & the Rumbles

Chet Orr - voc (11/4/43; Superior)
Dennis Konkel - ld gtr
Dave Lindemann - rh gtr (12/4/46; Fargo, ND)
John Rookey - bs
Don Fenn - dr   **John Grindal** - bs

Studio City	1012	Be Satisfied/Please Free Me

Chet Orr, who also plays drums, joined Duluth's XL-5 Minus One, who recorded on Cove.

Unrelated Rumbles: Capitol, Dad's, GNP/Crescendo, Lemon, Magic, Mercury, Sire, Soma
Sources: Jack Casper telephone interview, 2/14/94
        Dave Lindemann telephone interview, 3/6/94
        Chet Orr telephone interview, 4/94

Eau Claire

AlDon & the EC's

Al Fremstad - voc
Don Cronkhite - gtr (dec)
Tex Hanson - gtr
Art Hestekin - gtr
Kip McFaul - sx
Tom O'Brien - dr

Gaity   173/174   So Lonely/Endsville   (/I)   9/59

Al for Al Fremstad, Don for Don Cronkhite, EC's for Eau Claire and no bass player. This was the city's first recorded rock 'n' roll group, released on a small Minneapolis label. _Lost And Found_ Magazine describes the record as an Everly Brothers style vocal coupled with an echo-laden, Duane Eddyish instrumental. The EC's broke up just a few months later and Al Fremstad later joined the Thundermen upon his release from military service. Don Cronkhite died in a parachuting accident in the fall of 1968.

Also see: Thundermen
Sources: Rick Hoehn letter, 4/93
        Tourville. _Wisconsin . . . Discography._
        Oldsberg, Jim. "Aldon & The E.C.s/Thundermen." _Lost and Found_

Burlington Express

Craig Heron - gtr
Ken Mattson - gtr   **Mark Lillis** - gtr
Bill Burling - bs (1/27/49; Ladysmith)   **Jeff Hilger** - dr
Dave Kappus - dr

Prod   01   Shake[1]/Three Time Loser[2]   4/68

---

[1]Sam Cooke, 1965

Burlington Express began as the Dimensions in 1964. The Express traveled through the Gary Van Zeeland Agency and their record enjoyed its greatest success in La Crosse. The band broke up circa 1969 and Bill Burling recorded in 1970 as a member of Cross Town Traffique. Burling is now a college professor in Springfield, Illinois.

Sources: Bill Burling telephone interview, 7/30/94
        Mickey Lynnes telephone interview, 6/12/94
        Tourville. Wisconsin . . . Discography.

Burlington Express: Bill Burling, Craig Heron, Ken Mattson, Dave Kappus (courtesy Bill Burling)

Jerry Dee & the Intruders

Jerry Dee (Wes Lamuska) (8/6/41; Joliet, IL) - voc
Olie Wahl - ld gtr
Wayne Toske - gtr
Mick Zirngible - bs
Mike Schelberger - dr

Sara   6352   Sugar Corsage/Bo Diddley[1]   5/63

---

[2]Wilson Pickett - *The Wicked Pickett* LP, 1967
[1]Bo Diddley, 1955

Wes Lamuska was given the stage name of Jerry Dee by manager Jack Nance. Nance, who worked with Conway Twitty and co-wrote "It's Only make Believe," took on Lamuska in late 1959. Backed by the Bill Black Combo, the singer did a demo session for Hi Records in Memphis. After returning to Eau Claire, Lamuska joined the Intruders and their record was produced by local DJ Dick Hoff. "Sugar Corsage" made the WAXX top 20. (Hoff later relocated to Green Bay where he also wrote and produced for several bands). Lamuska eventually left the Intruders and went on the road as a single, again managed by Jack Nance. Voice problems in the early 70's forced him to leave the business.

Also see: Shandells (Mick Zirngible)
         Dupries, Rhythm Royals - Green Bay (Dick Hoff)
Unrelated Jerry Dee: Darem
Sources: Wes Lamuska telephone interview, 6/18/94
         Mickey Lynnes, 1994
         WAXX survey - courtesy Rick Hoehn
         Osborne-Brown. Rockin' Records.

Jaguars/Up-Stairs
(Chippewa Falls)

Tom Sumner - ld gtr (2/23/47; Chippewa Falls)
Dave Peterson - rh gtr   **Howie Market** - dr
Jim Flynn - bs   **Curt Johnson** - org
Paul Nebel - dr

Cuca	6542	Boney Maronie[1]/I've Had It[2]	4/65
Sara	6583	What's The Use Of Love/Things We Said Today[3]	8/65
Cuca	1309	Operator Please/Be My Baby[4]	1/67
		(Up-Stairs)	

"We were kind of fans of the Thundermen," says Tom Sumner, explaining how the Jaguars version of Boney Maronie was patterned after the Thundermen's "Money." The Jaguars played mostly teen gigs and beer bars from 1963-67, changing their name to the Up-Stairs in their later stages.

Sumner then went on to some noteworthy musical accomplishments in Los Angeles. Several of his tunes were used on TV shows, including the _Partridge Family, Cagney & Lacey_ and _Murder_

---

[1]Larry Williams, 1957
[2]Bell Notes, 1959
[3]Beatles - _Something New_ LP, 1964
[4]Ronettes, 1963

She Wrote. Another was recorded by the DeFranco Family (a group that charted three singles in 1973-74). "The one I'm most proud of is called 'Happy Birthday, U.S.A.'," relates Sumner. "It was performed on the Johnny Carson Show by Pat Boone." The song was also recorded by Donnie Brooks as the title cut on a bicentennial LP on 20th Century. Still, without a major breakthrough, Sumner eventually returned to Eau Claire as a radio announcer, later shifting to the sales end of the business.

Sources: Tom Sumner telephone interviews, 8/14/94, 8/23/94
        Jim Kirchstein, 1994

Shandells

Jeff Gottheardt - ld gtr
(Charles) Grant Gilbertson - rh gtr (3/25/46; Eau Claire)
Mick Zirngible - bs (6/1/45; Bremerton, WA)
Jim Coggins - dr

Bangar	0659	Gorilla/Hey Little One[1]	/65
Studio City	1037	Here Comes The Pain[2]/Summertime Blues[3]	/66

Though members Gottheardt and Coggins claimed writing credit for "Gorilla," the song was apparently derived from the Ideals' "The Gorilla" which bubbled under in 1963. Mick Zirngible, who was never aware of the latter record, was amazed to hear the song done by Milwaukee's Dynasty's at a 1994 reunion concert in La Crosse.

Gottheardt was from Milwaukee where he was influenced by the Legends, accounting for the fact that three of the Shandells' four sides had been previously recorded by that band. The Shandells lasted for about five years and toured with the Gene Pitney Shower of Stars where they opened for many name artists. They also recorded with Cannibal & the Headhunters in Minneapolis.

Also see: Jerry Dee & the Intruders (Mick Zirngible)
Sources: Grant Gilbertson telephone interview, 8/25/94
        Mick Zirngible telephone interview, 8/29/94
        John Beilfuss, 3/94
        Mickey Lynnes telephone interview, 6/12/94
        Tourville. Wisconsin . . . Discography.

---

[1]Dorsey Burnette, 1960
[2]Legends, 1964
[3]Eddie Cochran, 1958; Blue Cheer, 1968; Who, 1970

Showmen with Bobby Lee

Bobby Lee - voc (1/24/46)
Mike Gutch - ld gtr
Bob "Snuffy" Smith - rh gtr
Terry Hoepner - bs
Dave Preston - dr

Coulee	113	Alright/Dawning	2/65

Later with Everyday People, Bobby Lee is now a partner in the Dagen & Lee Entertainment Agency.

Unrelated Bobby Lee: This Bobby Lee has no connection with any other Bobby Lee recording.
Unrelated Showmen: Airecords, Amy, BB, Imperial, Liberty, Minit, Sam, Swan, Texas,
     Twin Town
Source: Bobby Lee letter, 11/4/93

Thundermen

Al Fremstad - voc
Rick Hoehn - gtr
Gerry Johnson - bs (8/2/43; Missoula, MT)   **Mike Marx** - gtr
Mickey Lynnes - dr   **Chuck Solberg** - pno

Soma	1194	Money[1]/Flyin' High[2]	(/I)	9/62
Cuca	6372	Night Train[3]/Blues Stay Away From Me[4]	(I/I)	7/63
		(Al & Gerry Jay & the Thundermen)		
Thundermen	1196	Money-1982/Aw She-Hey She		8/82
	1197	Don't-A-Come-A My House/Starfreighter Lullaby		8/83
	1199	Great Balls Of Fire/Little Darlin'		8/85
	1201	Mule Skinner Blues/Rock & Roll Medley		12/86
	1208	Good Golly Miss Molly/Chantilly Lace		6/89
LP's:				
Thundermen	1195	Rick Hoehn, The Thundermen & Money		8/82
	1203	The Works, 1962-1986		3/86

---

[1]Barrett Strong, 1960; Kingsmen, 1964
[2]Bobby Vee & the Shadows, 1959
[3]Buddy Morrow, 1952; Viscounts, 1960; James Brown, 1962
[4]Owen Bradley, 1949; Ace Cannon, 1962

Up-Stairs: Jim Flynn, Tom Sumner,
Curt Johnson, Howie Market
(courtesy Tom Sumner)

Thundermen: Al Fremstad, Rick Hoehn, Gerry Johnson, Mickey Lynnes (courtesy Mickey Lynnes)

The Thundermen became stars in Eau Claire when their self-produced version of "Money" climbed all the way to the top spot at WAXX on October 27, 1962 - even with some wrong words. The group had been evolving for about 2-1/2 years and they became inspired with a performance of the song by Roscoe & His Little Green Men at Fournier's Ballroom. (The Green Men had a single on it about two years earlier).

In September the Thundermen and a couple of musician friends drove to Kay Bank Studios in Minneapolis and recorded all four of the songs that comprised their two singles. The session included the services of Don Cronkhite on harmony vocal and Mike Marx on lead guitar. The boys paid for it all, owned the master, and did all their own promotion, including sending a review copy off to Billboard Magazine. When it was listed with a four-star review, the band members jumped into Gerry Johnson's Chevy and covered as many of the area radio stations as they could. Despite all this, the Soma label remained uninterested. The Thundermen waited until the following summer to release their follow-up, this time taking the tapes to Cuca for pressing.

By 1964 the Thundermen had disbanded and all but Mickey Lynnes eventually dropped out of the business. However, in 1980 Rick Hoehn began working on a project that included the re-recording of "Money" (with the same wrong words!). The effort resulted in an album and a reuniting of the original Thundermen after 18 years. A second LP includes the four original cuts from 1962. After a few years of occasional gigs, all but Lynnes have since returned to other occupations. Hoehn continues with the recording studio, however, along with his own label and a mail-order record business.

Also see: AlDon & the EC's (Al Fremstad, Don Cronkhite)
Unrelated Thundermen: Kiski
Sources: Rick Hoehn letter, 4/93
       Tourville. <u>Wisconsin . . . Discography.</u>
       Oldsberg. <u>Lost and Found</u>
       Osborne-Brown. <u>Rockin' Records.</u>

Twilights

Gene Frazier - ld gtr
Dan Dernbach - rh gtr (3/31/46; Eau Claire)
Bob Grizb - bs
Donnie Winget - dr (3/9/48; Eau Claire)

On the snowy highway down to Sauk City in early 1965 the Twilights lost control of their van and went off the road. Fortunately, after receiving some help from a farmer (awakened at 3AM), they made the recording session. The intended title for the "007" side was "Gestapo" but that was nixed by label owner Jim Kirchstein. (Perhaps he was uneasy after his early episode with the Swastika label - see Cuca Story). Donnie Winget later spent several years with Doc & the Interns who booked through Al Schultz but never recorded.

Bangar	0634	Why, Why, Why/Tears	/64
Cuca	6531	You Make Me Feel So Good[1]/007	3/65

Unrelated Twilights: Aqua, Capitol, Destination, Felice, Parkway, Parrot, Roulette, 6 Star, Twilight

Sources: David Stanton telephone interview, 7/2/94
Don Winget telephone interview, 8/5/94
Dan Dernbach telephone interview, 8/7/94
Osborne-Brown. Rockin' Records.

Stevens Point/Wausau

Chosen Few
(Stevens Point/Milwaukee)

Warren Groovy (Mittlestadt) - org (3/27/47; Chicago)
Gary Huboldt - ld gtr
Des (Desmond) Smith - rh gtr (3/10/47; Milwaukee)
Dave Huegel - bs
John Baker - dr

Denim	1092	Stop In The Name Of Love[2]/Pink Clouds And Lemonade		/66
Related:				
Desmond	100	Ruthy's Run/Knowing Yourself	(Winfield Road)	/76

The Chosen Few have turned out to be rather plentiful. There are Chosen Few records on several labels from various parts of the country, undoubtedly representing quite a few different groups. The strangest entry is another Chosen Few release on the same Denim label, which apparently precedes this one (#1082). Neither Des Smith nor Warren Mittlestadt professed any knowledge of this or any other Chosen Few recordings. It's possible that bassist Dave Huegel may have carried on the name when he moved east, and could have a connection with some later recordings. There was also an unrelated (and unrecorded) Chozen Few in Milwaukee.

Though some of this band's members were also from the Milwaukee area, the Chosen Few got together while attending college in Stevens Point and worked mostly around the state. They got a break filling in for the Kingsmen (of "Louie, Louie" fame) at a U.W. homecoming dance when the latter group was delayed by an auto accident. This created a showcase opportunity resulting in full time bookings by Gary Van Zeeland.

---

[1]Zombies, 1964 (flip of "She's Not There")
[2]Supremes, 1965

Mittlestadt got drafted and later worked extensively (under the name Warren Groovy - how's that for a 60's name?) with Jules Blattner. Des Smith formed his own record label before going into the jewelry business. In 1976 the original Chosen Few, minus Gary Huboldt, reunited as Winfield Road for the single "Ruthy's Run." With a lyric about a Colorado skiing site, the song reportedly did well in that area.

Unrelated Chosen Few: Autumn, Bandit, B.F.D., Canusa, Canyon, Co-Op, Crystal, Dart,
      Denim 1082, Liberty, Maple, North Beach, Playboy, Phonograph, Power International,
      RCA, Roulette, Talum Stereo
Also see: Jules Blattner (Warren Mittlestadt)
Sources: Warren Mittlestadt telephone interview, 2/13/93
      Des Smith telephone interview, 8/14/93
      Tourville. <u>Wisconsin . . . Discography.</u>
      Osborne-Brown. <u>Rockin' Records.</u>

Chosen Few: Warren Mittlestadt,
Gary Huboldt, John Baker, Dave Huegel,
Des Smith (courtesy Des Smith)

Furys
(Stevens Point)

Jimmy Delwood (Sturgel?) - voc
Myrna   - rh gtr

Dee Jay   1097   Run To Him/Jenny   7/62

This band is not connected with the Furys covered in the Sheboygan section.

Unrelated Furys: Aura, Cuca, Diamond, Fleetwood, Laurie, Lavender, Liberty, Mack IV,
        Manor, World Pacific
Sources: Tourville. <u>Wisconsin . . . Discography.</u>
        Osborne-Brown. <u>Rockin' Records.</u>

Dick Hiorns (high'-rons)
(Wausau)

Cuca   1047   The Gods Were Angry[1]/I'm Movin' On[2]   9/61
                      (Side 2 reissued on *The Cuca Story, Vol 1*)
Sara   6566   Alimony/Everytime The Phone Rings   5/66
Cuca   6815   Cattle Call/Columbus Stockade Blues   1/68

Hiorns was a nightclub owner in Wausau and had booked in Jimmy Sun & the Radiants, who
provided the backing on his first record.

Also see: Fendermen (Jimmy Sun & Radiants)
Source: Jim Sundquist telephone interview, 7/3/94

Ray Kannon & the Corals
(Wausau)

Ray Kannon (Kannonberg) - voc (dec)
Denny Bloom - ld gtr
Dick Bartig - rh gtr   **Jim Marcotte** - gtr (5/15/44; Milwaukee)
Buddy Bradford - bs   **Tom Litzer** -dr
James "Curley" Cooke - dr (11/12/44; Wausau)

Cuca   1078   Muleskinner Twist[3]/Please Don't Leave Me   5/62
                      (Side 1 reissued on *The Cuca Story, Vol 2)*
               1106   Little Baby/Dance   8/62
               1122   Rendezvous/Barbara   1/63
               1164   Let's Surf/Dianne   4/64

---

[1]Eddie Kirk, 1948; Margaret Whiting & Jimmy Wakely, 1950
[2]Hank Snow, 1950; Ray Charles, 1959; Don Gibson, 1960
[3]Fendermen, 1960 ("Mule Skinner Blues")

Corals

| Big Sound | 308 | Blue Moon[1]/Everyday[2] | /66 |
| | 311 | Baby My Heart/Stand By Me[3] | /67 |

Curley Cooke is the member of this group who went on to the most noteworthy musical accomplishments, recording with Steve Miller, Boz Scaggs, Chuck Berry and many others, while switching from drums to bass and guitar.

Cooke was on bass with Robin Lee's Launchers in 1964, then joined Tim Davis' Chordairs as the guitarist. That group disbanded when Davis, Cooke and bassist Dick Personett got the call to join Steve Miller on the West Coast. Cooke has also recorded with James Cotton, Tracy Nelson, A.B. Skhy, Jerry Garcia, and Ben Sidran. He is the writer of Tim Davis' sole chart single and has had several other songs covered on various albums. His solo LP, "Gingerman" (First American 7767) came out in 1980.

Unrelated Corals: Cheer, Rayna (There is also no connection with Candy & the Corals/Dupries)
Also see: Tim Davis, (Curley Cooke, Jim Marcotte)
       Launchers - Robin Lee (Curley Cooke)
Sources: James Cooke letters, 1/94
       Tourville. <u>Wisconsin . . . Discography.</u>

Robin Lee/Lavenders/Launchers
(Roger Schenzel; 8/3/32; Merrill)

Pfau	--	We Are Meant To Be/Alone	/57
		(Roger Schenzel & the Fav-O-Rites)	
Northland	7003	I Want To Be Loved By You/Ever Ever True	/58
		(Roger Winston & the Plaids)	
Circle Dot	103	Pretty Patti/Walk Away	/60
Karrye	842	Summertime's Finally Here/Bye Bye	/61
		(Robin Lee & the Lavenders)	
Reprise	20068	Gambling Man/Angel With A Broken Wing	5/62
		(with the Jordanaires)	
	20111	Dream Drifter/If That's For Me	1/63
		(with the Anita Kerr Singers)	
Cuca	1130	Aw Shucks/Down By The Sea	4/63
		(Lavenders) (Side 1 reissued on *Badger A Go Go* LP)	

---

[1]Glen Gray, Benny Goodman, 1935; Marcels, 1961; many others; w: Rogers-Hart
[2]Buddy Holly, 1957 (flip of "Peggy Sue")
[3]Ben E. King, 1961; many others

Cuca	1152	(They Call The Wind)Maria[4]/White Lightnin' Effin' (Lavenders) (Side 2 reissued on *The Cuca Story, Vol 3*)		11/63
Cite	5010	The Puppet/Space Cowboy	(Launchers)	9/64
	5011	I See Her Face/Maria And The Stranger	(Launchers)	1/65
Big Sound	300	Barbara Jo/Carnival Of Love	(with the Night Beats)	/65
	302	Feet Of Clay/Medal Of Honor		/65
	307	Little Boy Blue/Blue Water		/66
USA	872	Pretty Patty[2]/Flyin' High	(with the Revels)	4/67
Tee Pee	4567/68	To Hell With Love/The Urge For Going		/68
At	684	Whatever Happened To Joey/The Bubble Gum Song (Royal Host)		/68
Pro-Gress	8357	Sure I Will/Your Whole World Is Falling Down (with the Royal Host)		/69
		Angel Brown/Come Dream With Me		/72
ESU	1003	What Goes Around Comes Around/Across The Table From Me		/91

LP's:

Strand	116	Robin Lee Sings	/64
Pro-Gress	2204	Robin Lee with the Royal Host	/69

Related:

Cuca	1206	That's All Right/I Still Love You (Rod & Terry - Rod Means & Terry Christian of the Lavenders) (Side 1 reissued on *Badger A Go Go* LP)	1/65

As he closes in on 40 years in the music business, Roger Schenzel continues to write songs and occasionally perform as a single. "Pretty Patti," his first record under the name Robin Lee, proved to be one of his most successful, selling well around Wisconsin. "Conway Twitty even liked it and called Everest Records in Minneapolis," recounts Schenzel. "They called me but I just didn't know what to do. I didn't have the know-how of the business at that time."

Not long after that, Schenzel sent some tapes to Buck Ram in Los Angeles. Ram, who was the manager of the Platters and had written many of their songs, liked the material and flew the singer to Nashville to record. The sessions featured backing by some of Nashville's finest, including the Jordanaires and the Anita Kerr Singers. About 10 songs were cut but, after two releases on Reprise fizzled, Ram sold the remainder to Strand for release on a budget album.

While still under contract to Reprise, Schenzel recorded for Cuca using the band's name, the Lavenders. Next came "The Puppet" for Jay Albrent's Cite label in Milwaukee, which brought another brush with greater success.

"RCA called me and wanted to redo it in their studio, so I called my friend in Milwaukee. He

---

[1]Mariners, 1951, from Broadway show *Paint Your Wagon* - Lerner & Lowe
[2]Remake of his own earlier release

said, 'Well, no, Mercury's going to do it. We've got it sewed up,' and it never happened. So I never called the guy back from RCA because he said there were too many fingers in the pie. So, it was another of those things. You're so close and so far away."

In more recent years, Schenzel has split time between owning a bar in Wausau and writing in Nashville, still hoping to pen that big one.

Lavenders:	Launchers:
Robin Lee - rh gtr	**Robin Lee** - rh gtr
Terry Christian - ld gtr	**Jerry Starr (Suchomski)** - ld gtr (Schofield)
Rodney Means - bs	**Curley Cooke** - bs (11/12/44; Wausau)
Bob Oestreich - dr	**Bob Oestreich** - dr

Although some personnel had changed, the Launchers were really still the Lavenders under a pseudonym. Bassist Curley Cooke had come from playing drums with the Corals and would soon leave to work with Tim Davis. An interesting oddity is the fact that Cooke wrote the Launchers's flip side, "Space Cowboy." He later worked with Steve Miller who recorded an unrelated song titled "Space Cowboy" in 1969.

Guitarist Jerry Starr had done his first recording with Duke Wright's polka band in Wausau. Starr, who had his name legally changed from Suchomski, had also toured with country artist Wanda Jackson. Sometime after the Launchers release, Starr got a call from George Jones. He toured and recorded off and on with the Jones Boys before settling in Albuquerque in 1967. Starr did some work with Tommy Strange & the Features and Kenny Vernon. Since then he has been playing Spanish and Mexican music and building string instruments.

Also see: Night Beats
     Ray Kannon & the Corals (Curley Cooke)
     Big Sound Records (Duke Wright)
     Cite Records (Jay Albrent)
Unrelated Robin Lee: Atlantic-America, Dot
Sources: Roger Schenzel telephone interview, 3/5/94
     James Cooke letter, 1/94
     Jerry Starr letter and telephone interview, 4/27/93, 6/93
     Tourville. <u>Wisconsin . . . Discography.</u>
     Clee. <u>American 45 R.P.M. Records.</u>

Orbits
(Stevens Point)

Ron Hanson - gtr
Eddie Merwin

Big Sound   304   Fuzzy/Make Me Feel Good   /66
Cuca   6744   Don't/Goodbye My Lover Goodbye[1]   4/67

This band is not to be confused with the Orbits from Portage who were also on Cuca (1006).

Unrelated Orbits: Argo, Cuca (1006), Dooto, Flair-X, Friddell, Gaity, Nu-Kat, Space, SSS Int.
Sources: Wayne Leitermann telephone interview, 7/29/94
        Osborne-Brown. Rockin' Records.
        Tourville. Wisconsin . . . Discography.

Starfires
(Wausau)

Forrest Jehn - ld gtr
Gary Van Sleet - gtr
Mike Reinicke - bs   **Dick Sternberg** - dr (11/29/43; Wausau)
Wayne Leitermann - dr/org (2/19/47; Milwaukee)

Big Sound   301   I'll Be Your Man/Please Go Away   /65

Starfires: Mike Reinicke, Gary Van Sleet, Wayne Leitermann, Forrest Jehn (courtesy Wayne Leitermann)

[1]Searchers, 1965

"We recorded that up in the Red Rail Room of the YMCA, where they used to have Friday night dances," says Wayne Leitermann, who switched from drums to organ for the Starfires. The band, formed around 1962, had one of the first releases on Big Sound and did most of their gigs in or near Wausau.

Also see: Night Beats (Dick Sternberg)
Unrelated Starfires: Accent, Apt, Bargin, Bernice, College, D&H, Decca, Duel, G.I., LaBrea,
     Ohio, Pace, Pama, Round, Sara, Sonic, Triumph, Yardbird
Sources: Dick Sternberg telephone interview, 7/12/94
     Wayne Leitermann telephone interview, 7/12/94
     Tourville. <u>Wisconsin . . . Discography.</u>

Around The State

American Tea Co.
(Marshfield)

Gary Testrake - voc (5/31/50; Marshfield)
Ken Rogers - gtr
Mark Nelson - org
Tim Haley - bs
Jim Schuh - dr

Golden Voice   2327   I Want You Now/Don't Leave Your Love   /69

American Tea Co. began in 1967 with the members still in high school. Their single was recorded at a small studio in East Pekin, Illinois, and spent seven weeks on WDLB's top 40 (Marshfield). The band did some touring through the Gary Van Zeeland Agency and broke up in 1970. The members reunited to play a set at their high school reunion in 1989.

Source: Gary Testrake letter 8/18/94

Attila & the Huns/Filet of Soul/Filet of Sound
(Thorp)

Mike Peace (Pease) - ld gtr (6/30/47; Alameda, CA)
Doug Deuel - rh gtr   **Benny Wisniewski** - rh gtr (Lublin)
Barry Berdal - bs   **Barb Spence** - voc (Abbotsford)
Walter Staniec - dr   **Dennis Lewan** - bs
     Rich LeGault - dr

Sara	6511	Cheryl/The Lonely Huns	1/65
Magic Touch	2009	Hula Shake/Hurry Back	11/67
	2070	Walking In The Vineyards/Here's Where I Get Off (Huns Of Time)	/69
	2071	Vineyards Of My Time/Here's Where I Get Off	/69

Filet of Soul

Dynamic	1002	Sweet Lovin'/Do Your Own Thing	/69
Magic Touch	2078	Proud Mary[1]/(Get Out, Get Out) We Want Peace (Mike Peace & Filet of Soul)	/69
Zap	002	Moving To The Country/But I'll Try	/70

Filet of Sound

Zap	EP 003	Rag Pickin' Man-That's How I Feel/Animal Jones-Riding White Horses	
Filet of Sound	4503	Oh Loretta/Now And Forever	/77
Wavemakers	001	The Tape Player Song/ (Mike Peace)	/84

LP's:

Moniquid Sound		Freedom (Filet of Soul)	/70
Filet of Sound	771	Live (8 track)	/75
	001	Prime Cuts	/77

Mike Peace (cassettes)

Wavemakers	002	These Wings Are Made To Fly	/86
	001	Peace Of Christmas	/88
	004	Reflections	/88

Attila & the Huns were born on April 4, 1964. The members' annual celebration has etched that date into Mike Peace's memory. With personnel and name changes, the band lasted into the 80's.

It was almost an accident that they landed on Lenny LaCour's Magic Touch label. After taking second place in a Wausau battle of the bands, they were contacted by an agency in Milwaukee. Arriving in town with the wrong address, they wound up at Dave Kennedy Studios. Kennedy referred them to LaCour, who liked their homemade tape and signed them. It was LaCour's idea to change the name to Filet Of Soul, to match their white soul style.

The group toured the U.S. and Greenland, finally settling in Chicago. Peace, who had the spelling of his name legally changed, says their Filet of Sound album "was a million seller - I've got a million in my cellar." Peace's 1984 solo single got airplay on Dr. Demento's syndicated show. Bassist Dennis Lewan is now a painter in Simi Valley, CA.

Unrelated Filet Of Soul: Mercury
Sources: Mike Peace telephone interview, 8/14/94
    Clee. American 45 R.P.M. Records.

---

[1]Creedence Clearwater Revival, 1969

Attila & the Huns: Benny Wisniewski, Dennis Lewan, Rich LeGault, Mike Peace (courtesy Mike Peace)

Bare Fat: (top) Randy Lindert, Steve Beau, (bottom) Jim White, Gene Diest, Kurt Kuzulka
(courtesy Kurt Kuzulka)

Bare Fat
(Waupun)

Jim White - voc (11/5/48; Waupun)
Kurt Kuzulka - ld gtr (2/28/49; Hustisford)
Steve Beau - rh gtr/kb (Fond du Lac)
Gene Diest - bs (Milwaukee)
Randy Lindert - dr (Mayville)

Bang   573   You Can All Join In[1]/Soft   11/69

It's a surprise to see a Waupun band pop up on New York's Bang label for their only release, but the connection came about through Bag Productions out of Milwaukee. The session was done at Dave Kennedy Studios and the record charted in Oshkosh, Waupun and Milwaukee. The label mistakenly credits the A-side writer as Danny Mason instead of Dave Mason.

Together for only a year, Bare Fat was formed with former members of the Warlords. Highlights include Milwaukee's *Summerfest* with James Brown, the Milwaukee Arena with Paul Butterfield and James Cotton, and the Iola Rock Festival. Kurt Kuzalka later did session work at his brother's studio and he continues to play in the 90's.

Also see: Warlords (Jim White, Randy Lindert, Steve Beau, Kurt Kuzulka)
Sources: Kurt Kuzulka telephone interview, 6/15/94
        Tourville. <u>Wisconsin . . . Discography.</u>

Benders
(Marinette)

Gerry Cain - ld gtr (9/5/46; Buffalo, NY)
Tom Noffke - rh gtr (Neenah)
Geno Jansen - bs (Antigo)
Paul Barry - dr (10/15/44; Berwyn, IL)

Big Sound   306   Can't Tame Me/Got Me Down   /66

The only record for this group of Stout University students is considered a "punk classic" by collectors of that genre. The disc was released with a picture sleeve that listed the name of a fictional manager to make the band appear more professional. The Benders operated their own club, the Pit, and later played at Pete's Pine Point and the Out-A-Sight.

Having grown up around Kenosha, drummer Paul Barry returned to the Milwaukee area to teach

---

[1]Traffic - *Traffic* LP, 1968

school. Around 1970 he formed Barry's Truckers, a popular oldies band that continues in the 90's. Barry also has his own studio and label, Lulu, formed to record local talent.

Also see: Why Four (Gerry Cain)
Unrelated Benders: Jamaka
Sources: Paul Barry telephone interview, 2/13/94
      Gerry Cain telephone interview, 5/4/94
      Prellberg. Lost and Found

Benders: Tom Noffke, Gerry Cain, Geno Jansen, (drums) Paul Barry (courtesy Paul Barry)

Blue Echoes
(West Bend/Kewaskum)

Probable members:
Larry Ruesel
David Sutton
Dave Skretney

Raynard   10019 Moonride/What I Say

Probably unrelated Blue Echoes: Bon, Bristol, Itzy, Lawn
Sources: Tourville. Wisconsin . . . Discography.
      Osborne-Brown. Rockin' Records.

Dick Campbell
(Monroe)

Betty	1212	Miami/	(Billy Stoker)	/64
Mercury	72511	Blues Peddlers/People Planners		11/65
Cuca	6962	Train To Hollywood/Sugar Ripe		6/69

LP:

Mercury	20160	Sings Where It's At	/65

Possibly related:

Great	4703	She's My Girl/	/63

"Dick Campbell used to ride his bike around town, dressed like a hippy, and he had a little bag that he carried his money in," says Jim Kirchstein Of Cuca Records. "He was quite a character. Everybody thought he was a little odd but one day he came in and I was very impressed."

Campbell did some engineering and producing at Cuca and eventually had his own label. He wrote and produced for other artists and may have also had additional releases of his own. Kirchstein believes he went to work for a publishing company in Los Angeles.

Also see: Cine Vista Records
       Talismen - Madison/Janesville
Unrelated Dick Campbell: Myra
Sources: Jim Kirchstein telephone interview, 6/19/94
       Phil Holzbauer, Ron Buchek, Ken Adamany, 1994
       Fred Masotti letter, 6/6/94
       Osborne-Brown. Rockin' Records.
       Clee. American 45 R.P.M. Records.

Counts

Key	15131	All Night/Sittin' Here Wonderin'

This may be a version of Vilas Craig's Viscounts who left him to record on their own.

Source: Tourville. Wisconsin . . . Discography.

Vilas Craig/Vilas Craig & the Viscounts
(12/21/38; Richland Center)

Rif	1148	Spring Fever/My One My Only Love		4/59
	2118/2119	My Heart/If I May		/60
International Artists				
	2120	Little Miss Mary/You Know How		4/60
	2122	The Spin/Blue Mist	(I/I)	/60

Cuca	1011	Don't You Just Know It[1]/Rotation		9/60
		(Six Shooters - Both sides reissued on *The Cuca Story, Vol 1*)		
	1072	Skinny Minnie Twist[2]/ (flip by the Badgers)		3/62
		(with the Royal Lancers)		
Fan Jr.	1706	Little Miss Brown Eyes/Poor Loser[3]		/62
	4729	Walkin' Down The Avenue/Don't Sweetheart Me		/62
International	6334	Gotta Find My Baby/Love You; If I May		3/63
Artists	6335	It's All Over/Chumba	(/I)	3/63
	6336	Heartbreak Hotel[4]/Black Out	(/I)	3/63
	6337	Poor Loser/Summer's Over		3/63
Sims	259	Unlucky Me/I'm Looking For A Girl		/65

In 1962, while our band was appearing at Madison's Shuffle Inn, we went in for a demo session with Skip Nelson of Fan Jr. Records. During a break he played Vilas Craig's "Little Miss Brown Eyes" and it sounded like a hit. A Rick Nelson-style teen pop tune written by Craig, it was a well-produced record with a tasty touch of strings and a smooth vocal. It proved to be the artist's closest brush with major success, receiving airplay on two powerhouse stations, KOMA (Oklahoma City) and KAAY (Little Rock), along with many Wisconsin outlets.

Craig was a farm boy whose musical beginnings included playing cornet in the high school band. When he formed his first country-western band, the early rock 'n' roll influences soon crept in. "Elvis is the one that got me off the farm," he says. Craig has expressed his belief that his was the first rock 'n' roll band in Wisconsin. While other sources may contradict this, it was probably the first in the southwestern part of the state, and very likely the first to travel to many small towns. Initially called the Kollege Kings, Craig's group eventually became an influence to many next-generation musicians in the area.

His first recording was done at Kay Bank Studios in Minneapolis on the same day that future star Bobby Vee was in cutting his debut "Suzie Baby." Craig created his own label for his first four releases, the second of which was also done at Kay Bank. He then began to use the new Cuca studios where he also produced Steve Sperry, Steve Mutimer & the Rhythm Kings, and the Furys.

Converting the area's audiences from old time country-western and polkas to rock 'n' roll wasn't easy. "They didn't like us - especially my father," he laughs. "We had to be very careful what rock 'n' roll songs we dared to do. If you did anything wild like 'Jailhouse Rock,' they frowned on that. We'd play 'That's All Right Mama' and they wouldn't know how to dance to it." Often,

---

[1]Huey Smith & the Clowns, 1958
[2]Bill Haley, 1958 ("Skinny Minnie")
[3]Rick Nelson - *Album Seven By Rick* LP, 1962
[4]Elvis Presley, 1956

to secure the booking, Craig had to guarantee that the band could play polkas.

"I'd go book the job and then run around the week before the dance and put up all the posters," says Craig. "That one year when I had my 1960 Buick convertible, I put 100,000 miles on that car." At one point, the miles caught up. On route from Mt. Horeb to Kendall, the car in which the band was traveling was hit head on by a drunk driver, taking the life of bassist Denny Radloff and injuring the others. After a hospital stay, Craig appeared in a wheel chair at a benefit in Madison featuring many area musicians. When he returned to action, he hired Milwaukee's Royal Lancers to back him.

"Little Miss Brown Eyes" gained the KOMA airplay when a DJ friend, Jay O'Day from Madison, moved to the Oklahoma station and asked for a copy of the record. Unfortunately, the small Fan Jr. label was unprepared for this magnitude of action outside the Wisconsin area. "It got to number two," claims Craig, "but we couldn't get a distributor in Oklahoma City."

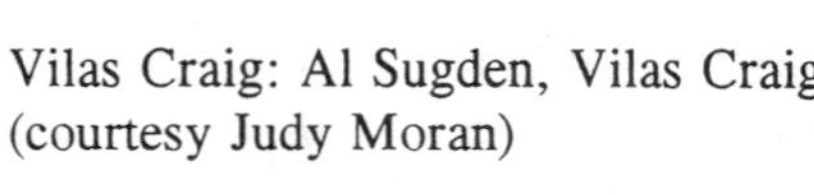

Vilas Craig: Al Sugden, Vilas Craig
(courtesy Judy Moran)

Craig attempted a variety of styles on record; mostly originals, a few remakes, four instrumentals, a barbershop quartet background, and one with a Four-Seasons flavor. His final release was done in Nashville with some top studio musicians, including Billy Grammer ("Gotta Travel On," 1958) on guitar.

Many musicians have passed through Craig's bands over the years, including Keith Knudsen who went on to major success with Doobie Brothers. Craig was apparently not always easy to work with. One source, after learning that Craig now works as a single, said, "Well, that's good - that way he can get along with himself." Craig works winters in Florida and summers in Wisconsin and Wyoming. His son Timothy has a rock band in Nashville.

Viscounts:

Ronnie McDonald - gtr	**Steve Prestigard** - pno
Dick Faith - gtr	**Pete Steele** - pno
Gary Kirschner -gtr	**Carl Gillingham** - bs
Bob Smitke - gtr	**Jim Chitwood** - bs
Jack Goodwiler - gtr	**Bobby Greenwood** - dr
Gene "Fuzz" Moller - gtr	**Bill McCorkle** - dr
Hal Block - sx	**Al Sugden** - bs
George Cash - sx	**Tom Levarda** - bs
Roger Hessling - gtr	

Also see: International Artists/Rif Records - Wisconsin Labels
    Fan Jr. Records - Wisconsin Labels (Skip Nelson)
    Royal Lancers - Milwaukee
    Furys - Sheboygan(Dennis Radloff)
    Ramrods (Pete Steele)
    Fortunes - Cuca (Roger Hessling)
Unrelated Viscounts: No separate Viscounts records have any connection with this band.
Sources: Vilas Craig letter and telephone interview, 5/93
    Phil Nee show, WRCO, 9/92 - courtesy Phil Nee
    Vilas Craig/Phil Nee interview, 9/15/93 - courtesy Phil Nee

Gord's Horde
(Rhinelander)

Gordy Gillman - gtr (2/13/46; Rhinelander)
Phil Van Goethen - org
Dan Nordall - org/gtr/sx (Park Falls)   **Cliff Fellows** - gtr/org
Dale Smith - bs/sx
Tom Price - dr

Hodag   0540   I Don't Care/Please Tell Me   6/66
        (Side 1 reissued on Pebbles _Highs In The Mid 60's, Vol 15_)

Dan Nordall wrote both sides of this band's only release. About the time he left, the name changed to T.H.E. Horde. Leader Gordy Gillman, now a fireman, says, "I guess as far as highlights go, other than the enjoyment and camaraderie of the band experience itself, our modest achievements included opening for a Kingsmen concert in Stevens Point and the same for a Turtles show in Ashland."

Sources: Gordy Gillman telephone interview and letter, 5/2/94, 5/8/94
    Tourville. <u>Wisconsin . . . Discography.</u>

I.M. Broke & the Taxpayers
(Fond du Lac)

Poverty   --   Wiped Out/Do The Washington   /69

Off beat novelty record reportedly produced at Milwaukee's Dave Kennedy Studios by a seemingly mysterious Chip Maze.

Source: Dale Luther telephone interview, 6/12/94

Individual Activity
(Fond du Lac)

Al Blau - ld gtr (6/27/47)
Brian Olson - kb
Bill Shaw - bs
Dennis Moore - dr

Tee Pee   73/74 Ten O'clock/Don't Let The Sun Catch You Crying[1]   11/68

This band worked around Wisconsin and Northern Illinois, previously as the Fabulous Temptations. Al Blau believes their record got a few spins on WLS.

Sources: Al Blau telephone interview, 6/18/94
         Dale Luther, 1994

Tommy King & the Starlites
(Lake Geneva)

Claremont   661 I'm Gonna Knock On Your Door[2]/Bop Diddle In The Jungle   /66

Source: Tourville. Wisconsin . . . Discography.

Madadors/Easy Street
(East Troy-Palmyra)

Phil Holzbauer - gtr (6/13/47; Milwaukee)
Larry Black - org   **Nels Christiansen** - dr/perc (7/17/44; Milwaukee)
Jerry Adams - bs   **Jerry Stefani** - bs
Gene Bell - dr   **Ron Buchek** - dr (6/28/46; Davenport, IA)

---

[1]Gerry & the Pacemakers, 1964
[2]Eddie Hodges, 1961

Madadors: Jerry Stephani, Larry Black, Ron Buchek, Phil Holzbauer (courtesy Phil Holzbauer)

Madadors

Feature	105	Girl Don't Leave Me/Alright[1]	/66
Easy Street			
Cine Vista	1003	Peter Pan/Boom-Bah	/68
	1004	Do You Hear The Magic Music/Walking In The Clouds	8/69
Paramount	0007	Do You Hear The Magic Music/Walking In The Clouds	/69

"We called ourselves the Mad Madadors," says Phil Holzbauer, explaining the spelling of this band's name. The group originated in the early 60's and metamorphosized into Easy Street in 1967. After an Alaskan tour with the Rascals, the band went in to record at Universal Studios in Chicago with producer Dick Campbell. Eventually one release got some action when Paramount picked it up. "It sold in Kansas City. I know it went number one there," says Ron Buchek. "It was hot in Northern Wisconsin but Dot (Paramount) just would never have enough records. I pushed the issue with Dot Records and they were just really cold to me, like, 'Hey, it's our business. We'll do what we want.' I don't know if we were a tax write-off or what we were."

---

[1]Searchers - *Meet The Searchers* LP, 1964; also Legends and many others

Nels Christiansen, previously of the Playboys, filled in when Buchek left for National Guard duty. Buchek has had a construction business since the early 70's. Organist Larry Black later moved to Denmark. Phil Holzbauer recorded with oldies band Solid Gold in the 70's.

Also see: Playboys (Nels Christiansen)
       Dick Campbell
Unrelated Madadors (Matadors): Chart Maker, Colpix, Feature, Forbes, Keith, Sue
Unrelated Easy Street: Capricorn
Sources: Nels Christiansen telephone interview, 5/7/94
       Phil Holzbauer telephone interview, 5/11/94
       Ron Buchek telephone interview, 5/21/94

Marshmellow Tugboat
(Merrill?)

Possible member: E.J. Sandas

Blue Coral   5474   Michelle, Be My Girl/Please Don't Go   /67

Sources: Mike Peace telephone interview, 8/14/94
       Tourville. <u>Wisconsin . . . Discography.</u>

Pitlik's Construction Co.
(Rhinelander)

Bob Moes - voc
John Pitlik - ld gtr
Jim Roehling - bs
Mike Vlahakis - dr (4/2/40; Rhinelander)

Mister Ed's Presents 7502   Your Nose Is Gonna Grow[1]/Sweet Little Sixteen[2]   /65

Guitarist John Pitlik went on to back many name artists on the road.

Source: Mike Vlahakis telephone interview, 8/4/94

---

[1]Johnny Crawford, 1962
[2]Chuck Berry, 1958

Rags Of Riches
(Ladysmith)

Webco   105   Up On The Roof[1]/First Train To California[2]   /69

This group chose Cryan Shames covers for both sides of their lone single. "Those were their heroes," recalls musician Bill Burling who knew the band.

Sources: Bill Burling telephone interview, 7/30/94
        Tourville. <u>Wisconsin . . . Discography.</u>

Ramrods
(Prairie du Chein)

Mike Farrell - ld gtr
Pete Steele -kb (1/7/40; Prairie du Chein)   **Zonnie Frichi** - sx
Chip Specht - bs   **Denny Lee (Sesso)** - ld gtr
Butch "Frog" Cavanaugh - dr

AD   70   Come Back Baby/Morado   /59

This band's only recording was done at Audio Deluxe in Oelwein, Iowa, at the urging of DJ Dale Wood. Keyboardist Pete Steele had also worked with Vilas Craig. A later version of the Ramrods included Milwaukee guitarist Denny Lee who continued in the business with many bands.

The Ramrods were part of a reunion concert in July 1993, to benefit the Prairie du Chein Rescue Squad and Fire Department. "We had a tremendous crowd," says Steele. "I can't believe that there is still such a strong interest in the 50's and 60's music. Large numbers of people told us it was the greatest thing that ever happened here. I really think the bands had more fun than anyone else."

Also see: Greenmen (Denny Lee)
        Vilas Craig (Pete Steele)
        TJ's/Caravans (Dale Wood)
Unrelated Ramrods: Amy, Fenton, Plymouth, Queen, R&H, Rampage
Sources: Peter Steele letters and telephone interview, 4/13/93, 8/9/93, 6/93
        Osborne-Brown. <u>Rockin' Records.</u>

---

[1]Drifters, 1963; Cryan Shames, 1968
[2]Cryan Shames - *Synthesis* LP, 1969

Rebounds
(Rhinelander)

Phil Jahnke
Steve Krueger

Hodag   6932   Summertime[1]/Don't Throw Your Love Away   /66

Unrelated Rebounds: Tower
Source: Michael Kuehl letter, 8/15/94
        Osborne-Brown. Rockin' Records.

Dick Ruedebush
(1924; Mayville - 5/5/68)

Andoll	2	Battle Hymn Of The Republic[2]/Love At Lunchtime	
Jubilee	5425	Autumn Leaves[3]/My Funny Valentine[4]	/62
	5432	Sugar Blues[5]/I Can't Get Started[6]	/62
	5448	Days Of Wine And Roses[7]/I Left My Heart In San Francisco[8]	4/63
	5547	Is Paris Burning/Goodnight Sweet Prince	/66
	5568	Chove Chuva/Lullaby For Trumpets	/67
	11925	Cottonfields[9]/Big Butter And Egg Men (juke box 33 single)	

LP's:

Jubilee	5008	Meet Mr. Trumpet	/62
	5015	Mr. Trumpet Remembers The Greats	/62
	5021	Dick Ruedebush, Mr. Trumpet	/63
Ascot	1307	Happy Horn	

Jazz trumpeter Dick Ruedebush played in the Army swing band at Ft. Slocum, New Jersey, and took whatever jazz gigs he could find around Madison after his discharge. Relocating to Milwaukee, he took his own group, the Underprivileged Five, into the Tunnel Inn downtown and remained there for five years.

---

[1]Gershwin standard
[2]Columbia Mixed Quartet, 1912; many others
[3]Roger Williams, 1955; many others
[4]w:Rodgers & Hart
[5]Clyde McCoy, 1931,1935; many others
[6]Hal Kemp, 1936; Bunny Berigan, 1938
[7]Andy Williams, Henry Mancini, 1963
[8]Tony Bennett, 1962
[9]Highwaymen, 1962

The band had a shot on the Ed Sullivan Show January 28, 1962, guest hosted that night by Sid Caesar. In 1965 Ruedebush joined Woody Herman's band and appears on two of their Columbia LP's. He also guested on "Music To Lure Pigeons By," an album by the Night Pastor & Seven Friends (Claremont 672). Ruedebush died of a heart attack at the age of 44.

Sources: Baker, Jack. "Dick Ruedebusch." Illustrated History Of Wisconsin Music. Milwaukee: MGC, 1991
     Clee. American 45 R.P.M. Records.

Spacemen
(Antigo)

Gene Fondow - ld gtr
Bob Jilek - org
Tom McMahon - rh gtr
John Schuster - bs (2/2/44; Antigo)
Loren Skaare - dr (Williston, ND)

Gemini	--	The Space Walk/Please, Please Me[1]	7/65
Big Sound	303	Modman/Retro	3/66
	309	Same Old Grind/Run For Your Life	9/66
		(Side 1 reissued on Pebbles *Highs In The Mid 60's, Vol. 10*)	

The Spacemen managed three releases in their brief, two year existence, garnering airplay on WRIG in Wausau and a few other areas. The band traveled around Wisconsin, Minnesota and Michigan. In the spring of 1967 they did their final gig at Mr. Roberts in Appleton. The Spacemen had an unusual age range, with 32-year old Bob Jilek in the lineup alongside 17-year old Gene Fondow.

Loren Skaare had previously traveled with country bands, including that of Les Cunningham who recorded for Decca. John Schuster, who says, "I've had my share of bars," put away his bass in 1992.

Unrelated Space Men/Spacemen: Alton, Era, Felsted, Jameco, Jubilee, Markey
Sources: John Schuster telephone interview, 5/22/94
     Prellberg. Lost and Found
     Osborne-Brown. Rockin' Records.

---

[1]Beatles, 1963, 1964

Warlords
(Waupun)

James White - voc (11/5/48; Waupun)
Kurt Kuzalka - ld gtr (2/28/49; Hurtisford)
Steve Beau - rh gtr (Fond du Lac)   **Larry Williams** - ld gtr
George Barrahas - bs (dec)   **Bill Shupe** - rh gtr
Randy Lindert - dr (Mayville)

Night Owl   6816   My Girl[1]/Sad Songs   1/68
                      (Side 2 reissued on *Badger A Go Go* LP)

The Warlords played all around the state from about 1966-68. After the breakup of the band, various members got back together as Bare Fat. George Barrahas went to New York where he recorded with Duke Jupiter.

Also see: Bare Fat (James White, Randy Lindert, Steve Beau, Kurt Kuzulka)
Unrelated Warlords: Thor
Sources: Kurt Kuzulka telephone interview, 6/15/94
        James White telephone interview, 6/19/94
        Tourville. Wisconsin . . . Discography.

Why Four
(Marinette)

Drew Lund - voc/hca
Gerry Cain - ld gtr (9/5/46; Buffalo, NY)
Ken Stone (Stoneberner) - bs
Terry Lund - dr

Rampro   118   Hard Life/Not Fade Away[2]   /66

"The Why Four was probably one of the first long, long hair bands in Wisconsin," claims Gerry Cain. "That's how the band got together. I was going to college and one of my friends said, 'Some of my friends in my hometown got hair as long as yours.' So we met and decided to form this band." Their record was produced at Cuca by Steve Sperry who also played organ on it. Cain and Lund both went on to work with Raw Meat, a Milwaukee band in the 70's. Cain had previously been with the Benders and had been about to join Bobby Lee's Showmen when Lee got drafted. He now teaches guitar in Menominee, Michigan.

---

[1]Temptations, 1965
[2]Crickets, 1958 (flip of "Oh Boy"); Rolling Stones, 1964

Also see: Benders
        Steve Sperry (On The Charts)
Sources: Gerry Cain telephone interview, 5/4/94
        Tourville. <u>Wisconsin . . . Discography.</u>

Various Artists

The following two compilation albums of Wisconsin artists were released in the *Pebbles - Highs In The Mid 60's* reissue series:

10017 Volume 10   <u>Original release</u>

The Shag	Stop And Listen	Capitol 5995
Wanderers Rest	The Boat That I Row	Wright 6771
Young Savages (Chicago)	The Invaders Are Coming	Dynamic Sound 2006
Faros	I'm Crying	Target 104
Lord Beverly Moss & Mossmen	Please, Please What's The Matter	Target 107
Noblemen	Dirty Robber	USA 1222
The Hinge	Come On Up	Tee Pee 75
Jack & the Beanstalks	Don't Bug Me	Le Ron 3601
Jack & the Beanstalks	So Many Times	Le Ron 3601
Trodden Path	Don't Follow Me	Night Owl 6711
Joey Gee & the Come-On's	She's Mean	Sara 6599
Deverons	On The Road Again	Raynard 1046
Love Society	You Know How I Feel	Target 1006
Rehabilitation Cruise	I Don't Care What They Say	(unknown)

10025 Volume 15

Baroques	Nothing Left To Do But Cry	Chess LP 1516
Shaprels	A Fool For Your Lies	Feature 103
Gord's Horde	I Don't Care	Hodag 0540
Cannons	Days Go By (correct title: Day To Day)	Night Owl 1312
Family	I Wanna Do It	Teen Town 119
Wanderer's Rest	You'll Forget	Wright 67101
Challengers	Take A Ride On The Jefferson Airplane	Night Owl 6794
Mustard Men	I Lost My Baby	Raynard 10036
Spacemen	Same Old Grind	Big Sound 309
Impalas	Spoonful	Feature 107
Mid-Knighters	Charlena	Paragon 814
Joey Gee & the Come-On's	You Know - Till The End Of Time	Sara 6599
Fugitives	Come On And Clap	Trend 101
Medallions (believed to be from Chicago)	Leave Me Alone	Warped 1001
Rehabilitation Cruise	Mini Skirts	(unknown)

And The Beat Goes On

Of course, it was only the stroke of midnight on December 31st that separated 1970 from 1969. It was difficult to draw that line that includes the December 1969 recording, but eliminates the one that came but a few weeks later. Even the borderline of the state - more defined, perhaps, than the borderlines of the decades - can be hard to pin down where the movement of people is concerned. Still, I had to stop somewhere. (It's a good thing there's a large lake on one side of the state!) For those who didn't make the cut, there is always more to be written.

Besides groups that became staples in the local 70's scene, there were some Wisconsin musicians, not yet recording in 1969, who stepped up to substantial national success. Darryl Stuermer (Gensis, Phil Collins) has been briefly mentioned in the context of other stories. One interesting young band, the Walkers, at various times included Bob Metzger[1] (Don MacLean, Spencer Davis, Leonard Cohen, many others), Jerry Harrison (Modern Lovers, Talking Heads), Jon Paris (national TV commercials, Link Wray, Johnny Winters, others), and Jerry or David Zucker (brother team who went on to produce or direct blockbuster films including Airplane, Naked Gun, Ghost and others).

Researching, compiling, and writing this book has been a fascinating, joyful, occasionally frustrating, and totally engrossing experience. It grew far beyond my expectations. I have learned much, found old friends, and made new friends. I've attempted to be as complete and accurate as possible but I'm sure there is more to learn. I welcome any additions and corrections.

August 1994

---

[1]Metzger had recorded prior to 1970, but as a session musician rather than a member of a band with its own release.

Appendix

The following records are believed to be from Wisconsin in the 50's & 60's, but I have been unable to find sufficient evidence to confirm that. All information comes from Tom Tourville's *They Couldn't Tame Us - The Wisconsin 60's Rock Discography*.

Apple Glass Cyndrom (Madison)
Column   691   Someday/Going Wrong   /69
Bossmen (Milwaukee)
Score   1001   Mashed Potatoes/Bad Boss Man
James Bryant & the Critters (Manitowoc)
Parrot   45016   Long Long Time/True Lovers Are Hard To Find   /65
Renee   108   Hey There You Girl/
Connie Campbell
KO   83568   Wind In The Willow/Lonely Dreams   /68
Colony
Sunderland   2293   Pseudo-Psycho Intuition/
Gene Jenkins
Trinity   Short Stuff/
Lunatics
Sunlight   1002   Mountains Of The Moon/
Nite Cappers (Sheboygan)
Pal   1150   Out Of Sight/T.P. Special
                9158   Everything/A Heartbreak
Pat Parker & the Way-Mates
Skyland   1000   Boy Watcher/Warm Glow
Satins (Milwaukee)
Aldon   8627   Get Out Of My Life/The Lonely
Shandells - The Fab Four
Sizzle   5130   Mary Mary/Caroline
Zeke Sheppard (Milwaukee)
President   831   Snow Surfin'/What Does Too Young Mean   /63
Society's People (Milwaukee)
Smile   432   That's The Way Of Our Day/O' Darlin'   /67
Sons Of Mourning
Midgard   204   Come On Everybody/I'm Not Worth It   /67
Spectrum
DCR   10203   For You/What Did I Do
Twin-Dells (Green Bay) (Probable members: M. Kacoyanis, C. Baslie)
Twin-Dell   Love 'Em And Leave 'Em/Nancy
Vice-Roys
USA   761   Liverpool/Tonk   (I/I)   /65
Acquarius   1004   Lame Duck/Heartbreak

Paul Vernon
Love   821   Keeps My Mind A-Wonderin'/For Carol
Marty Wyte
Brush   7000   Queen Of The Mardi-Gras/The Ho-Bo Song
Shammy   501   Queen Of The Mardi-Gras/The Ho-Bo Song

Order Form

To order additional copies of *Do You Hear That Beat*, use or copy this order form.

....

<u>Quantity</u>

Do You Hear That Beat	_______	@ $27.90	=	_____________
Discount: 5-9 copies = less 10%, 10 or more = less 20%			=	_____________
Subtotal			=	_____________
Shipping/Handling (see chart below)			=	_____________
California residents add 8.25% sales tax ($2.30) per book			=	_____________
Total (Enclose check or money order, do not mail cash)			=	_____________

If money order or cashier's check, books shipped within three days, if personal check, allow extra 10 days to clear.

Ship to:

Name   ____

Address   ____

City/State/Zip ____

Mail order form and payment to:

Hummingbird Publishing
P.O. Box 4777
Downey, CA 90241-1777

....

Shipping/Handling:

Book Rate:	One book	$2.05
	2 - 4 books	3.95
First Class	One book	3.30
	2 - 4 books	5.25

For larger quantities or overseas shipping, please write for rates.